MAKING SENSE OF MENTAL HEALTH AND WELLBEING IN PRIMARY SCHOOLS

Building on the latest research in developmental neuroscience, this book provides an evidence-based, accessible and practical roadmap for those looking for more effective ways to support primary school pupils' mental health and wellbeing.

The guide begins by analysing current approaches before presenting a new, comprehensive framework for mental health and wellbeing curricula in primary schools. Focusing on building up mental health knowledge and key skills of children in a neuroscience-informed and age-appropriate way, the book:

- Translates key developmental processes in the mind and brain into learning outcomes, knowledge and skills with focus on Reception stage, KS1, and lower and upper KS2.
- Lays out a 7-step, trauma-informed pedagogical approach for teaching mental health and wellbeing and provides a plethora of relevant activity examples.
- Looks at the implementation of the curriculum framework as a whole school approach in primary schools, including its positioning within wider social contexts.
- Explains key terms, with case studies and reflection opportunities throughout.

This innovative book is a must-have guide for primary school educators interested in understanding the mental health and wellbeing development of their pupils and finding research-based ways to effectively support them long-term. It is also valuable reading for pastoral leaders in schools, mental health professionals and policy makers.

Dusana Dorjee is a Senior Lecturer (Associate Professor) in Psychology in Education at the University of York where she is heading the Well Minds Lab. A psychologist and cognitive neuroscientist, she conducts research in translational developmental neuroscience, investigating processes in the mind and brain underpinning mental health and wellbeing. She 'translates' this understanding into educational practice and policy. Her research has been applied to the development of two primary school mental health and wellbeing curricula in the UK. Dusana has also contributed to education policy initiatives in Wales and internationally. This is her third book published by Routledge.

MAKING SENSE OF MENTAL HEALTH AND WELLBEING IN PRIMARY SCHOOLS

A Practical Neuroscience-Based Guide

Dusana Dorjee

LONDON AND NEW YORK

Designed cover image: Getty Images

First published 2026
by Routledge
4 Park Square, Milton Park, Abingdon, Oxon OX14 4RN

and by Routledge
605 Third Avenue, New York, NY 10158

Routledge is an imprint of the Taylor & Francis Group, an informa business

© 2026 Dusana Dorjee

The right of Dusana Dorjee to be identified as author of this work has been asserted in accordance with sections 77 and 78 of the Copyright, Designs and Patents Act 1988.

All rights reserved. No part of this book may be reprinted or reproduced or utilised in any form or by any electronic, mechanical, or other means, now known or hereafter invented, including photocopying and recording, or in any information storage or retrieval system, without permission in writing from the publishers.

Trademark notice: Product or corporate names may be trademarks or registered trademarks, and are used only for identification and explanation without intent to infringe.

British Library Cataloguing-in-Publication Data
A catalogue record for this book is available from the British Library

ISBN: 978-1-041-00298-7 (hbk)
ISBN: 978-1-041-00287-1 (pbk)
ISBN: 978-1-003-60908-7 (ebk)

DOI: 10.4324/9781003609087

Typeset in Interstate
by Deanta Global Publishing Services, Chennai, India

CONTENTS

Acknowledgments	vii
Introduction	1
1 The What, Why and How of School Mental Health and Wellbeing	6

PART I
GUIDING ATTENTION

2 Emotional Awareness	29
3 Managing Distractions	50

PART II
MANAGING EMOTIONS

4 Managing Reactivity	73
5 Habitual Thoughts and Emotions	98
6 Managing Rumination and Worry	118

PART III
NURTURING CONNECTIONS

7 Shared Humanity	143
8 Connections	163
9 Making a Difference	186

PART IV
FINDING DIRECTION

10 Purpose in Life and Self-Concept   213

11 Implementing the ATTEND Framework   238

Index   259

ACKNOWLEDGMENTS

This book is a culmination of 15 years of my research into the processes in the mind and brain that underpin mental health and wellbeing development, and ways to foster these processes effectively in schools. This research also provided numerous opportunities for me to learn from teaching staff and pupils about the challenges and opportunities to foster mental health and wellbeing in primary schools which I was able to build on in this book. A Knowledge Transfer Project with the PSHE Association, in which we worked on translating my research into a primary school curriculum, provided further inspiration for the book as a way of sharing, in a comprehensive yet accessible way, my framework for teaching mental health and wellbeing with educators. And whilst working on the book, helpful suggestions and feedback from my skilled Routledge editor, Clare Ashworth, made the book more engaging and less dense with scientific jargon. Last but not least, I am grateful to my two amazing daughters for teaching me about mental health and wellbeing development what I wouldn't find in research papers, and inspiring me to think about practical and effective ways to support children's mental health and wellbeing long-term.

INTRODUCTION

Why This Book?

The primary school years are a developmental period when the processes underpinning mental health and wellbeing are most malleable. It is a key time to foster mental health and wellbeing skills to prevent mental ill-health later on. Schools are ideally suited for such learning, but this potential has so far not been fully harnessed. One of the reasons for this is that teachers are often faced with the daunting task of selecting the right mental health and wellbeing programmes and the right set of skills for their pupils from amongst 'a jungle' of available approaches. The aim of this book is to enable you, as a primary school teacher or pastoral lead, to navigate this 'jungle' of mental health and wellbeing concepts and resources.

This book provides a roadmap for understanding which mental health and wellbeing knowledge, skills and strategies need to be fostered at each of the primary school stages. This can in turn enable you to see how different approaches to mental health and wellbeing can be meaningfully combined in the classroom within and across primary school years. The set of knowledge, skills and strategies, and their progression, presented in this book is based on a rigorous review and integration of psychological and neuroscientific research on how the processes in the mind and brain underpinning mental health and wellbeing develop.

The research evidence on which this book builds is presented in a research article titled 'Conceptualising Child and Adolescent Mental Health and Wellbeing Neurodevelopment' (Dorjee, 2024), which you can read if you are interested in a deeper dive into the underpinning research. This book focuses on presenting some of the key research evidence in an accessible form and specifies ways the research can be translated into learning in a primary school classroom in the form of a comprehensive mental health and wellbeing curriculum framework.

Is This Book about Mental Health or Wellbeing?

Throughout this book I use the terms mental health and wellbeing together. This is because the current definitions of both of these terms highlight their overlaps. For example, a definition of mental health provided by the World Health Organization (2022) says that mental health is 'a state of mental well-being that enables people to cope with the stresses of life, realize their abilities, learn well and work well, and contribute to their community'. So being mentally healthy doesn't simply mean an absence of mental ill-health and also involves an element of flourishing – wellbeing linked to accomplishing one's potential. Research with children in schools also supports the overlapping nature of mental health and wellbeing, better mental health is often (even though not always) linked to higher wellbeing (Lereya et al., 2022). For these reasons the term mental health and wellbeing (MHW) is used in this book.

Given the overlaps between mental health and wellbeing, the knowledge, skills and strategies presented in this book have three overlapping aims – to prevent mental ill-health, strengthen mental health and enhance wellbeing. While not all of the MHW knowledge, skills and strategies you will find in the book accomplish all three aims equally, they are all to be fostered because they build on each other and can meaningfully complement each other.

Why Is This Book Neuroscience-Based?

As an educator, you have most likely come across some references to the brain when exploring different approaches to teaching MHW knowledge and skills to your pupils. One of the reasons why neuroscience is often included in such teaching is because it seems to provide a more 'scientific' basis for this type of teaching and learning. The challenge is that the neuroscience included in many of the approaches is oversimplified and often inaccurate. This book aims to provide a more accurate and complete account of the neuroscience underpinning MHW in primary school children in an accessible way.

There are two other reasons why stronger knowledge of the underpinning neuroscience can be beneficial to MHW teaching and learning in schools. First, better understanding of MHW neuroscience can support you, as a teacher, in your understanding of how MHW processes develop in primary school children. Research shows that teachers who have stronger understanding of MHW development can better support their pupils in acquiring MHW knowledge and skills (Schonert-Reichl, 2017). In addition, teaching children relevant neuroscience in an accessible age-appropriate way can have therapeutic effects in itself – by providing children with a 'neutral' language to understand and talk about their experiences.

However, the neuroscience content and evidence is not used in the book to suggest that such evidence is always 'stronger' or more 'rigorous' than psychological evidence. As a neuroscientist I myself do not view neuroscience evidence in this way. In my research I find that understanding the brain processes underpinning MHW can often, but not always, provide a more complete picture of these processes, alongside psychological evidence. I also find that looking at the brain processes can sometimes lead to new insights into how different MHW knowledge, skills and strategies overlap and build on each other. I included examples of this in the book.

Book Overview

This book presents a comprehensive framework for formulating and teaching MHW curricula, called the ATTEND framework. Chapter 1 introduces the reasoning and research evidence behind the framework. This includes an introduction to the two key capacities underpinning MHW - the self-regulation capacity and the self-world capacity. You will learn how these two capacities can explain overlaps across common MHW concepts such as self-regulation, resilience, emotion regulation, mindfulness, empathy etc. The chapter then explains how understanding of these two capacities can be translated into the ATTEND framework and guide MHW learning in schools. Finally, you will learn that the ATTEND framework can be implemented in your lessons using the 7-step approach - a pedagogical strategy for teaching MHW in schools. This will in turn enable you to start seeing the first features of the 'roadmap' that can guide MHW teaching in your classroom.

The following chapters then elaborate on how the ATTEND framework, presented in the form of the ATTEND Pyramid of MHW knowledge and skills, can be taught in schools, step-by-step. Part I includes two chapters explaining the first tier of the ATTEND pyramid (the 'ATT') - the MHW knowledge, skills and strategies fostering children's abilities to manage and guide their attention. These include emotional awareness and skilful ways of managing distractions. Building on this learning, Part II of the book presents in three chapters the second tier of the ATTEND Pyramid (the 'E'), which cultivates children's knowledge and skills in managing their emotions. This involves learning to manage reactivity, habitual thoughts and emotions, and rumination and worry.

Building up the MHW knowledge and skills further, Part III of the book outlines the third tier of the ATTEND Pyramid (the 'N'). This tier focuses on developing children's knowledge and skills of relational MHW - described as nurturing connections. In this tier, presented in three chapters, children learn to recognise the shared humanity of our experiences, cultivate gratitude and awe linked to a wide range of connections in our lives, and learn how prosocial behaviours (helping, sharing, volunteering etc.) can support their MHW. Expanding their learning further, Part IV of the book specifies the final tier of the ATTEND Pyramid (the 'D') that focuses on finding direction in one's life. The only chapter of this tier (Chapter 10) describes how to support children in developing a sense of purpose in their lives and cultivate a flexible sense of self to work with change in support of their MHW.

Each of the chapters in Parts I to IV of the book includes an overview of research evidence underpinning the MHW knowledge, skills and strategies discussed in that particular chapter. This is followed by specification of how the knowledge and skills develop and how they can be fostered in an age-appropriate way across the primary school key stages following the 7-step approach. This approach outlines a progression of learning from recognising different strategies in examples from stories or cartoons to increasing emphasis on exploring how the strategies can be applied in children's own experience. In the final steps of the 7-step approach children embed the strategies into their school experiences and outside of school. Learning about key MHW concepts and underpinning neuroscience is woven into the seven steps. To exemplify different aspects of MHW learning and challenges of teaching MHW in the classroom, each chapter also includes case studies that will enable you to relate the research evidence and knowledge/skills explanations to real-world examples.

Finally, the last chapter of the book (Chapter 11) focuses on implementation of the new curriculum framework as a whole school approach in primary schools. From this perspective, the chapter explains the interactive impacts of fostering the two MHW capacities in children, their peers, teachers and parents. This chapter also includes responses to frequently asked questions about the ATTEND framework and guidance on how to maintain and enhance long-term effectiveness of the ATTEND framework implementation. Finally, we will explore how the knowledge, skills and strategies of the ATTEND framework can support children in managing their MHW in the face of current societal challenges – from climate change to polarisation.

How to Work with This Book

Since the book builds up your understanding of MHW development and corresponding knowledge, skills and strategies, the way to start working with the book is by reading it from the beginning to the end. After the first read, you may want to zoom-in onto Parts I to IV and read them with specific focus on the age group you are working with. Here you may want to focus on the developmentally appropriate sections of the 7-step approach for each of the 10 chapters. Then once you have formulated a plan for delivery of the MHW curriculum to your pupils, you may consider ways of expanding its embedding to the whole school, as described in the last chapter.

It is important to keep in mind that the knowledge, skills, learning outcomes and strategies presented in each chapter build on the knowledge, skills and strategies presented in previous chapters. So while you may have good reasons to pick-and-choose particular skills or strategies for teaching MHW in your classroom, it is important to consider if children already have the foundational knowledge and skills presented in the tiers of the ATTEND framework preceding the chapter you selected. For example, children may find it difficult to learn about ways to manage rumination and worry if they don't have the foundational knowledge, skills and strategies of emotional awareness and managing reactivity. This is because managing rumination and worry requires the ability to notice thoughts and emotions in a non-judgmental way and the ability to manage reactivity to emotions effectively in the moment.

Once you are closely familiar with mental health and wellbeing development in the age group you work with and with the ATTEND framework, you may want to start exploring how other approaches you learned about outside of this book fit the wider 'roadmap' of the ATTEND framework. For example, you may recognise that some of the strategies presented in a resilience curriculum you have been working with map onto some of the tiers and strategies of the ATTEND framework, but there also are some gaps which the ATTEND framework may help you cover. You may also notice that another programme you are familiar with, for instance one fostering empathy, fits well with some of the skills and strategies of the ATTEND framework presented in Part III of the book and you can expand learning in your classroom with further strategies from the empathy programme. However, you will now understand why such programmes need to be introduced after children have developed foundational skills of self-regulation in Parts I and II of the ATTEND framework.

A Personal Note

I have spent the last 15 years researching how processes in the mind and brain that underpin MHW in children and adolescents develop. I always approached this research with the intention of contributing to better understanding of these processes so that we can improve prevention and early interventions for mental health support in schools. For this reason, I engaged in conversations with policy makers and contributed to educational MHW policy developments in Wales and England and to international UNESCO initiatives. But I gradually realised that the research seemed to make the most difference when I was able to reach teachers directly, through research collaboration, workshops and curriculum co-development.

Therefore, I was pleased to have the opportunity to work with a leading provider of MHW curricula to schools in England, the PSHE Association, over two years on translating my neurodevelopmental research into a primary school curriculum. This collaboration inspired me to specify the knowledge, skills, strategies and learning objectives for what became the ATTEND framework and resulted in this book. It is my hope that, presented in this format, rigorous research on MHW will be able to make a difference to your pupils more directly and readily through helping you make sense of MHW in primary schools.

References

Dorjee, D. (2024). Conceptualising child and adolescent mental health and wellbeing neurodevelopment: an integrative brain networks framework. Preprint, 4 November. https://doi.org/10.31234/osf.io/7vx45

Lereya, S. T., Patalay, P., & Deighton, J. (2022). Predictors of mental health difficulties and subjective wellbeing in adolescents: a longitudinal study. *JCPP Advances*, 2(2), e12074.

Schonert-Reichl, K. A. (2017). Social and emotional learning and teachers. *The Future of Children*, 27(1), 137-155.

World Health Organization. (2022). Mental health. www.who.int/news-room/fact-sheets/detail/mental-health-strengthening-our-response

1 The What, Why and How of School Mental Health and Wellbeing

Introduction

Prevention of mental ill-health has many advantages compared to interventions to address mental illness, both from individual and societal perspectives. For a child, effective prevention can shift their life-long trajectories of mental health with ripple effects on fulfilment of their potential, including their academic and workplace success and overall quality of life (Moffitt et al., 2011). From the societal perspective, investing in prevention of mental ill-health is much more cost effective in comparison to the cost of productivity lost to mental ill-health across the population and the cost of mental ill-health interventions which are often needed in the long term. Indeed, poor mental health is one of the leading causes of disability across the world (Kieling et al., 2024).

Yet, the mental health crisis in youth has been worsening (Newlove-Delgado et al., 2023) and is regularly making the headlines. While those headlines often focus on difficulties in access to mental health services, the role of schools in addressing the mental health crisis is also part of these conversations. Over the last decade, most of the efforts to support child and adolescent mental health in schools focused on improving mental health literacy and signposting to mental health services. This is clearly an important role schools take on in the chain response of supporting child and adolescent mental health. However, schools have a much wider potential in making a difference to young people's mental health and wellbeing (MHW).

What does this wider potential of schools entail? Not surprisingly, it focuses on mental ill-health prevention and involves learning! As this book shows, there is a particular set of MHW knowledge and skills that can be systematically fostered across school years. The reasons why we haven't so far fully harnessed the potential of schools in teaching such knowledge and skills are many. They range from lack of prioritisation of MHW in school evaluations and policies to the overwhelming pressures on teachers' time and responsibilities. We will consider these limitations more extensively in the last chapter of the book.

However, what is rarely acknowledged is that we are not very good at teaching MHW in schools because we lack effective curriculum frameworks for this type of learning. Such curriculum frameworks need to specify the developmental progression of MHW knowledge and skills. How can teachers effectively teach MHW knowledge and skills if there are no clear guidelines about what these are and how they develop? Therefore, as a starting point of making sense of MHW in primary schools, this chapter introduces key MHW knowledge and skills for children to learn in primary schools, based on relevant research.

Case Study: Choosing the Right MHW Approach for your Classroom

Kathryn is a teacher in Year 4. She is currently planning MHW lessons for the next academic year. Those lessons will run over a half-term. To start with, Kathryn looked at the guidelines for teaching mental wellbeing provided by the Department for Education. The guidelines include some useful starting points, but without much detail. They mostly emphasise the need to foster emotional awareness and self-regulation in primary school children, but they do not provide much guidance on how this should be taught.

So Kathryn goes online in search of further information. She finds lots of different teaching resources, from social and emotional learning through resilience programmes to mindfulness training. The amount of information is a bit overwhelming and Kathryn doesn't know how to choose the right materials for her class. She is wondering if the resources are of good quality – they all claim to be scientifically-based, so it is hard to know if some of them have a stronger grounding in research evidence than others. It is also not clear which of the resources are intended for year 4 children. Kathryn is wondering if it is ok to combine the resources, since they all seem to contain some relevant information, but none of them is sufficient to cover the learning over six weeks.

Next day, Kathryn decides to ask her teacher colleagues for help and guidance. She also talks to the pastoral lead in the school. She finds out that her colleagues, including the pastoral lead, have been struggling with the same challenges. They all share that during their teacher training they learned very little, if anything, about child MHW development and ways to foster it. They also reflect on some of the CPD training they received; while some of it was useful it didn't provide sufficient information on child mental health development and ways to distinguish and combine different approaches to fostering it. So Kathryn relies on her intuition and combines the materials based on her current understanding and decides to try out what will work in the classroom. But she hopes to find a resource or attend CPD training that would help her make more informed choices about teaching MHW skills in her year 4 classroom.

Questions for reflection:

- How do you decide which MHW resources are most suitable for your classroom?
- Do you know enough about child MHW development to guide your decisions about what MHW content to teach to your pupils?
- Do you know how MHW learning should build up across lessons?
- What is your pedagogical approach to teaching MHW?

The Three Pillars of MHW School Curricula

If you ever found yourself in a similar position as Kathryn in the case study above, the starting point of making sense of the various psychological concepts and approaches might be to consider the three pillars of MHW development. Keeping these three principles in mind builds the foundation of any considerations about fostering children's MHW in your primary school. One could think of these three principles as the three support pillars for the MHW curricula, if one of the pillars is not solid enough the curriculum provision will be out of balance and possibly crumble – meaning it will be ineffective. The three principles are: nourishing root systems of MHW, developmental continuity of MHW learning and real-world contextualising of MHW learning. We will now introduce each of these pillars in detail.

Nourishing the Root Systems of MHW

The first principle involves looking deeper into the 'root systems' of MHW. Let's metaphorically think about children's MHW as a tree that needs to be nourished. Now if we think about what we are currently doing in schools, it can be likened to nourishing some of the 'branches' of a tree. This means, for example, that we are mostly focusing on teaching children to notice thoughts or behaviours that might be indicative of poor mental health and how to seek help. Similarly, we may teach them a few strategies to manage some of the subclinical symptoms (take care of the branches), such as some simple practices to help them settle when feeling stressed or anxious. Or we may tell them what it means to be resilient.

What these examples share is that they mostly focus on isolated strategies aimed to tackle particular problems. Such an approach inevitably misses some (possibly a lot) of the tree branches. Most importantly, this approach doesn't focus on the key part of a tree that needs nourishing if we want it to grow well – its root systems! This is because most of the current approaches don't look deep enough, they don't focus on understanding and fostering the processes in the mind and brain that underpin MHW – its root systems. And for this reason, they also don't take care of the tree in a systematic way – they don't get the ingredients needed for nourishing the tree right, and from the ingredients that they select, they don't 'feed' the tree in the right order for it to flourish.

Now looking closer, what are these root system processes in the mind and brain that need to be fostered to effectively support children's MHW? There is cutting-edge research that helps us answer this question. This research suggests that across mental ill-health symptoms there are some shared processes in the mind and brain – these are called transdiagnostic processes (Snyder et al., 2019). For example, difficulties in managing where we place our attention are shared across symptoms of anxiety and depression and problematic social media use. In anxiety or depression they can manifest as difficulties in disengaging from repeated thoughts of worry or self-criticism or sadness. In problematic social media use it is the difficulty in disengaging attention from social media scrolling.

This book focuses on several key transdiagnostic processes that need to be fostered, as the root systems of MHW, during child development to prevent mental ill-health and to address subclinical symptoms early on. These transdiagnostic processes are explained in a new developmental theory of MHW – the Neurodevelopmental Theory of MHW Capacities

(NDeTeC) (Dorjee, 2024). As you will see, neuroscience research can also be helpful in understanding these root system processes of MHW and clarify the overlaps, interactions and complementary learning across mental health approaches. For example, you will learn that the root system processes underpinning both self-regulation and resilience closely overlap. Understanding these overlaps may enable you to go beyond the labels that different approaches highlight, and combine them or build on them in more effective ways.

Key Term

The *Neurodevelopmental Theory of MHW Capacities* (NDeTeC) explains the 'root system' processes in the mind and brain underpinning MHW development.

Developmental Continuity of MHW Learning

The focus on the root systems of MHW has another advantage. It may enable us to design MHW programmes for schools that meaningfully nourish the root systems of MHW step by step in a developmentally-appropriate way. After all, in any other subject, from learning to read to learning maths, we build up children's knowledge and skills gradually in this way. Indeed, teaching and learning of reading or maths builds on psychological theories of the processes in the mind and brain underpinning maths and reading knowledge and skills – their root systems. In this book, we are applying the same approach of developmental continuity to MHW learning, enabled by the NDeTeC theory.

The developmental continuity manifests in the NDeTeC theory, and translates into the ATTEND framework for school curricula, in two ways. First there is a 'general' developmental continuity in learning MHW knowledge and skills at any age. This continuity involves a progression of complexity in learning from foundational MHW knowledge and skills to the more complex ones. For example, the ability to become aware of thoughts and emotions in a non-judgmental way is a foundational skill for any further learning of MHW strategies. If we start with mental health strategies, such as reappraisal of emotions involving changing our ways of thinking, before we have developed non-judgmental awareness of thoughts and emotions, the learning will most likely not be very effective.

The second type of developmental continuity is about understanding the limitations brain development, and associated cognitive and emotional development, places on the abilities of children to learn different MHW strategies. This involves knowing what children can and can't effectively do when it comes to managing their emotions and behaviour at different ages. Lack of such understanding currently manifests in primary schools both in terms of limited MHW teaching to younger age groups and lack of build up in MHW knowledge and skills across the year groups. Any effective MHW curriculum needs to foster a progression of age-appropriate MHW knowledge and skills that systematically builds up across the primary school years. Just like we wouldn't expect children to learn to read without such a systematic and developmentally sensitive approach, we can't expect them to build up strong MHW knowledge and skills without it.

Finally, we need to recognise that effective mental ill-health prevention and fostering of wellbeing particularly involves learning of *MHW skills*. We currently tend to approach MHW learning mostly from a knowledge-based perspective. But telling children what MHW is about is much less effective than teaching them actual skills they can apply in their lives to manage their MHW. Again, just like with learning to read, we don't just teach children about reading, most of the learning involves practising reading skills. Similarly, most of the learning for MHW needs to involve development of skills in managing attention, emotions, behaviour and relationships embedded in children's lives.

> Questions for reflection:
> - Can you distinguish simpler emotion regulation strategies from more complex ones?
> - In your classroom, do you mostly teach children MHW knowledge or skills?
> - Do you think it might be possible to approach teaching MHW knowledge and skills in the same way we approach teaching reading or maths across primary school years?

Contextualising MHW Learning in the 'Real World'

Most current approaches to MHW in schools focus on teaching children a few strategies to manage their emotions and behaviour from an 'isolationist' perspective. Such a perspective is prevalent in the biomedical model of MHW which focuses on 'fixing the individual' without considering how different social factors impact one's MHW and how one's MHW can have social impacts. For example, rigorous studies show that factors such as poverty (Palacios-Barrios & Hanson, 2019) and discrimination (Njoroge et al., 2021) are major negative influences on child and adolescent mental health development. And recent research also highlights the need to acknowledge how one's pursuit of happiness or wellbeing can impact others' wellbeing from a sustainability perspective, particularly if it involves consumerism (Kjell, 2011). In other words, how one's choices of activities that support their wellbeing impact on others (e.g. overtourism or activities with high environmental footprint).

Can we build school MHW curricula that factor in these contextual influences? The ATTEND framework presented in this book aims to do so in two ways. First, you will find throughout the book that for each set of MHW skills and knowledge we also consider how development of these skills is impacted by societal factors. We will explore what this means for teaching the skills in the classroom. For example, learning about managing distractions will involve also learning about the attention economy – how our attention is pulled in different directions on social media through techniques that aim to capture our attention for monetary gain. Knowing about these techniques and how to resist them is part of the MHW skills children need in the current era of online overstimulation.

Second, we will explore how children's MHW skills can also have a positive impact on others and the world, and how this can in turn further enhance their MHW. For example, research shows that having a greater sense of connection with nature can support our MHW. And fostering such connections can also involve greater awareness of sustainable actions which can counter feelings of climate anxiety and hopelessness in the face of the climate crisis. Another example, prosocial actions aimed at benefiting others have also been shown to benefit children's wellbeing and can have a positive impact on others when they involve sharing, helping or volunteering. Such a wider perspective on MHW can also foster the transfer of MHW knowledge and skills from the classroom to the 'real world' and thus make MHW school curricula more effective in the long term.

> Questions for reflection:
> - How can we make learning MHW knowledge and skills more relevant to the 'real-world'?
> - Do you think MHW learning needs to consider the impact of our wellbeing choices on others?
> - Can you think of examples when MHW activities can also be good for 'the world'?

Introducing Capacities Underpinning MHW

Now that we have introduced the three pillars of MHW school curricula we can explore in more depth what the processes in the mind and brain underpinning MHW - its root systems - are. In the NDeTeC framework, which we are building on in this book, the root systems are described as MHW capacities. The term 'capacities' designates that these processes can be changed and shaped by learning and that they represent the potential for strong mental health and flourishing wellbeing. Based on extensive synthesis of relevant research, the NDeTeC specifies two key MHW capacities - the Self-Regulation Capacity and the Self-World Capacity. We will now introduce these two capacities in more detail.

The Self-Regulation Capacity

Self-regulation is usually described as the ability to manage one's behaviour in alignment with one's goals. It is one of the main and most consistent predictors of MHW in childhood and adolescence. For example, one study showed that children with lower self-regulation were more likely to experience symptoms of anxiety and depression as adolescents (Klinge et al., 2023). In addition, there is robust research evidence that higher self-regulation predicts a range of health, social and economic outcomes, including better physical health, grades, income and lower likelihood of engaging in criminality (Moffitt et al., 2011). All this evidence together makes self-regulation a key target for MHW interventions. In the context of the NDeTeC, the self-regulation capacity is defined in terms of psychological and neural processes 'that need to be fostered during child and adolescent development to enable adaptive management of thoughts, emotions and behaviour in alignment with one's goals in support of long term MHW' (Dorjee, 2024, p. 10).

12 *Making Sense of Mental Health and Wellbeing in Primary Schools*

> **Key Term**
>
> The *Self-Regulation Capacity* is the first 'root systems' capacity in the NDeTeC framework. The self-regulation capacity specifies the processes in the mind and brain that enable adaptive management of thoughts, emotions and behaviour in alignment with one's goals in support of long-term MHW.

Interestingly, when looking at the psychological and neural processes underpinning MHW (the root systems), one can see a close overlap between self-regulation and other MHW concepts (depicted in Figure 1.1). For instance, self-regulation builds on the ability to notice and recognise different types of emotions from a non-judgmental perspective. It also includes the ability to let go of immediate impulses and work towards longer-term goals. These abilities are also emphasised in mindfulness (as the ability to pay non-judgmental attention to experience) and in resilience (the ability to bounce back from adversity). Similarly, self-regulation involves effective problem solving and decision making, because these are instrumental to being able to plan for achievement of one's goals. And better problem solving and decision making is linked to better MHW. These overlaps are also evident when looking at programmes and interventions that can foster self-regulation and these other concepts – the same types of programmes and interventions are often 'prescribed' across these concepts.

Neuroscience of the Self-Regulation Capacity

These overlaps are even more evident when looking at the neural underpinnings of self-regulation and the related psychological concepts we just mentioned. The brain processes underlying self-regulation are often considered in terms of two interacting mechanisms

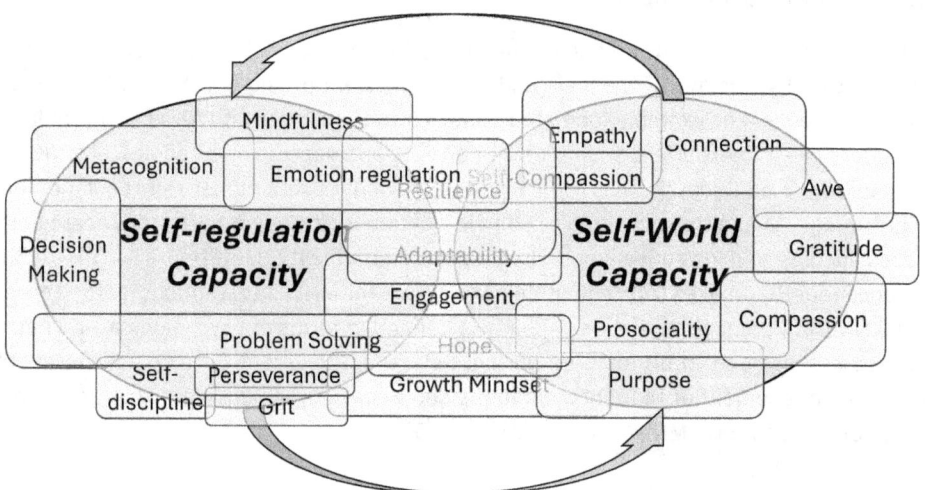

Figure 1.1 Overlaps across MHW concepts.

(Palacios-Barrios & Hanson, 2019). The first key mechanism (bottom-up stream of self-regulation) is more automatic. Broadly speaking, it reflects ways we react, mostly automatically, to external stimuli, our thoughts and emotions.

There are three key brain regions involved in these reactive bottom-up self-regulation processes. The first brain region, amygdala (right and left amygdalae), produces fast responses to emotionally strong stimuli which are often threat-related – such as when we are worried, anxious, angry or stressed. Another brain region involved in reactive responding is the ventral striatum (VS). The VS is active during rewarding experiences. Such experiences can be the result of an achievement, positive experiences in relationships, helping behaviours towards others etc. However, strong activity in the VS may also make it difficult for children to self-regulate, particularly when this involves a delayed reward or when a reward interferes with another goal. The final brain region involved in the bottom-up stream of self-regulation is called the hippocampus (left and right hippocampi) and is associated with learning and memory processes.

Spot bottom-up self-regulation in your classroom:

- Can you think of an example from your classroom when a child reacted 'without thinking' to something another child said to them? This could have been an immediate strong positive response (giggle or excitement) or a negative one (frown or even a punch). These would be examples of bottom-up reactive self-regulation facilitated by the amygdalae.
- Or you could think of instances when children keep chatting in the classroom when they are asked to focus on a task. This is because speaking to their friend is more rewarding for them in the moment, it activates the VS more strongly than the 'future reward' of completing their task, even though they may feel 'bad' about not completing the task afterwards. This is another example of automatic bottom-up self-regulation.
- Finally, can you think of some patterns of responding some of the children in your classroom have? This could be a child that always withdraws when they have a disagreement with their classmate. It could be an example of bottom-up self-regulation the child learned from seeing others behaving in the same way. Or the child might have learned that such a response helped them manage their emotions in the past in a similar situation. The activity in the hippocampi would facilitate these repeated responses.

These three examples show that bottom-up self-regulation is often maladaptive. But it can be adaptive too. For example, when we quickly jump out of the way when seeing an approaching car (supported by amygdalae). Or when we learn habitual ways of automatically responding to our own distress in a caring and self-compassionate way (enabled by hippocampi).

In comparison to the first stream of more automatic and reactive bottom-up self-regulation, the second group – the top-down stream of self-regulation – involves more voluntary, goal-oriented and controlled management of thoughts, emotions and behaviour. This group of self-regulation processes relies on brain regions underpinning our ability to notice thoughts, emotions and bodily sensations and reflect on our behaviour. It also involves inhibiting irrelevant information and responses, shifting attention at will, setting appropriate goals and making plans, problem solving and making well-considered decisions.

One of the three main brain regions supporting these top-down self-regulation processes is the anterior cingulate cortex (ACC) – underpinning monitoring of thoughts, emotions and behaviour, attention control including inhibition of irrelevant stimuli (letting go of distractions) and regulation of emotions. Effective self-regulation also involves a brain region called the insula (right insula and left insula or insular cortex). Insula contribute to effective self-regulation by supporting awareness of emotions and bodily sensations associated with emotions (e.g. children may notice having a 'nervous tummy'). Insula work together with the ACC and another brain region, the prefrontal cortex (PFC), in support of top-down self-regulation. The PFC is involved in goal setting, planning and decision making. It enables us to think through and regulate our thoughts, emotions and behaviour at will, in a controlled and situation-appropriate manner.

> Spot top-down self-regulation in your classroom:
>
> - Can you think of an example from your classroom when a child managed to control their immediate reaction to another child being mean to them? Instead of shouting back or acting out, the child might have said to the other child that they are being mean and calmly alerted a teaching assistant? This would be an example of top-down self-regulation, where a child was able to harness their ACC to 'calm down' their amygdalae and let go of an urge to shout back. The child also used their PFC to think through an appropriate response.
> - And how about a situation where a child is disrupted by their friend during a task and wants to chat to their friend but then remembers to focus on the task and asks their friend to wait until the break? This would be another example of top-down self-regulation where the child was able to 'downregulate' the activity in the VS by recruiting ACC and PFC and stay focused on the task. The child probably understood that in this way they will have both the reward for completing the task and the reward of chatting to their friend, just a bit later.
>
> Top-down self-regulation is usually the adaptive preferred way of self-regulating. Therefore, much of what we will cover in the book will focus on this type of self-regulation. However, the challenge with top-down self-regulation is that the PFC develops slowly, so children are not fully able to harness this type of self-regulation independently, but can do so with guidance. There are also some self-regulation strategies that don't rely heavily on the PFC, falling somewhere between bottom-up and top-down self-regulation, and thus younger children can use them more readily. These strategies can be, for example, mindfulness- and distraction-based.

While it can be helpful to outline the roles of particular brain regions in bottom-up and top-down self-regulation, as we have done above, it is equally important to recognise that brain regions never work in isolation. They often support self-regulation in coordinated fashion across brain regions, for example, some brain regions such as PFC downregulate activity in the amygdalae when we manage anxiety or anger. Therefore, in this book, when considering the neural underpinnings of the self-regulation and self-world capacities in more depth in the following chapters, we will also describe particular brain networks linked to each capacity. This will also include more detailed explanations of the roles of the brain regions mentioned above, together with their roles in the networks they are part of and associated psychological processes and MHW knowledge and skills.

Facets of the Self-Regulation Capacity

Building on the basic understanding of self-regulation and underpinning neuroscience research, we can now consider how the self-regulation capacity can be fostered in the classroom. This is where it becomes helpful to think about the facets of the self-regulation capacity describing specific processes of self-regulation that can be cultivated in support of MHW. The facets of the self-regulation capacity start with emotional awareness and basic emotion regulation strategies of naming and describing emotions in the *Facet of Emotional Awareness* and then progress towards more complex self-regulation strategies. Building on the skills of emotional awareness, the second facet, the *Facet of Managing Distractions*, specifically focuses on working with distractions and anchor-based emotion regulation strategies, such as anchoring attention by focusing on things of a certain colour in one's environment.

> **Key Term**
>
> The facets of the *Self-Regulation Capacity* are: emotional awareness, managing distractions, managing reactivity, working with habitual thoughts and emotions and managing rumination and worry.

Expanding on the foundational skills developed in the first two facets, the third facet – the *Facet of Managing Reactivity* – describes the processes of managing reactivity through basic stress-management including mindful paced breathing. Then the fourth facet, the *Facet of Habitual Thoughts and Emotions*, encourages children to explore ways of working with the negativity bias (tendency to notice and remember negative events more than positive) and savouring positive experiences. The fifth (and last) facet of the self-regulation capacity, the *Facet of Managing Rumination and Worry*, specifies a more complex emotion regulation strategy of cognitive reappraisal, changing one's way of thinking to manage emotions, and explores links between thoughts-emotions-behaviour. Each of these facets will be considered in detail in chapters 2 to 6, together with associated age-appropriate MHW knowledge and skills.

The Self-World Capacity

While there is an increasing emphasis on self-regulation in MHW school curricula, it is rarely acknowledged that self-regulation is not enough to support children's MHW. There is another group of mental health concepts and approaches that focus on the relational aspects of wellbeing – such as our sense of connection with others, prosocial behaviour and sense of purpose and meaning in life. These concepts and approaches are less well researched and often fragmented, but there is rigorous research supporting their strong contribution to child and adolescent mental health. For example, research on prosocial emotions such as gratitude shows benefits of gratitude training in schools to MHW of children (Obeldobel & Kerns, 2021). Similarly, initial studies show strong links between greater sense of meaning in life and lower levels of social-emotional difficulties in primary school children (Shoshani & Russo-Netzer, 2017).

To make sense of this emerging research on relational wellbeing qualities, the NDeTeC framework proposed a second group of root system processes called the self-world capacity. This capacity is about our sense of self in relation to others – including family relationships, peer-relationships, connections to our culture, spiritual or religious tradition, nature and the world broadly speaking. Reflecting the contextualised approach to MHW, this capacity is 'ethically-grounded' in prosocial emotions including not only gratitude, but also compassion as well as purpose in life linked to contributing meaningfully to greater good. Thus, the self-world capacity can be defined in terms of the 'root systems' as 'processes that need to be fostered to enable development of a connected, flexible, ethically-grounded and purposeful sense of self in support of child and adolescent long-term MHW' (Dorjee, 2024, p. 22).

> **Key Term**
>
> The *Self-World Capacity* is the second 'root systems' capacity in the NDeTeC framework. The Self-World Capacity specifies the processes in the mind and brain that underpin a connected, flexible, ethically-grounded and purposeful sense of self.

The self-world capacity integrates a range of existing relational wellbeing concepts – such as empathy, connections, self-compassion, engagement, hope, prosociality, purpose, gratitude, compassion and awe (see Figure 1.1 above). It also enables for the overlaps across these concepts to be more visible. For example, teaching children empathy skills is often emphasised in wellbeing curricula, but it is rarely acknowledged that empathy can lead to distress. This can arise when we relate to the suffering of others without taking empathy one step further, towards compassion and prosociality. As a result, empathically relating to others' difficulties can sometimes make us feel hopeless, for instance when thinking about the effects of climate change or war or illness of a friend. But compassion and prosociality can extend empathy towards compassionate thoughts and actions which turn empathic distress into positive emotions and actions benefiting our mental MHW (Singer & Klimecki,

2014). In this way, the self-world capacity enables us to recognise how relational wellbeing qualities can complement each other.

> Questions for reflection:
> - Can you think back of instances when children in your classroom experienced gratitude, awe or compassion and reflect on how this impacted their MHW?
> - Did you know that prosocial behaviours such as helping and sharing can support children's MHW?
> - Did you know that having a purpose in life can protect MHW and can be taught as early as in primary schools?

Facets of the Self-World Capacity

Just like in the case of the self-regulation capacity, there is a progression of processes across the facets of the self-world capacity. The first facet, the Facet of Shared Humanity, introduces the shared nature of human experience to counter feelings of isolation and excessive self-criticism symptomatic of anxiety and depression. In this facet new techniques are presented which can enable one to provide balanced and caring support to others and oneself during difficult experiences. Then the second facet, the Facet of Connections, explores in more depth the different types of connections in our lives and relates these to strategies fostering gratitude, awe and interconnectedness.

Expanding the scope of previous learning, the Facet of Agency (Making a Difference) describes the differences between empathy and compassion, and links these to cultivation of different types of prosocial behaviour to support MHW. Building on the learning in the first three facets, the Facet of Purpose in Life explores the sense of meaning and purpose in life linked to extrinsic (fame, beauty, wealth) and intrinsic values (personal growth, contribution to community etc.). Finally, the Facet of Flexible Self integrates the processes across the facets and explores whether we and others can change and how this relates to our MHW. This facet cultivates a flexible sense of self which has been associated with good MHW, in contrast to a rigid sense of self which is linked to poor MHW (Snyder et al., 2019).

> **Key Term**
>
> The facets of the Self-World Capacity are: shared humanity, connections, making a difference, purpose in life and flexible self-concept.

Neuroscience of the Self-World Capacity

The neuroscience underpinning the self-world capacity builds on and expands the neuroscience underlying the self-regulation capacity. The processes across the self-world capacity facets involve the mentalising network of the brain linked to our ability to recognise and reason about our and others' thoughts, feelings and behaviours. These are processes sometimes described as the 'theory of mind' and 'perspective taking' – laying the foundations for our ability to relate to others, connect with each other, develop a sense of purpose and identity, and act prosocially. The mentalising network involves brain regions such as the TPJ (temporo-parietal junction) and regions in the PFC (medial PFC).

Further brain networks underpinning the self-world capacity include the empathy and prosocial networks but also the reward network which activates in response to rewarding social experiences linked to connecting with others in compassionate and prosocial ways. Finally the default mode network, which also supports self-regulation, is involved in processes shaping our sense of purpose in life and our sense of self. We will consider each of these networks in detail, including their key brain regions, when we introduce the self-world capacity facets in Chapters 7 to 10.

The ATTEND Framework

Coming back to the challenges Kathryn is faced with in the scenario from the beginning of this chapter, the previous sections would have provided her with the 'roadmap' of MHW learning – in terms of the key pillars of MHW and the two key capacities underpinning MHW development. She may also now have a better understanding of the different overlaps and relations across different mental health concepts and approaches. However, it may not be clear to her how to translate this understanding into an actual framework for lessons with learning outcomes and corresponding knowledge, skills and strategies. To enable such 'translation' of the NDeTeC into educational practice, the facets of the two capacities are in this book presented in four groups of processes, and associated knowledge and skills, to be fostered in schools: Guiding **ATT**ention, Managing **E**motions, Nurturing Co**N**nections and Finding **D**irection. All four groups together give rise to the ATTEND framework for school MHW curricula.

> **Key Term**
>
> The *ATTEND framework* 'translates' the research in the NDeTeC theory specifying the Self-Regulation and Self-World Capacities into a framework for MHW curricula in schools.

In short, the acronym ATTEND means that we 'show up' to our experience by noticing it in an accepting and kind way and that we 'own' our experience in a sense of managing our thoughts, emotions and behaviours skilfully in support of our MHW. ATTEND also means 'to stand up and be counted' meaning that we recognise the shared nature of our human experiences, the multitude of connections we have with others and nature, and choose to make a difference, day in day out, using our strengths. This can in turn foster our sense of purpose in life (direction) that involves contributing to goals that make the world a better place, and our sense of self (identity) that is accepting, virtue-grounded and flexible.

Guiding ATTention

Fostering attention processes is the foundation of any MHW skill or strategy. This is because what we pay attention to and how we pay attention strongly influences our MHW. We have a natural tendency to notice and remember threatening events, this is called the negativity bias – an evolutionary bias to keep us safe. For instance, when we eat some food that makes us ill we need to remember not to eat the same food again. However, excessive negativity bias, such as repetitive thinking about something unpleasant that happened earlier in the day or repetitive self-critical thoughts, can undermine our MHW. So noticing what we pay attention to and choosing activities where we can pay attention to what supports our MHW is a foundational skill for other MHW skills and strategies.

Similarly, how we pay attention matters, particularly when we pay attention to our thoughts, emotions and behaviours. This is because paying attention to our experiences in a judgmental rigid way can worsen our MHW. Learning to pay attention to our experiences in an kind, accepting and non-judgmental way is another foundational skill for fostering MHW. Therefore, in the ATTEND framework children develop the knowledge, skills and strategies of 'what' and 'how' we pay attention to our thoughts, emotions and behaviours in the first two facets of the framework – the Facet of Emotional Awareness and the Facet of Managing Distractions. These two facets form the first tier of the ATTEND Pyramid (see Figure 1.2).

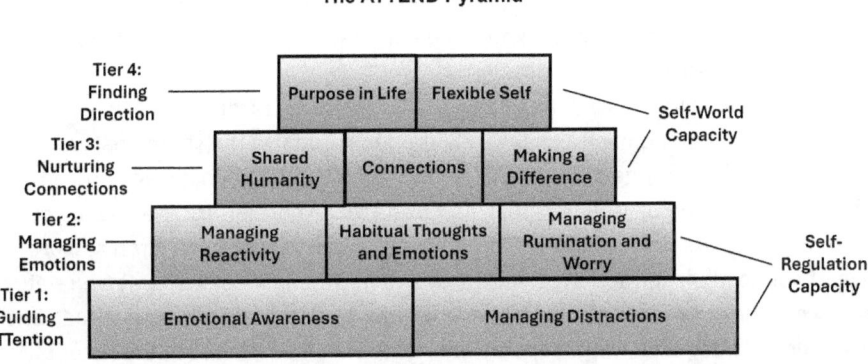

Figure 1.2 The ATTEND Pyramid of MHW knowledge and skills.

Managing Emotions

Building on the knowledge and skills in guiding attention, the second tier of the ATTEND Pyramid aims to develop the abilities of managing emotions. Neuroscience research shows that brain regions involved in guiding attention and managing emotions overlap. So after children have strengthened their attention skills, they are able to engage in further fostering of their emotion regulation skills more readily. In this tier, children gradually develop the knowledge and skills of the three remaining facets of the self-regulation capacity – Managing Reactivity, Working with Habitual Thoughts and Emotions and Managing Rumination and Worry.

The progression of the three facets in this tier reflects increasing complexity in emotion regulation strategies. For example, in the Facet of Managing Reactivity children learn simple emotion regulation strategies involving paced breathing and progressive muscle relaxation. These require less cognitive resources than strategies that involve recognising and managing habitual emotion regulation patterns or managing rumination (repetitive negative thinking) and worry. This is because these latter strategies rely more extensively on metacognition (noticing one's thoughts and emotions), working memory (holding information in our mind) and decision making. These abilities are underpinned by the PFC which has a protracted maturation trajectory until the age of 25, but children from the age of four can start using some of these strategies with support and fall back on simpler strategies when needed.

Nurturing CoNnections

After children have strengthened their attention and emotion regulation abilities, they can more effectively engage with learning strategies aiming to foster their relational wellbeing. This is because being able to manage attention and emotions are prerequisites for being able to communicate and engage with others effectively. For example, children who are not able to effectively manage distractions or are more reactive will find it more difficult to engage in play with other children or group activities both in and outside of the classroom. In the tier of nurturing connections, children build on their attention and emotion regulation skills to gradually develop the knowledge and skills in the facets of shared humanity, connections and making a difference.

The knowledge and skills again build up across the three facets of this tier. The learning in the facet of shared humanity enables children to recognise the shared nature of human experiences across a range of emotions – from happiness, through anxiety and anger. This counters the feelings of isolation that can exacerbate normal experiences of moderate anxiety and sadness, for example. Then building on this learning, children explore a wide range of connections in their lives, including and beyond immediate personal relations. In this process they work with strategies developing prosocial emotions of gratitude and awe. These emotions, together with empathy and compassion developed in the Facet of Making a Difference are then applied 'to fuel' prosocial action. Children learn across the facets how the emotions discussed and prosocial actions can support their MHW and develop skills in applying them in their lives.

Finding Direction

Finally, the tier of Finding Direction builds on all the previous learning in the preceding three tiers to foster a sense of purpose and a flexible sense of self in children. Having a sense of purpose and meaning in life is one of the main predictors of MHW, even physical health, across the lifespan. Now that children have developed strong self-regulation abilities and relational wellbeing skills, they can explore how all these skills can be brought together in cultivating their sense of direction in life. They explore different types of life goals and are encouraged to consider how they can contribute to greater good in society through their skills and goals. They also start exploring pathways to achieving such goals, from volunteering through studying to engagement in climate action and other wholesome causes.

This exploration is intertwined with further fostering of the self-concept in the facet of a flexible sense of self. Children start to recognise their strengths and aspects of self they may want to change. They consider how they could build up their strengths and use them in line with their direction in life, their developing sense of purpose. They also start to recognise – from a perspective of shared humanity, acceptance and non-judgment – that we all have some aspects of ourselves that we may want to work on and that we can change. They may start setting realistic goals to develop some qualities they would like to strengthen, such as patience or kindness or confidence, and are supported in cultivating these qualities. In this process they can harness the wide range of skills in attention regulation, managing emotions and nurturing connections they built up previously.

The 7-Step Approach

So now that we have specified the ATTEND framework, you might be wondering (just like Kathryn probably would be too), about the pedagogical approach to teaching the knowledge, skills and strategies of the framework. In other words, you might be thinking about the actual steps of teaching the ATTEND framework in your classroom. This is a key point, because for the learning to be effective, the teaching approach needs to be systematic – gradually scaffolding and fostering children's MHW knowledge and skills to enable them to apply what they have learned in everyday life within and outside of school. The process of teaching the MHW skills also needs to be non-probing, ensuring that the learning content and process doesn't trigger underlying trauma experiences and mental ill-health symptoms. For these reasons, the ATTEND framework is in this book presented for implementation in the classroom via the 7-Step Approach.

> ### Key Term
>
> The *7-Step Approach* specifies the pedagogy for teaching MHW knowledge and skills detailed in the ATTEND framework.

The 7-Step Approach follows two key principles. The first principle describes a progression of learning from external examples of MHW knowledge, skills and strategies to exploration of how this knowledge, skills and strategies might be applicable to one's own experience. Accordingly, in the following chapters, for each of the ten facets of the ATTEND framework, there will be a progression from examples presented in cartoons or stories or public life examples to exploration of how these examples might be relevant to children's own experiences. The second principle describes a progression from practice of knowledge, skills and strategies in 'artificial' scenarios in the classroom to 'real world' application of the knowledge, skills and strategies during the school day and outside of school. This ensures that children develop life-long MHW competencies embedded in their lives since this is the only way the MHW knowledge, skills and strategies they acquire can protect their MHW in the long term.

In what follows, I will introduce each of the seven steps in general terms. These steps are applied to each of the ten facets of the ATTEND framework in the following chapters. The first three steps focus on developing knowledge about the key MHW concept for each facet and associated strategies based on external examples, such as stories and cartoons. The following four steps develop skills where children apply the knowledge about the concept and strategies to their own experience.

Step 1

Objective: To learn the key MHW concept of a facet and know how it relates to MHW based on external examples

The first step of learning in each of the facets involves children familiarising themselves with the key concept/concepts to be explored in each facet based on external examples. For example, in the first facet of the ATT (Guiding Attention), children learn about emotional awareness. Based on examples from cartoons or stories, the teacher explains to children what emotional awareness means – noticing emotions in a non-judgmental way. Children then practise themselves recognising instances of emotional awareness in further examples from cartoons or stories. They also learn how noticing emotions can support MHW based on examples from cartoons and stories.

Step 2

Objective: To learn about the strategy/strategies linked to the key MHW concept and know how it/they can support MHW based on external examples

In the second step, children build on their learning about the key concept from the first step and expand it further by learning about a strategy associated with the key concept based on external examples. For instance, in the case of emotional awareness, children learn that naming emotions can help us manage them based on examples from stories or cartoons. They learn that naming an emotion decreases the intensity of the emotion (its strength). To prepare children for applying naming of emotions as a strategy in Steps 4-7, in this step children also learn to recognise and name a wider range of emotions based on examples from stories and cartoons, as appropriate for their age.

Step 3

Objective: To learn basic neuroscience underpinning the key MHW concept and the associated strategy/strategies

Learning about neural underpinnings of MHW can be a useful tool for children in making sense of how they feel. It can provide vocabulary that encourages decentring (healthy distancing) from thoughts and feelings as part of emotion regulation. Research from the Well Minds Lab suggests that primary school children enjoy learning about neuroscience of MHW, and use their neuroscience understanding in reflecting on and managing their thoughts, emotions and behaviours. Another reason to teach children neuroscience of MHW is to empower them through understanding that they can develop considerable control over how they think and feel through acquiring relevant knowledge and skills and applying them in everyday life.

Therefore, in the third step children learn the neuroscience underpinning the particular concept and strategy. For example, in the Facet of Emotional Awareness, children learn that there is a brain region called the ACC which helps us notice our emotions. As children progress through primary school years they also learn that another brain region, called the insula, helps us notice feelings in the body linked to our emotions. And older children learn that ACC and insula are part of the salience network in the brain which helps us notice and recognise our emotions. They also learn how these brain regions, through enabling emotional awareness, can support MHW. In this step, children work with the examples introduced in Steps 1 and 2 when expanding their understanding through relevant neuroscience knowledge.

Step 4

Objective: To start applying knowledge about the key MHW concept to own experience in support of own MHW

This is the first step that involves learning of relevant skills associated with the key MHW concept by starting to apply the knowledge learned in Steps 1-3 to children's own experience. In the case of emotional awareness, in this step children are guided in practices that encourage them to explore if any of the examples of emotional awareness from stories and cartoons relate to their own experiences. Teachers can provide children with different individual and pair/group activities that provide opportunities for age-appropriate exploration of similarities and differences between the emotional awareness examples and children's own experiences.

Step 5

Objective: To start applying knowledge about the strategy/strategies linked to the key MHW concept to own experience in support of own MHW

In Step 5 children are guided through activities that encourage them to apply the strategies they learned about based on external examples to their own experience. For instance, in the Facet of Emotional Awareness, children will be encouraged to name their emotions following the examples of characters from stories or cartoons. Teachers can facilitate this by providing children with a list of emojis or emotion words children can choose from. Children are then encouraged to recognise how naming an emotion makes them feel and explore how this could support their MHW. They can practise these skills further, in age-appropriate ways, in pairs or groups.

Step 6

Objective: To start using knowledge about neuroscience underpinning the key concept and associated strategy/strategies in supporting own MHW

In the sixth step, children further practise applying the knowledge and skills they learned in previous steps to their own experience by weaving in their neuroscience knowledge. For example, in the Facet of Emotional Awareness children can practise explaining how they are applying recognising and naming emotions to managing their attention and emotions using references to the ACC, insula and the salience network. Including neuroscience in reflections on their experience can have 'therapeutic effects' in itself, as it provides a decentred language to verbalise how they feel. It also further solidifies their understanding of emotional awareness and naming of emotions as a way of supporting their MHW.

Step 7

Objective: To apply the new knowledge and skills about the key MHW concept and associated strategy/strategies, including neuroscience, in everyday life

Finally, in the last step, children are encouraged to apply the knowledge and skills they learned in their everyday life, both in the classroom and at home. This can be achieved through teacher prompts during classes and breaks, reflective practices at the end of the day recalling how they were applying the particular strategy during the day and plans/reflective practices on how children are applying the strategy at home. For emotional awareness, children would be reminded by teachers and teaching assistants in everyday situations to notice their emotions in the moment when appropriate and name their emotions as a way of regulating them. Children could also create logs where they track their use of the naming of emotions strategy outside of school for a week and reflect on how this impacted their MHW. They use neuroscience references in their reflections and descriptions of experience if they find that helpful.

Conclusion

This chapter outlined the key concepts and approaches that we will be applying throughout this book as we introduce each of the facets of the ATTEND framework. If you could relate to the case study about Kathryn, a teacher in year 4 trying to 'make sense' of the myriad of MHW concepts and approaches in preparing lessons for her pupils, hopefully the chapter provided you with an initial roadmap of the ATTEND approach. Perhaps you now have a bit more clarity about how the different MHW concepts overlap and how we can organise them in a meaningful way if we follow the 'matrix' of facets of the self-regulation and self-world capacities. You may also be able to start seeing the 'big picture' based on the ATTEND Pyramid, outlining a progression of MHW learning based on the underpinning processes in the mind and brain. Finally, the 7-Step Approach hopefully provided a practical pedagogical approach to translating the ATTEND Framework into learning in your classroom. In the following chapters, we will now explore the research underpinning each of the ten facets of the ATTEND Pyramid and translate it into learning objectives, knowledge and skills based on the 7-Step Approach.

Key chapter points:

- There are 'root systems' of MHW, which we call MHW capacities in this book, that need to be fostered across primary school years to effectively support children's MHW.
- There are two key MHW capacities: the Self-Regulation Capacity and the Self-World Capacity.
- There is a progression of MHW knowledge and skills corresponding to the two capacities that can be taught across primary school years, just like learning to read or do maths.
- The ATTEND Framework explains how we can build up children's MHW knowledge and skills in four tiers of MHW learning.
- The 7-Step approach specifies how the MHW skills and knowledge of the four tiers of the ATTEND Pyramid can be systematically, effectively and safely taught in the classroom.

References

Dorjee, D. (2024). Conceptualising child and adolescent mental health and wellbeing neurodevelopment: an integrative brain networks framework. Preprint, 4 November. https://doi.org/10.31234/osf.io/7vx45

Kieling, C., Buchweitz, C., Caye, A., Silvani, J., Ameis, S. H., Brunoni, A. R., ... & Szatmari, P. (2024). Worldwide prevalence and disability from mental disorders across childhood and adolescence: evidence from the global burden of disease study. *JAMA Psychiatry, 81*(4), 347-356.

Kjell, O. N. (2011). Sustainable well-being: a potential synergy between sustainability and well-being research. *Review of General Psychology, 15*(3), 255-266.

Klinge, J. L., Warschburger, P., Busching, R., & Klein, A. M. (2023). Self-regulation facets differentially predict internalizing symptom trajectories from middle childhood to early adolescence: a longitudinal multimethod study. *Child and Adolescent Psychiatry and Mental Health*, *17*(1), 120.

Moffitt, T. E., Arseneault, L., Belsky, D., Dickson, N., Hancox, R. J., Harrington, H., ... & Caspi, A. (2011). A gradient of childhood self-control predicts health, wealth, and public safety. *Proceedings of the National Academy of Sciences*, *108*(7), 2693-2698.

Newlove-Delgado T, Marcheselli F, Williams T, Mandalia D, Dennes M, McManus S, Savic M, Treloar W, Croft K, Ford T. (2023). *Mental health of children and young people in England, 2023*. Leeds: NHS England.

Njoroge, W. F., Forkpa, M., & Bath, E. (2021). Impact of racial discrimination on the mental health of minoritized youth. *Current Psychiatry Reports*, *23*, 1-7.

Obeldobel, C. A., & Kerns, K. A. (2021). A literature review of gratitude, parent-child relationships, and well-being in children. *Developmental Review*, *61*, 100948.

Palacios-Barrios, E. E., & Hanson, J. L. (2019). Poverty and self-regulation: connecting psychosocial processes, neurobiology, and the risk for psychopathology. *Comprehensive Psychiatry*, *90*, 52-64.

Shoshani, A., & Russo-Netzer, P. (2017). Exploring and assessing meaning in life in elementary school children: development and validation of the meaning in life in children questionnaire (MIL-CQ). *Personality and Individual Differences*, *104*, 460-465.

Singer, T., & Klimecki, O. M. (2014). Empathy and compassion. *Current Biology*, *24*(18), R875-R878.

Snyder, H. R., Friedman, N. P., & Hankin, B. L. (2019). Transdiagnostic mechanisms of psychopathology in youth: executive functions, dependent stress, and rumination. *Cognitive Therapy and Research*, *43*, 834-851.

PART I
Guiding Attention

2 Emotional Awareness

Introduction

The first 'building block' in the foundational tier of Guiding ATTention in the ATTEND Pyramid, aims to foster children's abilities of emotional awareness. The learning focuses on developing knowledge and skills of non-judgmentally noticing thoughts and emotions, recognising different types of emotions and using naming of emotions as a basic emotion regulation strategy. Noticing emotions is a bedrock of emotion regulation, because emotions that are not noticed can't be regulated readily. The process of noticing emotions largely builds on attention processes in the mind and brain, that's why emotional awareness is a key part of the Guiding ATTention tier of the Pyramid. Recognising and naming emotions takes emotional awareness one step further, enabling children to manage their emotions using this simple strategy.

In this chapter, we first explore the differences between emotions, feelings and moods, and then consider the research evidence linking emotional awareness with mental health and wellbeing (MHW). Next, we examine the processes in the mind and brain that underpin emotional awareness and naming of emotions, and explain how these processes develop in children. Finally, the chapter outlines ways we can teach emotional awareness in the primary school classroom in an age-appropriate way and step-by-step following the 7-Step Approach. But first, let's consider an example of a real-world school scenario exemplifying the challenges of teaching emotional awareness in primary schools.

Case Study: Teaching Emotional Awareness across Primary School Years

Anya is a pastoral lead in her primary school. At the last meeting with the school leadership it was decided that there is the need to improve their school's MHW strategy. In that meeting, Anya presented to her colleagues the key points from the government guidance on supporting MHW in primary schools. The guidance mostly mentioned two key abilities that need to be fostered in children of this age – emotional awareness and self-regulation. Anya and her colleagues agreed that they will expand the MHW provision in their school to include more focus on fostering these two abilities in pupils. Anya has been tasked with developing a detailed strategy to accomplish this.

DOI: 10.4324/9781003609087-4

To start with, Anya went back to the government guidance on MHW, but there were very few details on how to foster emotional awareness and self-regulation in primary school children. So she looked up more information online, but it was still fairly basic. Most of the information on emotional awareness highlighted the importance of teaching children vocabulary that would enable them recognise and name a range of emotions. Anya already knew this. But she didn't find much information on why this would improve children's MHW. She was also wondering whether fostering emotional awareness in children could actually undermine their MHW, since they may start noticing negative emotions they were not aware of before. She found no information on that online.

Anya was also looking for some research-based information on how to foster emotional awareness in primary school children in a developmentally appropriate way. She was aware that MHW strategies are most effective if they are cultivated continuously across primary school years, but didn't know how this could apply to fostering emotional awareness. She did not want the learning across the years to be repetitive, but meaningfully built-up. She found virtually no guidance on developmental progression in acquiring emotional awareness knowledge and skills.

Questions for reflection:

- Do you know how and why emotional awareness can support children's MHW?
- How do you approach teaching emotional awareness in your classroom?
- How would you build up the knowledge and skills of emotional awareness across the primary school years if you were to face the same task as Anya?

Distinguishing Emotions, Feelings and Mood

To start with, it might be helpful to draw distinctions across common psychological terms related to emotional awareness: emotions, feelings and mood. In research literature all three of these terms fall under the broad label of 'affect'. However, *emotions* are a more short-lived kind of affect and usually arise in response to a particular event. Emotions consist of several components (Frijda, 1987; Scherer, 2009; Mulligan & Scherer, 2012). While we often think of emotions in terms of how they make us feel, *feelings* are only one aspect of emotions related to how we experience emotions. Another component of emotions is an *action tendency*, when emotions motivate us to act/behave in a certain way. For example, when we are angry we may want to 'act' on that feeling by shouting or when we are happy we may want to hug others or jump etc.

In addition, emotions are linked to particular types of thoughts and thought patterns – that's their *cognitive component*. For instance, when we are sad we might keep on thinking about an event that made us feel sad or if we feel gratitude we may think about what we are grateful for. The feelings, action tendency and thought patterns are also associated with *neurophysiological changes* in the body, such as changes in heart rate, sweat patterns, stress response in general and brain activity patterns. Just think about how it feels in the body when you are angry, sad, joyful, grateful or calm. Finally, all these components are usually also associated with particular *facial and vocal expressions* – we can often tell if somebody is anxious, angry, sad, joyful, calm simply from their face or from their voice.

Now how do emotions differ from feelings and moods? *Feelings* can be considered as the experiential side of emotions, what emotions feel like. So feelings are a part of emotions, but emotions also include the other components mentioned above. In contrast to emotions and feelings, *moods* are longer-term affective experiences where we sometimes might be able to point to an event that led to a change in our mood but often we don't know why we are experiencing a particular mood. Here it might be useful to acknowledge that in the clinical context, mood disorders, such as depression, are typically associated with longer-term experience of a particular mood (e.g., sadness) with its impact on one's ability to function in everyday life. In comparison with moods, emotions change more often, we can experience different emotions in one day.

> **Key Terms**
>
> - *Emotions* are a kind of short-lived affect, often in response to a particular event. We can experience several emotions in a day. Emotions have four components – feelings (what emotions feel like), thoughts, action tendency (behaviour) and neurophysiological changes (including bodily sensations).
> - *Feelings* are the experiential part of emotions, what it feels like to experience a particular emotion.
> - *Mood* is a longer-term affective experience, often we don't know why our mood changed.
> - *Affect* is an overarching psychological category including emotions, feelings and moods.

How Is Emotional Awareness Relevant to MHW?

In the scenario we started with, Anya was wondering how and why emotional awareness can support children's MHW. We have already mentioned that emotional awareness is a prerequisite for applying any further emotion regulation techniques. However, this is only the case if emotional awareness is non-judgmental and accepting. Otherwise, greater awareness of emotions could lead to negative rumination or worry and exacerbate feelings of anxiety or depression. Therefore, it is essential to equip children with knowledge and skills of emotional awareness that support rather than hinder MHW.

The Healthy Kind of Emotional Awareness

Kind non-judgmental awareness of emotions means that we notice our feelings without judging them as good or bad, they are just feelings we are experiencing right now. It also means that we notice how our emotions feel in the body, again, in a gentle non-judgmental way. For example, when we are angry we usually frown and may have clenched fists. Noticing how emotions make us act/behave is also part of emotional awareness. And finally, we can notice how different emotions impact our brain and body – for instance, make us feel full of energy when we are happy, give us sweaty palms when we are anxious or make us feel lethargic when we are sad. Noticing these different aspects of emotions in a kind, gentle and non-judgmental way can help us notice earlier when we start experiencing an emotion, and then we can start managing the emotion earlier too. This is often easier than managing an emotion when it is very strong.

Indeed, research shows that adaptive emotional awareness (with the qualities of kindness and acceptance) is one of the main 'root system' processes in the mind and brain underpinning MHW. One study found that those children and adolescents (7-19-year-olds) with higher emotional awareness were less likely to experience psychopathology (e.g. anxiety and depression). The study also reported that over time low emotional awareness 'enabled' worsening in mental health, particularly in girls (Weissman et al., 2020). Therefore, the study concluded that low emotional awareness might be a transdiagnostic mechanism underpinning poor mental health.

There is another potential benefit to emotional awareness. Given that a lot of MHW learning in schools focused on mental health literacy over the last decade, some researchers raised the concern that this may have led to 'overpathologising' of a normal range of emotional experiences (Foulkes & Andrews, 2023). For example, when children learn about symptoms of mental ill-health as part of mental health literacy lessons, they may incorrectly infer that any feelings of sadness or worry or anxiety mean they have a mental health disorder. This tendency can be further exacerbated by presentations of disclosures about mental health difficulties being perceived as socially rewarding on social media, following celebrity examples (Lind & Wickström, 2024). Effective teaching of emotional awareness in schools may help children recognise a healthy range of emotional experiences, while drawing clear differences between pathology and normal variations in emotions.

Benefits of Naming Emotions

Such acquisition of emotional awareness knowledge and skills can be further enhanced, and safeguarded, by teaching children simple strategies of regulating their emotions via naming their emotions. While mostly based on research findings from studies with adults, there is also evidence from studies with adolescents showing that naming emotions, either by speaking or in writing, can reduce the intensity of emotions (their strength) and associated distress. For example, in one study girls named their emotions in a diary and their parents noticed a reduction in their anxiety levels (Thomassin et al., 2012). This is a very simple strategy that doesn't require strategic thinking and analysis of emotions or thoughts, which makes it particularly suitable for children.

So how does naming emotions work as an emotion regulation strategy? The short answer is that we don't know for sure, but there are a couple of plausible explanations (Torre & Liberman, 2018). One of them is closely linked to the healthy kind of emotional awareness because noticing emotions in a kind and accepting way can also foster healthy distancing from emotions. This is a strategy particularly cultivated in mindfulness which also emphasises kind and accepting awareness of thoughts, emotions and sensations. As a result, we are less immersed in our thoughts and emotions and less reactive to them. But there are also other explanations, for example one theory suggests that when we name emotions, we are reducing uncertainty about what we are experiencing and this reduces activity in the amygdalae. Regardless of which of the theories turns out to be most supported by research findings, there is sufficient rigorous evidence to encourage children to use naming of emotions in managing their emotions.

Questions for reflection:

- When is emotional awareness helpful and when can it be unhelpful?
- What does the research on the effects of emotional awareness on MHW show?
- How can naming emotions support emotion regulation?

Neuroscience of Emotional Awareness

Emotional awareness is underpinned by the salience network, encompassing a coordinated activity across a range of brain regions involved in bottom-up and top-down self-regulation. The ATTEND Framework particularly emphasises the role of two key brain regions in emotional awareness – the ACC and the insula – even though other regions such as VS and amygdalae are also part of this network. The ACC stands for the anterior cingulate cortex. The dorsal part of the ACC (dACC) is particularly involved in the salience network. The ACC enables us to notice where we are placing our attention and guides our attention to what we want to focus on. It also monitors our attention focus, enabling us to notice when we are focusing on something else than what we want to focus on. The ACC integrates information from different brain regions, putting together information about the different components of emotions and thus enabling us to notice and differentiate emotions.

The insula are particularly involved in noticing sensations in the body that are linked to emotions. For example, when we are anxious we may feel tension in our tummy and notice that the palms of our hands are sweaty. And when we are relaxed we may notice the tightness in our shoulders loosening up and our body posture being more straight. Insula (particularly its anterior part) enables us to notice these changes in our body and feelings. It works together with the ACC and other brain regions of the salience network to help us notice and distinguish emotions, and this in turn enables effective emotion regulation.

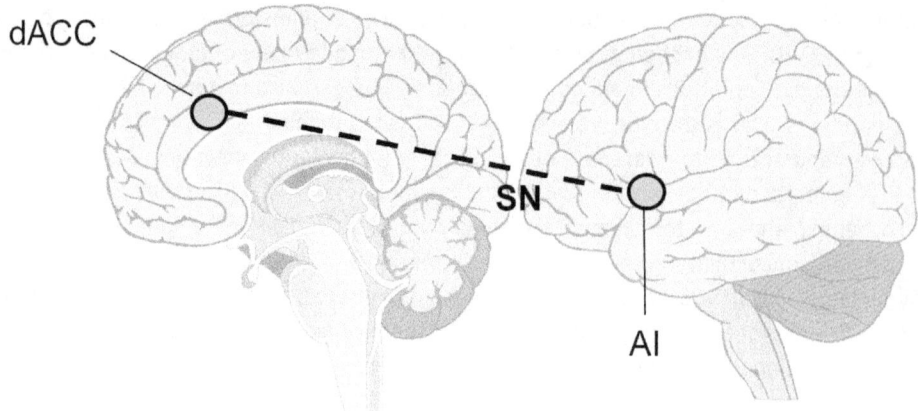

Figure 2.1 The salience network - SN: dACC - dorsal Anterior Cingulate Cortex, AI - Anterior Insula. Source: adapted with permission from Dorjee (2024)

> **Salience Network and Emotional Awareness at the Playground**
>
> Joe is a little boy in year 2. Anya, who is the pastoral lead in the school, noticed that when she asks Joe about how he is feeling he usually mentions only two types of emotions – sad or happy. Joe also has sometimes difficulty managing his emotions when playing with others; after a disagreement with his friends at the playground he often runs off and withdraws, playing by himself. So Anya advised the teacher of the year 2 class to teach children more strategies of emotional awareness.
>
> Following Anya's advice, children were guided to recognise what different basic emotions may feel like in their body. The teacher also explained that we need to be kind and gentle to ourselves when noticing our emotions. She explained to children that emotions are usually not good or bad, they are just trying to tell us how we feel so that we can take care of ourselves. Just like a rumbling tummy may tell us that we are hungry, a tight belly can tell us that we are a bit scared and we need to relax or find safety. The teacher also encouraged children to name the new emotions they noticed to help manage them in the moment.
>
> Anya knew, and explained to the teacher and teaching assistants, that this type of learning would 'strengthen' the salience network in children. She was also aware that repetition was the key to increasing the activity in the developing salience network. So she asked teaching assistants to encourage children in the year 2 class, including Joe, to notice and name their emotions in different situations in the classroom and on the playground. After a couple of months Anya observed that Joe was withdrawing from the play with his classmates less often at the playground. The class teacher and teaching assistant confirmed this when Anya asked them, they also noticed that other children in the year 2 class started to notice and manage their emotions more readily.

The above example of the effects increasing emotional awareness can have is aligned with neuroscience research showing that healthy development of the salience network contributes to MHW. Specifically, childhood trauma has been linked with aberrant development of the salience network (McLaughlin et al., 2019). One study showed that adverse childhood experiences were associated with maladaptive changes to the salience network observed in adolescence (Rakesh et al., 2023). In the same study researchers found that abnormalities in the salience network were related to higher likelihood of depression. This raises the possibility that improving the functioning of the salience network in childhood could prevent mental health difficulties in adolescence.

> **Key Neuroscience Terms for Emotional Awareness**
> - The *anterior cingulate cortex* (ACC) is a brain region located on the surface of the brain, but in its middle part (closer to the forehead) surrounding the connection between the two brain hemispheres (the corpus callosum). The ACC helps us notice our emotions by putting together the different types of information about the different components of emotions. It also helps us monitor and guide our attention, making it easier to notice and differentiate our emotions.
> - *Insula* (or *insular cortex*) are located deeper in the brain, on its sides, under the intersection between temporal, parietal and frontal lobes. The insula enable us to notice sensations in the body that help us distinguish emotions and manage them (e.g. tension in our tummy or sweaty palms).
> - The *salience network* involves the ACC (specifically dACC), insula and other brain regions. It enables us to notice our thoughts, emotions and bodily sensations and monitor what we are focusing on.

How Can Children Acquire the Knowledge and Skills of Emotional Awareness?

Now that you know why emotional awareness and naming emotions can support children's MHW, you might be wondering, just like Anya did in our case study, how you can effectively teach these MHW skills in your classroom. The first steps in fostering emotional awareness in children involve learning from examples of others how they noticed their thoughts and emotions and how this helped them manage these better. This is accompanied by learning age-appropriate vocabulary and learning how to recognise different emotions, including understanding that emotions usually involve thoughts, affective feelings, feelings in the body and tendency to act in a certain way.

Learning about differences across emotions can be further facilitated by introduction of the Pleasantness and Intensity scales/graph. Emotions have been traditionally described and distinguished using these two dimensions (Yarwood, 2022). For example anger is often an unpleasant and high intensity emotion. In contrast, feeling lethargic is a low intensity unpleasant emotion. Feeling excited is often a pleasant high intensity emotion. And feeling calm can be a pleasant low intensity emotion. Distinguishing emotions based on these dimensions can enable children to fine-tune their understanding of emotions. It can also enable them to notice more accurately changes in these emotional dimensions after they use emotional awareness and naming emotions, thus supporting their MHW. And together with learning relevant neuroscience, such understanding can enable children to further explore emotions from a more decentred perspective.

> **Key Strategy for Emotional Awareness**
>
> Naming Emotions is a simple emotion regulation strategy where we put a word label on our emotional experience, in speaking or writing.
>
> - Pleasantness (valence) of emotions can be evaluated on a scale from very unpleasant to very pleasant.
> - Intensity of emotions can be evaluated on a scale from very weak to very strong.

After acquiring this foundational knowledge about noticing thoughts and emotions together with relevant vocabulary and neuroscience, children are encouraged to use naming of their emotions and describing the process of noticing emotions in a non-judgmental way in everyday situations. They explore how this may be helpful in managing their emotions. However, it is useful to keep in mind that excessive noticing of thoughts and emotions followed by rumination is often associated with mental ill-health. Therefore, children need to be encouraged to notice their emotions and name them, then return to their usual activity. In case further regulation of emotions is needed, children should be then guided in other emotion regulation strategies encouraging self-care (neutral mindful anchors or imagining soothing safe space or other attention-shifting strategies) which will be discussed in the following chapter.

Developmental Differences in Fostering the Knowledge and Skills of Emotional Awareness in Children

Learning age-appropriate emotion vocabulary is recommended as the foundation for other emotion regulation strategies across the primary school year groups. Children can also be encouraged from an early primary school age to learn to notice their thoughts and feelings and how these associate with feelings in the body and processes in the brain. As you will see in the 7-Step Approach, this learning would be very simple in reception and nursery, becoming more specific and detailed as children progress through the primary school years. Children can also be guided to use the 'naming emotions' strategy from early years, together with guidance on noticing how this strategy changes the way they feel.

> **Terminology: Feelings and Emotions**
>
> In descriptions of the 7-Step Approach the terms 'feelings' and 'emotions' are used in the following ways throughout the book:
>
> - In reception and KS1 the term 'feelings' is used instead of the term 'emotions' for easier grasp.
> - In lower and upper KS2 the term 'emotions' is used.

However, children can typically begin to effectively use metacognitive strategies, where they notice their thoughts and emotions and apply a certain strategy to manage them, from around the age of seven due to maturation of brain areas, mostly in the prefrontal cortex, and their connections with other brain areas including the salience network. Therefore, younger children will use the naming of emotions strategy less frequently and typically with support of adults. The ability to use naming of emotions as an emotion regulation strategy more effectively and independently increases as children progress through primary school.

> Questions for reflection:
>
> - Would you know how to teach emotional awareness skills to children in KS1?
> - What is the approximate range of emotions children can learn in KS2?
> - Can you describe the developmental progression of learning emotional awareness and naming emotions skills in primary school children?

Acquiring the Knowledge and Skills of Emotional Awareness: The 7-Step Approach

The acquisition of the knowledge and skills of emotional awareness follows the two principles of the 7-Step Approach we introduced in Chapter 1. Accordingly, the first three steps detailed below will focus on equipping children with foundational knowledge about emotional awareness and naming emotions, including relevant neuroscience. They will also learn how emotional awareness and naming of emotions can support MHW based on external examples from stories and cartoons. In the following four steps children will apply this knowledge in developing their own skills of emotional awareness and naming emotions. They will progress from practising these skills in 'artificial' scenarios in the classroom to applying the new skills increasingly in everyday life in school and at home. Each of the seven steps will describe age-appropriate knowledge and skills for the four primary school age group: reception (4–5-year-olds), KS1 (5–7-year-olds), lower KS2 (7–9-year-olds), upper KS2 (9–11-year-olds).

Step 1: Learning How Noticing of Thoughts and Emotions Relates to MHW

The learning objective of this first step is for children to acquire the knowledge that will enable them to understand that noticing our thoughts and emotions (and behaviours) in a non-judgmental way can help us manage them and improve our MHW. The learning is based on impersonal examples from stories, cartoons and public life.

In *reception*, children begin to understand that it can be useful to notice what we are feeling and thinking in a kind and non-judgmental way. To foster basic familiarity with the concept of emotional awareness, the teacher can provide children with simple examples from cartoons or use a story involving a puppet. Then children start practising recognising (with support) instances where characters noticed their thoughts and feelings in the same examples. Children are then provided with new examples and they practise recognising instances of noticing thoughts and feelings further. Finally, the teacher explains that noticing thoughts and feelings can help us feel better using the same or new examples of characters or stories. Children then practise recognising the link between noticing thoughts and feelings and feeling better in examples provided with teacher support.

In contrast to children in reception, pupils in *KS1* will be able to recognise instances of characters noticing their thoughts and feelings in a kind and non-judgmental way more readily in examples. They can now also begin to recognise that our feelings are linked to feelings in our body. A teacher can provide examples of noticing thoughts and feelings, and associated feelings in the body, in a story. Children can then practise pairing up feelings with thoughts and feelings in the body in simple examples, e.g. for feelings such as happy, sad, calm and angry. Once children are comfortable recognising instances of emotional awareness in the story characters, the teacher can start pointing out the link between emotional awareness and MHW. This can be done through examples where noticing feelings was the first step for the character in adaptively managing their feelings. Children can then practise identifying the link between noticing feelings and managing them (feeling better) on their own. They can, for example, prepare drawings depicting the link between noticing feelings and managing them better for basic feelings based on the examples provided in class.

In *lower KS2*, children are able to work with a greater range of examples that are more nuanced in describing emotional awareness in characters. They understand readily from examples that emotions are often linked to thoughts and feelings in our body. They also start recognising the links between emotions, thoughts, feelings in the body and behaviour in examples provided. They are able to come up with some examples of these links on their own, with support. When the teacher explains that emotional awareness can help us manage our emotions, thoughts and behaviours, children are able to identify these links in examples provided readily. In pairs, they can practise thinking of their own examples of emotional awareness that helped a character manage their emotions and made them feel better. They can share some of these examples with the whole class if they are comfortable.

Increasing the complexity and nuance of learning, *upper KS2* children can be provided with examples from stories or public life (celebrities, sportswomen and sportsmen, influencers ...) talking about emotional awareness and how it supports their mental health. Children can be provided with examples of how thoughts, emotional feelings, feelings in the body, our actions (behaviour) are all parts of emotions. They can practise recognising the four components of emotions in short written fictional scenarios. The teacher then explains how recognising these different components of emotions can support our MHW by enabling us to manage our emotions earlier on, before they get very strong. Children can then practise identifying the links between emotional awareness and MHW by writing their own short fictional scenarios. Finally, the teacher can explain to children the difference between emotions and moods and link this to mental health literacy. This can, for example, involve explaining that we all experience a range of emotions during a day, but significant changes in mood are what is typically more relevant to mental ill-health.

Step 2: Learning Emotion Vocabulary and that Naming Emotions Can Help Us Manage Them Better

The learning objective in the second step is for children to acquire age-appropriate vocabulary for naming emotions and to understand that naming emotions can help us manage them, and therefore improve our MHW. Children also learn that we can describe emotions by their pleasantness (feels good) and intensity (strength).

Building on the first step, children in *reception* learn names of basic emotions/feelings (happy, sad, angry, scared). They also learn that saying the name of the feeling can help one to feel better. To accomplish this, the teacher can prepare activities encouraging children to name 'feelings' of characters in cartoons or stories. These can be the same cartoons and stories children are already familiar with from step 1. Children are then provided with further cartoon/story examples and practice naming the characters' feelings. Afterwards, children are introduced to the 'feel good' and 'strength' aspects of feelings. The teacher can use the 'Feels Good Scale', for this age group it can be an emoji scale, to show children how the 'feel good' aspect of emotions can be assessed in the examples they worked with previously. Children practise 'guessing' how good the character felt using the scale in new examples. Then the teacher introduces the Emotion Strength Scale to measure how strongly a feeling was experienced by a character in a cartoon or story. Children practise 'guessing' this aspect of feelings too. In the final phase of this step, children are provided with very simple examples of how naming of a feeling helped characters manage them. They practise recognising this in further examples, with support.

> **Terminology: Feels Good/Pleasantness (Valence) and Strength/Intensity of Emotions**
>
> - The term 'feels good' with the 5-gradient Emoji Scale is used in reception and KS1 to describe valence (pleasantness) of emotions.
> - The term 'strength of an emotion' with the 5-gradient Emotion Strength Scale is used to describe intensity of emotions in reception and KS1 for easier comprehension.
> - The terms 'pleasantness of an emotion' and 'intensity of an emotion' are used in lower KS2 and upper KS2 together with the Pleasantness of Emotion Scale, Intensity of Emotion Scale (lower KS2) and Pleasantness and Intensity of Emotion Graph (upper KS2). These scales and graph use a 10-gradient assessment of emotions.

In *KS1*, children will be able to learn to recognise and name a wider range of feelings (6–8 different feelings) and will be able to understand more readily that naming feelings can help us feel better. The teacher can work with the examples from Step 1 to exemplify recognising feelings. Children can then practise recognising feelings with further examples. Once children are comfortable with the new emotion/feeling vocabulary, the teacher can provide them with examples showing that naming a feeling can help us feel better, it can help us manage the feeling. Children then practise recognising this in further examples on their own, with support. Finally, the teacher introduces the 'feel good' and 'strength' aspects of feelings using examples they worked with before. Children can practise recognising the feel good and strength aspects of feelings using the Emoji Scale and the Emotion Strength Scale. They can then try to recognise the emotions in the drawings they made in Step 1 and assess them using the two scales, with support.

In *lower KS2*, children are able to learn to differentiate a greater range of emotions (8–10 emotions) and they can readily recognise and rate the pleasantness and intensity of these emotions. They will also be able to readily understand that naming emotions can help us manage them. The teacher can work with previous examples from Step 1 and introduce new examples from stories and movies depicting the different emotions. The teacher can show children how to evaluate pleasantness and intensity of the emotions using the Pleasantness and Intensity Scales. Children then practise recognising and evaluating emotions on these two dimensions using new examples the teacher provides. Once children have a good level of competency in using the new emotion vocabulary and recognising the two dimensions of emotions, they are introduced to naming of emotions as an emotion regulation strategy using examples. Children then work in pairs and support each other in recognising the effects of naming emotions on the character's ability to manage their emotions.

Finally, children in the *upper KS2* further expand their emotion vocabulary and learn to distinguish 10-12 different emotions. They are also able to assess these emotions independently using the pleasantness and intensity dimensions. They can articulate mostly independently why naming emotions can help us manage them better. The teacher can work with the examples provided in Step 1 and introduce further examples to help children understand the differences across a wide range of emotions. The teacher and children can use references to the components of those emotions in drawing differences across emotions. The teacher can then encourage children to evaluate the emotions using the Pleasantness and Intensity of Emotions Graph, demonstrating how emotions fall into the four quadrants. Children can then work with the fictional scenarios they prepared in Step 1 and expand them further by specifying the emotions experienced by the characters and evaluating the emotions using the Pleasantness and Intensity of Emotions Graph. Once the teacher has explained to children that naming emotions can decrease their intensity, children further elaborate their scenarios by describing how naming emotions impacted the characters' experience of the emotions. They can use changes in intensity of emotions from before to after naming an emotion to quantify the impacts of emotion naming and further expand on how using naming of emotions as a strategy could impact the characters' MHW.

Step 3: Learning Neuroscience Underpinning Emotional Awareness and Naming Emotions

The learning objective in the third step is for children to acquire the knowledge enabling them to understand, in an age-appropriate way and based on impersonal examples, what happens in the brain when we notice thoughts and emotions and when we name emotions. They also learn to relate neuroscience underpinning emotional awareness and naming of emotions to MHW.

In the third step children in *reception* begin to link their learning about emotional awareness to learning about the brain. In this young age group, the learning can start with very simple explanations of where the brain is and what it helps us do. Then this can be linked to previous learning about noticing thoughts and feelings. The teacher can bring to the class a child-friendly model of the brain or a drawing of the brain. Children can then point to the model or the poster of the brain when they are learning about noticing thoughts and feelings, and naming feelings.

Children in *KS1*, will be able to start referring to specific brain regions when learning about emotional awareness. The teacher can explain to children that there is a part of the brain called the ACC that is active when we notice our thoughts and feelings. Children can try to write the letters ACC or act them out with their hands or arm postures. When the teacher is encouraging children to notice thoughts and feelings in cartoon or story examples, the teacher can also prompt children to remember that noticing feelings is linked to the part of the brain called the ACC. Pointing to the ACC in simple models of the brain or in a poster depicting the brain can also help children link noticing feelings to the ACC. This can be then further linked to

their understanding that noticing and naming feelings, enabled by the ACC, can help us manage them better.

In *lower KS2*, children can engage with slightly more detailed explanations of the neuroscience underpinning emotional awareness and naming of emotions. First, they can be introduced to the ACC – the teacher can elaborate that the ACC helps guide our attention so that we can notice our thoughts and emotions. This can be related to the examples from stories and movies introduced in Steps 1 and 2. Then the teacher explains that another brain region, called the insula, helps us notice how we feel and think. The insula are particularly helpful in enabling us to notice how emotions feel in the body. Again, this can be related to examples children worked with before. Children are then encouraged to practise referring to the ACC and insula when discussing examples of noticing thoughts, emotions, behaviours and naming emotions. They can also be provided with a simple brain drawing where they colour-in the ACC and insula brain regions.

Finally, *in upper KS2*, children are introduced to the ACC and insula regions and also learn that they are part of the salience network. They learn that the ACC stands for the Anterior Cingulate Cortex and that this brain region plays a key role in guiding and monitoring our attention - knowing where our attention is and moving it to where we want it to be. That's why it supports noticing emotions, thoughts and behaviours. The teacher also explains that insula are a brain region that enables us to notice bodily sensations linked to emotions. The ACC and insula work together in helping us notice and recognise emotions as part of the salience network, which also includes other brain regions. This learning is linked to the examples children learned about in the previous two steps and are further supported by explanations of where the ACC and insula brain regions are using brain posters. Children then elaborate the scenarios they prepared in Steps 1 and 2 with further references to the ACC, insula and the salience network. They can also practise explaining to each other in small groups their scenarios, so that they can use the neuroscience terms more independently. They are now able to describe what is happening in the brain when the characters in the scenarios are noticing thoughts and emotions using the terms ACC, insula and salience network. They can also link these neuroscience explanations to the effects of emotional awareness and naming emotions on MHW.

Step 4: Learning Skills of Emotional Awareness in Own Experience

The learning objective in the fourth step is for children to develop the skills that will enable them to non-judgmentally notice their own emotions and thoughts, and to start recognising and articulating how this may enable them to manage them skilfully and support their MHW.

Building on the knowledge children acquired based on examples from cartoons and stories in the previous three steps, they can now start applying this knowledge to their own experience and learn skills of emotional awareness. In *reception*, children can start recognising some of their thoughts and feelings, with support and encouragement. Building on the examples from cartoons or stories, the teacher can guide children to start noticing their own thoughts and feelings in a kind and non-judgmental way. The teacher can come up with a gesture that children can use as a sign to indicate that they noticed what they were thinking and feeling.

Pupils in *KS1* will be able to recognise their thoughts and feelings in a kind and non-judgmental way more readily. They will be able to start recognising how different emotions feel in their body. They can also understand more readily from their own experience that noticing feelings and thoughts can help us manage them better. The teacher can build on the examples used previously and guide children in noticing their own feelings and thoughts just like some of the characters did. This can include exploring how different feelings feel in their body. Then again, following the examples of characters they are familiar with, children can start recognising that noticing their own feelings and thoughts can help them manage them. Children can also make a drawing depicting the link between noticing feelings and managing them based on their own experience. The teacher can also remind children that it is OK to experience a range of different feelings during the day.

In *lower KS2*, children are able to understand readily from their own experience that emotions are linked to thoughts and feelings in the body. They also start recognising the links between emotions, thoughts, feelings in the body and behaviour in their own experience. They understand more independently that noticing emotions, thoughts and behaviours can help us manage them more effectively and make us feel better. The teacher can guide children through a series of exercises where children start noticing their emotions and thoughts from a non-judgmental and kind perspective, following the examples of characters they discussed in class previously. When children are comfortable with this, the teacher starts encouraging them to explore how noticing emotions and thoughts can help them manage these skilfully. The teacher also reminds children that we can experience a range of emotions throughout the day.

Finally in *the upper KS2*, children are able to independently understand, based on their own experience, that emotional awareness involves non-judgmental and kind noticing of emotions and thoughts, feelings in the body and behaviours linked to those emotions. They also understand from their own experience, and can articulate, how emotional awareness can help support their MHW. The teacher can encourage children to start recognising the four components of emotions in their own experience. They can practise this in writing scenarios describing emotions they noticed during the day, including their four components, and reflect on how emotional awareness can support their MHW. These personal scenarios are not to be shared with others, but the teacher can comment on them, from a non-judgmental and supportive perspective. They should not be evaluated as a standard school assignment due to their personal sensitive nature. The teacher can then remind children that it is normal to experience a range of emotions during the day and that emotions differ from moods.

Step 5: Learning to Use Naming of Emotions to Support Own MHW

The learning objective in the fifth step is for children to be able to use age-appropriate emotion vocabulary and naming of emotions in supporting their own MHW. They will also start using ratings of pleasantness and intensity of emotions in this process to expand their MHW skills.

 With support and reminders, children in the *reception* start using the naming of emotions strategy to manage their feelings. They also start exploring how naming their feelings can help them manage these feelings. The teacher can build on the examples provided in Step 2 and explain to children that just like the character in the cartoon or story used naming of their feelings to feel better they will now try to practise the same. During a circle time children can be gently invited to notice and name their feelings. After they are comfortable with this task, the teacher can also invite them to evaluate the 'feels good' and the 'strength' dimensions of their feelings using the 'Feels Good Scale' and 'Emotion Strength Scale'. After children get used to naming and evaluating their feelings using the scales, they can be encouraged to start noticing how naming their feelings makes them feel.

 Children in *KS1* will be able to recognise and name a wider range of their own feelings (6-8 different emotions). They can practise this during circle time or similar activities and the teacher can refer to the examples they worked with previously to enable transfer of that knowledge into children's MHW skills. Children will also be able to use the naming emotions strategy more readily, but still with guidance. They will be able to recognise more readily from their own experience that naming feelings can help them manage their feelings. Once they have gained sufficient competency in using the newly learned emotion vocabulary and are more effective in using the naming emotions strategy to manage their feelings, the teacher can encourage children to start recognising the 'feel good' and 'strength' dimensions of emotions in their own experience. Children can practise rating how they feel using the 'Feels Good Scale' and the 'Emotion Strength Scale' with growing confidence.

 In *lower KS2*, children are able to differentiate a greater range of emotions (8-10) in their own experience, and they can readily recognise and rate pleasantness and intensity of their emotions. They are able to readily understand from their own experience that naming emotions can help them manage them. Building on the examples from stories or movies, the teacher will encourage children to start naming their emotions during classroom practice sessions. A poster with names of all the emotions children learned about can support this. They can also practise writing down names of their emotions, this can be equally helpful in managing emotions as naming them out loud. The teacher will then encourage children to rate their emotions using the Pleasantness and Intensity of Emotion scales. Children can start using the scales to evaluate how the pleasantness and intensity of their emotions changes from before to after using the emotion naming strategy. They also start reflecting on how using

Emotional Awareness 45

this strategy during the school day and outside of school could support their MHW. They are encouraged to start using emotional awareness and naming of emotions to manage their emotions during the school day.

Finally, children in the *upper KS2* will be able to use the expanded emotion vocabulary to name their emotions independently. They will be able to assess their emotions on pleasantness and intensity dimensions without support. They will also be able to articulate mostly independently how naming of emotions can help them manage their emotions and support their MHW. The teacher can encourage children to name the emotions they are experiencing and distinguish the four comments of their emotions during classroom exercises. This can be supported by a poster depicting the emotions they learned about and components of emotions or a handout with the same information. Children can also practise comparing different emotions they experience using the Pleasantness and Intensity of Emotion Graph. Here they can use the graph to plot their different emotions. Children can use the graph to compare how naming of emotions changed the pleasantness and intensity of the emotions they were experiencing. They can describe how they are using emotional awareness and naming emotions to manage their emotions during the day in writing. They can also reflect in writing how this is helping them to support their MHW.

Step 6: Learning to Apply Neuroscience Knowledge as Part of Emotional Awareness Skills

The learning objective in the sixth step is for children to be able to use their understanding of the neuroscience underpinning emotional awareness and the naming emotions practice in enhancing their MHW skills. They will be able to recognise and articulate how using neuroscience in this way can support their MHW.

With support and guidance, children in *reception* begin to use their understanding that the brain supports emotional awareness and naming emotions when noticing and naming their feelings. The teacher may use a gesture, such as pointing to the brain or use a simple brain model to prompt children to link noticing and naming feelings to brain activity. Children can now practise noticing and naming feelings together with linking these skills to what is happening in the brain in very simple terms.

In *KS1*, children are able to use their understanding of neuroscience underpinning noticing and naming emotions to help them develop their new MHW skills. They learned previously that noticing of feelings is supported by a brain region called the ACC. Now the teacher can encourage them to remember that the ACC supports their own noticing and naming of feelings. Children can be guided to sign the letters ACC when they are practising noticing and naming their feelings during the day. They can also be reminded that by supporting noticing and naming feelings the ACC is involved in enabling them to manage their feelings more easily.

In the *lower KS2*, children are able to use their understanding of the neuroscience underpinning emotional awareness and naming emotions more independently to deepen and enhance their MHW skills. When practising emotional awareness and naming emotions, the teacher can remind children about the ACC and its role in guiding our attention so that we can notice our thoughts and emotions. The teacher can use a brain model to point to the brain region and children are encouraged to recognise that their own ACC is supporting their ability to notice thoughts and emotions. Then the teacher reminds children about the insula and their role – particularly in supporting our ability to notice how emotions feel in the body. Children are then invited to refer to the ACC and insula when they are naming their emotions during classroom activities.

Finally, in the *upper KS2*, children are able to use their understanding about the neuroscience underpinning emotional awareness and naming emotions independently to support their MHW skills. They are also able to articulate how the different brain regions (ACC – anterior cingulate cortex and insula) and salience network support their emotional awareness and naming of emotions. They are able to independently describe, using neuroscience terms they learned, how emotional awareness and naming emotions can support their MHW. The teacher can use brain models or posters to help children describe their new MHW skills in neuroscience terms. Children can be encouraged to add neuroscience terminology to the scenarios they have written previously where they were describing their experiences of using emotional awareness and naming emotion to manage their emotions in support of their MHW.

Step 7: Applying Skills of Emotional Awareness and Naming Emotions in Everyday Life

The learning objective in the seventh step is for children to be able to apply their knowledge and skills of emotional awareness and naming emotions, including relevant neuroscience understanding, in supporting their MHW in everyday situations.

In *reception*, children begin to apply, with support and guidance but increasingly more readily, their knowledge and skills of noticing and naming emotions, including references to the brain, in everyday situations. They are also increasingly able to recognise that using these skills helps them manage their feelings better. Teaching staff encourages pupils during the day, whether in the classroom or at the playground etc., to use their new skills of emotional awareness and naming feelings to manage their emotions when upset or overexcited. This can be done by using previously established gestures children learned in practice activities as a prompt or by guiding children through noticing and naming feelings if needed. The more children practise these skills in everyday situations, the more internalised and automatic the use of these skills becomes.

Emotional Awareness 47

 In *KS1*, children are able to apply their knowledge and skills of emotional awareness and naming emotions more readily, supported by their neuroscience understanding (the ACC), in everyday situations. The teaching staff can remind children in everyday situations during the school day when they are upset, angry or over excited to notice and name their emotions. They can also encourage children to describe what is happening in their brain when they are noticing and naming feelings. Children can then be encouraged to rate how they feel after applying the naming strategy using the 'Feels Good Scale' and 'Emotion Strength Scale'. This may solidify children's understanding that the new skills of emotional awareness and naming feelings can help them manage their feelings. Children can also be reminded to use their new skills before breaks and before home time – to encourage using the skills at home.

 In the *lower KS2*, children are able to apply their knowledge and skills of emotional awareness and naming emotions, including relevant neuroscience they learned (the ACC and insula), to manage their attention and emotions in support of their MHW mostly independently. The teacher can remind children to use their new skills during morning registration, before and after breaks and before home time. The teacher also encourages children to remember to keep using the Pleasantness of Emotion Scale and Intensity of Emotion Scale to recognise the change in their emotions after using the new skills. They are also reminded again that we experience a range of emotions during the day and that's normal. Just when the emotions are becoming too strong, we can use emotional awareness and naming emotions to manage them. Children are able to recognise from their own experience when applying these skills helps them manage their emotions and understand from their own experience how this can support their MHW in the longer term. They are encouraged to keep using the new skills beyond the school day.

 Finally, children in the *upper KS2*, are able to use their new knowledge and skills of emotional awareness and naming emotions, including relevant neuroscience (ACC, insula and the salience network) independently during everyday situations. The teaching staff can remind children to use their new skills throughout the school day. The teacher also encourages children to support each other by reminding and guiding each other to use the new skills in situations when stronger emotions arise for them. Children can start tracking their use of the new skills by noting at the end of the day situations when they used their skills and making a plan how they want to further improve the use of their skills the next day. They can also use the Pleasantness and Intensity of Emotion Graph to plot changes in their emotions as a result of using emotional awareness and naming emotions, and recognise how this can support their MHW in the long term if sustained. This can be repeated until children are able to use these skills without further prompts from the teaching staff.

Conclusion

Emotional awareness is a foundational skill enabling children to notice their thoughts, emotions and associated bodily feelings and behaviours. This skill enables further steps in self-regulation and therefore is the first building block of the first tier in the ATTEND Pyramid. If you were wondering, just like Anya the pastoral lead in the scenario at the start of the chapter, how specifically emotional awareness relates to children's MHW, hopefully this chapter provided you with the relevant understanding. You may have also learned that emotional awareness can be readily combined with the skills of naming emotions which can provide children with a simple but effective way to start managing their emotions skilfully. Following the 7-Step Approach children will be able to acquire and solidify the skills of emotional awareness and naming emotions effectively in an age-appropriate way across the primary school years.

Key chapter points:

- Emotional awareness, as the ability to notice and recognise emotions in a kind and nonjudgmental way, is a key prerequisite for other emotion regulation strategies.
- Better emotional awareness has been linked to better mental health.
- Naming of emotions is a simple but effective emotion regulation strategy that can be used by children in primary schools to reduce the intensity of their emotions.
- There is a developmental progression of learning emotional awareness and naming emotions skills in primary school children, from low range of emotions and support in naming emotions to wider range of emotions recognised and independently named.

References

Foulkes, L., & Andrews, J. L. (2023). Are mental health awareness efforts contributing to the rise in reported mental health problems? A call to test the prevalence inflation hypothesis. *New Ideas in Psychology*, 69, 101010.

Dorjee, D. (2024). Conceptualising child and adolescent mental health and wellbeing neurodevelopment: an integrative brain networks framework. Preprint, 4 November. https://doi.org/10.31234/osf.io/7vx45

Frijda N. H. (1987). Emotion, cognitive structure, and action tendency. *Cognition & Emotion*, 1, 115-143.

Lind, J., & Wickström, A. (2024). Representations of mental health and mental health problems in content published by female social media influencers. *International Journal of Cultural Studies*, 27(2), 217-233.

McLaughlin, K. A., Weissman, D., & Bitrán, D. (2019). Childhood adversity and neural development: a systematic review. *Annual Review of Developmental Psychology*, 1(1), 277-312.

Mulligan, K., & Scherer, K. R. (2012). Toward a working definition of emotion. *Emotion Review*, 4(4), 345-357.

Rakesh, D., Allen, N. B., & Whittle, S. (2023). Longitudinal changes in within-salience network functional connectivity mediate the relationship between childhood abuse and neglect, and mental health during adolescence. *Psychological Medicine*, 53(4), 1552-1564.

Scherer, K. R. (2009). The dynamic architecture of emotion: evidence for the component process model. *Cognition & Emotion*, 23, 1307-1351.

Thomassin, K., Morelen, D., & Suveg, C. (2012). Emotion reporting using electronic diaries reduces anxiety symptoms in girls with emotion dysregulation. *Journal of Contemporary Psychotherapy, 42*(4), 207-213.

Torre, J. B., & Lieberman, M. D. (2018). Putting feelings into words: affect labeling as implicit emotion regulation. *Emotion Review, 10*(2), 116-124.

Weissman, D. G., Nook, E. C., Dews, A. A., Miller, A. B., Lambert, H. K., Sasse, S. F., ... & McLaughlin, K. A. (2020). Low emotional awareness as a transdiagnostic mechanism underlying psychopathology in adolescence. *Clinical Psychological Science, 8*(6), 971-988.

Yarwood, M. G. (2022). *Psychology of human emotion: an open access textbook.* Affordable Course Transformation, Pennsylvania State University. https://psu.pb.unizin.org/psych425/chapter/circumplex-models/

3 Managing Distractions

Introduction

The second facet of the foundational 'Guiding Attention' tier of the ATTEND Pyramid cultivates the knowledge and skills of managing distractions because working with distractions in a skilful adaptive way is essential for effective self-regulation. The facet of Managing Distraction aims to develop the knowledge and skills enabling children to recognise, evaluate and manage external (such as interruptions by others, social media) and internal (thoughts, emotions, bodily sensations) distractions more adaptively and effectively. It also aims to foster an understanding that distractions can be useful for managing emotions and self-care, and encourages children to develop new skills in relating to and working with distractions in a more informed and discriminating manner to support their mental health and wellbeing (MHW).

This chapter first explores the role of distractions in children's MHW, showing how distractions can both undermine MHW and support it. Next, we consider the processes in the mind and brain underpinning adaptive managing of distractions. Building on this research, we then examine how children can acquire the knowledge and skills that would enable them to work with distractions skilfully in support of their MHW. Finally, the chapter presents a detailed outline of ways to foster healthy management of distractions across primary school years following the 7-Step Approach.

Case Study: How to Teach Children Skills of Managing Distractions Skilfully

John is a teacher in year 5. From his own experience of working with pupils in his class he knows that his students would benefit from learning to manage distractions in their lives better. He also knows from talking with parents that most pupils in his class go on their phones right after school and parents are worried about the impact of the constant distractions online on their children's mental health and school work.

John previously attended a course on teaching digital literacy in primary schools. The course was useful but did not really discuss the links between online distractions and mental health. So John tried to look up more information online, but again, found very little guidance on how to teach children skills to manage distractions. Most of what he found was about tips on restricting time children spend online and setting up parental controls on the content children view.

John was also thinking that distractions are probably not always bad when it comes to mental health. He noticed that when some of the children in his classroom get a bit anxious or fidgety, it helps them when they are given an engaging task that distracts them from their worries or restlessness. When talking to colleagues in the school, they said they intuitively use similar strategies with some pupils, but, just like John, do not know much about the links between this approach and MHW.

Questions for reflection:

- Do you know why managing distractions skilfully can support children's MHW?
- From your experience, can distractions sometimes support children's MHW?
- What strategies do you use in your classroom to foster children's skills in managing distractions?

How Is Managing Distractions Relevant to MHW?

Research shows that higher rates of distractibility by thoughts that are not related to a task (for example during a reading task in class) are linked to a worse mood, higher stress, and lower life satisfaction in children and adolescents (Mrazek et al., 2013). Other studies indicated that higher distractive mind wandering, particularly if the distracting thoughts are negative, is linked to lower mood and more difficulties in emotion regulation (Webb et al., 2021). This pattern holds for both children with ADHD who are more susceptible to distractibility and neurotypical children (Frick et al., 2020).

In addition, robust research with children suggests that better ability to manage both positive and negative distractions is closely related to better self-regulation and a range of positive long-term outcomes, including less likelihood of mental ill-health in adolescence and adulthood (Palacios-Barrios & Hanson, 2019). Children who can manage negative distractions more readily and delay gratification from positive distractions tend to have better outcomes both academically and with respect to their MHW (Tangney et al., 2018). Building on this and further research evidence, the facet of managing distraction targets development of attention control and decision making skills which underpin the ability to discern unhelpful internal distractions and disengage from them in support of children's emotion regulation.

When it comes to external distractions, social media, and online content in general, are major sources of distraction even for children. Indeed, a survey by the BBC (2024) found that 38% of 5-7-year-olds and more than a half of under 13-year-olds uses social media. Concerningly, little less than one third of year 3 pupils use social media regularly and this increases to two thirds of pupils in year 6. Research suggests that the roll out of social media negatively impacted mental health of young people (Braghieri et al., 2022) and adolescents are particularly vulnerable to problematic social media use which undermines their mental health (Maza et al., 2023). This is due to maturational changes in their brain that increase adolescents' sensitivity and reactivity to emotional content, particularly if it is peer-related, combined with difficulties in disengaging from such distractions. There is much less evidence available on the impacts of social media on children, but it is unlikely that the pattern of impacts on their mental health differs much from the findings in adolescents. This is why there has been increasing emphasis on digital literacy in schools. But such teaching typically doesn't take into account that children's abilities to manage distractions are different at different ages. Similarly, their susceptibility to different types of distractions changes with age. This undermines the effectiveness of common digital literacy approaches.

The Attention Economy

In the process of developing the knowledge and skills to manage distractions, particularly those linked to social media use, we first need to acknowledge that getting distracted is natural for everyone and sometimes disengaging from distractors can be quite difficult. This is where learning about the attention economy and neuroscience underpinning managing distractions can be helpful, and is therefore part of learning in this facet. In practical terms attention economy means, for example, that most of the content online is designed to capture our attention because spending time on the content translates into financial profit for the content creators. To capture users' attention, content creators often aim to invoke in users strong emotions and use perceptually captivating content such as vibrant colours and loud sounds. As a result, on a daily basis children are bombarded with excessive amounts of stimuli aiming to capture their attention, most of which are not relevant to their everyday lives. This overstimulation can undermine one's ability to self-regulate and negatively affect MHW, with stronger effects in children and adolescents due to developmental brain vulnerabilities (Maza et al., 2023). This further highlights the importance of developing the knowledge and skills to manage attention effectively to decrease susceptibility to distractions from an early age.

Positive Effects of Distractions

However, distractions can also support one's safety and MHW. For example, a police car or ambulance siren sound tells us to move out of the way, and a school bell captures children's attention to signal the end of a break or lesson. In addition, we all sometimes get distracted by interesting creative ideas that can help us solve problems. Specifically in relation to MHW, distraction-based emotion regulation strategies can be effective in managing emotions and are readily applied from early childhood (Simon et al., 2020). For instance, some techniques for managing negative thoughts or intense emotions use distraction in redirecting attention to neutral or positive thoughts and activities. Some such techniques (such as 'spot three things' and cognitive defusion) are detailed in the following sections and in the outline of the learning outcomes and activities for managing distractions across primary school age groups.

Positive use of distraction strategies can also involve engaging in activities that are distracting but can support one's MHW if applied at the right time and for appropriate duration. For instance, children may distract themselves when having negative thoughts by art activities, being physically active, watching cartoons, playing non-violent computer games or chatting with a friend. If the activities are active and neutral or positive, they are more likely to have a positive impact on MHW. The duration of the activity matters too, some activities may feel good in the moment, but across age groups can make us feel tired or emotionally worse if we spend excessive time on them (e.g. social media).

One of the key self-care skills is being able to recognise which activities support one's wellbeing and how long to engage in them to benefit. That's why the Facet of Distractions places emphasis on recognising both usefulness of distractions and their negative impacts to enable gradual development of more informed decisions about what children focus on, when and for how long.

> Questions for reflection:
>
> - Can you describe some of the research evidence linking greater distractibility to poor MHW?
> - What are some of the positive effects of distractions on children's MHW?

Neuroscience of Managing Distractions

The abilities to recognise, evaluate and manage distractions are underpinned by the executive network (referred to in research as the executive attention network or central executive network) involving primarily the ACC and PFC regions (Rueda et al., 2005). However, these two brain regions work closely with the information provided by the insula in regulating the activity in the regions of the automatic reactive stream of self-regulation (mainly amygdalae and the VS). We have discussed the roles of ACC and insula in self-regulation in the previous chapter. As a reminder, these two regions are part of the salience network enabling us to notice and monitor our emotions, thoughts and behaviours. As such the salience network enables us to notice distractions as a prerequisite of managing them. In this process the salience network works together with the executive network.

> ### The Executive Network and Managing Distractions in the Classroom
>
> The executive network presents the next step in top-down self-regulation, after noticing emotions, thoughts and behaviours via the salience network. For example, a teacher might be asking children in a class to do a reading task. A child in the second row does

not understand the task fully and starts worrying about not being able to complete it. A teaching assistant notices that the child is a bit fidgety, looking around instead of doing the task, and walks up to them. The assistant kindly asks the child what is going on. In response, the child says that they are worried about not being able to do the task. The teaching assistant first encourages the child to name the emotion they are experiencing. This makes the child feel a bit less worried. Then the teaching assistant supports the child in doing the 'spot three things' practice. The child looks around the room and notices three things in yellow colour. This shifts their attention away from the anxious thoughts.

This shifting of attention towards the three things in yellow colour and away from anxious thoughts was enabled by the executive network. The ACC helped the child notice the conflict between wanting to focus on a task and being distracted by anxious thoughts. Then the PFC was involved when the child was shifting attention away from their anxious thoughts. Since the executive network is still developing in children, the child needed guidance from the teaching assistant to recruit the executive network. But with practice and repetition they will most likely learn to engage the executive network more independently.

The above example demonstrates how executive function contributes to top-down self-regulation. This includes the ability to recognise conflicts linked to distractions and shift attention away from distractions towards what one wants or needs to pay attention to in the moment in alignment with one's goals (Rothbart et al., 2011). These are processes where we use conscious decisions and will. Therefore, they require what we call in research 'cognitive

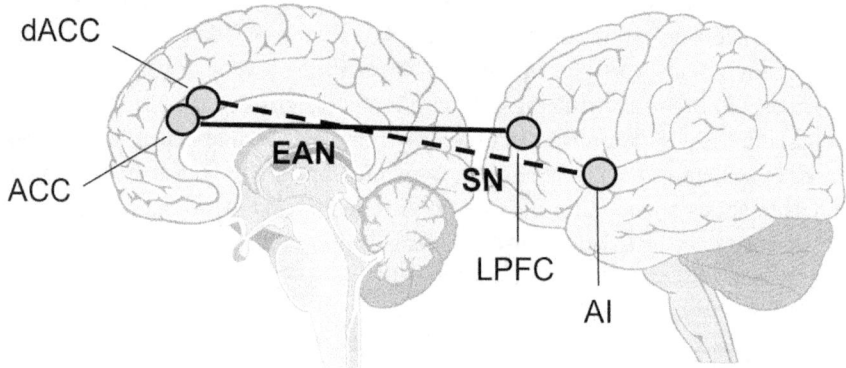

Figure 3.1 The executive network - EAN: ACC - Anterior Cingulate Cortex, LPFC - Lateral Prefrontal Cortex. The salience network - SN: dACC - dorsal Anterior Cingulate Cortex, AI - Anterior Insula.

Source: adapted with permission from Dorjee (2024)

effort' – there is an element of striving when we first try to shift attention away from distractions. But this becomes easier with practice and can be trained (Davis et al., 2016).

These processes are in the brain particularly underpinned by the lateral PFC working with the ACC. As we mentioned in Chapter 1, PFC is a large part of the brain supporting our ability to make decisions, problem solve, plan, resolve conflict and shift our attention at will. These abilities include making decisions in the moment about how to work with distractions. As in the example above, this involves shifting attention away from thoughts and emotions that may undermine MHW.

> **Key Neuroscience Terms for Managing Distractions**
>
> - ACC stands for the *anterior cingulate cortex*. It is a brain region involved both in the salience network and the executive network. Aside from helping us to notice our emotions, thoughts and behaviour, it also enables us to notice when there is a conflict between how we feel and how we want to feel (e.g. feeling anxious when we want to feel settled) or between what we are doing and we want to do (e.g. scrolling on social media instead of doing a homework). It helps guide our attention where we want it to be.
> - PFC stands for *prefrontal cortex*. It is the part of the brain behind our forehead that enables us to shift attention away from distractions. PFC is also involved in decision making, problem solving and planning.
> - The *executive network* involves the ACC, PFC and other brain regions. It enables us to 'take control' of our attention by noticing 'conflicts' and redirecting attention in support of our MHW.

How Can Children Acquire the Knowledge and Skills of Managing Distractions?

Coming back to the scenario from the start of this chapter, John would now have a better understanding of how managing distractions relates to children's MHW. He would now be probably wondering how this research can be translated into teaching relevant knowledge and skills in the classroom. Following the 7-Step Approach introduced in Chapter 1, learning to manage distractions follows the progression from acquisition of the relevant knowledge based on external examples to gradual development of skills in managing distractions in children's own experience.

As the first step in developing such knowledge and skills, children are encouraged to recognise distractions in examples from cartoons, stories and the public domain. They also explore whether the distractions were external or internal and whether they were useful (sometimes they are, for example when sensations in our body tell us that we need to eat or when we hear the sound of a fire engine while crossing the road) or not useful (when feeling anxious or over excited interferes with our ability to engage in activities fully). Children also start to notice ways the characters in stories or figures in public life (sportsmen and sportswomen, singers, influencers) manage the distractions they encounter. They then learn neuroscience underpinning the recognition, evaluation and managing of distractions, which provides them with a vocabulary that can facilitate a decentred perspective on experiences of being distracted.

Building on the foundation of such knowledge about distractions, children then develop skills in recognising, evaluating and managing external and internal distractions they encounter in their experience. They start by noticing their experiences of distraction during school activities, such as listening to a story or watching a movie, and learn to evaluate the usefulness of the distractions. They then acquire skills in managing external distractions first, since these are typically less emotionally charged and probing, by setting realistic goals and using positive feedback to encourage positive management of distractions (such as spending time online). Children are also encouraged to use the technique of naming emotions learned previously in managing their distractions in the moment and acquire new techniques that are distraction-based. These include the 'spot three things' technique involving noticing three things in one colour, noticing three sounds and noticing three parts of their body. In the first example children look around their environment and try to find three things in a certain colour to interrupt the process of distraction and then redirect their attention to what they want to focus on. This can be extended by noticing three sounds and three parts of their body, e.g. by bringing attention to their shoulders, hands and feet.

Key Strategies for Managing Distraction

- *Spot three things* – children are guided to notice three things in one colour in their surroundings, notice three sounds and/or notice three parts of their body.
- *Cognitive defusion* – encourages children to build healthy distance from their distracting thoughts by imagining these are pop-up adverts (or thoughts being carried away by balloons or clouds in the sky that float away) which they can choose to ignore or engage with as they wish (see Self-Help Toons, 2020).

Older children also learn psychological techniques such as cognitive defusion, encouraging children to create a healthy distance from their distracting thoughts by imagining these are pop-up adverts which they can choose to ignore or engage with as they wish. The emotion evaluation scales introduced in Chapter 2 and applied in the previous chapter can also be used to support evaluation of distractions in an experimental explorative way. In the final step of the training, children are invited to apply the knowledge and skills they learned in managing distractions in their everyday lives. Simple logs helping children to keep track of their progress in using these techniques can support children in applying the new skills they learned in everyday activities. It is important that the training to manage distractions is delivered from a non-judgmental perspective, acknowledging that we all get distracted and that we can learn to manage our distractions more skilfully with practice.

Developmental Differences in Fostering the Knowledge and Skills of Managing Distractions in Children

The ability to manage distractions increases during development in alignment with maturational changes in the executive network. Younger children often need adult support in managing distractions because the PFC has a protracted maturational trajectory until the mid-20s. In contrast, the amygdala and the VS regions mature earlier which makes children susceptible to more automatic immediate responding to situations, thoughts and emotions. Nevertheless, research shows that children as young as 5 years old can benefit from attention training targeting the executive network and improve their attention control abilities (Rueda et al., 2005). Further research showed that attention training can improve self-regulation in primary school children even if they have unfavourable genetic predisposition and are growing up in unfavourable socio-economic conditions (Isbell et al., 2017).

Distraction-based strategies to manage emotions are used by children as early as during the first year of life, even though they are not voluntary or effortful. For example, children may be upset about something but then orient their attention to the sound of a rattle or something else that captures their attention in the environment and this downregulates their emotions. This more automatic strategy relies on the orienting network, which involves parietal areas of the brain maturing earlier than the brain regions of the executive network (Rothbart et al., 2011). In contrast, the executive network enables children to shift their attention to manage their emotions in a more strategic way, as in the 'spot three things' technique, by delaying gratification or by choosing to engage in an activity that supports their MHW.

The ability to use these strategies increases with age, still they are less cognitively demanding than some other emotion regulation strategies, such as cognitive reappraisal which involves changing the way one thinks about experience or event (Simon et al., 2020). Therefore distraction-based strategies are suitable for use during the primary school age, initially with support from adults in reception and KS1 and then increasingly independently in KS2. Around the age of seven, children can link the distraction-based strategies with more metacognitive awareness of when such strategies work well for them and apply them more effectively and independently. Further goal setting and cognitive defusion based strategies can be introduced for children in KS2 to expand the repertoire of strategies they can use to manage external and internal distractions more flexibly and strategically.

Acquiring the Knowledge and Skills of Managing Distractions: The 7-Step Approach

Just like in learning skills of emotional awareness, the 7-Step Approach applied to managing distractions progresses from impersonal examples, such as the experience of characters in stories and cartoons (Steps 1-3), to development of one's own skills in managing distractions in everyday life (Steps 4-7). There is also a progression from learning about external distractions to internal distractions across the steps. Further progression in learning involves practising managing distractions in 'pretend' classroom practice situations and then increasingly in everyday school situations. In the final step children integrate their learning across the steps and apply their new knowledge and skills in everyday life, in and outside of school, with increasing independence. The developmental progression of learning is reflected in age-appropriate specification of learning objectives and practice activities across the four primary school age groups: reception (4-5-year-olds), KS1 (5-7-year-olds), lower KS2 (7-9-year-olds), upper KS2 (9-11-year-olds)

Step 1: Learning about External Distractions and Their Impact on MHW

The learning objective in the first step is for children to acquire the knowledge that will enable them to understand the difference between focusing and distraction based on impersonal examples and to learn that external distractions (environment, others, social media) can be both useful and not useful. Children will also gain foundational knowledge in relating distractions and their effects to MHW.

Starting with *reception*, children in this age group can begin to understand the difference between focusing and getting distracted by external distractions. They can start to notice distractions in impersonal examples provided. Such examples can include cartoon clips where characters are focusing and getting distracted (e.g. by noise outside). The teacher can first point out the difference between focusing and distraction. Children can then be encouraged to spot the distractions in further examples. After acquiring basic understanding of the differences between focusing and distraction, children can be provided with examples demonstrating how the characters skilfully dealt with the distractions. Teachers can describe this for children based on the cartoon example and then children start to recognise and describe, in simple terms and with support, ways the characters managed distractions.

In comparison to reception, children in *KS1* will be able to notice external distractions more readily and begin to distinguish between useful and not useful external distractions based on impersonal examples. They start to recognise in the examples provided that getting distracted can relate to how we feel. They begin to recognise ways distractions can be managed to support wellbeing. Such learning can be enabled through activities where pictures depicting situations with different external distractions are provided and children try to reason which ones are useful and which ones are not useful (e.g. car honking versus interruptions while doing a task). They can also be provided with examples from cartoons showing how external distractions make one feel (can use 'Feels Good' and 'Strength of Emotion' scales) and how they can be managed. Teachers can guide children in naming emotions the characters experienced when being distracted and help them describe a couple of simple ways the characters managed distractions in support of their wellbeing.

 Children in the *lower KS2* will be able to work with a greater range of impersonal external distractions in examples provided than children in KS1. They will also be able to consider with greater accuracy and independence which distractions are useful and which ones are not useful. They will begin to articulate more independently, using examples from stories or movies, how distractions make one feel (impact one's wellbeing) and how they can be managed. Activities supporting development of such knowledge will encourage children to identify external distractions in stories or movies more independently and categorise them based on how useful or not useful they are. Children can then explore how the distractions made the characters feel; they can use the Pleasantness of Emotion Scale and Intensity of Emotion Scale to quantify the character's feelings. Finally, they can explore how the characters managed the distractions in a more detailed way. Children can work in pairs or small groups during such activities and then share what they have found with other groups or pairs.

 Finally, in the *upper KS2* children can learn to recognise a wider range of external distractions from everyday life using impersonal public domain examples, for example from sportsmen, sportswomen, celebrities or influencers. Due to their increased ability for complex reasoning children in this age group can be taught in simple terms about the attention economy so they start to understand how distractions in adverts or social media are set up to capture our attention because paying attention translates into money for those who create the content. Children in upper KS2 will also be able to explain independently how different types of distractions relate to mental health based on public domain examples (e.g. Tom Holland and his experience with the impact of social media engagement on mental health). They can use the Pleasantness and Intensity of Emotion Graphs to quantify the effects of distractions on MHW. They will also be able to articulate in more detail how the distractions can be managed based on such examples.

Step 2: Learning about Internal Distractions and Their Impact on MHW

The learning objective in the second step is for children to acquire the knowledge that will enable them to understand, based on impersonal examples, that distractions can also be internal (thoughts, emotions, bodily sensations), and that these internal distractions can be useful or not useful. They also learn how internal distractions relate to MHW, and how they can be managed skilfully.

Building on learning in the first step, in the next step children in *reception* can begin to understand that sometimes we can get distracted by feelings (emotional and bodily). Cartoon or story examples of characters getting distracted from a task by being too excited or experiencing other emotions, including feeling uncomfortable in their tummy when upset, can be used to exemplify this. The teacher can first describe the distractions in the examples and then encourage children to notice distractions in new examples. After children acquire basic understanding of what internal distractions are, further examples can show how the characters in the cartoons or stories manage internal distractions adaptively. After teacher explanations, children are encouraged to start recognising in basic terms how the adaptive ways of dealing with distractions made the cartoon/story characters feel.

Children in *KS1* will be able to notice some internal distractions in stories or cartoons more readily than children in reception. They also begin to recognise that some internal distractions are useful (feeling hungry) and some are not useful. Children explore internal distractions through examples in stories or cartoons and practise recognising which one's were useful and which ones' were not and why. They also recognise with more nuance how such distractions made the characters feel and how the characters managed them. Children can use naming of a wider range of emotions (they learned in the first step) and the 'Feels Good' and 'Strength of Emotion' scales to try to quantify how the characters felt. They can also try to come up with their own similar stories with fictional characters in small groups, providing examples of distractions and ways to manage them.

Children in the *lower KS2* are able to recognise a wider range of internal distractions in stories or movies and can distinguish which ones were useful and which ones were not useful increasingly independently. They also recognise with greater nuance and independence how the distractions made the characters feel and how they dealt with the distractions. In this step, children are encouraged to recognise two main strategies for managing distractions: using naming of emotions and distraction-based strategies such as the 'spot three things' technique. If children grasp these two strategies well, teachers can introduce them to cognitive defusion too. In fostering their knowledge in this facet, children can work in pairs and prepare a list of internal distractions they noticed in a story and categorise them into those that were useful and those that were not useful. Afterwards, children can describe to each other in basic terms examples of how the distractions made the characters feel (can use the Pleasantness of Emotion Scale and Intensity of Emotion Scale). They can also practise describing how the characters managed distractions using naming, distraction-based strategies and/or cognitive defusion.

In the *upper KS2*, children can be first introduced to some examples of internal distractions and ways to manage these from the public domain - using stories from athletes or celebrities or influencers from the public domain. Children can then discuss in small groups whether the distractions were useful (creative thought) or not useful (worry, anxiety, anger) and how they impacted the person's MHW (can use the Pleasantness and Intensity of Emotion Graph). Children are then encouraged to discuss ways the person in the example dealt with the distractions (using naming, distraction based strategies or cognitive defusion). Groups can present their observations to the whole class to learn further from each others' examples. For homework, children can look for further examples from the public domain they encountered and then discuss these examples in pairs in class. This will further solidify

Managing Distractions   61

their ability to articulate independently and confidently what internal distractions are, what makes them useful or not, how they impact on MHW and how the three strategies can be used to manage distractions.

Step 3: Learning Neuroscience Underpinning Managing Distractions

The learning objective in the third step is for children to acquire the knowledge that will enable them to understand, in an age-appropriate way and based on impersonal examples, what happens in the brain when someone gets distracted and when they apply some of the strategies they learned about to manage distractions. Children also learn to relate the neuroscience underpinning distractions and their regulation to MHW.

Children in *reception* begin to understand, using the previously introduced examples from stories and cartoons, that when someone gets distracted, just like the characters did, this also changes what is happening in their brain. Similarly, when someone skilfully manages distractions, they use their brain to do so. To link the previous learning to neuroscience in very basic terms, teachers can remind children that our brains get distracted to protect us, as in the story and cartoon examples. However, sometimes the brain's reactions to distractions are not useful and we can use our brains to manage such distractions. Teachers can use a child-friendly model of the brain introduced in the Facet of Emotional Awareness when they discuss links between managing distractions and the brain.

Children in *KS1* were introduced to the ACC in the Facet of Emotional Awareness and teachers can link this learning to the Facet of Distractions by explaining to children that the ACC helps us notice distractions too. Then children are introduced to a new brain region - the PFC - which helps us decide if the distractions are useful or not. The PFC also supports our ability to choose where we want to focus and apply some of the distraction-based strategies learned. This new neuroscience knowledge can be linked to the previous story and cartoon examples of characters noticing and managing distractions. Children can be encouraged to think about what happened in the brains of the characters, and use references to the ACC, and PFC to explain in basic terms the process of distraction, evaluating if a distraction was useful or not, and changing attention focus away from distractions using the strategies learned. They can also point to the forehead on a model or their forehead as a location of the PFC.

Children in the *lower KS2* can build on the neuroscience knowledge they acquired when learning about Emotional Awareness. They expand their understanding by learning that the ACC and insula help us notice distractions. Then teachers can introduce children to the new brain region called the prefrontal cortex (PFC), the full name together with the acronym can be used for this age group. Teachers explain that the PFC works with the ACC to decide if a distraction is useful or not. Children also learn that the PFC supports our ability to change attention focus when we are using strategies such as naming of emotions, the 'spot three things' technique or cognitive defusion. Other brain regions called the Amygdalae help us quickly notice distractions that might mean danger or excitement (such as a honk of a car, ambulance noise, thunder or fireworks), so that we can act fast if needed. But the PFC and ACC can redirect our attention and help us calm down if it is a false alarm (e.g. a toy car honking).

Children can be encouraged to recognise increasingly independently which parts of the brain were active when the characters in previous stories noticed distractions: insula – bodily distractions, amygdalae – potential danger and strong automatic emotional responses including anxiety, anger or excitement. Then they can be supported in recognising which brain areas helped characters to evaluate if the distractions were useful and when they managed their responses using the strategies discussed earlier – the ACC and PFC. Brain maps can be used for children to point to the relevant brain regions and they can also have a go at adding new brain regions to brain drawings they started in the previous facet.

Children in the *upper KS2* first apply their previous neuroscience learning to Managing Distractions and are able to understand that the insula helps us notice bodily and emotional distractions and amygdalae alert us to potential danger or strong emotions. They can learn about a new brain region called the VS (ventral striatum) which is activated for the 'feel good' rewarding distractions. They understand that the ACC (anterior cingulate cortex) and the PFC (prefrontal cortex) help us decide whether the distraction is useful or not and redirect our attention to what we want to focus on using naming, the spot three things technique, cognitive defusion or other adaptive distractions (e.g. dancing, music). They also learn that the ACC and PFC are parts of the executive network (the boss) that helps us make decisions and manage our attention and emotions.

Children in this age group can use references to the brain processes and brain regions involved in noticing, evaluating and managing distractions independently when describing somebody (from the public domain examples) getting distracted, e.g. references to insula when referring to bodily distractions, amygdalae signalling potential danger or strong emotions and VS (ventral striatum) for rewarding distractions. They can refer to the PFC and ACC (using both full names of these brain regions and their acronyms) and the executive network when describing how these were involved in the examples of managing distractions. They can independently link these descriptions to impacts on MHW of the public figures from the examples. Brain models and brain maps as examples provided and/or created by the pupils can be used to support learning in this step in small groups.

Step 4: Learning to Manage External Distractions in Own Experience

The learning objective in the fourth step is for children to develop the skills that will enable them to notice and recognise a range of external distractions in their own experience and start managing them skilfully. Children will also be able to understand and articulate from their own experience how external distractions and their management can support their MHW.

Managing Distractions 63

 Building on learning in the previous three steps, children will now start applying what they have learned so far to their own experience. Specifically, children in *reception* acquire basic skills in noticing when they get distracted and with support are able to come back to a task. Teachers guide children in noticing when they get distracted and provide positive feedback to encourage such behaviour. In the process of learning, teachers can refer back to the examples from stories and cartoons and support children in applying the same approaches to their own experience. New practices can be used as well, for example, children can listen to the singing bowl sound (or a song) and raise their hand when they notice that they got distracted. They are also encouraged to get back to their task after getting distracted and receive positive feedback when they do so.

 With guidance, children in *KS1* will be able to notice getting distracted during a task more readily and start distinguishing in their own experience whether the distractions were useful or not. They can also start recognising how the distractions made them feel. They can use the 'Feels Good' and 'Strength of Emotion' scales to assess their own experience in relation to the distractions in a playful way. With support, children can then be encouraged to start applying the naming of emotions technique as well as simple strategies from the story and cartoon examples to manage external distractions in their own experience. They can also explore in basic terms how using the strategies made them feel, how it changed their feelings. The 'Feels Good' and 'Strength of Emotion' scales can be used here too.

 In comparison to KS1, children in the *lower KS2* will be able to recognise a greater range of external distractions when trying to focus on a task and distinguish between useful and not useful distractions more independently. They will also be able to discern with more accuracy how the different types of distractions make them feel and relate this to their wellbeing. They can use the Pleasantness of Emotion Scale and Intensity of Emotion Scale logs to track their experience of distractions. They will be encouraged to start using simple strategies, including naming of emotions and strategies from the example stories and movies such as simple mnemonics or gestures, to manage external distractions. They can also start practising setting realistic goals and begin to recognise how long they can focus well on a task. Children can explore how it feels to stay focused and how it feels getting distracted and how their feelings change when they apply some of the strategies to manage external distractions (possibly using the Pleasantness of Emotion Scale and Intensity of Emotion Scale). They can be encouraged to explore how managing distractions more skilfully can support their MHW.

 Children in the upper KS2 will be able to recognise independently in everyday life a wide range of external distractions, including adverts and social media distractions. They can discern with good accuracy which of the distractions are supportive of their MHW and which are not. They will be able to link the distractions to their basic understanding of the attention economy and use this knowledge in supporting their management of distractions. They will start using effective techniques in

setting realistic goals to stay focused on a task or activity when they want to. Children also start using techniques of naming emotions, mnemonics or gestures or other strategies from the impersonal examples to return readily back to a task when they get distracted. They can articulate how focusing on a task and being distracted impacts their own MHW. To support learning in this step, children can conduct an 'experiment' where they track their distractions for a couple of days a week using a log that records date, time, type of external distraction, how long they were distracted for, how it made them feel (can use Pleasantness and Intensity of Emotion Graph), what they did about it and what they want to do next time the same distraction arises. They can describe what they found out about their external distractions in relation to their MHW from 'the experiment' in a homework assignment.

Step 5: Learning to Manage Internal Distractions in Own Experience

The learning objective in the fifth step is for children to be able to notice internal distractions in their own experience and use naming emotions and distraction-based strategies to manage them. Children will also be able to understand and articulate how internal distractions and their regulation impacts their MHW.

The learning in the fifth step builds on the knowledge and skills children acquired in the previous steps and expands it towards regulation of internal distractions in their own experience. In *reception*, children begin with noticing internal distractions (such as getting over-excited or upset) during the school day in their own experience with support from their teachers. Children are then guided in using naming the emotion experienced and/or simple distraction-based strategies, such as noticing three things in their environment that are a certain colour or counting to five, to manage these emotions. With support, they begin to notice how applying these strategies changes their feelings.

In *KS1*, children are able to notice internal distractions more readily (including both distracting emotions and some distracting thoughts) and start recognising which of the internal distractions are useful and which are not. They also start using the new distraction-based strategies (and naming) to manage the distractions that are not useful more frequently with some support. They may particularly need reminders, guidance and encouragement to use the strategies more consistently during the school day. Building on examples from cartoons and stories introduced earlier, children can try to notice internal distractions in their own experience more often and apply naming and new distraction-based strategies (such as spot three things or counting to 10) to manage their thoughts and feelings in the moment. They can explore, using the 'Feels Good' and 'Strength of Emotion' scales, how applying the strategies makes them feel.

Managing Distractions 65

In the *lower KS2*, children notice in their own experience a greater range of internal distractions (emotions and thoughts) and can use naming of emotions and distraction-based strategies more independently to manage these. The strategies include the technique spot three things, counting backwards from 5 or 10 or thinking about a place where they feel happy and safe. In year 4, or earlier if they are ready, they can start to use a new strategy of cognitive defusion for managing distracting thoughts and emotions, e.g. imagining they are pop-up adverts and choosing which ones to attend to. To practise these skills children can engage in activities where they are provided with an example situation (e.g. while listening to a story or watching a movie), and make a list of internal distractions they experienced. They can note if the distractions were useful or not and what technique they used to get back to listening to the story (naming or distraction-based techniques including spot three things, counting backwards, imagining a safe place or cognitive defusion); they should not describe their personal experience in a group but can simply indicate number of distractions, types of strategies used and how using the strategies made them feel (using the Pleasantness of Emotion Scale and Intensity of Emotion Scale).

Children in the *upper KS2* are able to notice in their own experience a wide range of internal distractions (bodily, emotional, thoughts) and independently assess their usefulness. They are able to apply strategies discussed in examples from the public domain and in class to own experience, including naming of emotions, distraction-based techniques such as spot three things or counting backwards from 10 or 15 or imagery of a safe place or cognitive defusion (thoughts and feelings as pop-up adverts one can choose to act on or ignore). They explore and recognise mostly accurately how feeling distracted by thoughts or emotions makes them feel and how using the techniques changes these emotions. They can articulate how internal distractions and their regulation impacts MHW based on their own experience. To develop these skills, children can prepare a log where they track their internal distractions over a couple of days per week, recording date, time, type of internal distraction, how long they were distracted, how it made them feel (can use Pleasantness and Intensity of Emotion Graph) and whether the distraction was useful or not, which technique they applied to manage the distraction if needed, how it changed their emotions and how they want to deal with the same type of distraction next time. They can write a homework assignment on this theme, not sharing the specifics in groups for confidentiality reasons. However, teachers can create a document where children can provide their general observations from this learning anonymously. Teachers can summarise the entries in front of the whole class.

Step 6: Learning to Apply Neuroscience in Managing Distractions in Own Experience

The learning objective in the sixth step is for children to be able to use understanding of the neuroscience underpinning managing distractions to regulate distractions skilfully in their own experience. Children will also be able to recognise and articulate how using neuroscience in this way can support their MHW.

66   *Making Sense of Mental Health and Wellbeing in Primary Schools*

 The sixth step solidifies and expands children's previous learning in managing external and internal distractions by integrating neuroscience into their strategies. In *reception*, children start to recognise that getting distracted and managing distractions involves processes in their own brain. Children can be supported in using references to the brain when getting distracted and managing distractions. They can then be repeatedly encouraged to refer to the brain when managing distractions to integrate this understanding with their distraction management skills through practice.

 In *KS1*, children can use references to the ACC and PFC when reflecting on noticing, evaluating the usefulness of and managing both external and internal distractions in their own experience. Teachers can provide example explanations of what happens in their brain when they get distracted and children can be guided to describe the brain processes when they get distracted. Children can be encouraged to use references to the ACC and PFC brain regions. Specifically, they can, for example, say that the ACC was active when they noticed that they got distracted by a thought about a movie they watched. They can then describe that the ACC and PFC were involved when they were choosing and applying one of the strategies to manage the distraction and come back to a task. Children can point to their forehead as the location of the PFC.

 In the *lower KS2*, children can increasingly independently use references to the ACC, insula and amygdalae when describing their own experiences of getting distracted and reflecting on what type of distraction it was (internal/external, useful/not useful). Children can also describe how amygdalae got activated by strong emotions linked to the distractions. They would then refer to the ACC and prefrontal cortex (PFC) when describing choosing and applying techniques to manage distractions. Teachers encourage children to refer to the different brain regions when reflecting on getting distracted and managing distractions in their own experience. To practise this, children can work in pairs and use non-triggering relatable examples such as getting distracted from a task by noise of others chatting or remembering something exciting that happened during the weekend while trying to focus on a task. They can relate, increasingly independently, the brain activity changes to MHW (how they felt). Brain maps they created in Step 3 can be used to support such activities.

 In the *upper KS2*, children will be able to independently use references to the brain regions they learned about in Step 3 when describing instances of getting distracted (with both external and internal distractions) and how they managed these. They can readily use references to the brain processes involved in getting distracted and evaluating the type of distraction as external, bodily, emotional or thought-related (ACC, insula, amygdalae and VS). Children can also describe the process of choosing a technique and managing distractions using references to the ACC and PFC which are part of the executive network. They will be able to use the acronyms or full names of the brain regions. They will also be able to articulate how the neuroscience descriptions relate to impacts of managing distractions on their MHW. Examples from the log children created in the previous two steps can be used to practise describing the brain

processes involved in noticing and managing distractions in writing. Teachers can use the anonymous examples created in Step 6 to exemplify how to relate neuroscience to some of the non-triggering examples of managing distractions. Teachers and children can use brain models and brain maps created previously as part of teamwork in Step 3 to support the activities in this step.

Step 7: Skilfully Managing Distractions in Everyday Life

The learning objective in the seventh step is for children to be able to readily notice external and internal distractions, evaluate their usefulness and skilfully manage them using naming of emotions, relevant neuroscience, distraction-based techniques and cognitive defusion in everyday life (in the classroom and outside of the classroom) to support their own MHW.

The seventh step integrates the learning across the previous six steps and encourages children to implement the new skills readily in their everyday lives. To support this process, children in *reception* are supported to notice distractions (external and internal) regularly and consistently during the school day. They are also guided to use the naming and distraction-based techniques to manage distractions during everyday activities, with support but increasingly more independently. Children are encouraged to use the naming and distraction-based techniques, plus references to the brain, in regulating their emotions during instances of distraction that occur in everyday situations and provided with positive feedback when they manage to do so.

Children in *KS1* will be able to notice distractions (external and internal) more readily, recognise if they are useful, and start managing them using naming, references to the brain and/or distraction-based techniques in everyday situations more effectively, with encouragement and some guidance. Teachers can create a mnemonic, a gesture or a sign, to remind children to manage distractions when they arise throughout the school day. During everyday activities, children are encouraged to recognise when they get distracted and distinguish the type of distraction readily, then choose a way to manage the distraction using naming, neuroscience and/ or distraction-based techniques. Children also begin to reflect more automatically on how this can be helpful (e.g. calming them down, staying focused); they will need some support and positive feedback to develop and solidify these skills.

In *lower KS2*, children will be able to recognise different types of distractions in their own experience (external and internal) more independently and in an increasingly more automatic and internalised way. They will more independently evaluate the usefulness of the distractions and apply naming, neuroscience descriptions, goal setting, distraction-based techniques and/or cognitive defusion to manage distractions mostly effectively in everyday situations. Teachers can remind children during everyday classroom situations, such as working on a task, to recognise distractions, evaluate their usefulness and apply the different techniques they learned to manage them. Consistency in such reminders and encouragement will be

essential for children to solidify use of the newly learned skills in everyday life. They will also start to explore which techniques work best for different distractions and situations and how using the strategies has been supporting their MHW. Teachers can use activities where they provide children with a range of distraction types that are non-triggering and children share in small groups how they managed these utilising peer-learning.

Finally, in the *upper KS2*, children will be able to independently recognise, evaluate and manage a range of distractions (both internal and external) in an internalised way using knowledge about the attention economy and neuroscience of distractions and techniques including naming of emotions, goal setting, distraction-based techniques and cognitive defusion. They will know which techniques work best for them in managing different types of distractions and situations in everyday life, both inside the classroom and outside of the classroom. They will be able to recognise independently and articulate the benefits of their new skills of managing distractions to their own MHW and school work.

Peer-led activities can be encouraged in this age group, with children supporting each other in recognising, evaluating and managing distractions in everyday life, including minor upsets, social media engagement and school work. Children can also share with each other tips for use of self-care distraction strategies and be encouraged to keep using logs to track the benefits of applying these skills to their MHW.

Conclusion

Many teachers seem to find it challenging to teach children skills that would enable them to manage distractions in their lives more skilfully. Hopefully, this chapter equipped you with a better understanding of the research explaining both the negative and positive effects of distractions on children's MHW. Based on the outline of the 7-Step Approach applied to teaching children distraction management, you may now also be able to envision in a more systematic way how you might teach these skills in your classroom in an age-appropriate way. Acquiring these skills may, together with the emotional awareness skills, enable children to build up a solid foundation for learning further emotion regulation strategies in the next three tiers of the ATTEND Pyramid.

Key chapter points:

- Distractions can be external (e.g. social media) or internal (thoughts and emotions).
- Sometimes distractions are useful and often they are not useful, therefore a key skill of managing distractions is recognising the usefulness of distractions.
- Managing distractions involves complex processes in the mind and brain of recognising where our attention is and redirecting it if needed; these processes are supported by the executive attention network including the ACC and the PFC.

- One approach to using distractions in support of one's wellbeing is the spot three things technique which is particularly helpful in managing anxiety.
- Cognitive defusion is a technique enabling us to perceive what is happening in our mind from a distanced perspective and this can be helpful in managing distracting thoughts and emotions.
- Primary school children can acquire age-appropriate skills in managing distractions, including the spot three things and cognitive defusion strategies, following the 7-Step Approach.

References

BBC (2024). Ofcom: Almost a quarter of kids aged 5-7 have smartphones. www.bbc.co.uk/news/technology-68838029

Braghieri, L., Levy, R. E., & Makarin, A. (2022). Social media and mental health. *American Economic Review, 112*(11), 3660-3693.

Dorjee, D. (2024). Conceptualising child and adolescent mental health and wellbeing neurodevelopment: an integrative brain networks framework. Preprint, 4 November. https://doi.org/10.31234/osf.io/7vx45

Davis, E. L., Quiñones-Camacho, L. E., & Buss, K. A. (2016). The effects of distraction and reappraisal on children's parasympathetic regulation of sadness and fear. *Journal of Experimental Child Psychology, 142*, 344-358.

Frick, M. A., Asherson, P., & Brocki, K. C. (2020). Mind-wandering in children with and without ADHD. *British Journal of Clinical Psychology, 59*(2), 208-223.

Isbell, E., Stevens, C., Pakulak, E., Hampton Wray, A., Bell, T. A., & Neville, H. J. (2017). Neuroplasticity of selective attention: Research foundations and preliminary evidence for a gene by intervention interaction. *Proceedings of the National Academy of Sciences, 114*(35), 9247-9254.

Maza, M. T., Fox, K. A., Kwon, S. J., Flannery, J. E., Lindquist, K. A., Prinstein, M. J., & Telzer, E. H. (2023). Association of habitual checking behaviors on social media with longitudinal functional brain development. *JAMA Pediatrics, 177*(2), 160-167.

Mrazek, M. D., Phillips, D. T., Franklin, M. S., Broadway, J. M., & Schooler, J. W. (2013). Young and restless: validation of the Mind-Wandering Questionnaire (MWQ) reveals disruptive impact of mind-wandering for youth. *Frontiers in Psychology, 4*, 560.

Palacios-Barrios, E. E., & Hanson, J. L. (2019). Poverty and self-regulation: connecting psychosocial processes, neurobiology, and the risk for psychopathology. *Comprehensive Psychiatry, 90*, 52-64.

Rothbart, M. K., Sheese, B. E., Rueda, M. R., & Posner, M. I. (2011). Developing mechanisms of self-regulation in early life. *Emotion Review, 3*(2), 207-213.

Rueda, M. R., Rothbart, M. K., McCandliss, B. D., Saccomanno, L., & Posner, M. I. (2005). Training, maturation, and genetic influences on the development of executive attention. *Proceedings of the National Academy of Sciences, 102*(41), 14,931-14,936.

Self-Help Toons. (2020). Cognitive fusion and defusion. www.youtube.com/watch?v=CpdVMs818AE.

Simon, E., Driessen, S., Lambert, A., & Muris, P. (2020). Challenging anxious cognitions or accepting them? Exploring the efficacy of the cognitive elements of cognitive behaviour therapy and acceptance and commitment therapy in the reduction of children's fear of the dark. *International Journal of Psychology, 55*(1), 90-97.

Tangney, J. P., Boone, A. L., & Baumeister, R. F. (2018). High self-control predicts good adjustment, less pathology, better grades, and interpersonal success. In R. F. Baumeister, *Self-regulation and self-control* (pp. 173-212). Routledge.

Webb, C. A., Israel, E. S., Belleau, E., Appleman, L., Forbes, E. E., & Pizzagalli, D. A. (2021). Mind-wandering in adolescents predicts worse affect and is linked to aberrant default mode network-salience network connectivity. *Journal of the American Academy of Child & Adolescent Psychiatry, 60*(3), 377-387.

PART II
Managing Emotions

4 Managing Reactivity

Introduction

Now that children acquired basic skills in managing their attention in the first tier of the ATTEND Pyramid, building on these foundational skills the second tier aims to foster children's knowledge and skills of Managing Emotions. The first building block in the second tier of the Pyramid considered in this chapter focuses on cultivating children's knowledge and skills of Managing Reactivity which are an essential part of self-regulation. Indeed, policy guidelines on supporting children's mental health and wellbeing (MHW) often refer to the need to teach children how to 'calm down'. The building block of Managing Reactivity provides specific guidance on how children can acquire the knowledge and skills needed for them to be able to effectively regulate maladaptive reactivity to external (external events including interactions with others) and internal stimuli (thoughts, emotions and bodily sensations).

The chapter first presents research explaining how managing reactivity relates to MHW and how it is impacted by different factors increasing stress – such as lack of sleep, conflict, poverty, discrimination etc. We then consider the processes in the mind, brain and body underpinning reactivity to better understand the chain reaction of reactivity and ways to regulate it. Next, we explore strategies that can enable children to manage reactivity and outline the developmental progression of the relevant processes, knowledge and skills. Finally, the second part of the chapter specifies ways children can acquire the knowledge and skills of managing reactivity in the classroom in an age-appropriate way across the primary school years, following the 7-Step Approach. But let's consider the following case study first.

Case Study: Teaching Children Effective Strategies to Manage Reactivity

Salma is a reception teacher in her primary school. She knows that the behavioural policy in her school aims to reduce instances where children behave aggressively, and the guidance is useful. But there are also situations of less severe reactivity she often encounters in her classroom. For example, when children have a disagreement and find it hard to calm down afterwards. Or children can get overexcited and find it difficult to settle down. Salma is wondering how to help children manage their emotions more skilfully in these circumstances.

Salma also noticed that children are often more reactive when they don't have enough sleep, or didn't have breakfast or their family is going through some difficulty. She wonders if more can be done to acknowledge and mitigate these effects on children's reactivity. She would like to understand better how this all links to children's longer-term MHW. She heard that this may have a lot to do with physiological effects of stress on children's development, but would like to know more.

And alongside addressing the wider factors impacting on children's emotions and behaviour, Salma is also wondering if there might be strategies children can learn beyond managing reactivity in the moment that would help them lower their stress levels overall. She knows that children are facing so many stressors – from bullying, through too much screen time to worrying about what is happening in the world, such as climate change. She thinks that having regular time to 'de-stress' and the skills to do so effectively might be essential for supporting children's MHW from a young age.

Questions for reflection:
- What strategies do you teach children in your class to help them manage reactivity?
- Do you know how stress impacts children's MHW?
- Can you think of any strategies children could use regularly to de-stress?

How Is Managing Reactivity Relevant to MHW?

Reactivity is an inevitable part of our lives. It enabled us to survive as a species throughout evolution since reactivity underpinned our ability to effectively deal with danger. Even nowadays, reactivity is important in everyday life, it enables us to mobilise our resources when we need it. But reactivity can also undermine our MHW when it is too strong as a result of a traumatic event or when it is chronic. That's why learning skills of managing reactivity is an essential part of MHW and children can start learning such skills early on. We will now explore in more detail when reactivity is useful and when it can undermine children's MHW.

When Reactivity Is Useful

Reactivity means that we respond quickly and often strongly to an event – it can be an external event or it can be our own thoughts, emotions or bodily sensations. Reactivity is a natural response enabling us to act fast in situations of danger. For example, if we see someone is about to trip up and fall or if we see a fast approaching bicycle when someone is crossing a road we may shout for them to be careful or to get out of the way, that's a reactive response. Or we can find ourselves in the same situations and adjust our movement to avoid falling or speed up to cross the road. So reactivity can be very helpful for our safety.

Reactivity is enabled by the HPA axis (hypothalamic-pituitary-adrenal axis) specifying the neural and endocrine connections underpinning the stress response across brain regions and the adrenal cortex. The HPA axis activity regulates the balance in the autonomic nervous system involving the sympathetic system response (fight, flight, freeze) and parasympathetic system response (rest and digest).

As part of the HPA axis, an increased activity in the amygdalae is typically the starting point of a chain reaction where other brain regions are activated and hormones released (see the next section on neuroscience of reactivity). This increases the activity of the sympathetic nervous system which results in increased heart rate and blood flow to our muscles for a quick reaction. Such changes enable us to 'escape' or 'fight' in a dangerous situation (fight/flight response), as in the examples above when one needs to cross the road quickly. This mobilisation of resources can also be useful in everyday situations that don't pose an immediate threat to our safety. For example, a moderate increase in anxiety ahead of a test can improve our ability to concentrate on the test and perform better.

As soon as we are safe again (or the test is over), brain regions such as the PFC initiate a reduction in the stress hormone release and soon the parasympathetic nervous system takes over, enabling relaxation and rest after a stressful event. During everyday situations the sympathetic and parasympathetic systems work in balance, increasing our alertness and motivation when needed (sympathetic nervous system) and reducing it, for example, when we rest and eat during a lunch break (parasympathetic nervous system).

Reactivity and Mental Health

However, the HPA activity is often activated not by immediate danger or a situation where we need to mobilise our resources and focus on a task, but by our thoughts and emotions. For example, children may react to a disagreement by anger and this will increase the activity in the amygdalae and result in HPA axis activation and a reactive response. Or they can be worried about something that happened in the morning and this will initiate the HPA axis activation, then result in reactivity during the day. In these instances reactivity may not be helpful and it is better to manage it since it is not serving a useful purpose.

If the HPA axis is activated too often, the PFC and hippocampus may lose their ability to downregulate the stress response (Lupien et al., 2009). This can happen when children have constant worrying thoughts or when they are frequently in stressful situations, for example due to bullying or due to conflicts at home because of financial difficulties. It can also happen due to lack of sleep or poor quality of sleep because some stages of sleep activate the sympathetic nervous system and others the parasympathetic nervous system, with the latter being essential for balanced HPA activity during the day. All these stressors are often associated with poverty (Evans & Kim, 2013).

Robust research linked such imbalances in HPA axis activity with poor mental health (Lupien, 2009). For example, chronic stress has been linked to higher likelihood of depression and anxiety in children. In contrast, strong acute stress linked to trauma has been linked to lower activity in the HPA axis, possibly as a protective mechanism. The effects of trauma can then manifest later in life. So the HPA axis activity can also be imbalanced in mental health difficulties associated with apathy, lack of motivation and lower alertness.

The Three Zones of Reactivity

We have now established that reactivity can be both useful and not useful, and it is closely linked to how we are able to manage our stress response. One useful way of thinking about the relationship between reactivity and stress can be in terms of three zones. The key zone is the zone of tolerance (based on the work of Dan Siegel) which we will call in this book *'the green zone'*. When children are in this zone, they feel that they can face the challenges of everyday life and cope well with normal stresses, they are not over-reactive or under-reactive.

Then there is *'the red zone'*, this is a zone where we react more strongly than usual, because of acute HPA axis imbalance (due to lack of sleep, feeling hungry or a stressful family event) or because of chronic stress (due to low SES or chronic worry/anxiety linked to excessive negative thinking and emotions). When the red zone expands, the green zone narrows and children are more reactive even in low-trigger situations. This imbalance, if it continues over time, can translate into a higher likelihood of poor mental health.

Finally, there is *the blue zone*, when children are apathetic or do not respond sufficiently to situations. This can be the result of trauma, sleep difficulties or other health problems or mental health problems (e.g. depression). So it can be both a symptom of mental ill-health and a consequence of other factors that may result in poor mental health.

Recognising these three zones can be a useful heuristic for teachers in understanding their pupils' MHW and poor mental health. Teaching children about the three zones can also become a useful tool in helping them manage their reactivity and stress levels. We will therefore use references to the tree zones as part of the strategies that can enable children to manage their reactivity in the second part of this chapter.

> Questions for reflection:
> - When is reactivity useful and when is it not useful?
> - How is reactivity linked to the stress response?
> - What do the three zones of reactivity describe and how can being in the green zone support children's MHW?

Neuroscience of Managing Reactivity

The HPA axis activation is the key neuroendocrine mechanism underpinning reactivity. The HPA axis involves the amygdalae, hippocampus, PFC and other brain regions. One of its main functions is regulation of the release and uptake of the hormone cortisol. While the HPA axis is primarily associated with the stress response linked to parasympathetic/

sympathetic system balance, there is also robust evidence linking dysregulation in the HPA axis with anxiety and depression.

The stress response associated with an increase in sympathetic system activity is typically initiated by increased activation of the amygdalae due to perception of an immediate threat in the environment or thinking about a possible threat (including worry, self-critical thoughts etc.). The increased amygdalae activity leads to activation in the hypothalamus, a brain region where corticotropin releasing hormone (CRH) is produced, leading to activation of further parts of the HPA axis.

The CRT hormone initiates the release of the adrenocorticotropic hormone (ACTH) in the pituitary gland and the ACTH travels through bloodstream to the adrenal cortex on the top of the kidneys where it stimulates the release of cortisol, a key stress hormone. This hormone then travels through the bloodstream back to the brain, reaching receptors in the hippocampus and prefrontal cortex which are sensitive to this hormone. Through the signalling of increased levels of cortisol, these two brain regions can then down-regulate the activity in the amygdalae where the stress-response started, leading to a reduction of activity in the HPA axis.

However, cortisol is also neurotoxic and an excessive acute stress response or a chronic stress response can diminish the ability of the hippocampi and the PFC to down-regulate the stress response. In addition, increased exposure to cortisol without appropriate down-regulation can impact on neurogenerative processes in these brain regions resulting in difficulties with concentration, decision making, learning, memory and disruption of the sleep cycle.

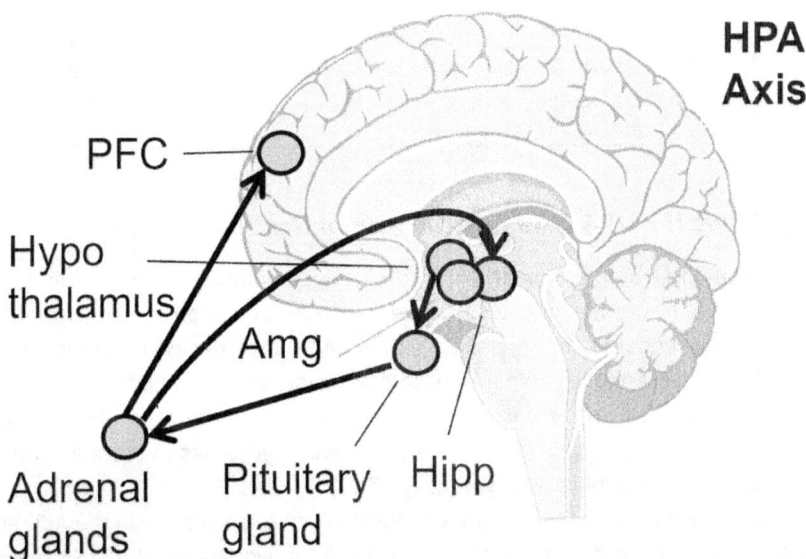

Figure 4.1 Neuroscience of reactivity. HPA axis: PFC - Prefrontal Cortex, Amg - Amygdala, Hipp - Hippocampus, Hypothalamus, Pituitary gland, Adrenal glands.

Source: adapted with permission from Dorjee (2024)

As we have mentioned earlier, the HPA axis is not only activated in response to stressful situations, abnormal activity just like the one observed in the chronic stress response has been associated with poor mental health, including anxiety and depression. The neuroendocrine processes described above are one of the key mechanisms underpinning the range of cognitive (e.g. difficulty with concentration and memory) and bodily symptoms (sweating, sleep difficulties, digestive problems) associated with anxiety and depression.

Key Neuroscience Terms for Managing Reactivity

- The *hypothalamic-pituitary-adrenal (HPA) axis* underpins the stress response linked to reactivity. The HPA axis involves a chain reaction of activation in brain regions including the amygdalae, PFC and other brain regions intertwined with release of stress hormones both in the brain and in the adrenal cortex (on the top of the kidneys). The HPA axis regulates the balance between sympathetic and parasympathetic systems.
- *Amygdala* (plural: *amygdalae*) are a brain region which automatically responds to strong emotions (both negative and positive), but particularly those emotions linked to stress. It can activate the HPA axis and lead to release of stress hormones.
- *Cortisol* is a key stress hormone released by the adrenal cortex (on the top of kidneys). It travels through the blood to other parts of the body, including the brain, and stimulates the sympathetic nervous system.
- The *sympathetic nervous system* mobilises our resources in response to a threat and is linked to the fight or flight response.
- The *parasympathetic nervous system* regenerates our resources and is associated with resting and digesting.

Downregulating the HPA Axis through Mental Health Strategies

Emotion regulation strategies – such as breathing techniques prolonging the outbreath, mindfulness and relaxation techniques – have been shown to adaptively downregulate HPA activity by increasing parasympathetic activation and thus reducing reactivity. For example, in one study children followed paced breathing guidance in an app for only one minute and the findings showed an increase in parasympathetic activity even after a few paced breaths (Obradović et al., 2021). Another study showed decreases in state anxiety in children practicing deep breathing (Khng et al., 2017).

These shifts in HPA axis activation are enabled by increased activity in the ACC and PFC. These brain regions have direct connections with the amygdalae and VS. As a reminder, amygdala responds automatically to emotional content, for example when we are anxious or overexcited. The VS activity increases when we perceive or experience something as rewarding – be it scrolling online, favourite food or enjoyable social interactions. The connections between the PFC and amygdala enable downregulation of activity in the amygdala to manage anxiety or over excitement etc. Indeed, a randomised controlled study with 11 year olds showed a reduction in the right amygdala activity and greater connectivity with the PFC after 8 weeks of school-based mindfulness training (Bauer et al., 2019).

The HPA Axis and Managing Reactivity in the Classroom

Isla is a child in Salma's reception class. Salma noticed that Isla has been more irritable and reactive than usual during school days over this half-term. Isla has also been having more difficulties in concentrating during class activities than before. Salma talked with Isla's parents a few days ago and found that the family has been going through a difficult time. Isla's mother also mentioned that Isla has more difficulties getting to sleep and wakes up during the night more often than before.

Based on what Salma knows about neuroscience of reactivity, she thinks that Isla's irritability, difficulties with concentration and sleep might be linked to an imbalance in the HPA axis due to family stress. Salma is aware that Isla might be experiencing overactivation of the sympathetic nervous system triggered by increases in amygdalae activity. Teaching Isla to increase the parasympathetic system activity might be a way to address the HPA axis imbalance.

Based on this understanding, Salma pays more attention to Isla when guiding children in the class through the paced breathing practice and through progressive muscle relaxation. Salma also instructed the teaching assistant to spend a bit of extra time in supporting Isla with these practices. Salma plans to talk to Isla's mother again and explain to her in an accessible way how she can support Isla in re-balancing her stress response through doing the paced breathing and progressive muscle relaxation practices at home. This may also help with Isla's sleep difficulties. Salma also plans to explore with Isla's parents other ways the school could help them manage the family difficulties they are experiencing as a way of supporting Isla through reducing family stress.

Similar mechanism works also for reactivity linked to difficulties to manage our impulses for getting something that we want. The connections between the PFC and the VS underpin the ability to delay immediate gratification in the moment to support our longer-term goals (Palacios-Barrios & Hanson, 2019). For example, when children may want to keep engaging in an activity they like even though it may make them overtired or interfere with their sleep and/or MHW later on, managing reactivity through paced breathing or mindfulness can be helpful.

How Can Children Acquire the Knowledge and Skills of Managing Reactivity?

The approach to acquiring the knowledge and skills of managing reactivity is the same as for the preceding facets, progressing from external examples to application of the new knowledge and skills to personal experiences. The first step in this process is for children to acquire basic understanding about the difference between relaxation and stress and how too much stress can be managed based on examples from cartoons, stories, movies and public life. They then learn about the green zone, and related concepts of the red zone and the blue zone, from further examples which will also link this knowledge to MHW.

Building on this learning and using further examples, children then learn about reactivity, both its useful aspects and not useful aspects. They are encouraged to recognise in external examples how the green zone links to reactivity and what can narrow down and expand our green zone and thus help us manage reactivity. Emojis indicating reactivity and emojis indicating that reactivity has been managed well can be provided to children as prompts to signal when they spot reactivity in examples. In the next step of learning, children acquire age-appropriate neuroscience knowledge about the stress response (the HPA axis) and relate this to the examples used previously, deepening their understanding.

In the next steps of learning, children begin to apply the knowledge they acquired to their own experience through learning new techniques for expanding the green zone (progressive muscle relaxation) and managing reactivity in the moment (flower-bubbles practice or a simple practice where children breathe in on a count of 4 and breathe out on a count of 6). Both techniques encourage increases in parasympathetic activity and research shows they can be readily implemented in the classroom (O'Donnell & Dunlap, 2019). During inbreath the sympathetic system is activated more strongly and during outbreath parasympathetic system takes over, so prolonging the outbreath reduces the stress response in the body.

Key Strategies for Managing Reactivity

- Flower-bubbles practice – children breathe in as if smelling flowers and breathe out as if blowing bubbles (with a slightly longer outbreath); this practice is for children in reception and KS1.
- 4-6 breathing – children breathe in on a count of 4 and breathe out on a count of 6; this practice is for children in KS2.
- The three zones:
    - Children are in the *green zone* when they feel that they can face the challenges of everyday life and cope well with normal stresses; they are not over-reactive or under-reactive (this is the zone to expand and foster in children).
    - Children are in the *red zone* when they react more strongly than usual to annoyances and tasks, or when the demands exceed their coping resources.
    - Children are in the *blue zone* when they are apathetic or do not respond sufficiently to situations (due to tiredness, illness or trauma).

> - Progressive muscle relaxation – a guided practice that involves systematically tensing and relaxing different parts of the body (look up Vimeo from the PSHE Association for guided progressive muscle relaxation practice instructions we co-developed).

The progressive muscle relaxation practice was developed over 100 years ago by Edmund Jacobson, an American physician. It is one of the most classic approaches to managing stress, currently recommended by the NHS for adults. Research with children shows that progressive muscle relaxation can be effective in improving their attention abilities (Jarraya et al., 2023) and children with behavioural problems can benefit too (Lopata, 2003). There are many adapted versions of progressive muscle relaxation for children. I have provided guidance on a progressive muscle relaxation practice which is part of the PSHE Association's Foundations for Wellbeing curriculum (can be found on Vimeo).

In a classroom format it is important that progressive muscle relaxation is delivered to children with their eyes open, and sitting rather than lying down (this is an attachment - and trauma-informed approach). While learning these new strategies, children are encouraged to assess, using the pleasantness and intensity scales, how their emotions changed from before to after applying these new techniques to indicate reduction in the stress-response (stress response being associated with higher intensity of emotions that are more likely to be unpleasant).

They can also make a graph with the three zones, the green zone being central (and ideally the boundaries of the zone being movable), and mark where they would position themselves within the zones, how their position in the zones changes in different situations and how the boundaries of the green zone change when they apply the new relaxation and breathing techniques as well as techniques learned in previous facets (KS2 children). Movement exercises, where children can move across the zones and act out feelings within each zone, can be used with younger children.

KS2 children can use logs to track their progress in expanding the green zone and managing reactivity. Children are encouraged to also apply their knowledge about neuroscience to their experience, helping them decentre and understand what happens in their brain and body when they apply relaxation techniques and other techniques to expand the green zone and manage reactivity. In the final step of learning, children are encouraged to apply the new techniques in everyday life, both during times of non-reactivity to expand their green zone through progressive muscle relaxation, and in moments of reactivity using breathing techniques (or techniques learned previously if some children find it difficult to focus on their breathing). Repetition is the key to internalising the use of these new concepts and techniques to support MHW in the long term (through neural plasticity to be discussed in the next chapter).

Developmental Differences in Fostering the Knowledge and Skills of Managing Reactivity

The two techniques children learn in this facet are accessible to children from reception onwards, so children will be able to engage with these readily across the age groups. The younger children can also try to enact the three zones if the teacher designates certain spaces in the classroom as the green zone, red zone and blue zone (these can be colour coded and face expressions associated with the zones can be used rather than the zone names). Children can try to imitate the feelings in the three zones and show how they move from one zone to another from before to after doing progressive muscle relaxation or breathing exercises for managing reactivity.

Older children can further map changes in their emotions from before to after applying these techniques using the scales/graph of pleasantness/intensity. They can also graphically depict the three zones and how they move across the zones when they practise the relaxation technique and other techniques they learned in the three facets. Children in the upper KS2 can also be encouraged to keep logs where they track their reactivity and how they managed it using pleasantness/intensity of emotions ratings and a new graph they prepared with the movable green zone.

Across the age groups children are also encouraged to use references to the neuroscience underpinning the stress response to decentre and better understand their reactivity, the three zones and ways to manage them. They are reminded that with repetition managing reactivity becomes easier and explore how managing reactivity in this way can support their MHW.

Acquiring the Knowledge and Skills of Managing Reactivity: The 7-Step Approach

The 7-Step approach applied to managing reactivity starts with the first three steps in which children learn to recognise reactivity and the three zones in external examples. They also learn how the flower-bubbles practice and progressive muscle relaxation can be useful in managing reactivity. Their knowledge about managing reactivity is further solidified through learning about neuroscience underpinning the stress response and its regulation. Building on this knowledge, the following four steps then aim to foster children's skills in managing their reactivity in everyday life. This starts by recognising instances of reactivity and the three zones in their own experience and is followed by applying the flower-bubbles practice (or the 4-6 practice) and progressive muscle relaxation in managing their reactivity. In the final step children bring together their newly learned skills of managing reactivity and relevant neuroscience in increasingly independently and effectively regulating their reactivity in everyday situations.

Step 1: Learning How Managing Reactivity Relates to MHW

The learning objective in the first step is for children to acquire the knowledge that will enable them to understand the difference between stress and relaxation, and relate this understanding to the red zone, green zone and blue zone distinctions. They learn that some practices and activities can expand the green zone and this can support MHW.

 In *reception* children begin to understand the difference between relaxation and tension (stress) and how this relates to the green zone as an optimal zone to be in for learning and play. The teacher can use cartoon examples of relaxation as well as the green zone in contrast to the red and blue zones to help children grasp these concepts. Emojis can be used too. Based on these examples children can practise stepping inside the three colour coded zones and acting out what it means to be in the red zone, green zone and blue zone. They can use the Feels Good Scale and Emotion Strength Scale with help to start recognising the pleasantness and strength of feelings while in the zones.

 In *KS1* children are able to understand what relaxation and tension (too much stress) mean more readily, based on examples. They can start assessing differences in pleasantness and strength between them and relate this to the green zone as an optimal zone for learning and play, in contrast to the red and blue zones. They can explore, with support, basic ways to expand the green zone in examples provided (progressive muscle relaxation).

Children can be encouraged to recognise when characters are relaxed or too stressed in cartoons or stories. They can also try to imitate them by stepping into the three zones (physical colour codes for zones in the classroom can be used). They identify how characters managed their feelings when they were in the red zone (progressive muscle relaxation) and start using the Feels Good Scale and Emotion Strength Scale to quantify the difference between green zone and red zone.

 In the *lower KS2* children are able to recognise more independently the difference between relaxation and too much stress in examples. They can, mostly independently, relate this difference to the three zones and understand from examples that the green zone is the optimal zone for learning and play. They also understand with help that the green zone can be expanded using some example techniques (progressive muscle relaxation) and can relate this to MHW in basic ways.

Children can practise recognising examples of relaxation and too much stress – including their features in expressions, feelings and behaviour – in stories or movies. They can then try to relate these examples to the three zones and possibly use the Pleasantness of Emotion Scale and Intensity of Emotion Scale to make the differences clearer. They start identifying mostly independently ways the characters expanded the green zone and how this made them feel.

In the *upper KS2* children can independently recognise and provide a range of examples from public life demonstrating the difference between too much stress and relaxation. They can relate these differences to the three zones and describe the differences in terms of the pleasantness and strength of emotions. In examples they find themselves they can identify ways the green zone was expanded and how this shifted emotions on the Pleasantness and Intensity of Emotion Graph. They can also relate this to MHW.

Using examples from the public domain or movies/stories, children are encouraged to identify (make a list) of differences between relaxation and too much stress and their manifestations in emotions and behaviour. They then relate this to the three zones by making a drawing and describing in it what emotions and behaviours are linked to each zone. They then describe examples of ways to expand the green zone and how this can support MHW.

Step 2: Learning to Recognise Reactivity and How it Can Be Managed

The learning objective in the second step is for children to acquire the knowledge that will enable them to understand what reactivity means and how it relates to the red zone, green zone and blue zone. They learn that the green zone can sometimes narrow down while the red zone expands and as a result we become more reactive. Children also learn from examples how reactivity impacts MHW and can be managed.

In *reception* children begin to understand what reactivity means based on examples. They can relate this to the red zone (colour-coding and emojis can be used to refer to each of the three zones). They learn with support that sometimes reactivity is helpful but often it is not helpful. Children can be provided with examples of reactivity (quick responses) that are helpful, e.g. somebody is about to slip on a wet floor and another person reacts quickly to warn them. Then they are introduced to examples when reactivity is not helpful, e.g. when a child snatches somebody else's toy or shouts to get something when it is not necessary. With guidance and support children learn to relate these examples to the coloured zones with emojis. They are also introduced to some examples of strategies for managing reactivity, such as the flower-bubbles practice.

In *KS1* children are able to identify more readily examples of reactivity and start to recognise that sometimes reactivity is helpful and often it is not helpful. They can relate reactivity to the three zones (less reactivity in the green zone, more reactivity in the red zone). They can also be provided with basic examples of how reactivity can be managed in the moment (flower-bubbles practice) and examples of expanding the green zone to manage reactivity in the longer term through progressive muscle relaxation.

Children can develop this knowledge through activities where they learn to recognise reactivity in examples from stories or cartoons and relate this to the three zones they learned about previously. They can consider examples when reactivity was helpful (warning of danger) and not helpful (over-reactivity to a remark or situation). They then learn about simple techniques (such as flower-bubbles practice) to manage reactivity in the moment and start exploring how expanding the green zone through progressive muscle relaxation and having enough sleep supports managing reactivity in the longer term.

In the *lower KS2* children are able to recognise reactivity mostly independently in examples from stories or movies and relate this to the three zones, understanding that being in the green zone enables less reactivity. They can recognise mostly independently when reactivity is helpful (situations of danger) and not helpful (overreacting to annoyances). Children can also recognise factors impacting on reactivity such as lack of sleep or worrying about something. They understand readily from examples how to manage reactivity in the moment using breathing techniques (breathing in to count of four breathing out to count of six and any of the previously learned techniques). They also begin to understand that practising progressive muscle relaxation regularly can expand the green zone and make us less reactive, and this supports our MHW.

To foster this knowledge, children can engage in activities where they can practise recognising examples of reactivity in stories or movies and how these were managed. They can also discuss, with guidance, how the three zones relate to the examples of reactivity and whether reactivity was useful or not useful in those cases. Children can make a list of ways to manage reactivity (including breathing techniques and previously learned techniques) and ways to expand the green zone (progressive muscle relaxation etc.). They can use the Pleasantness of Emotion Scale and Intensity of Emotion Scale to explore the effects of these techniques.

In the *upper KS2* children are able to recognise reactivity independently in examples from public life and can relate this to the three zones. They understand that being in the green zone enables one to be less reactive. They can also recognise independently when reactivity is helpful (situations of danger) and not helpful (overreacting to annoyances). Children recognise factors impacting on reactivity such as lack of sleep or worrying about something or too much scrolling on social media or playing violent computer games. Based on examples they know how to manage reactivity in the moment using breathing techniques (breathing in to count of four breathing out to count of six three times) and any of the previously learned techniques. They can understand that good sleep, eating well, regular practices such as progressive muscle relaxation and managing distractions as they arise can expand the green zone (can use the Pleasantness and Intensity of Emotion Graph to evaluate the change in examples) and make us less reactive. This can then support our MHW.

To foster this knowledge, children try to find examples from public life (athletes, celebrities, influencers) of reactivity and how it was managed. They can explore useful and not useful cases of reactivity and what public figures do to expand their green zone such as getting enough sleep, eating well, practising relaxation techniques (see further examples in the general description of this facet). They can use the Pleasantness and Intensity of Emotion Graph to evaluate the changes from before to after applying relevant techniques to manage reactivity and expand the green zone. They also practise recognising how managing reactivity and green zone relate to MHW.

Step 3: Learning Neuroscience Underpinning Managing Reactivity

The learning objective in the third step is for children to acquire the knowledge enabling them to understand what happens in the brain and body during the stress response and to be able to relate this to the concepts of reactivity and the three zones. Children also learn how engaging in strategies and activities that reduce stress and reactivity modifies the stress response and supports MHW.

 In *reception* children begin to understand with support that the brain makes it easier for the body to quickly respond in moments of reactivity, that's why we feel full of energy and ready to run or shout when we are reactive. However, we can also use the brain to calm down when we are not in danger and want to be in the green zone and less reactive. The teacher can guide children in simple activities where some children pretend to be the brain and other children to be receiving signals from the brain and act based on the signals they receive. Children can practise acting fast and moving quickly when the brain tells them to be reactive and then practise calming down and settling when the brain tells them to relax and slow down. This can also be linked to the concepts of the three zones.

 In *KS1* children are able to understand more readily that the stress response involves a new brain region called the amygdala and this brain region helps us detect danger and makes us reactive. Other brain regions including the PFC and ACC help us decide whether it is useful to be reactive or whether we don't need to be reactive, e.g. when we see a toy spider and we jump back or when we notice we are reactive when we don't need to be in response to everyday annoyances). We can use the PFC and ACC to calm down the reactive response, (e.g. when we do the flower-bubbles practice or use other strategies learned before) and also to stay longer in the green zone.

To develop such knowledge, children can make a model or draw two maps of the stress response in groups depicting what happens when someone is reactive (possible links to characters from stories and cartoons) with the amygdala showing strongest activity, and what happens when we calm down (relax) with the PFC, ACC being activated more strongly. They can use emoji stickers that can be placed next to the brain region names to describe their roles and this can be more explicitly linked to the breathing strategy, previous strategies and also the three zones.

 In the *lower KS2* children are able to understand mostly independently that amygdalae are more active when we are reactive and in the red zone and that amygdalae can start a bodily response (the stress response) which makes us ready to fight or run away from danger. They also learn that we can use the PFC and ACC to reduce the activity in the amygdalae and calm down the stress response though practices such as the 4-6 breathing or strategy. This loop connecting the amygdalae, ACC and PFC, and the body is called the HPA axis and we can control activity in the HPA axis by engaging the PFC and ACC when applying the strategies we have learned, thus making the HPA axis activity more balanced (green zone).

Practising techniques such as the progressive muscle relaxation also helps to calm down the HPA axis activity in the long term so that we can expand the green zone and reduce general reactivity to support MHW.

To foster this knowledge, children can be assigned roles based on the different brain regions plus the body and create a chain (linking hands) symbolising the HPA axis (red zone) acting out what happens during the stress response. When the amygdalae and the body become more active (negative emotions or overexcitement) there is less activity in the other brain regions. Whereas when we are in the green zone and/or applying the techniques learned, the most active regions in the HPA axis are PFC and ACC reducing activity in the amygdalae and the fight/flight response in the body. This leads to balanced non-reactive experience. Children can also recognise that factors such as lack of sleep or feeling upset about something make it easier for amygdalae to be activated and start the chain stress response, this can also be linked to the ratings on the Pleasantness of Emotion Scale and Intensity of Emotion Scale, and in turn to MHW.

In the *upper KS2* children are able to understand independently, and can describe, the chain of processes involved in the HPA axis underpinning the stress response. This starts with the amygdalae, which detect danger (real or imagined) and then activate other brain regions that release hormones travelling through the blood to the adrenal glands where stress hormone cortisol is released (responsible for sweating, increased heart rate getting us ready to fight or run away, blood flow into muscles and digestive changes - stomach shrinking feelings). These changes can be associated with the stress response when they are too strong or last too long (red zone) and reactivity.

But when we notice being reactive (insula) and decide that the situation doesn't require us to fight or run away, we can use the ACC and PFC to downregulate the activity in the amygdalae (using the 4-6 breathing or other strategies). This leads to lower release of cortisol and balances out the activity in the HPA axis (lowers stress response). Children can also recognise that factors such as lack of sleep, worrying or excessive scrolling on social media can increase the HPA axis activity. Regular practising of techniques such as progressive muscle relaxation can balance out the HPA axis activity (widen the green zone) supporting our MHW.

To cultivate this knowledge, children can use examples from the public domain they found previously and try to describe what was happening in the brain and body in those examples, including the activity in the HPA axis (outlined above), and how this linked to reactivity. They can then describe what happened when breathing techniques or other strategies were applied to reduce reactivity, how the HPA activity changed as a result and how this supported MHW of those in the examples. Brain map drawings of the HPA axis can also be used to support the descriptions, with links to the Pleasantness and Intensity of Emotion Graph ratings and changes in them.

Step 4: Learning Skills of Managing Reactivity in Own Experience

The learning objective in the fourth step is for children to develop the skills that will enable them to recognise in their own experience the difference between feeling stressed and feeling relaxed. They learn to recognise the three zones in their own experience and can apply simple relaxation strategies to shift from the red zone to the green zone. They understand from own experience how this links to MHW.

In *reception* children begin to be able to recognise with support in their own experience the different feelings associated with relaxation and tension (stress) during practices such as progressive muscle relaxation. They begin to relate the three zones to their own experience (using colour signals or emojis) and start applying relaxation techniques with guidance to expand the green zone. The teacher can guide children in the progressive muscle relaxation practice, delivered in a fun way, with eyes open and sitting or standing, not lying down – this is a trauma/ACE/attachment sensitive delivery. The teacher can encourage children to notice the difference between tensing and relaxing muscles in their own experience and relate this to how they feel when they are in the three colour coded zones with emojis.

In *KS1* children are able to recognise more readily in their own experience the difference between relaxation and tension (too much stress) during guided progressive muscle relaxation practices. They begin to recognise differences in pleasantness and strength between relaxation and tension and can relate this to the three zones. They also start to recognise, with support, how practising progressive muscle relaxation and other techniques (see general description) can expand the green zone and that this helps them feel better.

To foster these skills, the teacher can guide children in the progressive muscle relaxation practice delivered in a fun way, with eyes open and sitting or standing, not lying down – this is a trauma/ACE/attachment sensitive delivery. This can help children recognise in their own experience the difference between tension and relaxation. Children can also experiment with other techniques from the examples they learned previously and rate the differences using the Feels Good Scale and Emotion Strength Scale. They can be guided to relate this to the three zones and explore in their own experience with support how it feels to be in the green zone and how this feeling can be more frequent and/or longer.

In the *lower KS2* children are able to recognise from their own experience during guided progressive muscle relaxation the difference between relaxation and too much stress and can do parts of the relaxation practice mostly independently. Using the Pleasantness of Emotion Scale and Intensity of Emotion Scale they can recognise the difference between too much stress and relaxation and relate this to the three zones. They recognise in their own experience what emotions (including bodily sensations – feeling less tense) the green zone is associated with. Children also start using strategies including progressive muscle relaxation (and other strategies

learned previously) mostly independently to expand the green zone. They understand mostly independently from their own experience that expanding the green zone can support their MHW.

To cultivate these skills, the teacher can guide children in activities where they learn progressive muscle relaxation, delivered with eyes open and sitting or standing, not lying down - this is a trauma/ACE/attachment sensitive approach. Children then try to practise progressive muscle relaxation independently under supervision. They can rate their emotional state using the Pleasantness of Emotion Scale and Intensity of Emotion Scale before and after the progressive muscle relaxation practice and relate this to the three zones. Children can also explore other ways to expand the green zone using techniques from the story/movies examples discussed earlier. They can relate the shifts in the green zone through the practices to own MHW with increasing independence.

In the *upper KS2* children can independently recognise and describe the difference between feeling stressed and feeling relaxed from their own experience and relate this to the three zones. They can describe from their own experience what it feels like to be in the green zone. They learn and can practise progressive muscle relaxation independently and explore other strategies from the public domain examples to expand the green zone. Children can also use the Pleasantness and Intensity of Emotion Graph to differentiate between relaxation and stress in relation to the green zone. They understand from their own experience how expanding the green zone through these strategies can support their MHW.

To foster these skills children can participate in activities encouraging them to describe in a few words from their own experience what feeling relaxed and feeling stressed means. This is best done anonymously using a Padlet or another software so that the focus is on group responses rather than individuals. Children then learn the progressive muscle relaxation practice with eyes open and sitting or standing, not lying down - this is a trauma/ACE/attachment sensitive approach to delivery of the practice. They can do simple evaluations using the Pleasantness and Intensity of Emotion Graph to further differentiate between stress and relaxation and the three zones. They can also use a graph with the three zones to try to place themselves within those spaces based on how they feel during the week (again, this is best done anonymously in a group format). Children can be encouraged to brainstorm how this can support their MHW in groups.

Step 5: Learning to Recognise Reactivity in Own Experience

The learning objective in the fifth step is for children to be able to recognise in their own experience instances of reactivity and differentiate between useful and not useful reactivity, then apply the new strategies to reduce reactivity in the moment and generally. Children also learn to recognise possible causes of reactivity and possible ways to address these, and understand how managing reactivity relates to MHW from their own experience.

90 *Making Sense of Mental Health and Wellbeing in Primary Schools*

 In *reception* children begin to recognise instances of reactivity in their own experience with support. With guidance they also start considering if these were useful or not, by relating this to the examples of cartoon or story characters provided previously. They try to apply new breathing techniques (if helpful can try to also use any previously learned strategies) to manage reactivity in the moment and begin to recognise how applying these techniques and strategies changes their feelings. To foster these skills, children can be encouraged to recognise reactivity in their own experience and with support evaluate if it was useful or not. They learn the flower-bubbles breathing technique guided by the teaching staff and are gradually prompted to use it when they are being reactive (some children may prefer other strategies learned earlier, that's ok). They can also use the emojis associated with the three zones to indicate how their feelings change when they apply the technique to manage reactivity - meaning they moved back to the green zone (colour coded).

 In *KS1* children recognise instances of reactivity in their own experience with support but more readily. With guidance they can evaluate if the reactivity was useful or not. They learn the flower-bubbles breathing technique guided by their teacher and start to use it in instances of reactivity, first supported by the teaching staff and then sometimes on their own. They sometimes recognise causes of their reactivity, e.g. not having enough sleep, and start to understand in their own experience that managing reactivity using the new techniques or other strategies can make them feel better.

To acquire these skills, children can be guided in the flower-bubbles technique and can use the Feels Good Scale and Emotion Strength Scale to recognise the shift in how they feel from before to after applying the technique. The teacher can explain that this can help them manage reactivity next time. Teachers and teaching assistants non-judgmentally encourage children to recognise reactivity when it happens and help them evaluate its usefulness. Then children are encouraged to apply the breathing technique or previously learned strategies to manage their reactivity and recognise how this changes the way they feel.

 In the *lower KS2* children are able to recognise reactivity in their own experience more readily and independently, and evaluate if the reactivity is useful or not. They learn and then apply the 4-6 breathing technique (and any of the previously learned techniques if preferred) when reactivity is not useful. Children can recognise more readily a few possible causes of reactivity and how these can be addressed. They also recognise in their own experience that feelings change when we are reactive and then change when we apply techniques such as the 4-6 breathing. They can use the Pleasantness of Emotion Scale and Intensity of Emotion Scale to quantify this if helpful. They are able to relate reactivity to MHW and understand mostly independently that less reactivity means feeling better.

To develop these skills, the teaching staff can guide children in the 4-6 breathing technique and encourage them to recognise that this can be helpful in instances when they are reactive. Then during the school day children can prepare a log reflecting twice a day on any instances of reactivity that occurred during the day, whether they were useful or not, how they responded to them and how they want to respond to them next time. They can also reflect on possible causes of not useful reactivity such as feeling annoyed by something that happened earlier or staying up too late the previous day. They can use the Pleasantness of Emotion Scale and Intensity of Emotion Scale in the logs to mark how they felt when they were reactive and how they felt after managing it. Children don't share the logs but could enter the numbers of reactivity cases and changes in pleasantness and strength of emotions in a group document anonymously so that the patterns in the class as a whole can be explored.

In the *upper KS2* children are able to readily and independently recognise instances of reactivity in their own experience and recognise whether they were useful or not. Then they readily apply the 4-6 breathing technique (or previously learned strategies if preferred) to manage reactivity increasingly in an internalised way. They use the Pleasantness and Intensity of Emotion Graph to evaluate how emotions change during reactivity and after applying techniques to manage reactivity. They can also recognise that reactivity gets worse with factors such as lack of sleep, playing violent computer games or watching content online for a long time. They recognise from their own experience that less reactivity is linked to better MHW.

To cultivate these skills, children first learn the 4-6 breathing technique to be applied during instances of not useful reactivity. Then they can prepare logs where they keep track of instances of reactivity over a couple of days, both instances in school (they reflect on this once during school day) and outside of school. In the log they record what the reactivity trigger was, whether reactivity was useful or not, whether there were any factors that impacted on it, how they managed reactivity, how they felt while being reactive and after managing reactivity (Pleasantness and Intensity of Emotion Graph) and how they want to manage reactivity next time (teachers can prepare a grid for this). Children can prepare cumulative scores of numbers of reactivity (useful and not useful) and how many times it was managed well and how pleasantness and strength of emotions changed, then share the scores anonymously in a Google Doc or Padlet with the whole class so that the progress of the whole class can be mapped and discussed.

Step 6: Learning to Apply Neuroscience Knowledge as Part of Managing Reactivity

The learning objective in the sixth step is for children to be able to use their understanding of neuroscience underpinning managing reactivity to maintain or expand the green zone and manage reactivity. Children learn to explain the effects of the strategies for managing reactivity applied to their own experience in neuroscience terms and relate this to supporting their MHW.

 In *reception* children begin to describe (with support) that when they are feeling reactive the brain is signalling to their body to be ready to run or shout, and when they are doing the flower-bubbles practice they use their brain to calm down the body. During the progressive muscle relaxation practice, children can describe that they are using their brain to expand the green zone (colour coded) so that they are less reactive. To foster these skills, the teacher first reminds children that they are using their brain to calm down the body to be more in the green zone. Children are then encouraged to explain in their own terms what is happening during the practice. Similarly, when practising the flower-bubbles technique, the teacher reminds children that they are using their brain to calm down reactivity and encourages them to remember this next time they do the practice and in real life situations when they are managing reactivity.

 In *KS1*, with teacher guidance children are able to use references to the changes in the brain associated with the stress response (amygdalae, PFC, ACC) in support of expanding the green zone during the progressive muscle relaxation practice and when managing reactivity using the flower-bubbles breathing technique. To cultivate these skills, children can be encouraged to describe what is happening in their brain during progressive muscle relaxation practices and when practising the flower-bubbles practice (amygdalae, PFC, ACC). Then during everyday activities they are encouraged to refer to the relevant parts of the brain when they are managing their reactivity. This can also help with decentring from their feelings and possibly triggering circumstances. They can also make a simple record of how many times a day they managed reactivity (using stickers).

 In the *lower KS2* children are able to use understanding of the neuroscience underpinning the stress response (references to the HPA axis involving the amygdalae, ACC and PFC) to explain changes in the brain when practising progressive muscle relaxation and/or the 4-6 breathing technique more independently. Based on their own experience, they can relate the neuroscience changes to improvements in their own MHW, for example, when comparing days during which they practised the techniques to days when they did not.

To cultivate these skills, children can be encouraged to draw two pictures, one depicting what happens in their brain when they are reactive and the other depicting what happens in their brain when they are applying the 4-6 breathing technique. They can use emojis to indicate the changes in emotions and relate this to the Pleasantness of Emotion Scale and Intensity of Emotion Scale ratings. Children are then encouraged to use references to the brain (if helpful) during instances of reactivity to decentre from their reactive emotions and the situation; this can enable more effective management of their emotions. Children can also be encouraged to take turns describing what is happening in their brain during regular progressive relaxation practices with teacher guidance. They are prompted to link the neuroscience descriptions to supporting their MHW.

In the *upper KS2* children are able to independently and readily use their understanding of neuroscience underpinning the stress response (HPA axis - amygdalae, PFC, ACC, cortisol) in guiding and motivating implementation of practises that maintain or expand the green zone and help them manage reactivity. They can readily describe what is happening in their brain when practising progressive muscle relaxation and the 4-6 breathing technique. They can relate the effects of these practices on the stress response to effects on their MHW.

To foster these skills, using examples from their everyday life, children can prepare two small comic books, one depicting what happened to the HPA axis (including all the relevant brain regions they learned about and cortisol) when they were reactive, and the other depicting changes in activity of the HPA axis when they were managing reactivity using the 4-6 breathing technique (or other strategies if preferred). They can use emojis and ratings on the Pleasantness and Intensity of Emotion Graph in the comic books too. The comic books should not be shared with peers but the teacher can provide feedback. Children can also take turns describing what is happening in their brains during teacher-guided practices of progressive muscle relaxation and the 4-6 breathing technique. They can share their observations about links between the neuroscience underpinning the stress response and MHW with each other, without details of personal experiences.

Step 7: Applying Skills of Managing Reactivity in Everyday Life

The learning objective in the seventh step is for children to be able to apply their knowledge about the stress response, three zones and reactivity, together with their new skills in managing reactivity and relevant neuroscience, to expand the green zone and manage reactivity effectively in everyday situations to support their MHW.

In *reception* children begin to notice instances of reactivity in their own behaviour, and with support start applying the flower-bubbles breathing technique (and/or previously learned strategies if preferred) together with references to the brain to manage their reactivity in everyday situations. In their own experience, with support, children start recognising in everyday situations when they are in the green zone and the red zone and apply techniques such as the progressive muscle relaxation with guidance to expand the green zone.

To cultivate these skills, in everyday situations, children are encouraged to recognise cases of reactivity in their behaviour (non-judgmental approach from their teachers needs to support this) and evaluate if the reactivity is useful or not. If not, they are reminded to use the flower-bubbles technique or any other previously learned strategy they may find helpful to reduce their reactivity. They can use references to the brain in the process to decentre from the situation. Children are also reminded in everyday situations to check whether they are in the green zone (e.g. after register or after a lunch break or after a busy activity) and are guided by their teacher to do regular practice of progressive muscle relaxation to maintain or expand their green zone.

In *KS1* children recognise instances of reactivity in their behaviour in everyday situations with teacher support (non-judgmental approach needed from teachers). They can more readily evaluate if reactivity is useful or not useful in a particular situation and with prompts start applying the flower-bubbles breathing technique (or any other strategy previously learned if preferred) to manage reactivity in the moment (may refer to the amygdalae, ACC and PFC to decentre). Children start to recognise the beneficial effects of the technique and notice that with practice managing reactivity becomes easier. Similarly, they recognise being in the green zone more readily and use the progressive muscle relaxation practice (or other strategies) to expand the green zone during the day.

To foster these skills, in everyday situations children are encouraged to recognise reactivity – the teacher could use sign prompts to indicate reactivity and another sign with two sides asking children if the reactivity is useful or not in that particular situation. They then apply the flower-bubbles technique (or other strategies if preferred) and use neuroscience to describe their experience. If there are the Pleasantness of Emotion and Intensity of Emotion Scales as posters in the classroom where the child is, they can also try to evaluate in the moment how they felt while being reactive and after managing reactivity. Similarly, children could indicate with signs in the morning during register which zone they feel they are in and then the teacher could guide them in the progressive muscle relaxation practice to expand the zone. Children can use the scale posters to evaluate how they felt before and after the relaxation practice or relate this back to the zones with signs.

In the *lower KS2*, children are able to recognise their own experience in everyday situations when they are reactive mostly independently. With very little support they can evaluate whether their reactivity is useful or not in a particular situation. They are able to apply the 4-6 breathing technique (or any other previously learned technique if preferred) to manage reactivity in the moment mostly independently and effectively. They can also notice the difference in emotion pleasantness and strength during reactivity and after applying the technique. They are able to refer to neuroscience (HPA axis, amygdalae, ACC, PFC) in describing their experience of reactivity and managing reactivity when helpful. Children notice mostly independently when they are in the green zone and when outside the zone, and can link this to possible factors such as lack of sleep or some earlier upset. They can practise progressive muscle relaxation to expand the green zone regularly, recognising that this can support their MHW.

To foster these skills, during everyday activities children are encouraged, by teaching staff and/or each other, to recognise being reactive. They evaluate if the reactivity is useful and if not apply the 4-6 breathing technique to manage it. They can be encouraged to describe their experience in neuroscience terms if helpful for decentring. Children can use the log to keep tracking their progress with managing reactivity and use the Pleasantness of Emotion and Intensity of Emotion Scales to see whether the technique is effective in changing how they feel. They can expand the log to track progress and factors impacting reactivity at home for a couple of days too (not sharing this in class). In class, children can take turns in small groups to lead the progressive muscle relaxation practice once or twice a day (e.g. after register, after a lunch break or at home time) and make a group record of how their emotions change from before to after the practice and whether their green zone expanded (or they feel more within the zone).

In the *upper KS2* children are able to independently and readily recognise instances of reactivity in their own experience during everyday activities, evaluate if reactivity was useful or not in a particular situation, and if not apply the 4-6 technique to effectively downregulate reactivity in the moment. They can clearly recognise the shift in pleasantness and strength of emotions after managing reactivity and can describe the changes in their emotions in neuroscience terms (HPA axis - amygdalae, cortisol, PFC, ACC). Children can readily recognise the three zones in everyday situations and independently practise progressive muscle relaxation (or other strategies if preferred) to maintain or expand the green zone couple during the day. Children also recognise how lack of sleep, peer-conflict, too much social media time or gaming can reduce the green zone and increase reactivity, and take action to manage these factors as needed. They recognise from their own experience how being in the green zone and reactivity impact their MHW and apply the strategies learned to support their MHW.

To foster these skills, children can be reminded at the start of the day (and before breaks) to notice reactivity in their behaviour during the day and manage reactivity, when it is not useful, using the 4-6 technique (other strategies if preferred). They are also encouraged to apply their understanding of neuroscience underpinning the stress response in managing reactivity. Children are also encouraged to guide each other in the 4-6 breathing technique in a supportive way during moments of reactivity. They can reflect on instances of reactivity and its successful management at the end of the school day. A class chart where they enter their reflections anonymously can be reviewed by their teacher with the whole class (both overall reductions in reactivity instances and cases of successful management out of overall reactivity instances are positive outcomes). Children can keep tracking their reactivity and management of it after school too and write a diary about their experience (not shared with others). They can be encouraged to take turns in guiding the class or guide each other in pairs in the progressive muscle relaxation practice to expand their green zone and anonymously plot changes in their emotions using the Pleasantness and Intensity of Emotion Graph on a class chart in Google Docs that the class as a whole can reflect on. Children can brainstorm in an anonymous class Google document how managing reactivity and expanding the green zone has been supporting their MHW; the teacher can review this with the whole class together so that children also learn from each others' insights.

Conclusion

Effective managing of reactivity is one of the key skills children need to be able to self-regulate. If you, just like Salma, were looking for a deeper understanding of why reactivity arises and how it links to MHW, this chapter might have provided you with a comprehensive research-based explanation. Building on this understanding, we have also considered ways to foster skills of managing reactivity in primary school children. These were presented in a systematic and age-appropriate way following the 7-Step approach and focused both on development of children's understanding of reactivity and acquiring of relevant skills via the flower-bubbles practice and progressive muscle relaxation. Hopefully you will now be able to help children in your class develop this knowledge and skills in a more systematic and effective way.

Key chapter points:

- Reactivity can be useful when responding to danger but is not useful in many other everyday situations that are not dangerous.
- Excessive reactivity to situations, thoughts or emotions has been linked to poor mental health.
- Reactivity is underpinned by chain reactions of the HPA axis and learning to manage reactivity involves learning to downregulate the stress response skilfully.
- Increasing children's understanding of the stress response and HPA axis activity can help them manage reactivity.
- Following the 7-Step Approach children can learn breathing strategies that can help them manage reactivity (and the stress response) in the moment.
- Regular progressive muscle relaxation practice can help children expand their green zone so that they can face normal everyday challenges skilfully without becoming over-reactive or under-reactive.

References

Bauer, C. C. C., Caballero, C., Scherer, E., West, M. R., Mrazek, M. D., Phillips, D. T., Whitfield-Gabrieli, S., & Gabrieli, J. D. E. (2019). Mindfulness training reduces stress and amygdala reactivity to fearful faces in middle-school children. *Behavioral Neuroscience, 133*(6), 569-585. https://doi.org/10.1037/bne0000337

Dorjee, D. (2024). Conceptualising child and adolescent mental health and wellbeing neurodevelopment: an integrative brain networks framework. Preprint, 4 November. https://doi.org/10.31234/osf.io/7vx45

Evans, G. W., & Kim, P. (2013). Childhood poverty, chronic stress, self-regulation, and coping. *Child Development Perspectives, 7*(1), 43-48.

Lupien, S. J., McEwen, B. S., Gunnar, M. R., & Heim, C. (2009). Effects of stress throughout the lifespan on the brain, behaviour and cognition. *Nature Reviews Neuroscience, 10*(6), 434-445.

Khng, K. H. (2017). A better state-of-mind: deep breathing reduces state anxiety and enhances test performance through regulating test cognitions in children. *Cognition and Emotion, 31*(7), 1502-1510.

Jarraya, S., Jarraya, M., & Engel, F. A. (2022). Kindergarten-based progressive muscle relaxation training enhances attention and executive functioning: a randomized controlled trial. *Perceptual and Motor Skills, 129*(3), 644-669.

Lopata, C. (2003). Progressive muscle relaxation and aggression among elementary students with emotional or behavioral disorders. *Behavioral Disorders, 28*(2), 162-172.

Obradović, J., Sulik, M, J., & Armstrong-Carter, E. (2021). Taking a few deep breaths significantly reduces children's physiological arousal in everyday settings: results of a preregistered video intervention. *Developmental Psychobiology, 63,* e22214. https://onlinelibrary.wiley.com/doi/10.1002/dev.22214

O'Donnell, P. S., & Dunlap, L. L. (2019). Teacher acceptability of progressive muscle relaxation in the classroom for the treatment of test anxiety. *Journal of Psychologists and Counsellors in Schools, 29*(2), 151-165.

Palacios-Barrios, E. E., & Hanson, J. L. (2019). Poverty and self-regulation: connecting psychosocial processes, neurobiology, and the risk for psychopathology. *Comprehensive Psychiatry, 90,* 52-64.

5 Habitual Thoughts and Emotions

Introduction

Now that children have learned the skills of emotional awareness, managing distractions and reactivity, they can start exploring more nuanced aspects of their mental health and wellbeing (MHW). Over time we all develop established ways of relating to and managing our thoughts, emotions and behaviours – these can become patterns of habitual thoughts and emotions. Children can acquire these habits in their family, mirroring how their parents/carers and siblings are managing their thoughts and emotions, or they can follow examples from peers and teachers in school. As children get older they can also start copying ways of managing thoughts and emotions they see online and in movies. There can be some habitual thought and emotion patterns children are also naturally inclined to follow due to their predispositions, some of these are universal predispositions of the human mind such as the negativity bias.

Being able to recognise our habitual thoughts, emotions and behaviours can help us strengthen those patterns that support our MHW and limit those that are not helpful. Therefore, this building block of the second tier of the ATTEND Pyramid, aims to foster the knowledge and skills needed to recognise and shift maladaptive habitual thoughts and emotions, including the negativity bias, and increase adaptive thoughts and emotions through managing reactivity and redirecting attention to neutral or positive thoughts and emotions and savouring of positive experiences.

The first part of this chapter explains the research behind formation of habitual thoughts and emotions, including relevant neuroscience with focus on neural plasticity. We particularly explore the effects of the negativity bias and savouring of positive experiences. This research is presented through the lens of impacts habitual thoughts and emotions have on children's MHW. Building on this understanding, we then explore ways to foster children's abilities of noticing their habitual thought and emotion patterns and downregulating the patterns that are not supportive of their MHW while upregulating those that are helpful. The second part of the chapter guides you, step by step, in teaching children the knowledge and skills of managing their habitual thoughts and emotions in an age-appropriate way following the 7-Step Approach. But first, it might be helpful to imagine how habitual thoughts and emotions are playing out in the classroom and what the main challenges of managing them might be.

Case Study: Negativity Bias and Savouring of Experiences in the Classroom

Michelle is a year 3 teacher in her primary school. She noticed that when some children have a disagreement with their peers early in the day, they tend to keep thinking about it throughout the day and don't engage well with others or in classroom activities. Michelle knows that this behaviour can have many different reasons, for example, the conflict with their peers may remind some children of difficulties at home. But she is wondering if this sometimes is related to the negativity bias she read about.

She knows from her own experience that at the end of the day she finds it much easier to remember the difficult situations that happened during the day, rather than all the positive things that occurred. Michelle has been wondering how the negativity bias links to MHW and whether teaching children ways to manage the negativity bias may also support their MHW. Perhaps children could be taught how to savour and remember positive experiences equally well? But Michelle is aware that she doesn't want to steer children towards 'toxic positivity', she is looking for a balanced approach.

This also made Michelle think about habits and MHW in general. She noticed that, just like all of us, different children have different habitual ways of coping. Some of these ways are more adaptive than others. So Michelle was wondering if there is a way to strengthen some of the positive habits of managing emotions and adjust or limit some of the maladaptive ways such as lashing out. She was thinking that with repetition some of the new MHW skills children learned previously – those that help them become more aware of their thoughts and emotions and manage distractions and reactivity – could turn into useful habits that could support children's MHW in the longer term.

Questions for reflection:

- Have you noticed different habitual ways of coping children use in your classroom?
- Do you see some instances of the negativity bias when children reflect on what happened during the school day?
- Do you know how habitual thinking and emotional experiencing patterns relate to MHW?

How Are Habitual Thoughts and Emotions Relevant to MHW?

Our dispositions, experiences in family and school, as well as examples of managing emotions, thoughts and behaviours we encounter in everyday situations often lead to development of usual (habitual) ways we respond to situations, relationships and our own thoughts, emotions and behaviours. Some of these habitual ways of responding can be adaptive, supporting our MHW, such as using the naming and distraction-based strategies mentioned in the previous chapters. But others can be maladaptive, undermining our MHW, such as repeated avoidance of situations, reactive ways of responding or habitual suppression of our emotions. Research shows that these maladaptive habitual ways of responding are associated with anxiety and depression and can even have negative impact on our physical health.

The challenge of adopting adaptive habitual ways of managing emotions and thoughts is made more difficult by our susceptibility to the negativity bias. We talked about pleasantness and strength of emotions in the chapter on Emotional Awareness. Research relevant to formation of habitual thoughts and emotions shows that if we experience two different emotions that are equally intense but one is negative and the other positive, our attention will be drawn to the negative one more strongly than to the positive one. We will remember situations and events associated with negative emotions better, and negative emotions also have a stronger impact on our decision making. This is because from an evolutionary perspective, it is more important for our survival to avoid potential danger than to engage with stimuli that can bring potential gain.

However, studies show that exacerbated negativity bias is a feature of mental ill-health conditions such as anxiety and depression (Williams et al., 2009). Research also shows that maladaptive habitual ways of experiencing and responding, including the negativity bias, can be modified towards more adaptive ones, linking to the concept of neural plasticity described below. For example, attention bias modification treatment targeting excessive negativity bias has been effective in treating anxiety disorders in children (Hakamata et al., 2010; Eldar et al., 2012). This computer-based training focuses on redirecting attention away from negative stimuli and towards neutral or positive stimuli.

Similarly, some of the latest approaches to treatment of anxiety and depression encourage non-judgmental noticing, recognising and shifting of attention towards stimuli and activities associated with positive experiences. Other approaches provide training in recognising and savouring simple lower intensity neutral and positive experiences (such as observing an animal in play or colourful leaves on a tree in autumn). This can extend and magnify the impact of such experiences on MHW (Samios et al., 2021). All these skills, if acquired early in the development, have the potential to support MHW in the long term.

> Questions for reflection:
> - Do you know what negativity bias is and why it may have given us an evolutionary advantage?
> - How can negativity bias become maladaptive and undermine MHW?
> - What are some possible ways of countering negativity bias?

Neuroscience of Habitual Thoughts and Emotions

Formation of habitual thoughts and emotions is underpinned by neural plasticity – neural changes in the brain as a result of repeated experiences. This is because repeated experiences can shift the likelihood of neurons firing together and result in creation of 'pathways' that carry neural signals more readily. These processes of neural plasticity can work both in ways that can support and undermine MHW. For example, they can enhance MHW when we form habits of observing our thoughts and emotions in a non-judgmental way or develop a habit of practising progressive muscle relaxation every day or habitually use the paced breathing techniques when we are reactive. But neural plasticity can also underpin maladaptive habitual thoughts and emotions – for instance, when children repeatedly have anxious thoughts every time the teacher mentions a test or some other school activity. Therefore repetition of positive habits is essential to their long-term effects, and shifting of maladaptive habits is the key to their 'extinction'.

One of the main brain regions underpinning formulation of habits via neural plasticity is the hippocampus, which is involved in bottom-up stream of self-regulation. It is a brain region located deep in the brain and there is one hippocampus in each brain hemisphere. Hippocampi support learning and memory processes. In relation to MHW, the hippocampi are involved in storing memories of how we responded in different situations that required regulation of our emotions, and what worked. For example, if children repeatedly experience that avoidance of a situation brought them emotional relief they may tend to repeat that response. Similarly, if children witness certain types of emotion regulation (adaptive or maladaptive) in their social environment – whether in their family, peer-group or community – they may acquire a tendency to respond in similar ways.

But the functioning of hippocampi can also be impacted indirectly, through experiences of stress, including stressors such as poverty or maternal depression. Neural cells in the hippocampi have receptors that are sensitive to stress hormones and acute extreme exposure to stress due to trauma, or longer-term exposure to stress hormones through chronic stress, reduces the ability of the neurons in the hippocampi to form new connections, resulting in worsening of memory and learning processes. The sensitive period for maturation of the hippocampi is during the first couple of years of a child's life and traumatic experiences or longer-term stress during this period can result in so-called programming effects, which predispose a child to increased reactivity to stressful experiences in the future (Lupien et al., 2009). This can, for example, result in higher likelihood, and an earlier onset, of mental health problems in adolescence or early adulthood.

> ### Key Neuroscience Terms for Managing Habitual Thoughts and Emotions
>
> - Hippocampus (plural: hippocampi) is a structure deep in the brain (in the temporal lobes) supporting learning and memory. This includes learning and memories of how we responded in different situations that required regulation of our emotions and what worked.

- Neural plasticity is the process of strengthening connections between neural cells that fire 'together' when we think, feel or respond repeatedly (habitually) to situations and experiences in the same way.
- The ventral striatum (VS) is a brain structure deep in the brain activated when we savour positive experiences; it is part of the reward network.
- The reward network involves the VS, amygdalae, hippocampi, some areas in the PFC (particularly the ventromedial PFC - vmPFC), ACC and other brain regions.

However, the hippocampi are also part of a brain network that enables us to shift negative habitual patterns of thoughts and emotions and savour positive experiences - the reward network (Sesack & Grace, 2009). This network involves the ACC and PFC working with the insula to adaptively regulate the activity in the amygdalae, the VS, the hippocampi and other brain regions. The reward network responds to a range of experiences that can be described as rewarding - from enjoying a good meal to positive social interactions with others.

Maladaptive activity in this network in response to potentially rewarding experiences has been linked to depression, both in adults and in children (Rappaport et al., 2020). And further research with adolescents suggested that adaptive functioning of the reward network can have protective effects on the likelihood of further depression episodes of depression in adolescents who experienced depression previously, and can thus be linked to resilience

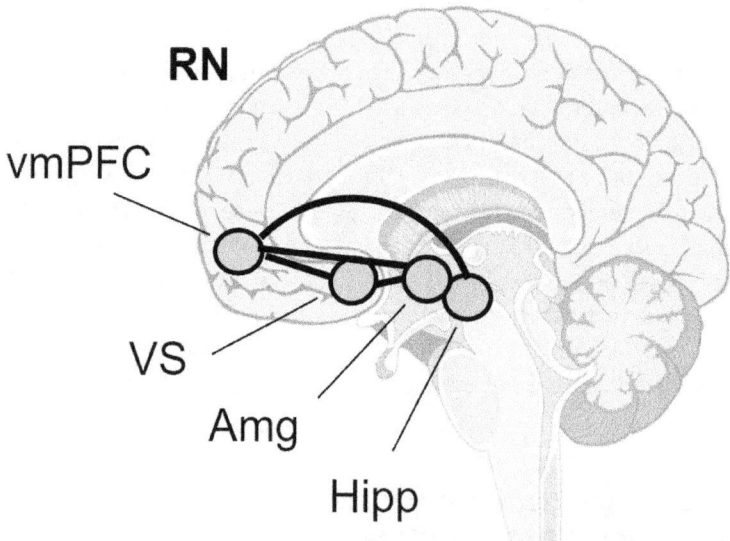

Figure 5.1 Neuroscience of habitual thoughts and emotions. Reward network: vmPFC - ventromedial Prefrontal Cortex, VS - Ventral Striatum, Amg - Amygdala, Hipp - Hippocampus.

Source: adapted with permission from Dorjee (2024)

(Fischer et al., 2019). For this reason some researchers suggested that abnormalities in the reward network could be considered as another transdiagnostic mechanism underpinning mental ill-health (Baskin-Sommers & Foti, 2015).

Finally, research on negativity bias suggested involvement of the executive network in managing the bias. One study found that increased activity in the PFC (particularly vmPFC) coupled with reductions in amygdala activation underpins the ability to downregulate the negativity bias (Carlisi & Robinson, 2018). This shows further overlap between the neural mechanisms involved in managing distractions and reactivity, and adaptive regulation of the negativity bias; it may also suggest that the adaptive neural processes fostered across the facets may have cumulative effects on strengthening children's MHW.

Neural Plasticity, the Reward Network and Managing Habitual Thoughts and Emotions in the Classroom

After learning about neuroscience underpinning habitual thoughts and emotions, Michelle started recognising more clearly the different habitual strategies children use to cope in her classroom. She also recognised how these strategies, even when not adaptive, get established more firmly if they help the child cope. For example, some children may become disruptive because they find it difficult to manage their emotions in the moment and when this leads to them being removed from the class, this may serve as a reward in some cases and reinforce such behaviour through activity in the hippocampus and neural plasticity. She knows that in such cases, working with children in developing more adaptive strategies to manage their emotions, which they also recognise as rewarding, can better support their MHW.

Michelle now understands that neural plasticity can work both in reinforcing unhelpful habitual ways of coping and in enabling children to develop new helpful ways of managing their emotions and thoughts. Repetition and reward are the key in both cases. She also understands now that the reward doesn't always have to be praise or a sticker. The reward system – including the VS, hippocampus, the PFC and ACC – becomes activated also when children enjoy an activity and savour it. Therefore, she has been guiding children several times a day during regular activities they enjoy – such as gardening or working on a group project or during a music class – in recognising their positive emotions and savouring them (expanding their duration though exploring the experience more closely).

She also regularly guides children in using previously learned strategies and new strategies of recalling positive memories, images or thoughts, when they find it hard to let go of something that upset them (often due to negativity bias). She knows that this can help disrupt neural plasticity working against children's MHW via repetition of negative thoughts and emotions. She noticed that children found it helpful when she taught them about the importance of using the strategies they learned again and again because this make it easier for their mind and brain to use the strategies next time due to neural plasticity.

How Can Children Acquire the Knowledge and Skills of Managing Habitual Thoughts and Emotions?

The first step in the process of learning to manage habitual ways of thinking and emotions is to start recognising that we tend to build up such habits. Children can acquire such knowledge through examples from cartoons, stories, movies (and everyday public life such as social media). In the next step they learn that it can often be easier to notice and remember negative 'things' (situations, events, words) because the brain responds more strongly to them, primarily to support our safety. Older children (KS2) also learn that this is called the 'negativity bias' and it is used in public life, including news and social media, to capture our attention. It is helpful for our MHW to balance out the negativity bias by learning to notice and savour positive experiences that are naturally noticed and remembered less readily.

Similarly, we can change unhelpful negative patterns in our thinking and emotions impacting on our behaviour (which we will explore more closely in the next chapter on Managing Rumination and Worry). The aim of learning in this chapter is not to encourage children to engage in 'toxic' positivity, rather to balance out negativity bias in our experience since it is actively used in our everyday life (news, media, movies) to capture our attention and can undermine our MHW. This can be referenced back to the attention economy children learned about in the building block of Managing Distractions. In addition, the individualistic success-focused culture we live in often encourages comparison resulting in self-criticism, thus further perpetuating the establishment of negative patterns of thinking and emotions that need to be balanced out.

To cultivate a more balanced way of experiencing, in the next step of learning children are encouraged to start recognising their own repeated patterns of thinking and emotions based on the examples previously discussed (from cartoon, stories, movies, public life), and KS2 children are also encouraged to recognise the negativity bias. At the same time, they are encouraged to apply skills in noticing neutral and positive experiences and savouring them. This can be done through increasing duration and exploring details of neutral and positive experiences. The emphasis here is on neutral or slightly positive simple experiences, that are lower intensity and associated with emotions of calm and content, such as observing a flower or an animal or enjoying a walk in nature or an art activity or learning something new. Children can be guided in exploring how these activities make them feel, what they notice (more detail) about the activity, which aspect of the activity they find most enjoyable, what makes them enjoy the activity more etc.

> ### Key Strategies for Working with Habitual Thoughts and Emotions
>
> - Noticing habitual thoughts and emotions is a strategy where children explore their own habitual ways of thinking, feeling and responding. This needs to be done from a non-judgmental perspective of emotional awareness.
> - Remembering negativity bias is a strategy where children learn that we notice and remember negative things more easily, that's just what our mind and brain do automatically.

- Savouring positive experiences is a strategy where we develop a habit of noticing, recognising and exploring further our positive and neutral experiences. This can be helpful in balancing out our negativity bias.
- Recalling positive thoughts, images, memories or words is another strategy that we can use to balance our negativity bias. We can find thoughts, images, memories and words that we can bring readily to our mind when we feel we need to counter some of our negative thoughts and feelings.

They also learn new strategies to counter negativity bias and unhelpful negative patterns of thinking and emotions, involving finding a calming or positive memory, image or words that they can recall readily when they want to shift negative thoughts or emotions. Children are encouraged to apply previously learned strategies (naming, distraction-based strategies and cognitive defusion) together with these new strategies and learn about neuroscience underpinning establishment of thinking and emotional patterns (neural plasticity) in support of this. This in turn fosters development of understanding that with repetition it becomes easier to manage our emotions and thoughts. Descriptions of experiences in neuroscience terms can further support decentring from negative experiences, enabling their effective regulation using these strategies.

Importantly, the teaching needs to be delivered from a non-judgmental perspective and the non-judgmental attitude needs to permeate children's learning of the relevant emotion regulation skills across the building blocks of the ATTEND Pyramid. This is essential throughout learning MHW skills, but particularly of importance in this facet where children may recognise possible negative patterns of their thinking and emotions. In this context, teachers need to emphasise the shared humanity of our experiences – everyone is susceptible to negativity bias and everyone has positive, neutral and negative patterns of thinking and emotions. We can choose to modify some of the negative patterns based on which ones we find less useful. This also invites children to understand experientially how the skills of shifting some patterns of thinking and emotions and savouring positive experiences can support their MHW.

Developmental Differences in Fostering the Knowledge and Skills of Managing Habitual Thoughts and Emotions

Children are naturally sensitive to rewards, this is because the brain regions of the reward network signalling rewards (particularly the VS) mature faster than other brain regions associated with responding to negative stimuli and managing emotions more generally (Martin & Ochsner, 2016). Harnessing this developmental 'imbalance', children can be encouraged, and are likely to positively respond to, activities involving savouring of lower intensity neutral and positive everyday experiences (such as exploring a leaf, listening to the sound of rain, enjoying learning something new). Bringing more awareness (attention) to such positive experiences and savouring them (extending their duration through exploring them in more detail) can prepare a useful foundation for countering the negativity bias that becomes more prominent with exposure to media and culture as children develop.

Older children can use more metacognitive approaches to recognising the negativity bias and their own habitual patterns of thinking and emotions (including relevant triggers) due to their ability to recruit more effectively the top-down self-regulation stream, including regions in the prefrontal cortex and the ACC. Learning about relevant neuroscience and articulating their experiences in neuroscience terms can provide a useful 'buffer' of decentring, reducing the likelihood of such reflections being more deeply clinically triggering. Across the age groups children are encouraged to recognise that repetition makes use of the emotion regulation strategies learned across the facets easier and more effective, as they acquire the concept of neural plasticity.

Acquiring the Knowledge and Skills of Managing Habitual Thoughts and Emotions: The 7-Step Approach

Similarly to the previous building blocks of the ATTEND Pyramid, learning to manage habitual thoughts and emotions involves three initial steps fostering relevant knowledge followed by four steps developing corresponding skills. The knowledge steps focus on cultivating children's understanding of the habitual patterns of thoughts and emotions we all have based on external examples, together with understanding of the negativity bias, savouring of experiences and strategies that can shift habitual patterns. This understanding is further solidified and expanded by learning about neuroscience underpinning habitual thoughts and emotions. In the steps fostering skills of managing habitual thoughts and emotions, children learn how to apply the knowledge they acquired in the previous steps to their own experience. They start recognising some of their own habitual patterns of thinking and experiencing emotions and ways they can shift some of them if they want to. In the final step, children apply the knowledge and skills they learned to managing their habitual thoughts and emotions in everyday situations to support their MHW.

Step 1: Learning How Managing Habitual Thoughts and Emotions Relates to MHW

The learning objective in the first step is for children to acquire the knowledge that will enable them to understand that repeated thoughts and feelings make it easier to think and experience the same thoughts and emotions over time. They also learn that we can change these patterns of thoughts and emotions and how this relates to MHW.

 In *reception*, children begin to understand with guidance that repeated thoughts and feelings make it easier for us to think in the same way and experience the same feelings in the future. They also begin to understand that we can change how we want to think and feel with repetition. To acquire such foundational knowledge children can be encouraged to recognise repetitive patterns of thinking and feeling in cartoons or stories. They can also be guided to begin recognising how the characters decided to change the negative patterns of thinking or feeling they experienced.

In *KS1* children understand more readily, but with support, that repeated thoughts and feelings make it easier for us to think and feel in the same way next time. They start to recognise the pleasantness/unpleasantness of the repeated thoughts and feelings in examples and ways the negative thoughts and feelings were changed. To foster such knowledge children can be encouraged to recognise the patterns of thinking and feeling in stories or cartoons and recognise their pleasantness, possibly using the Feels Good Scale. They then notice ways the negative patterns were changed in the examples and rate how the characters felt afterwards using the scale.

In the *lower KS2* children are able to recognise mostly independently that repeated thoughts and emotions make it easier for the same patterns of thinking and emotions to be experienced again. They can describe the pleasantness of the observed patterns of thinking and emotions and how they made the characters feel. They recognise more independently, based on examples provided, how the patterns were changed to support characters' MHW. To cultivate such knowledge, children are encouraged to recognise patterns of repeated thinking and emotions in a story or movie examples and rate them using the Pleasantness of Emotion Scale. Then they rate how the characters felt after they changed the patterns. Children can try to describe how the patterns of thinking and emotions made the character feel, how they changed them and how that made them feel.

In the *upper KS2* children can recognise a range of patterns of thinking and emotions independently and understand that with repetition they become more established and easier to experience again. They know how the patterns can be changed based on examples and how this relates to MHW. Using examples from movies, stories or the public domain that children find, they can exemplify established repeated patterns of thinking and emotions and how they were easily repeated. Then they practise recognising how these patterns were changed and how this supported the characters' MHW. They can use the Pleasantness and Intensity of Emotion Graph during the exercise. Children can practise describing independently to each other what they have learned about recognising habitual thoughts and emotions, how these were changed and how this impacted the characters' MHW.

Step 2: Learning about Negativity Bias in Relation to MHW

The learning objective in the second step is for children to acquire the knowledge that will enable them to understand what negativity bias is and its evolutionary basis. They also learn how negativity bias and negative habitual patterns of thoughts and emotions can be countered and how this links to MHW.

108   *Making Sense of Mental Health and Wellbeing in Primary Schools*

 In *reception* children begin to understand with guidance that we can often choose if we want to think of something positive and feel good and when we repeatedly practise savouring our positive experiences it becomes easier to feel this way again. To cultivate this knowledge, children can work with examples from stories or cartoons where a character either shifted from negative to positive experience or savoured their positive experience and explore how the character did this and how this made them feel.

 In *KS1* children begin to understand more readily that it is often easier for us to notice and remember negative things because this can keep us safe. However, sometimes this is not useful so it is good to be able to shift to neutral and positive thoughts and feelings instead and to savour positive feelings when we have them. They begin to understand that with repetition this becomes easier. To foster this knowledge the teacher can guide children in activities encouraging children to notice negativity bias in stories or cartoons and ways the character shifts the pattern towards neutral or positive thoughts and feelings. They explore how the character felt before and after the change, possibly using the Feels Good Scale. Similarly, examples of savouring positive experiences can be used and evaluated using the Feels Good Scale and Emotion Strength Scale.

 In the *lower KS2*, children are able to recognise more independently the negativity bias in stories or movies more readily and recognise specific strategies the characters used to shift it including those strategies children learned in previous two facets (naming, distraction based strategies, cognitive defusion) and new strategies such as positive memory, image or words. They can use the Pleasantness of Emotion Scale and Intensity of Emotion Scale to quantify the shifts. They are also able to understand that shifting negativity bias and savouring positive experiences becomes easier with repetition and is good for our MHW.

To develop this knowledge, children can engage in activities encouraging them to recognise negativity bias in stories and movies and using a list provided. They can make notes recording which particular strategy characters used to overcome the bias. Children can also explore examples of savouring positive experiences and how this made the characters feel and how it became easier with repetition. The Pleasantness of Emotion Scale and Intensity of Emotion Scale can be used to quantify this.

 In the *upper KS2*, children can recognise independently examples of negativity bias in everyday life, such as negativity bias in news and doom scrolling on social media. They also recognise ways to counter negativity bias, through strategies learned in previous facets and new strategies including naming negativity bias and associated emotions, paced breathing, and shifting attention to neutral or positive content, memories, images or words. They understand how developing a habit of noticing and savouring positive experiences helped those in the examples overcome negativity bias and how this supported their MHW. To foster such understanding, children can work in small groups or pairs and discuss examples of negativity bias

from news, social media, stories or movies. They can record ways the characters managed the negativity bias including strategies learned previously and new strategies including shifting attention to positive and neutral content, memories, thoughts, images or words. They explore examples of how savouring of positive experiences repeatedly developed into a habit that supported others' MHW.

Step 3: Learning Neuroscience Underpinning Habitual Thoughts and Emotions

The learning objective in the third step is for children to acquire the knowledge enabling them to understand what happens in the brain when we establish habitual patterns of thoughts and emotions, and how these patterns can be changed from a neural perspective (neural plasticity). They can link this understanding to improving ones' MHW.

In *reception*, children begin to understand with guidance that the brain changes when we repeatedly think and feel the same way and this makes it easier to feel and think the same way again in the future. To develop such understanding, the teacher can use simple sand play exercises demonstrating that if we pour water on the same place again and again, next time it flows down the sand hill faster, just like our repeated thoughts and feelings.

In *KS1* children understand more readily that with repetition of thoughts and feelings the brain changes and this makes it easier to think and feel the same way in the future. They learn that a new region of the brain called the hippocampus helps us learn and remember our thoughts and feelings. They also understand that the ACC and PFC can help us change the repeated thoughts and feelings. To foster this knowledge, children can colour in a simple map of the brain including the PFC, ACC and the hippocampus and relate it to maintaining and changing the way we think and feel based on character experiences from a story or cartoon they discussed in previous steps.

In the *lower KS2* children understand mostly independently that insula help us notice the patterns in our thoughts and emotions and that the amygdalae are more active when we repeatedly have thoughts and feelings that are negative, including due to the negativity bias. A brain region called the VS is active when we have positive thoughts and feelings and another brain region called the hippocampus helps us repeat the patterns by learning and remembering. The PFC and ACC enable us to shift negative patterns of thinking and emotions (including negativity bias) towards neutral or positive patterns and with repetition neural plasticity involving VS and hippocampus supports these changes. To foster this knowledge, children can engage in activities where they practise in small groups describing habitual patterns of thoughts and emotions of characters in stories or movies in terms of underlying neural activity of the relevant brain regions. They can also describe which brain regions were active when the characters changed their thoughts and emotions towards more neutral/positive ones. Brain maps and colouring-in can be used to support the activity.

In the *upper KS2* children understand independently that insula enable us to recognise the habitual patterns of thoughts and emotions. They also know that more negative patterns, including the negativity bias, increase activity in the amygdala, whereas savouring of positive experiences activates the VS. They understand that habitual patterns are established and sustained through neural plasticity involving associations between the aforementioned brain areas and the hippocampus plus ACC and PFC which can shift the habitual patterns. Children know that these regions together are part of the reward network of the brain. To develop this knowledge, the teacher can use brain models and colour in maps to familiarise children with the reward network. Children can then practise the relevant neuroscience by explaining to each other examples of neuroscience underpinning the negativity bias and habitual patterns of thinking and emotions using examples from movies and social media/public life. They can link neuroscience to MHW.

Step 4: Learning Skills of Recognising Habitual Thoughts and Emotions in Own Experience

The learning objective in the fourth step is for children to develop the skills that will enable them to start recognising their own habitual patterns of thinking and emotions and their triggers from a non-judgmental perspective. They also start understanding from their own experience how these patterns may link to their MHW.

In *reception* children begin to recognise with support in their own experience that we all have some patterns of thinking and feeling that we repeat. They also begin to recognise in very simple terms and with guidance that it can be helpful to notice what these patterns are so that we can keep repeating those that are useful and try to change those that are not useful. To develop such understanding the teacher can guide children in activities encouraging them to notice if any of the patterns of thinking and feeling from the cartoons and stories were similar to those they have experienced.

In *KS1* children begin to recognise more readily, in their own experience, some repeated patterns of thinking and emotions and what their triggers are from a non-judgmental perspective. The teacher can remind children that we all have some habitual patterns, some of them are useful and some of them are not useful, and we can choose which patterns we want to make stronger. To cultivate these skills, the teacher can use previously learned examples from stories and cartoons to encourage children to start recognising their own patterns of thinking and feeling. Children can also be guided to notice some patterns that were not in the examples. With guidance children can start exploring triggers for these patterns and possible ways of changing those that may not be useful based on the examples provided and how this makes them feel. In this process they can use the Feels Good Scale and Emotion Strength Scale.

In the *lower KS2* children recognise somewhat independently a wider range of repeated positive, neutral and negative patterns in their own thinking and emotions. They also recognise possible triggers for these from a non-judgmental perspective. The teacher should remind children that everyone has some patterns that are useful and some that are less useful. Children also explore possible ways of shifting patterns that are not useful based on examples provided. They understand from their own experience how such shifts can support their MHW.

To foster these skills, children could work with a grid of possible negative, positive and neutral patterns of thinking and behaviour they recognised in examples from movies and stories and tick which ones are similar to those they experience. They can add further examples and add triggers to the patterns. They can explore whether they could use some of the ways the characters used to shift their repeated patterns and how this makes them feel, possibly using the Pleasantness of Emotion Scale and Intensity of Emotion Scale.

In the *upper KS2* children can recognise independently a wider range of habitual positive, neutral and negative patterns in their own thinking and emotions. They can link these to possible triggers from a non-judgmental perspective. It is important to remind children that everyone has some patterns that are useful and some that are less useful. They recognise and can articulate how this can be useful in choosing which patterns to shift and consider possible ways of shifting them based on examples provided. They understand from their experience how changing some of the patterns can support their MHW.

To develop these skills, children can prepare a log with a list of patterns they observed in the examples from stories, movies and public domain and then, in comparison, track patterns they observe in their thinking, emotional experiencing and behaviour over a couple of days. They can record their valence and intensity using the Pleasantness and Intensity of Emotion Graphs. Children can also record possible triggers for these patterns and then try to identify which patterns they may want to change and how based on the examples provided. Children do not share the logs in class due to their personal nature. Only cumulative ratings for different types of strategies they used to manage habitual thoughts and emotions can be shared anonymously in the class.

Step 5: Learning to Shift Habitual Patterns of Thoughts and Emotions

The learning objective in the fifth step is for children to be able to apply previously learned emotion regulation skills and new strategies in shifting negativity bias and habitual patterns of thoughts and emotions (if they are not useful) to support their MHW.

In *reception* children acquire basic skills in noticing and savouring positive experiences with teacher guidance. They begin to understand (with prompts) that with repetition it can be easier to notice and savour positive experiences in the future and that thinking about something nice can help make us feel better when we feel a bit down. To foster these skills, the teacher can encourage children during activities such as a walk in nature to notice different colours of leaves, notice flowers or animals and recognise how that makes them feel. Acknowledging and expanding the pleasant feelings can be the first step in encouraging savouring such experiences and linking them to how we feel.

In *KS1* children can begin, with guidance, to apply previously learned strategies (naming, distraction-based strategies, paced breathing, progressive muscle relaxation) to shifting some habitual patterns of thinking and feelings that are not useful. They also begin to use new strategies that shift attention to positive thoughts and emotions (positive memory, image or words). As they notice positive experiences more often, they are encouraged to savour them. To cultivate these skills, children can be encouraged during activities such as doing art or gardening or sports to notice and acknowledge positive experiences and savour them. This can be done by increasing their duration though exploring different aspects of the experience. They are also encouraged to come up with a positive memory, image or words they can recall when feeling a bit down to feel better. Children can also be guided in using previously learned strategies to shift their habits that are not useful.

In the *lower KS2* children are able to recognise negativity bias in their own thinking and emotions more often and are able to more readily apply some of the previously learned strategies (naming, distraction-based strategies, cognitive defusion) and new strategies (shifting towards positive thoughts, images or memories) in changing them. They notice increasingly more independently positive experiences and use savouring to increase their duration to develop positive habits of thinking and emotions. They recognise more frequently that this supports their MHW. To cultivate these skills, children can be encouraged to note down one or two positive thoughts, images or memories (keeping these to themselves) and rate how thinking of them feels using the Pleasantness of Emotion Scale and Intensity of Emotion Scale. They can also be encouraged to savour positive experiences during some feel good activities (e.g. baking and tasting what they made). While listening to a story children could note down any instances when they noticed possible negativity bias in their experience and be encouraged to apply the strategies they learned, including the new ones.

In the *upper KS2* children are able to independently recognise negativity bias in their own thinking and emotional experiences (and externally, e.g. in media reporting). They increasingly internalise applying some of the previously learned strategies (naming, distraction-based strategies, cognitive defusion) and new strategies (shifting towards neutral or positive thoughts, images, memories or words) in changing them. They readily and independently notice positive experiences and often use savouring to increase their duration to develop positive habits of thinking and emotions. Children also recognise based on their own experience that this can support their MHW. To foster these skills, the teacher can use activities inviting children to prepare a log where they observe their experience over a few days and note down some instances when they noticed negativity bias and not useful patterns of thinking or emotions. Then they note down ways they managed them in the moment and how this made them feel, they could use the Pleasantness and Intensity of Emotion Graph. They might start recognising which strategies were most helpful and how this supported their MHW. Children do not share the logs in class due to their personal nature.

Step 6: Learning to Apply Neuroscience Knowledge in Managing Habitual Thoughts and Emotions

The learning objective in the sixth step is for children to be able to use their understanding of the neuroscience underpinning neural plasticity and negativity bias in recognising and shifting habitual patterns of thinking and emotions. They learn to explain how this can support their MHW.

In *reception* children begin to recognise, with support, that when we choose to savour our positive experiences we are also changing our brain in positive ways making it easier for our brain to notice and savour experiences in the future. To develop these skills, children can be reminded during savouring activities that they are also changing their brain to help them feel better in the future. The teacher can also use a prompt, a symbol or a gesture to make it easier for children to remember this.

In *KS1* children begin to use references to the hippocampus when referring to habitual patterns and how they get established with repetition. When applying strategies to change not useful patterns, with guidance but increasingly more readily, they use references to the ACC and PFC as the regions of the brain enabling this. To foster these skills, children can be encouraged to make a drawing about savouring one of their positive experiences and add to the drawing references to the hippocampus, ACC and PFC. These can be symbolic references depending on writing skills levels.

In the *lower KS2* children are able to describe their own experience of noticing negativity bias and habitual patterns of thinking in neuroscience terms mostly independently. They can refer to the insula as the underpinning of noticing the bias or patterns, refer to amygdalae in relation to negativity bias and not useful patterns of thoughts and emotions, and to VS when describing positive patterns of thoughts and emotions and savouring of positive experiences. They recognise mostly independently the role of hippocampus in forming these patterns and that PFC and ACC help change the bias and patterns using different strategies through neural plasticity.

To cultivate these skills, children could write a simple story where they describe the activity of their brain as they were noticing (insula) and responding to a negativity bias or changing an unuseful pattern of thinking or emotions (ACC and PFC). They could relate brain regions such as amygdalae and VS to how they were feeling when experiencing negativity bias and after they have changed the way they felt. They can also describe how the hippocampus can support longer-term change towards more positive experiences through repeatedly savouring positive experiences, also referring to neural plasticity.

In the *upper KS2* children are able to use relevant neuroscience terminology independently when describing their experience of noticing (insula) negativity bias (amygdalae) and their patterns of thoughts and emotions (amygdalae and VS). They can also articulate how habitual thoughts and emotions are established through neural plasticity (hippocampus) and shifted (ACC and PFC). They can describe how the reward network is involved in savouring experiences and that neural plasticity supports establishing neutral and positive patterns of thinking and emotions that support their MHW. Children also know what the acronyms for the different brain regions stand for. To strengthen these skills, children can write a story describing, using neuroscience terms, an instance of their savouring of a positive experience or an instance of overcoming a negativity bias or a not useful pattern of thinking and emotions using an emotion regulation strategy. They can link this to longer-term impacts on supporting their MHW.

Step 7: Applying Skills of Managing Habitual Thoughts and Emotions in Everyday Life

The learning objective in the seventh step is for children to be able to apply their knowledge about habitual thoughts and emotions and negativity bias, together with skills in recognising such patterns and shifting them, to support their MHW. This includes application of relevant neuroscience understanding, previously learned strategies and new strategies.

In *reception* children begin to recognise positive experiences and savour them in everyday situations, mostly with a prompt but gradually more without it. With guidance, they begin to use previously learned strategies of naming and distraction-based strategies in managing emotion patterns and begin to recognise the value of practice in this with references to the brain and repetition. In everyday situations and activities, such as sand play and outdoor play, children are encouraged to recognise and savour positive experiences. When encountering an upsetting experience, they are reminded to apply previously learned strategies and that with repetition managing their feelings becomes easier.

In *KS1* children begin to recognise positive experiences in everyday situations more readily, with guidance, and savouring them more habitually. With support, they start to apply basic understanding of their patterns of thinking and feelings in everyday situations, knowing some of their triggers and which strategies can help. These include naming of emotions, distraction-based strategies, paced breathing, and the newly learned strategies including a positive memory, image or words and neuroscience descriptions. Children start to recognise that this can help them feel better in the moment and becomes easier with repetition.

To foster these skills, children are regularly reminded to notice and savour positive experiences during the day using a prompt. In situations of conflict or other upset they are encouraged to use previously learned emotion regulation strategies including naming of emotions, distraction-based strategies and new strategies – recalling a positive memory, image or words. They are reminded to use neuroscience to talk about their experience from a more decentred perspective to support down-regulation of emotions.

In the *lower KS2* children can use their knowledge about negativity bias and the importance of savouring positive experiences together with skills in noticing and savouring positive experiences and shifting away from negativity bias and negative patterns of thinking and emotions more readily and independently in everyday situations. They use a range of previously learned strategies including naming of emotions, distraction based strategies, cognitive defusion, paced breathing, relevant neuroscience and newly learned strategies (shift towards positive thoughts, images or memories) in working with negativity bias and negative patterns of thoughts and emotions. They are able to recognise that with repetition this becomes easier and supports their MHW.

To cultivate these skills, children are encouraged to recognise negativity bias and positive experiences (savouring these) during everyday activities such as gardening club, playtime or learning something new that is exciting. They can prepare a class chart where they note instances of savouring positive experiences everyday. Children are encouraged to apply naming of emotions, distraction-based strategies, paced breathing, recalling positive memory, image or words when trying to shift negativity bias or negative patterns in everyday situations and explore how this can support their MHW with repetition.

In the *upper KS2* children are able to recognise independently negativity bias and unhelpful negative patterns of thinking (including their triggers) and emotions readily in everyday situations. This can include social media and news. They are able to effectively apply appropriate previously learned emotion regulation strategies (including naming of emotions, distraction-based strategies and cognitive defusion, paced breathing), their neuroscience understanding and new strategies (positive or neutral memories, thoughts, images or words) to manage these. Children recognise that with repetition this is becoming easier (this indicates they are internalising these skills) and that it can support their MHW.

To strengthen these skills, children can be encouraged to support each other in noticing negativity bias in everyday situations and applying relevant strategies to modify it. Peer-led activities can encourage noticing and savouring positive experiences in everyday situations such as team work. Logs can further support tracking and implementation of the strategies in everyday situations in school and outside of school.

Conclusion

We all have habitual ways of thinking and experiencing emotions. Some of these habits can support our MHW and some of them are not helpful. Understanding which patterns of thoughts and emotions are useful and which are less useful, then learning strategies to shift those that are not useful, can provide children with effective tools to protect and enhance their MHW in the longer term. This is particularly the case if they also understand the impact of the negativity bias and savouring of positive experiences on their MHW, and can skilfully work with these. If you were, just like Michelle, wondering at the start of this chapter how to support children in developing healthy MHW habits, this chapter hopefully provided you with the understanding and guidance on teaching relevant knowledge and skills to children in your classroom. As the chapter highlighted, repeated application of these skills in everyday life is the key to maintaining any beneficial effects of the strategies introduced in this book.

Key chapter points:

- We all have positive, negative and neutral habitual ways of thinking, feeling and responding.
- Negativity bias is a habitual way of thinking and feeling that makes it easier for us to notice and remember negative experiences, to protect us from danger in the future.
- Some of these habits can support our MHW and others, such as negativity bias in many instances, are not helpful.
- We can learn to counter negativity bias and shift other unhelpful habitual thoughts and emotions through various strategies, such as savouring of positive and neutral experiences or bringing to our mind comforting thoughts, images or words.
- Development of habits is enabled by neural plasticity and savouring of experiences activates the reward network.
- Following the 7-Step Approach, children can acquire healthy MHW habits in an age-appropriate way.

References

Baskin-Sommers, A. R., & Foti, D. (2015). Abnormal reward functioning across substance use disorders and major depressive disorder: Considering reward as a transdiagnostic mechanism. *International Journal of Psychophysiology, 98*(2), 227-239.

Carlisi, C. O., & Robinson, O. J. (2018). The role of prefrontal-subcortical circuitry in negative bias in anxiety: translational, developmental and treatment perspectives. *Brain and Neuroscience Advances, 2*, 2398212818774223.

Dorjee, D. (2024). Conceptualising child and adolescent mental health and wellbeing neurodevelopment: an integrative brain networks framework. Preprint, 4 November. https://doi.org/10.31234/osf.io/7vx45

Eldar, S., Apter, A., Lotan, D., Edgar, K. P., Naim, R., Fox, N. A., ... & Bar-Haim, Y. (2012). Attention bias modification treatment for pediatric anxiety disorders: a randomized controlled trial. *American Journal of Psychiatry, 169*(2), 213-230.

Fischer, A. S., Ellwood-Lowe, M. E., Colich, N. L., Cichocki, A., Ho, T. C., & Gotlib, I. H. (2019). Reward-circuit biomarkers of risk and resilience in adolescent depression. *Journal of Affective Disorders, 246*, 902-909.

Hakamata, Y., Lissek, S., Bar-Haim, Y., Britton, J. C., Fox, N. A., Leibenluft, E., ... & Pine, D. S. (2010). Attention bias modification treatment: a meta-analysis toward the establishment of novel treatment for anxiety. *Biological Psychiatry, 68*(11), 982-990.

Lupien, S. J., McEwen, B. S., Gunnar, M. R., & Heim, C. (2009). Effects of stress throughout the lifespan on the brain, behaviour and cognition. *Nature Reviews Neuroscience, 10*(6), 434-445.

Martin, R. E., & Ochsner, K. N. (2016). The neuroscience of emotion regulation development: Implications for education. *Current Opinion in Behavioral Sciences, 10*, 142-148.

Rappaport, B. I., Kandala, S., Luby, J. L., & Barch, D. M. (2020). Brain reward system dysfunction in adolescence: current, cumulative, and developmental periods of depression. *American Journal of Psychiatry, 177*(8), 754-763.

Samios, C., Catania, J., Newton, K., Fulton, T., & Breadman, A. (2021). Stress, savouring, and coping: the role of savouring in psychological adjustment following a stressful life event. *Stress and Health, 36*(2), 119-130.

Sesack, S. R., & Grace, A. A. (2010). Cortico-basal ganglia reward network: microcircuitry. *Neuropsychopharmacology, 35*(1), 27-47.

Williams, L. M., Gatt, J. M., Schofield, P. R., Olivieri, G., Peduto, A., & Gordon, E. (2009). 'Negativity bias' in risk for depression and anxiety: brain-body fear circuitry correlates, 5-HTT-LPR and early life stress. *Neuroimage, 47*(3), 804-814.

6 Managing Rumination and Worry

Introduction

Now that children have developed a range of knowledge and skills helping them to regulate their attention and emotions more skilfully, the final building block of the second tier of the ATTEND Pyramid aims to bring together all the knowledge and skills acquired across the preceding facets in managing rumination and worry. It also introduces new skills of reappraisal of thoughts and emotions and shifting attention to sensory experiences in regulation of negative rumination as the key symptom of depression and worry as the key symptom of anxiety. The previously learned skills were needed for children to strengthen their self-regulation so that they are now able to engage with rumination and worry more directly.

Without the foundations built up in the previous building blocks of the Pyramid, children may not be able to effectively engage with strategies intended for managing rumination and worry because they require more complex cognitive processing and engagement with emotions. Not having the basis of the preceding mental health and wellbeing (MHW) knowledge and skills may also increase the likelihood of learning about rumination and worry triggering some symptoms of depression or anxiety. Therefore, it is not recommended that learning in this facet is implemented in the classroom in isolation without the knowledge and skills introduced in the previous chapters.

This chapter starts with a review of research linking rumination and worry to MHW, particularly in relation to depression and anxiety. We will then consider the processes in the mind and brain underpinning rumination and worry, and their regulation. Next, the chapter explores strategies for managing rumination and worry, with a particular focus on reappraisal – changing the way we think about a situation we ruminate or worry about. Finally, the second part of the chapter outlines in detail how children in different primary school age groups can acquire knowledge and skills they need to effectively manage their everyday rumination and worry so it doesn't spiral into mental ill-health. But first, we will consider a common scenario teachers face in their classrooms when trying to teach children how to manage their rumination and worry.

Case Study: Teaching Children Skills of Managing Rumination and Worry

Sarah is a year 6 teacher in her primary school. She has noticed that over the school year children in her class have been increasingly more anxious. They have been struggling with worries about a range of things in their lives – from quarrels with their classmates, through comments online, to their appearance. This has been particularly the case for girls. And most of the children are also worried about the upcoming tests and the transition to their secondary school.

In addition, several children in the class shared that they are very worried about their future. They are aware of the effects of climate change and war; and worry about the situation worsening in the coming years and decades. This makes them question their own prospects. These concerns are also reflected in what parents have been saying during parent evenings.

So Sarah has been wondering how to best support children in managing their worries. She has been encouraging children to practise the skills they learned previously, such as paced breathing and some distraction-based strategies. This has been helping children cope better with their worries. But Sarah is thinking that there might be further ways to bring together all the MHW skills they have learned so far, and building on these skills teach children further strategies particularly intended for dealing with worry.

Questions for reflection:

- Have you noticed instances in your class where children are worried about something that may happen in the future or keep thinking about an event that happened earlier in the day?
- Are there any skills you currently teach children in your class to help them manage their rumination and worry?
- How could children use the skills outlined in the previous chapters to manage their rumination and worry?

How Is Managing Rumination and Worry Relevant to MHW?

Both rumination and worry describe patterns of repetitive unhelpful thinking which are difficult to manage (let go of) (e.g. Verstraeten et al., 2011). Rumination and worry often overlap but a key difference between them is that rumination tends to be about events or experiences from the past (e.g. something that happened during the day and we keep thinking about it in the evening) whereas worry is future-oriented (worrying about an exam or visit to the dentist). Both rumination and worry have a strong negative self-focus element.

Rumination often involves negative self-critical thoughts, and worry involves thinking about future threats to one's sense of self.

Even though rumination can be both positive and negative, the term 'rumination' is typically used in psychology to refer to negative rumination. Here a further distinction needs to be made between rumination and self-reflection. While rumination is typically 'destructive', undermining our sense of self-worth, self-reflection is 'constructive' helping us learn from mistakes and experiences (Child Focus, 2023).

Robust and extensive body of research has associated increased negative rumination and worry with poor MHW (Verstraeten et al., 2011). This finding holds across age groups, including children. While negative rumination is primarily linked with depression, worry is a key cognitive symptom of anxiety. However, both negative rumination and worry often overlap, just like anxiety and depression often co-occur together.

Both negative rumination and worry are linked to changes in all facets of the self-regulation capacity. With regards to emotional awareness, negative rumination and worry are associated either with lack of emotional awareness or with increased emotional awareness of negative thoughts, emotions and situations (perceived as a threat). Negative rumination and worry are also linked to reduced ability to manage distractions, particularly internal distractions in the form of negative thoughts and emotions – one can often feel caught up in negative thoughts or emotions without the ability to shift attention away from (or change) them towards neutral thoughts, emotions or activities.

The way of experiencing linked to rumination and worry, leads to establishing of negative habitual patterns of thinking and emotions with repetition, enabled by neural plasticity. These patterns of thinking and feeling activate readily in the face of minor setbacks or reminders of past or possible future negative events. This can also be associated with increased negativity bias in perceiving one's own thoughts, emotions and behaviour, and often also situations and others' behaviour and actions. As a result, the green zone reduces and the red zone or the blue zone expands, resulting in increased reactivity or apathy.

For all these reasons, learning skills in managing rumination and worry is an essential aspect of mental ill-health prevention and fostering wellbeing. The goal of this facet is to equip children with relevant knowledge and skills for managing rumination and worry, building on the knowledge and skills they acquired in the previous facets.

> Questions for reflection:
> - Do you know the difference between rumination and worry?
> - Why does negative rumination and worry undermine MHW?
> - How does rumination and worry relate to emotional awareness, managing distractions, reactivity and habitual thoughts and emotions?

Neuroscience of Managing Rumination and Worry

Negative rumination and worry have been repeatedly associated with a range of neural and neuroendocrine changes. This includes dysregulation in the salience network linked to increased sensitivity to negative thoughts (Marchitelli et al., 2024) and emotions, and reduced activation of the executive network which can regulate negative rumination and worry. In addition, rumination and worry are associated with dysregulation in the reward network linked to anhedonia (lack of joyful or pleasurable feelings) (Webb et al., 2023), and increased activation of the HPA axis linked to the stress response (Vergara-Lopez et al., 2024).

Yet, a neural hallmark of rumination worry is an increased activity/connectivity of the default mode network associated with self-referential processing (thinking about one's own thoughts, emotions, experiences and memories). The default mode network primarily reflects brain activity when we are not focusing on a particular task. It involves several brain regions including medial Prefrontal Cortex (mPFC), posterior cingulate cortex (PCC) involved in emotion regulation, temporo-parietal junction (TPJ) supporting reasoning about our own and others' mental states and precuneus associated with awareness of mental states, imagery and memory (Ho et al., 2015). The increase in connectivity of the

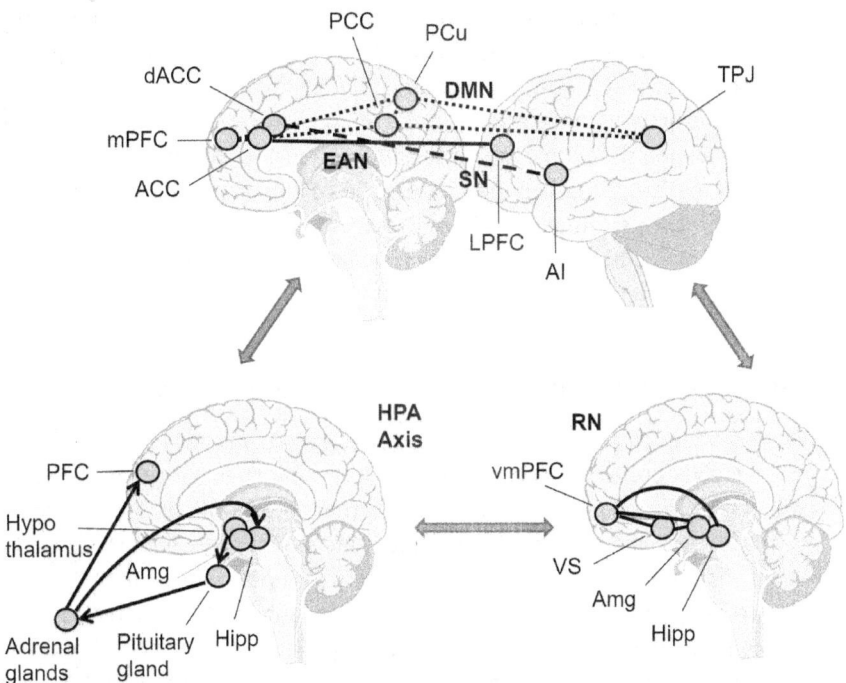

Figure 6.1 Neuroscience of managing rumination and worry SN - Salience network: dACC - dorsal Anterior Cingulate Cortex, AI - Anterior Insula; EAN - Executive network: ACC - Anterior Cingulate Cortex, LPFC - Lateral Prefrontal Cortex; DMN - Default mode network: mPFC - medial Prefrontal Cortex, PCC - Posterior Cingulate Cortex, PCu - Precuneus, TPJ - Temporoparietal Junction; RN - Reward network: vmPFC - ventromedial Prefrontal Cortex, VS - Ventral Striatum, Amg - Amygdala, Hipp - Hippocampus; HPA axis: PFC - Prefrontal Cortex, Amg - Amygdala, Hipp - Hippocampus, Hypothalamus, Pituitary gland, Adrenal glands.

Source: adapted with permission from Dorjee (2024)

default mode network in anxiety and depression is typically associated with repetitive negative self-critical thinking (negative rumination) and self-focused concerns about the future (worry). Therefore, aberrant processing the in the default mode network has been suggested as another possible transdiagnostic mechanisms underpinning poor mental health and wellbeing in children and adolescents (Whitfield-Gabrieli & Evins, 2021).

In contrast, reappraisal (noticing and changing thinking) and mindful emotion regulation strategies grounding attention on sensory experiences (rather than focusing on thoughts) can decrease negative rumination and worry (Volkaert et al., 2020). Effects of these strategies have been in adults (in the absence of studies with children) linked to reduced activation in the default mode network and increases in activity in the salience and executive networks (Westbrook et al., 2023). This involves balanced salience network activity enabling emotional awareness as a starting point of emotion regulation, and increased activity in the executive network enabling top-down self-regulation and application of emotion regulation strategies. Reappraisal and mindfulness are also linked to balanced activity in the reward network associated with healthy savouring of positive experiences and less negativity bias, and reduced activity in the HPA axis which relates to expansion of the green zone.

Neural plasticity also plays a key role both in maintaining and shifting habitual patterns of rumination and worry. With repetition, rumination and worry can become automatic responses to challenging situations, thoughts and emotions. However, neural plasticity can also be employed to disrupt the habitual patterns of rumination and worry through reappraisal and sensory-focus strategies. While employment of these strategies can be effortful at the start, with practice they become easier to apply due to changes in neural pathways linked to these adaptive forms of emotion regulation.

Key Neuroscience Terms for Managing Rumination and Worry

- The default mode network involves several brain regions including a part of the PFC – medial prefrontal cortex – mPFC. This network is activated during self-referential processing – thinking about own thoughts, emotions, experiences and memories. Activity in this network typically increases in rumination and worry.
- Rumination and worry is also linked to increases in activity in the salience network in response to negative situations, thought and emotions; as well as reduced activity in the executive attention network.
- Rumination and worry are often also associated with less activity in the reward network (less rewarding experiences) and increased activity in the HPA axis (increased stress response).
- Emotion regulation strategies such as reappraisal and sensory-focus strategies can reverse these dysfunctional patterns of brain activity. They often lead to increased activity in PFC regions, ACC and insula, alongside reductions in amygdalae activity.

In terms of brain regions, these strategies have been shown to reduce activity in the amygdalae associated with less negative affect, increased activity in the insula, PFC (McRae et al., 2012) and ACC associated with the ability to notice thoughts and emotions and shifting attention away from negative rumination towards more adaptive thought patterns or sensory experience (Martin & Ochsner, 2016). Reappraisal and mindfulness are also liked to reductions in the HPA axis activation (reduced cortisol levels or more balanced pattern of cortisol release) and reductions in neural reactivity to negative emotions (Kaunhoven & Dorjee, 2021). Other research suggested changes in the hippocampus linked to the neural plasticity underpinning these adaptive changes when these strategies are used repeatedly.

The neuroscience in this facet also explores how thinking, emotions and behaviour impact each other. This implies that we can change how we feel by changing any of these three aspects of our MHW (e.g. by thinking differently about an event, changing the way we feel by naming our emotions or applying distraction-based strategies, or doing progressive muscle relaxation, breathing practices, etc.).

Again, each of these self-regulation strategies whether they primarily focus on thinking, emotions or behaviour involves all the five networks we discussed in the first two tiers of the ATTEND Pyramid. They rely on increased activity in the top-down self-regulation brain regions such as insula, PFC and ACC and downregulate the activity in the amygdalae and the HPA axis (and associated cortisol release), thus reducing sympathetic system activity and increasing parasympathetic system activity and restoring balance between the two systems. Hippocampus supports regulation of the HPA axis and further enables neural plasticity changes underpinning adaptive self-regulation.

Default Mode Network and Managing Rumination and Worry in the Classroom

After learning about their neural underpinnings, Sarah can see more clearly the effects rumination and worry have on children's thinking, emotions, behaviour and learning. She knows that rumination and worry can increase activity in the default mode network and decrease children's ability to recruit the executive network that helps them focus. She is also aware that the salience network becomes more responsive to negative experiences – such as overwhelm about upcoming tests and minor upsets during the day. This can further increase children's negativity bias and their reactivity linked to imbalanced HPA axis activity (stress response). Such changes can undermine both their MHW and their ability to learn and perform well academically.

Knowing this, Sarah is also aware how the different MHW strategies of the ATTEND Pyramid children learned so far, together with reappraisal and sensory-focus strategies, can shift these maladaptive patterns. She knows that these strategies can strengthen children's executive network and shift their negativity bias, reactivity and stress response. Because of this, she decided to always dedicate time during the day to guide children in cognitive reappraisal and sensory-focus practices. She also reminds children at the start and the end of the day to think of MHW strategies they will be using throughout the day to manage their rumination and worry. She uses references to neuroscience of managing rumination and worry to motivate children in applying these strategies during the day.

> Sarah also spoke to teaching assistants, explained some of the neuroscience underpinning rumination and worry to them. She asked them to remind children during breaks and other situations during the day when they become worried or ruminate to practise the strategies of reappraisal, sensory-focus or any other strategies they learned and find helpful in managing their rumination and worry. She explained to the teaching assistants that repeated use of the strategies is the key to supporting children's MHW during this stressful time due to changes in in neural pathways of rumination of worry with neural plasticity.

How Can Children Acquire the Knowledge and Skills of Managing Rumination and Worry?

The most effective strategies for managing negative rumination and worry are reappraisal and shifting attention to sensory experiences. Reappraisal – it is a form of emotion regulation where we change interpretation of events in a way that adaptively changes our emotional response. In other words, we think about what we are concerned about from a different perspective and this can change our emotional response.

For example, if a child worries about performing in a school play, they can be encouraged to think about it in a different way, as an opportunity to have fun with their friends and show what they have learned. Similarly, if they ruminate about an event that happened in the morning, perhaps being late for school, they can be encouraged to think about it as something that has happened already and making a plan to not be late next time (if it is under their control). Children can be guided to let go of thinking about the event because this is not helpful, doesn't help them not being late next time if they have already made a plan to be on time next time.

Reappraisal is a key emotion regulation strategy applied in cognitive-behavioural therapy (CBT) and across different therapeutic approaches because it has been shown to effectively manage emotions and is associated with adaptive physiological processes such as downregulation of the HPA axis activity linked to stress response. In the therapeutic context, reappraisal is often introduced together with the triangle of thoughts, emotions and behaviour – inviting an exploration about how the three angles of the triangle influence each other. It can be particularly useful to explore how changing the way we think about something that happened or will happen can change our emotions and behaviour.

In the classroom context, children can be introduced to the concept of the triangle, with thoughts, emotions and behaviours as its angles – and explore from examples and then from their own experience how changing the way of thinking about an event changes our emotions and behaviour. In CBT this is often explored with children using the 'helpful thoughts technique' which I have adapted in this chapter for teaching in a whole-class format.

> **Key Strategies for Managing Rumination and Worry**
>
> - Reappraisal is an adaptive emotion regulation strategy where we change our way of thinking about a situation or experience, and in this way we change our emotions and behaviours.
> - The 'helpful thoughts technique' guides children in exploring how their thoughts impact their emotions and behaviours.
> - Sensory-focus strategies involve redirecting one's attention from thinking and analysing towards sensations – sounds, details of what we can see, touch, smell or taste – without much thinking.

When guiding children in the 'helpful thoughts technique', younger children can be provided with a toy and asked to think about helpful thoughts the toy is thinking and how this makes them feel and behave. Then they think about some unhelpful thoughts the toy might be having and how this makes them feel and behave. Then they can try to apply the same principles to starting to observe their own thoughts and behaviour from a non-judgmental kind perspective.

Similar techniques can be applied with older children, for example using a cartoon or story character. Children can also be provided with various hypothetical non-probing scenarios, such as waiting in a queue, and explore how different ways of thinking in those situations can impact the way one feels and behaves. The teacher can also use different prompts to demonstrate how looking at things from different angles can change our perception of them, for example they could use some figure-ground images where what we see changes based on what aspects of the figure we focus on. This can encourage children to explore different ways of thinking about events and recognising which ways of thinking might be more helpful than others. Children then apply these skills and techniques to their everyday experiences.

The other strategy for managing rumination and worry involves shifting focus to sensory experiences thus redirecting attention from thinking and analysing towards our sensations such as listening, seeing, sense of touch or smell or taste without much thinking. In children this could be accomplished through activities that involve focusing on listening to music or playing a musical instrument, watching animals, activities such as sand play, crocheting, sculpting or gardening and physical activities such as dancing or playing a ball game. Children can be guided to explore their sensations instead of particular goals in those activities.

These strategies are relatively easy for children to implement because they don't require lots of effortful attention which relies on PFC regions that are still maturing. In contrast, reappraisal is a more cognitively demanding strategy relying on the PFC (Kaunhoven & Dorjee, 2021). With repetition these activities can lead to healthy habits of the mind – when children notice ruminating or worrying they can choose to engage in an activity with sensory focus to manage their repetitive thinking and emotions.

There is also a specific sensory-focus technique recommended as a way to interrupt negative rumination and worry in the moment. This technique is an extension of the Spot

3 Things technique introduced in Chapter 3 where children were asked to find three things of a certain colour in their environment. The extended version of this technique is called the 3-3-3 technique, because it invites children to find three things of a certain colour, then notice three sounds in their environment and then make three different body movements (such as moving their arms, fingers and toes). This 'in the moment' technique can then be followed by reappraisal. Again, repetition is the key to effective use and internalising of these to manage one's MHW.

Developmental Differences in Fostering the Knowledge and Skills of Managing Rumination and Worry

Children of all primary school age groups can learn reappraisal and sensory focus strategies to manage their rumination and worry. However, reappraisal is a cognitively more complex strategy relying on the prefrontal cortex which is undergoing maturation throughout the primary school years and beyond. As a result, younger children will need more support in applying reappraisal whereas older KS2 children will be able to apply reappraisal independently. Reappraisal is an emotion regulation strategy often exemplified in educational programmes for children, the BBC series *Woolly and Tig* is a good example of this and clips from this programme might be very useful in supporting young children's understanding of reappraisal.

Older children can engage more readily with real world situation examples of reappraisal they can come up with. In comparison, the sensory focus strategies require less complex effortful self-regulation control relying on the prefrontal cortex, so they are easier for children to implement from a younger age. These strategies also naturally link to the curriculum content for younger children, including exploration of sensory experiences. Emphasis on repeated use of these strategies to make it easier for children to implement them (references to neural plasticity) will be helpful here as with any of the other strategies learned previously.

Acquiring the Knowledge and Skills of Managing Rumination and Worry: The 7-Step Approach

Learning to manage rumination and worry follows the first three steps which cultivate relevant knowledge and the four steps that translate the knowledge into practical MHW skills children can apply increasingly to manage their thoughts in everyday life. The knowledge steps initially focus on developing children's understanding of what rumination and worry is, in terms of unhelpful and helpful thoughts, using external examples. Children then learn how rumination and worry can be managed using reappraisal and sensory-focus strategies from external examples. This learning is complemented with development of understanding of the processes in the brain that underpin rumination and worry and the strategies that enable us to manage them. Children then gradually start applying this knowledge about rumination, worry, reappraisal and sensory-focus strategies in managing their own rumination and worry. In that process they start recognising the links between thoughts, emotions and behaviours in their own experience. In the final step, children apply the new knowledge and skills to managing rumination and worry in their everyday lives, in and outside of school.

Step 1: Learning How Managing Habitual Thoughts and Emotions Relates to MHW

The learning objective in the first step is for children to acquire the knowledge that will enable them to understand, based on examples, what rumination and worry is (linking this to repetitive thinking being helpful or unhelpful), and how it impacts emotions and behaviour. They learn that unhelpful thoughts in rumination and worry can undermine MHW by impacting emotions and behaviour. They understand that it is useful to notice such unhelpful thoughts and manage them to support our MHW.

In *reception* children begin to understand, with support, that we have both helpful and unhelpful thoughts and that these impact our emotions and behaviour. They begin to understand that we can manage our thoughts to feel better.

To develop such knowledge, the teacher can provide children with examples of rumination and worry that can be used to exemplify the difference between helpful and unhelpful thoughts. Children can also start exploring, with guidance, links between thoughts, feelings and behaviour in the examples. For example, the teacher can ask children what the character thought, how it made her feel (emotions) and what she did as a result (behaviour). Visual prompts can be used for thoughts, feelings and behaviour in a triangle.

In *KS1* children understand more readily the difference between helpful and unhelpful repetitive thinking and can link this to rumination and worry with help of examples and teacher support. They understand more readily that our thinking impacts our feelings (including bodily feelings) and behaviour and therefore it is good to manage our unhelpful thoughts, especially if they are repeated, to feel better. To foster this knowledge, using a toy children can be asked to brainstorm about possible helpful thoughts the toy may have and how these would make the toy feel and behave. Children can then do the same for unhelpful thoughts and how those would make the toy feel and behave; they can work with a figure of a triangle with angles of thoughts, emotions and behaviour, with support of symbols for each corner.

In the *lower KS2* children are able to recognise and distinguish rumination and worry in examples mostly independently and know the difference between them, in terms of helpful and unhelpful thoughts and their past or future orientation. They also understand mostly independently how helpful and unhelpful thoughts, referring to rumination and worry with teacher support, impact our emotions and behaviour and that we can learn to manage unhelpful thoughts in rumination and worry. This can in turn improve how we feel (emotions) and change our behaviour to support our MHW.

To cultivate this knowledge, children can be asked to brainstorm about helpful and unhelpful thoughts a cartoon character can have in a certain situation, they can practise distinguishing between rumination and worry. They can then brainstorm how these helpful and unhelpful thoughts can impact the character's emotions and behaviour, drawing clear differences between the impact of helpful and unhelpful thoughts. They can practise recognising from the examples that it is useful to be able to manage those unhelpful thoughts (rumination and worry) to feel better and understand in basic terms that this can support MHW.

In the *upper KS2* children are able to understand and can describe independently what rumination and worry is, how they link to helpful and unhelpful thinking and how they differ (past versus future orientation). They can also describe independently, using examples, how rumination and worry impact emotions and behaviour and can draw clear distinctions between the impacts of unhelpful thoughts in rumination and worry, and helpful thoughts. They understand that rumination and worry can make MHW worse but that we can learn to manage them and have more helpful thoughts.

To foster this knowledge, children can be provided with examples of helpful and unhelpful thoughts in response to an everyday situation and their links to emotions and behaviour by their teacher. Then they can work in small groups where they are provided with different situations for each group and brainstorm first about helpful and unhelpful thoughts in those situations, then they link the helpful and unhelpful thoughts to possible impacts on emotions and behaviour; groups then report back to the whole class and think together about impacts of helpful and unhelpful thoughts on MHW. They also learn that it is possible to change unhelpful thoughts to support MHW.

Step 2: Learning about Strategies to Manage Rumination and Worry

The learning objective in the second step is for children to acquire the knowledge that will enable them to understand what reappraisal is and how it can change unhelpful thoughts in rumination and worry, and positively impact emotions and behaviour. They learn that there are also other strategies one can apply to manage negative rumination such as doing activities where we focus on our senses. They understand that all these strategies can positively impact thinking, emotions and behaviour, and support MHW.

In *reception* children begin to understand, based on examples and with support, how unhelpful thoughts can be changed to more helpful thoughts. They start to notice with support how this changes feelings and behaviour. Children who find this difficult can explore sensory focus strategies and their impact on emotions and behaviour. Based on examples from children's programmes children can explore how the character changed her way of thinking and how this made her feel better and changed her behaviour. Children could use the Feels Good Scale and Emotion Strength Scale to make the impact of the change in thinking, from before to after reappraisal, on feelings clearer. Children that find it difficult to engage with reappraisal can do the same exercise with sensory focus strategies.

Managing Rumination and Worry   129

In *KS1* children understand more readily, based on examples and with some support, how unhelpful thoughts can be changed to more helpful ones and how this change can impact how one feels and behaves. Building on existing knowledge from the other facets they can also start to recognise that strategies shifting attention to senses can also be useful in managing unhelpful thoughts and help one feel better as well as impact behaviour positively. To foster this knowledge, the teacher can use activities where children brainstorm about ways a character from a story or a cartoon could change their thinking in a particular situation to feel better. They can use the Feels Good Scale and Emotion Strength Scale to understand the difference between feelings of the character before and after the change in thinking and also link this to changes in behaviour of the character. Children can then explore whether strategies with sensory experience focus could also make the character feel better.

In the *lower KS2* children know readily what reappraisal is, based on examples, and understand how reappraisal can change unhelpful thoughts in rumination and worry to helpful thoughts. With little support they can explain, based on examples, how reappraisal impacts emotions and behaviour. They understand that sensory focus strategies can also be helpful in managing rumination and worry and describe with little support how they impact emotions and behaviour. They understand that using these strategies repeatedly can help support MHW in the longer term.

To develop this knowledge, the teacher can use a prompt that looks different from different angles, ideally more positive from one angle and more negative from another, and explain that similarly we can change our thoughts about the same event from unhelpful to helpful. The teacher can exemplify reappraisal through thinking of a character in a story. Children can then draw a triangle where they explore how the thinking of the character impacted the character's emotions and behaviour before reappraisal and how reappraisal changed this. They can also use the Pleasantness of Emotion Scale and Intensity of Emotion Scale to quantify this. Children can do the same exercise with practices that focus on sensory experience to manage rumination and worry. They explore the longer-term impact of using such strategies in basic terms in relation to MHW.

In the *upper KS2* children understand independently what reappraisal is and are able to use this term correctly. They can provide examples how reappraisal can change unhelpful thoughts in rumination and worry to helpful thoughts and how this impacts emotions and behaviour. They also understand that sensory focus strategies can also be helpful in managing rumination and worry and similarly impact emotions and behaviour. They can articulate using examples how repeated use of reappraisal and sensory focus strategies can support one's MHW.

To cultivate this knowledge, the teacher can use the figure-background images to demonstrate how our perceptions can change based on our thinking. Similarly reappraisal can change how we perceive a situation or experience its impact on our emotions and behaviour. Children then think in pairs of real world situations where it might be helpful to use reappraisal and are provided with two triangles and two Pleasantness and Intensity of

Emotion Graphs where they describe what someone thought in that situations, how they felt as a result and how they behaved before and after reappraisal. They also assess how pleasantness and strength of that person's feelings changed from before to after reappraisal. Children can then explain to other pairs their example and the other pair reciprocates. They explore how using reappraisal repeatedly can impact MHW in the longer term.

Step 3: Learning Neuroscience Underpinning Managing Rumination and Worry

The learning objective in the third step is for children to acquire the knowledge enabling them to understand what happens in the brain during rumination and worry (with focus on the default mode network but integrating neuroscience learning across the self-regulation capacity facets) and when we use reappraisal or strategies relying on activities where we focus attention on our senses rather than thinking. They learn how these changes in the brain and body can support MHW.

In *reception* children begin to understand, based on examples, that by changing unhelpful thoughts to helpful thoughts we are also changing what is happening in our brain to feel better. Similarly when we focus on our senses different brain regions are active from those that are involved in unhelpful thoughts. With repetition we are changing our brain to make it easier to manage our unhelpful thoughts next time. During practices where children learn from children's programmes what reappraisal is and how it works, the teacher can also remind children (or ask them) what part of the body the character uses to change unhelpful thoughts to helpful thoughts. The teacher can also remind children that as the character repeatedly changes their unhelpful thoughts to helpful thoughts or uses sensory focus strategies they are making it easier for their brain to do the same next time and can feel better this way.

In *KS1* children understand more readily that the brain regions we have talked about previously are also involved in managing rumination and worry. When we are worried or ruminate there is more activity in the amygdalae and less activity in the PFC and ACC, whereas when we change unhelpful thoughts to more helpful ones or focus on sensory activities the activity in the PFC and ACC increases and the activity in the amygdalae decreases. The hippocampus helps us remember that these strategies of managing rumination and worry make us feel better and with repetition, relying on neural plasticity, this becomes easier and makes us feel better in the longer term.

Children can use simple print outs of the brain with the amygdalae, PFC, ACC and hippocampus depicted in them and shine flashlight through the region of the brain that is more active when we have unhelpful thoughts (amygdalae) and then the brain regions that are more active when we are changing unhelpful thoughts to helpful thoughts or use sensory focus activities (ACC and PFC). They could shine the flashlight through the hippocampus to link this to neural plasticity reminding themselves that with repetition it becomes easier to change unhelpful thoughts to helpful ones.

In the *lower KS2* children understand mostly independently that rumination and worry activate the amygdalae and therefore the HPA axis. The insula help us notice unhelpful thoughts when we are ruminating or worrying, and when we are managing rumination through reappraisal or focusing on senses we activate the PFC and ACC. Helpful thoughts are more likely to activate the VS. The hippocampus helps us remember to apply reappraisal or focus on senses when we have unhelpful thoughts in rumination or worry and through repetition this becomes easier via neural plasticity supporting our MHW in the longer term.

To foster this neuroscience knowledge, children can use the triangles they created in the task where they explored changes in thinking, emotions and behaviour from before and after reappraisal and this time try to elaborate the triangles further with drawings of the brain. They can outline brain areas that were predominantly activated before the reappraisal and after the reappraisal. They can do the same for strategies with sensory focus. Children can also explore, guided by their teacher, how these changes in the brain relate to MHW and how neural plasticity involving the regions underpinning reappraisal and sensory focus strategies can support MHW in the longer term.

In the *upper KS2* children understand independently and can describe the neuroscience underpinning rumination and worry with references to increased activation of the amygdalae, the default mode network and HPA axis (including increased cortisol levels). They know what happens in the brain when we apply reappraisal, or sensory focus strategies, to manage rumination and worry – starting with increased activity in insula and the salience network enabling us to notice rumination and worry, then increased activity in the PFC and ACC of the executive network enabling shift away from rumination and worry and towards reappraisal or sensory focus. An increase in helpful thoughts resulting from application of the strategies activates the VS and the reward network and reduces HPA axis, meaning lower amygdalae activity and cortisol, and default mode network activity. The hippocampus via neural plasticity can further establish the healthy and adaptive patterns of brain activity and support MHW in the longer term.

To foster this understanding, children can go back to the pair work they have done and in pairs try to explain to each other using neuroscience terms what happened in the brain when the person in the situation was ruminating or worrying and then what happened in the brain when they applied reappraisal or sensory focus strategies. The teacher then goes over the explanation of what happened in the brain before and after reappraisal or sensory focus strategies using an example and children compare their responses to the example. Children then brainstorm what happens in the brain when these reappraisal or sensory focus strategies are applied repeatedly and try to relate this to impact on MHW in the longer term. They can have a google doc where they share their ideas and the teacher then discusses these with the whole class.

Step 4: Learning Skills of Managing Rumination and Worry

The learning objective in the fourth step is for children to develop the skills that will enable them to notice and recognise rumination and worry (unhelpful thoughts) in their own experience as well as links between rumination and worry, emotions and behaviour. They learn to compare these effects to the impacts of helpful thoughts on emotions and behaviour. They also learn to recognise in their own experience that rumination and worry can be unhelpful for MHW but they can manage them to support their MHW.

In *reception* children can build on the previous examples and with teacher support begin to notice and recognise unhelpful thoughts in their own experience. They start exploring the links between thoughts, feelings and behaviour. They begin to compare the effects of unhelpful thoughts to the effects of helpful thoughts. They also start to recognise with guidance that unhelpful thoughts can make us feel sad or angry, but we can change those thoughts to feel better.

To foster these skills, children can practise making a triangle posture and assigning thoughts, feelings and behaviour to each of the corners. They can move up on their toes when exploring thoughts at the top of the triangle, bend their torso to the left when thinking of feelings and to the right when considering behaviour. They can be reminded by their teacher of examples of unhelpful thoughts and how they make us feel and behave. Then they can be reminded of helpful thoughts and how they make us feel and behave, combined with the posture and movements. Teaching staff then start reminding children of the triangle and helpful/unhelpful thoughts during everyday situations so that children begin recognising the links between the three corners of the triangle more often.

In *KS1* children notice more readily helpful and unhelpful thoughts and are able to link these to rumination or worry in their own experience. With some support they explore the impact of these on their feelings, including bodily sensations, and behaviour. They start to recognise from their experience that unhelpful thoughts in rumination and worry can change the way we feel and behave, and are reminded that we can change unhelpful thoughts to helpful thoughts to feel better. To develop these skills, with teacher's guidance children can learn a gesture of a triangle or make a small triangle prompt they can use to remind themselves of the links between thoughts, feelings and behaviour. Using the prompt teacher encourages children to notice helpful thoughts and how they make us feel and behave and unhelpful thoughts and how these make us feel and behave. The teacher can use some simple not-sensitive everyday scenarios such as having to wait or losing a pencil and children raise their hand if they felt the same as the feelings described. Children are then encouraged to notice unhelpful thoughts and remember that these can be changed.

In the *lower KS2* children are able to recognise rumination and worry in their own experience mostly independently and distinguish them based on their past or future orientation and unhelpful nature. They also recognise in their own experience the impact of unhelpful thoughts in rumination and worry on emotions and behaviour in comparison to impacts of helpful thoughts. They understand that they can change unhelpful thoughts to helpful thoughts to support their MHW.

To develop these skills, children are reminded about the character from previous examples having helpful and unhelpful thoughts. This can be linked to rumination and worry through non-sensitive everyday classroom examples. Then children consider if they can recognise having similar thoughts sometimes. When they have identified some thoughts that were similar to the character's thoughts, they draw the triangle to link the thoughts to emotions and behaviour – one triangle for helpful thoughts and another for unhelpful thoughts. They can also use the ratings of Pleasantness of Emotion Scale and Intensity of Emotion Scale to evaluate the differences in feelings in the two triangles. Children recognise that unhelpful thoughts in rumination and worry can make us feel worse but are also reminded that they can change the unhelpful thoughts to helpful thoughts to support their MHW.

In the *upper KS2* children are able to notice and recognise, readily and independently, rumination and worry (unhelpful thoughts) in their own experience. They are able to distinguish rumination from worry and describe their effects on emotions and behaviour from their own experience. They are also able to compare the impacts of unhelpful and helpful thoughts. They recognise from their own experience how rumination and worry can impact MHW but also know that the unhelpful thoughts in rumination and worry can be changed to support their MHW.

To develop these skills, children can be provided with examples of unhelpful thoughts in rumination and worry and their impacts on emotions and behaviour and have an anonymous vote whether they had a similar experience to those examples. Then the teacher can comment on the class results. The teacher can then provide examples of helpful thoughts and how these impact MHW and children again vote which examples were similar to their experience and teacher comments on the cumulative pattern of the vote for the class. Children can then do a writing task where they, using the triangles and the Pleasantness and Intensity of Emotion Graph, describe an example of helpful thoughts and an example of unhelpful thoughts from their own experience. They also describe how their emotions and behaviour were impacted in both examples and how this links to their MHW (contents of these writing tasks are not to be shared with the whole class).

Step 5: Learning to Apply Strategies of Managing Rumination and Worry to Support Own MHW

The learning objective in the fifth step is for children to be able to start using reappraisal in managing their rumination and worry and recognise how reappraisal can change their emotions and behaviour. They can also explore in their own experience other strategies for managing rumination and worry, such as those involving activities with sensory focus. They explore how applying these strategies impacts their own MHW.

134 *Making Sense of Mental Health and Wellbeing in Primary Schools*

With support, encouragement and guidance children in *reception* can begin to change unhelpful thoughts to helpful thoughts in their own experience and begin to recognise with support how this can change their feelings and behaviour. Children who find this too difficult can be guided to use sensory focus strategies instead. To foster these skills, children can build on the previous learning where they recognised helpful and unhelpful thoughts and their impact on their feelings and behaviour. The teacher can provide children with a simple accessible and non-sensitive example of an unhelpful thought, children describe how it makes one feel and behave – they can use the triangle posture and movements. Then the teacher asks children how they could change the unhelpful thought to a helpful one and how this changes their feelings and behaviour. Next, children are encouraged to start changing their thoughts from unhelpful to helpful increasingly more readily in everyday situations. Children who can't use reappraisal can use sensory focus strategies instead to change their feelings and behaviour.

In *KS1* children can understand from their own experience but with some support how to change unhelpful thoughts – they start to recognise that these link to rumination and worry in simple terms – to helpful thoughts. From their own experience they are able to recognise more readily how changing unhelpful thoughts to helpful thoughts changes their feelings and behaviour. They explore in their own experience how sensory focus strategies can also change how we feel and behave when we are ruminating or worrying. They start to explore how noticing unhelpful thoughts and changing them to helpful ones or using the sensory focus strategies can make them feel better.

Learning in this step can build on previous learning where children learned to use the triangle gesture to signify links between thoughts, feelings and behaviour. Children can now explore, using common everyday examples of unhelpful thoughts the teacher provides, how they would change them into helpful thoughts and how this would change their feelings and behaviour. Children can use the Feels Good Scale and Emotion Strength Scale to quantify the change in feelings from before to after changing unhelpful thoughts to helpful ones. They can do similar exercises with sensory focus strategies.

In the *lower KS2* children are able to understand from their own experience what reappraisal is and start using it in managing their unhelpful thoughts in rumination and worry more independently. With little support (or reminders) they can describe how changing unhelpful thoughts to helpful thoughts (in rumination and worry) using reappraisal can shift their emotions and behaviour. Children also explore in their own experience how sensory focus strategies may help them change the way they feel and behave when having unhelpful thoughts. They start recognising how applying these strategies repeatedly can help support their MHW.

To support children in developing these skills, the teacher provides them with everyday non-sensitive classroom based examples of unhelpful thoughts and children draw one triangle to explain how this would impact their emotions and behaviour. Then, with some suggestions from their teacher, children can draw a second triangle showing how they would change the unhelpful thoughts through reappraisal and how this would change their emotions and behaviour. They can use the Pleasantness of Emotion Scale and Intensity of Emotion Scale to quantify the difference from before to after applying reappraisal. Children can do similar exercises with sensory focus strategies. Finally as a class, children brainstorm together how applying the reappraisal and/or sensory focus strategies could support their MHW in the longer term, their teacher can make a list of the possible benefits for class display.

In the *upper KS2* children understand from their own experience what reappraisal is and start using it readily and independently to manage their rumination and worry. They can articulate how reappraisal changes their feelings and behaviour. They also explore in their own experience sensory-focus strategies to manage rumination and worry and how these impact their emotions and behaviour. Children start to recognise the longer-term impact of applying these strategies on supporting their MHW.

To foster these skills, children can be provided with examples of everyday non-sensitive unhelpful thoughts in rumination and worry, and are asked to describe in writing how they would change them to helpful thoughts and how this would change their emotions and behaviour (using the triangles). They can use the Pleasantness and Intensity of Emotion Graph to quantify the change in their emotions. They are then asked to write down examples of thoughts or situations from their experience where they could use reappraisal. Similar exercise can be done with sensory focus strategies. These writing tasks are not shared with the whole class. Then children are asked to write down in a google doc (anonymously) how they think applying reappraisal or sensory focus strategies could support their MHW in the longer term and their teacher summarises the suggestions to the whole class.

Step 6: Learning to Apply Neuroscience Knowledge as Part of Managing Rumination and Worry

The learning objective in the sixth step is for children to be able to use their understanding of the neuroscience underpinning rumination and worry, reappraisal and activities focusing on senses in managing their rumination and worry. They also learn to use integrated understanding of neuroscience underpinning all the self-regulation facets in managing their rumination and worry and recognise how this can support their MHW in the longer term.

In *reception* children begin to use, with support, references to the brain when changing unhelpful thoughts to helpful thoughts, recognising that this also changes the brain. Similarly when using sensory focus strategies children may be encouraged to acknowledge that this helps us feel better also because different parts of the brain than those involved in unhelpful thoughts take over. Children are reminded that every time we use these strategies we are changing our brains a little bit and making it easier to change our thoughts and feelings next time.

To develop these skills, children could use brain stickers to remind and reward themselves every time they change unhelpful thoughts to helpful thoughts or every time they use one of the sensory focus strategies to manage their unhelpful thoughts. The use of stickers would gradually decrease as children start to use the strategies in more internalised ways, albeit still with guidance. They are encouraged to remember that each time they use these strategies they are changing their brain to make it easier for them to manage their unhelpful thoughts next time and feel better.

With reminders, or using a brain map depicting relevant brain regions, children in *KS1* are able to use references to the brain regions underpinning unhelpful thoughts (amygdalae) to describe in basic terms and mostly correctly what is happening in their experience when ruminating or worrying. They can also describe what happens in the brain when changing unhelpful thoughts to helpful thoughts (PFC and ACC). Similarly they can apply neuroscience in describing their experience of sensory focus strategies. They understand that with repetition, relying on the hippocampus and neural plasticity, it becomes easier to change unhelpful thoughts and feel better.

To support children in developing these skills, their teacher can use an example of changing an unhelpful thought to a helpful one 'in their experience' in describing how they used neuroscience (amygdalae, PFC, ACC) in the reappraisal process to encourage children to do the same. Then building on the examples children can start applying reappraisal to their experience. They can now be encouraged, with support and guidance, to add neuroscience explanations to those examples of changing unhelpful thoughts to helpful thoughts. A similar exercise can be used for sensory focus strategies. Children are reminded that hippocampus and neural plasticity make it easier for us to change unhelpful thoughts with repetition.

In the *lower KS2* children are able to use understanding of neuroscience underpinning unhelpful thoughts in rumination and worry (amygdalae, HPA axis) and reappraisal (insula, PFC, ACC, VS) mostly independently when managing their unhelpful thoughts. In similar terms they can describe the brain processes involved in sensory focus strategies when using these to manage rumination and worry. Children are able to recognise that with repetition it becomes easier to manage rumination and worry in this way due to neural plasticity and with support of hippocampus and this can support their MHW in the longer term.

To foster these skills, children can use the triangles describing how they would manage unhelpful thoughts they previously prepared and add to them which parts of the brain are involved when they are having unhelpful thoughts and which parts of the brain are active when they are using reappraisal. A similar activity can be used for sensory focus strategies. Children are then encouraged to use neuroscience during everyday references to reappraisal and sensory focus strategies to decentre. They are also reminded regularly when applying the strategies that it becomes easier over time to apply these due to neural plasticity and this can support their MHW in the longer term.

In the *upper KS2* children are able to use references to what is happening in the brain independently to guide and motivate recognising (insula) unhelpful thoughts in rumination and worry (amygdalae, HPA axis, cortisol, default mode network) and when applying reappraisal or sensory focus strategies to manage

them (ACC, PFC). They can also integrate references to the five networks in describing the neuroscience underpinning management of rumination and worry. They use references to neural plasticity and the hippocampus to motivate their repeated use of these strategies to support their MHW in the longer term.

To cultivate these skills, children can prepare a comic book version of the write up about their experience of applying reappraisal (or sensory focus strategies) they prepared previously. In the comic book they include references (or drawings) to relevant neuroscience - their teacher can support this by listing all the relevant brain regions and networks on the board. Children can further elaborate the comic book to explain in neuroscience terms what is happening in their brains when they are using reappraisal and/or sensory focus strategies repeatedly and how this can support their MHW in the longer term. The whole class can then prepare a poster where they draw on what they prepared in the comic books in an impersonal way to summarise in neuroscience terms why it can be helpful for MHW to use reappraisal and sensory focus strategies in the longer term.

Step 7: Applying Skills of Managing Rumination and Worry in Everyday Life

The learning objective in the seventh step is for children to be able to apply their knowledge and skills of managing rumination and worry, including reappraisal and strategies focusing on the senses, together with relevant neuroscience, in everyday life. They are able to recognise how application of these strategies can support their MHW in the longer term.

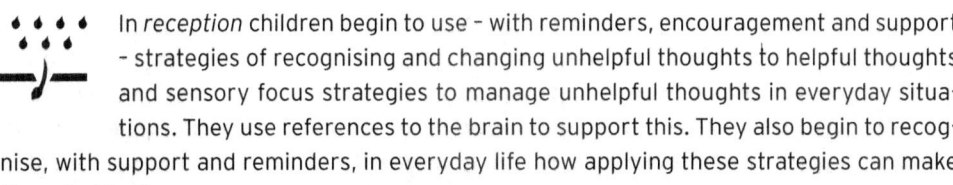

In *reception* children begin to use - with reminders, encouragement and support - strategies of recognising and changing unhelpful thoughts to helpful thoughts and sensory focus strategies to manage unhelpful thoughts in everyday situations. They use references to the brain to support this. They also begin to recognise, with support and reminders, in everyday life how applying these strategies can make them feel better.

To develop these skills, children are reminded in everyday situations in the class to use reappraisal; this can start with the triangle body posture, to manage their thoughts, emotions and behaviour. The class can prepare a symbol prompt to make the reminder easier. Similarly, children can be prompted to use sensory focus strategies if they can't engage with reappraisal usefully. Children are reminded to use the strategies repeatedly because it becomes easier with practice, references to the brain can be used to support this.

In *KS1* children are able to recognise more frequently instances of unhelpful thoughts linked to rumination and worry with teacher support in everyday situations. With encouragement and reminders, they apply reappraisal or sensory focus strategies to manage these. They are also able to use neuroscience to decentre when applying these strategies. They recognise from their own experience more frequently that applying these strategies makes them feel better, start to notice which strategies work better for them, and that it becomes easier with repetition to apply these strategies.

To foster these skills, children can be reminded to use the triangle gesture to recognise unhelpful thoughts linked to rumination and worry in everyday situations. Then they can be encouraged and guided to apply reappraisal or sensory focus strategies together with their neuroscience understanding to manage these thoughts. They could use the Feels Good Scale and Emotion Strength Scale, if they are displayed on the wall in the classroom, to recognise how applying reappraisal or sensory focus strategies changed their feelings and behaviour. Children can also be guided to develop a mnemonic to remind themselves that with repetition it becomes easier to apply these strategies to feel better in the longer term.

In the *lower KS2* children are able to recognise in everyday situations when they are ruminating or worrying, and this enables them to apply mostly independently reappraisal, sensory focus strategies and relevant neuroscience to manage unhelpful ruminative or worry thoughts. They are also able to recognise more readily and independently in their own experience the change in pleasantness and strength of emotions from before to after applying these strategies. They recognise more readily in their own experience which strategies work best for which types of thoughts or situations. They also recognise in their own experience that applying these strategies repeatedly can support their MHW in the longer term.

To cultivate these skills, children are encouraged during everyday activities to notice unhelpful thoughts and reminded to apply reappraisal or sensory focus strategies to manage these. They can also be encouraged to use neuroscience descriptions to decentre from rumination or worry if they find it helpful. Children can be encouraged to keep a diary where they write down their rumination/worry thoughts and then draw a triangle with the unhelpful thoughts and a triangle with the reappraised helpful thoughts to support use of reappraisal in managing these unhelpful thoughts. They can also use the Pleasantness of Emotion Scale and Intensity of Emotion Scale in the diary to help them see how reappraisal changed the way they were feeling and their behaviour. Children can be reminded to develop a habit of using the new strategies in everyday life and keeping a diary (or a log) to use the strategies in the longer term to support their MHW.

In the *upper KS2*, children are able to recognise, readily and independently, their own experience in everyday situations when ruminating or worrying. They are also able to apply in a mostly internalised way reappraisal, sensory focus strategies and relevant neuroscience to manage unhelpful ruminative or worry thoughts. They are able to recognise readily and independently in their own experience the change in pleasantness and strength of emotions from before to after applying these strategies. They also recognise readily and independently in their own experience which strategies work best for which types of thoughts or situations. They understand from their experience that applying these strategies repeatedly can support their MHW in the longer term and develop prompts to encourage habitual routine use of these strategies in everyday situations.

To strengthen these skills, children can be guided by their teacher in preparing either a log or a written diary or a comic book diary that they will use to motivate, encourage and track the use of reappraisal, sensory focus strategies (and any of the other strategies they learned about previously) in everyday life with continuity beyond the classroom learning. The teacher can suggest different options for what to include in the log, written diary or comic book diary, including the date, worry or rumination description, rating of emotions using the Pleasantness and Intensity of Emotion Graph, neuroscience description, strategy applied to manage them (reappraisal or sensory focus or other). They can also track the change in Pleasantness and Intensity of Emotion Graph after applying the technique and refer to the relevant neuroscience, then write a note to themselves about how to manage the same thought/situation next time. Teacher encourages children to keep the log or diary regularly and explores with children how keeping it may support their MHW in the longer term.

Conclusion

Rumination and worry are the key symptoms of depression and anxiety. Therefore, managing subclinical instances of rumination and worry effectively can be an essential skill preventing mental ill-health in children and adolescents. This chapter might have provided you with a clearer understanding of the links between rumination and worry, and mental ill-health. Knowing this, just like Sarah, the teacher in year 6 in the case study from the beginning of this chapter, you may have been wondering how to enable children in your classroom to develop knowledge and skills of managing rumination and worry systematically. You now may also have a deeper understanding of strategies, particularly appraisal and sensory-focus strategies, that can help children manage rumination and worry skilfully. Explanations of the neural changes underpinning rumination and worry, and changes in these underpinnings with application of these strategies, further reinforced this understanding. The chapter then provided detailed guidance on how these strategies can be taught in primary school classrooms across the school years in an age-appropriate way. As you have seen in this guidance, acquiring the knowledge and skills of managing rumination and worry also offers useful opportunities to integrate children's learning across the first two tiers (first five building blocks) of the ATTEND Pyramid. Altogether, this knowledge and skills can provide children with a solid foundation for life-long strengthening of their MHW.

Key chapter points:

- Rumination and worry are key symptoms of depression and anxiety, respectively, across the lifespan.
- While rumination is past-oriented, worry is future-oriented.
- Rumination and worry have been linked to increased activity in the default mode network which underpins self-referential mental processes, and dysfunctional activity in the other brain networks we have discussed.
- Reappraisal and sensory-focus strategies can help children manage rumination and worry and shift the maladaptive brain activity.
- Children can develop the skills of using reappraisal and sensory-focus strategies in managing their rumination and worry following the 7-Step Approach.

References

Child Focus. (2023). What is the difference between self-reflection & rumination? www.child-focus.org/news/what-is-the-difference-between-self-reflection-and-rumination-constructive-vs-destructive-thoughts.

Dorjee, D. (2024). Conceptualising child and adolescent mental health and wellbeing neurodevelopment: an integrative brain networks framework. Preprint, 4 November. https://doi.org/10.31234/osf.io/7vx45

Ho, T. C., Connolly, C. G., Blom, E. H., LeWinn, K. Z., Strigo, I. A., Paulus, M. P., ... & Yang, T. T. (2015). Emotion-dependent functional connectivity of the default mode network in adolescent depression. *Biological psychiatry, 78*(9), 635-646.

Kaunhoven, R. J., & Dorjee, D. (2021). Mindfulness versus cognitive reappraisal: the impact of mindfulness-based stress reduction (MBSR) on the early and late brain potential markers of emotion regulation. *Mindfulness, 12,* 2266-2280.

Marchitelli, R., Paillère Martinot, M. L., Trouvé, A., Banaschewski, T., Bokde, A. L., Desrivières, S., ... & IMAGEN consortium. (2024). Coupled changes between ruminating thoughts and resting-state brain networks during the transition into adulthood. *Molecular Psychiatry, 29*(12), 3769-3778.

Martin, R. E., & Ochsner, K. N. (2016). The neuroscience of emotion regulation development: implications for education. *Current opinion in behavioral sciences, 10,* 142-148.

McRae, K., Gross, J. J., Weber, J., Robertson, E. R., Sokol-Hessner, P., Ray, R. D., ... & Ochsner, K. N. (2012). The development of emotion regulation: an fMRI study of cognitive reappraisal in children, adolescents and young adults. *Social cognitive and affective neuroscience, 7*(1), 11-22.

Vergara-Lopez, C., Scalco, M. D., Gaffey, A. E., Reid, B. M., Bublitz, M. H., Lee, S. Y., ... & Stroud, L. R. (2024). The interactive effects of rejection and rumination on diurnal cortisol among adolescent girls: A preliminary daily diary study. *Cognitive Therapy and Research, 48*(5), 1027-1034.

Verstraeten, K., Bijttebier, P., Vasey, M. W., & Raes, F. (2011). Specificity of worry and rumination in the development of anxiety and depressive symptoms in children. *British Journal of Clinical Psychology, 50*(4), 364-378.

Volkaert, B., Wante, L., Van Beveren, M. L., Vervoort, L., & Braet, C. (2020). Training adaptive emotion regulation skills in early adolescents: The effects of distraction, acceptance, cognitive reappraisal, and problem solving. *Cognitive Therapy and Research, 44*(3), 678-696.

Webb, C. A., Israel, E. S., Belleau, E., Appleman, L., Forbes, E. E., & Pizzagalli, D. A. (2021). Mind-wandering in adolescents predicts worse affect and is linked to aberrant default mode network-salience network connectivity. *Journal of the American Academy of Child & Adolescent Psychiatry, 60*(3), 377-387.

Webb, C. A., Murray, L., Tierney, A. O., Forbes, E. E., & Pizzagalli, D. A. (2023). Reward-related predictors of symptom change in behavioral activation therapy for anhedonic adolescents: a multimodal approach. *Neuropsychopharmacology, 48*(4), 623-632.

Westbrook, C. A., Dutcher, J., Kusmierski, S., Creswell, J. D., Akpan, E., & Hallion, L. S. (2023). Neural correlates of mindful disengagement from worry. *Journal of Psychopathology and Clinical Science, 132*(1), 38.

Whitfield-Gabrieli, S., & Evins, A. E. (2023). Tuning the default mode network with behavioral interventions to address the youth mental health crisis. *Nature Mental Health, 1*(10), 695-696.

PART III
Nurturing Connections

7 Shared Humanity

Introduction

Now that children's self-regulation capacity has been strengthened in the first two tiers of the ATTEND Pyramid, the next two tiers of the pyramid gradually cultivate the key knowledge and skills of relational wellbeing. The first building block in the tier of 'Nurturing CoNnections' focuses on fostering the knowledge and skills of shared humanity. These are needed for enabling children to develop a balanced, non-judgmental, understanding and kind attitude towards their own and others thoughts, emotions and behaviours through exploring the shared humanity of experiences. This can in turn reduce feelings of isolation and excessive self-criticism which are increasingly common in children and young people and undermine their mental health and wellbeing (MHW). Some aspects of shared humanity were explored implicitly in the facets of the self-regulation capacity (particularly in the facet of Emotional Awareness), but in the facet of Shared Humanity they are cultivated with explicit strategies and in greater depth.

The first part of this chapter introduces the concept of 'shared humanity' and presents research evidence supporting the beneficial effects of cultivating shared humanity on children's MHW. We then explore the neuroscience processes underpinning shared humanity and their implications for teaching relevant knowledge and skills in the classroom. Next, we consider specific strategies for fostering shared humanity in primary schools and specify the developmental progression of shared humanity knowledge and skills. Finally, the second part of the chapter provides nuanced guidance on how to cultivate the knowledge and skills of shared humanity across primary school years following the 7-Step Approach. But first, to exemplify the importance and challenges of fostering shared humanity in primary schools, let's consider the following case study.

Case Study: Supporting Children Who Feel Isolated or Are Too Self-critical

Claire is a pastoral lead in her primary school. She recently developed a new set of teaching materials and guidance for teachers in her school on how to teach mental health literacy. Most of the guidance focuses on recognising mental ill-health symptoms, seeking support and signposting. There is further content in the guidance focusing on removing the stigma of mental ill-health.

But Claire would like to include in the materials more about ways children can support each other when they are going through difficulty. Children often instinctively comfort each other when someone is upset and that's encouraged in their school. But Claire is wondering if there is any further guidance on what to say to a friend and how to support them when they are upset.

Claire also noticed that some children often feel isolated in how they feel when they are going through a hard time. They may be reluctant to talk about what they are experiencing and sometimes seem to suggest that they feel others wouldn't understand. Girls in the final primary school years also seem to start being strongly self-critical of themselves, particularly when comparing themselves to others on social media. Claire would like to know more about ways to support children who are having these feelings of isolation and/or self-criticism.

Questions for reflection:

- What does mental health guidance in your school say about teaching children to support each other in times of difficulty?
- How do you support children in your class when they seem to feel isolated in what they are experiencing?
- Do you know how to support children who are excessively self-critical?

How Is Shared Humanity of Experiences Relevant to MHW?

Shared humanity overlaps with the concept of common humanity often used in psychology in the context of cultivating self-compassion. Common humanity is typically described as viewing one's experiences not as isolating but as part of a larger human experience (Neff, 2003). The concept of self-compassion includes, aside from common humanity, also self-kindness as an antidote to self-judgment and mindfulness to counter over-identification with experiences (Neff, 2003). Some aspects of these two other components of self-compassion are also included in the concept of shared humanity applied in this facet. However, over-identification with experiences was addressed as part of learning across the self-regulation facets (e.g. cognitive defusion, reappraisal, sensory-focus activities) and is also implicitly targeted across the last two tiers of the ATTEND Pyramid.

Yet, the concept of shared humanity as used in this facet of the self-world capacity has also inclusive and wider meaning than self-compassion. As described in the definition of this facet, shared humanity refers to cognitive and affective processes that underpin a balanced, non-judgmental, understanding and kind attitude towards others' and one's own thoughts, emotions and behaviours. The difference between self-compassion and shared humanity is the closer relational focus of the shared humanity concept, encouraging non-judgmental, understanding and kind attitude equally towards oneself and others.

Accordingly, the facet of shared humanity places more emphasis than self-compassion on perspective taking – being able to consider others' thoughts and emotions (Singer & Klimecki, 2014; Chatterjee Singh & Duraiappah, 2020). In this way, the concept of shared humanity counters some of the criticism, and also misunderstandings, around the concept of self-compassion linked to possible excessive self-focus. Another reason why the term self-compassion is not used here is that 'self-compassion' is sometimes criticised as an amalgamate, thus not unique, concept since it mostly entails mindfulness and decentring combined with explicit discussion about self-focused kindness and compassion.

While there might be good reasons not to use the term self-compassion as such in this facet, research shows that the characteristics covered by the concept of self-compassion (and also included in the concept of shared humanity) are positively related to MHW. For example, research on self-compassion with adolescents showed that it is positively associated with connectedness and secure attachment and negatively associated with depression and anxiety (Neff & McGehee, 2010). Another study with adolescents showed that increased self-compassion is positively linked with life satisfaction. In contrast, lower self-compassion is linked with negative affect and perceived stress (Bluth & Blanton, 2014). Self-compassion seems to be a particularly important target for mental health interventions with girls, since older adolescent girls typically score lower on self-compassion than boys (Bluth & Blanton, 2015; Bluth et al., 2017).

> Questions for reflection:
> - How is shared humanity different from self-compassion?
> - Why does shared humanity support MHW?
> - How does shared humanity in children link to positive affect, satisfaction with life, anxiety and depression?

Intervention studies showed that self-compassion components can be trained in adolescents. For example, a six-week mindful self-compassion training for teens evaluated in an RCT resulted in increased self-compassion, life satisfaction and lower depression scores in the training group (Bluth et al., 2016). Another study showed improvements in self-compassion after an 8-week self-compassion course in adolescents (Bluth & Eisenlohr-Moul, 2017).

While studies on self-compassion with primary school children are rare, there is initial evidence showing that higher self-compassion in 8-12-year-olds is associated with higher satisfaction with life and positive affect, as well as lower scores of anxiety and depression (Sutton et al., 2018). In addition, perspective taking has been developmentally linked to a range of social-emotional competencies, including empathy, which have been in turn associated with better MHW outcomes (Chatterjee Singh & Duraiappah; 2020).

Neuroscience of Shared Humanity

The Facet of Shared Humanity is underpinned by processes in some of the brain regions outlined for the self-regulation capacity – such as insula supporting emotional awareness, ACC enabling us to notice emotions and PFC supporting the ability to recognise emotions. Noticing and recognising emotions in ourselves and others is a prerequisite for us being able to understand their shared nature.

In addition, another brain region called the temporo-parietal junction (TPJ) particularly helps us think about others' thoughts and emotions and also reflect on our own emotions, thoughts and behaviours. In this way the TPJ can help us recognise the characteristics of shared humanity – including non-judgment, understanding and kindness – when we are relating to others' experiences.

> **Key Neuroscience Terms for Shared Humanity**
>
> - The *temporo-parietal junction* (TPJ) is a brain region on the surface of the brain linked to perspective taking – the ability to reason about others' thoughts and emotions and reflect on our own thoughts and emotions.
> - The *mentalising network* involves the TPJ, medial prefrontal cortex (mPFC), precuneus and other brain regions. It supports perspective taking processes.
> - Activity in the ACC has also been linked to shared humanity (self-compassion), likely due to its role in noticing emotions and in empathy.

The TPJ, together with some areas of the PFC (particularly mPFC) is part of the mentalising network. This network underpins our ability to reason about others' thoughts and emotions, and undergoes fast development during the first few years of life (Richardson et al.,

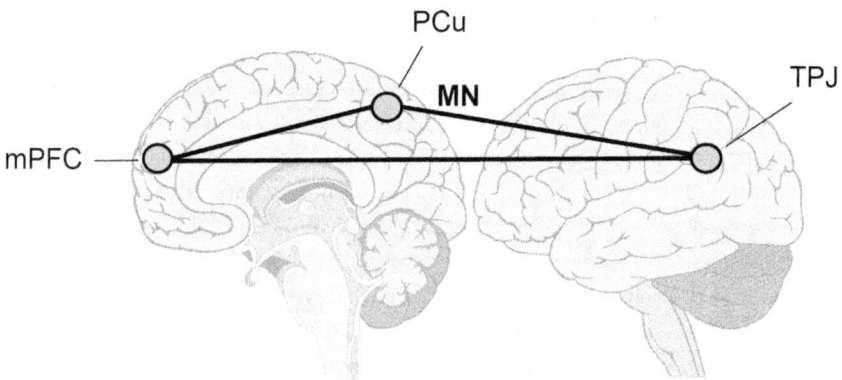

Figure 7.1 Neuroscience of shared humanity. MN – Mentalising network: mPFC – medial Prefrontal Cortex, PCu – Precuneus, TPJ – Temporoparietal Junction.

Source: adapted with permission from Dorjee (2024)

2018). Around the age of 4 children are able to utilise this network for reasoning about others' intentions, thoughts and emotions with higher degree of sophistication.

Studies with adolescents also show that self-compassion increases activity in the mentalising network, possibly due to mental activity related to working with self-judgment. Self-compassion also increases activity in the ACC (dACC) (Liu et al., 2022) which might be linked to both noticing emotions and empathy. There have been no neuroscience studies on shared humanity or self-compassion with children thus far.

> ### The Mentalising Network and Shared Humanity in the Classroom
>
> When reflecting on neuroscience of shared humanity, Claire realised that teaching children mental health literacy needs to include more content on perspective taking and shared humanity. She understood that the processes supported by the mentalising network, including being able to reflect on others' and own thoughts and emotions, are necessary prerequisites for mental health literacy learning to be effective. Claire came to the conclusion that without fostering these processes, the mental health literacy learning will likely be 'too shallow' – it will not result in deeper understanding and relating to what it means to experience mental health difficulties.
>
> She also recognised that reflecting on own and others' thoughts and emotions involves intertwined processes of the mentalising framework. Thus shared humanity means being kind and non-judgmental both towards one's own and others' experiences. She thought that such experiential understanding, supported by neuroscience, can further enrich children's mental health literacy. Therefore, she made plans to share her new understanding of mental health literacy with teaching staff in her school. She also expanded the guidance in preparation for the upcoming mental health literacy lessons with content on the mentalising network and shared humanity.

How Can Children Acquire the Knowledge and Skills of Shared Humanity?

Coming back to the case study from the start of the chapter, Claire would perhaps now have a better understanding of why recognising shared humanity of experience can support children's MHW, but she wouldn't necessarily know how to translate this understanding into teaching resources. Here it might be helpful for Claire to remind herself that the processes in the mind and brain underpinning the Facet of Shared Humanity undergo fast development during primary school years. This involves perspective taking, metacognitive skills and skills involved in self-regulation such as managing own thoughts and emotions to support interactions with others. The teaching needs to reflect these developmental changes.

Therefore, training of the relevant knowledge and skills in this facet starts by familiarising children with the concept of shared humanity in an age-appropriate way, using examples from stories and cartoons and encouraging children to recognise the qualities of non-judgment, understanding and kindness in those examples. The concepts of shared humanity and non-judgment are explicitly introduced only to children in KS2 whereas the qualities of understanding and kindness are introduced across the age groups. After gaining basic familiarity with the concept of shared humanity, children are encouraged to engage with examples of the 1-2-3 practice which builds on shared humanity and can be used to support others during times of difficulty and also oneself when facing difficulties (the application of own experience is appropriate for children from year 1 onwards).

> **Key Strategies for Fostering Shared Humanity**
>
> - 1-2-3 practice (What would a good friend say?) in relating to others is a strategy of supporting someone who is going through a difficult time in a kind and non-judgmental way. In three steps it describes recommendations on what to say and do in such instances.
> - 1-2-3 practice (What would a good friend say?) in relating to one's own experience is the same strategy as above but applied to one's own experience. We can imagine what a good friend would say to us in the situation we are going through, following the three steps of non-judgmental kind support.

1-2-3 Practice (What Would a Good Friend Say?)

Here is a brief description of the practice applied in supporting others:

Step 1 Validate feelings of your friend by saying things like, 'That sounds hard'. This is a balanced response, not overreacting or underreacting, but acknowledging that you understand what your friend is experiencing. In this way you can show 'shared humanity', by being non-judgmental, understanding and kind.

Step 2 Using distraction to shift focus to a positive activity. After acknowledging your friend's experience, you may want to see if you can support your friend further by doing something together that could make them feel better, maybe playing a game or listening to music together etc.

Step 3 Help your friend solve the problem they are facing if it is appropriate for the difficulty they are experiencing. This can be done by brainstorming about possible solutions and, if relevant, writing down their pros and cons. Such activity can help your friend come up with a suitable solution to the problem and make them feel better.

The same practice can also be used to support one's own MHW by asking oneself 'What would a good friend say to me?' and working through the steps, ideally in writing, applied to own specific situation. A less structured version of this practice is often used in self-compassion courses.

After learning about the 1-2-3 practice based on examples, children are encouraged to practise this technique through role-playing and writing tasks, then apply it to supporting others and oneself during everyday situations. Children also learn relevant neuroscience to support decentring from experience as in the facets of the self-regulation capacity and are encouraged to use the neuroscience to conceptualise and manage their thoughts and feelings using shared humanity attitude and practice.

Developmental Differences in Fostering the Knowledge and Skills of Shared Humanity

There is a developmental progression in introducing the different aspects of the concept of shared humanity due to complexity of the concept and associated practice and developmental maturational changes in the brain that underpin perspective taking, metacognition and self-regulation (and a progression from concrete thinking to more abstract thinking). For this reason, the concept of shared humanity is explicitly introduced only to children in KS2 together with all three of its qualities – non-judgment, understanding and kindness. In KS1 children are introduced only to the qualities of understanding and kindness in responding to others. While children across the year groups are encouraged to learn the 1-2-3 practice, they will be able to engage in it with different degrees of readiness, independence and complexity. Children in lower KS1 will need guidance on what the 1-2-3 steps mean for longer and they will need to be provided with a couple of simple examples that they can apply in everyday situations for each step to make the steps as concrete as possible. Their engagement in step 3 involving problem solving will be limited, mostly involving seeking an adult's help and most children in this age group will not be readily able to use the 1-2-3 practice in reference to themselves. However, from upper KS1, children will be able to recognise and apply the qualities of shared humanity and the 1-2-3 practice increasingly more independently, gradually across a wider range of situations and also apply the practice to their own experience with increasing independence. Ideally, children will be able to use the practice in an internalised way with practice and repetition.

Acquiring the Knowledge and Skills of Shared Humanity: The 7-Step Approach

The first three steps of the 7-Step Approach applied to cultivating the knowledge and skills of shared humanity will focus on equipping children with a foundational understanding of what shared humanity means and how it can support our MHW. They will also learn about the 1-2-3 practice and neuroscience underpinning shared humanity based on examples from cartoons, stories, movies or public life. In the following four steps they will apply this knowledge to their own experience, gradually progressing towards embedding the new skills of shared humanity in their everyday lives.

Step 1: Learning How Shared Humanity Relates to MHW

The learning objective of this first step is for children to acquire the knowledge that will enable them to understand what the concept of shared humanity means in the context of MHW based on examples (the concept of shared humanity is explicitly introduced only in KS2). Children learn to recognise shared humanity's qualities of non-judgment, understanding and kindness in the context of shared nature of human experience. They will be able to understand how shared humanity can counter feelings of isolation, when we are not feeling well, and thus support our MHW.

 In *reception*, children begin to understand the concept of shared humanity (the concept as such is not introduced explicitly) based on examples and with support. They begin to recognise the characteristics of kindness and being understanding in the examples and begin to understand the difference between feeling isolated and shared humanity feelings. The teacher can provide children with simple cartoon examples of characters feeling isolated in how they are feeling (sad for example) and then contrast it with examples when they are feeling sad but feel they are not alone in how they are feeling (shared humanity). Children are encouraged to recognise the difference, possibly identifying kindness in the later examples. They can also use the 'Feels Good' and 'Strength of Emotion' scales to rate the differences if helpful.

 In *KS1*, children are able to understand more readily the concept of shared humanity in relation to how one feels based on examples provided (the concept as such is not introduced explicitly). They begin to recognise the qualities of non-judgment, kindness and shared feelings in the examples and can differentiate more readily between examples of feelings of isolation and feelings of shared humanity in relation to wellbeing. Children can be provided with contrasting stories where the character experiences the same difficulty (e.g. feeling upset about not getting something) but in one scenario the character feels isolated in their feelings and in the other example they view their experience from the perspective of shared humanity. Children try to identify the feelings of non-judgment, kindness and shared experience in the examples and relate these to ratings on the 'Feels Good' and 'Strength of Emotion' scales.

 Expanding their knowledge further, children in the *lower KS2* are able to understand what the concept of shared humanity means and start to accurately use it to describe examples provided. They recognise the qualities of non-judgment, understanding, kindness and shared nature of human experience in the examples mostly independently. They also understand mostly independently how shared humanity can counter feelings of isolation when one is not feeling well and thus support MHW. Based on examples from stories or movies children can contrast feelings of isolation and feelings of shared humanity. They can be provided with a list or cut outs with names of characteristics describing feelings of isolation and shared humanity (including non-judgment, kindness and shared nature of experience) and link these to the relevant example scenarios, then describe how these link to MHW (the Pleasantness of Emotion Scale and Intensity of Emotion Scale can also be used here).

 Finally, in the *upper KS2*, children are able to fully understand what the concept of shared humanity means and can independently and correctly use it to describe experiences of characters in examples. They start to provide their own examples from public life that demonstrate the concept of shared humanity and can describe the qualities of non-judgment, kindness and shared nature of human experience in those examples. They are also able to contrast examples of feeling isolated versus feelings of shared humanity and link these to MHW while describing the reasoning behind the links. Children can be provided with examples of characters experiencing isolation versus shared humanity (from movies, stories or public life) and be asked to contrast these using the characteristics of non-judgment, kindness and shared human experience and their antonyms. Children are then encouraged to come up with examples they encountered in movies or public life (not their own experience) demonstrating the same. They rate the emotions experienced using Pleasantness and Intensity of Emotion Graph and based on this make links to MHW.

Step 2: Learning about the 1-2-3 Strategy and How it Can Support Shared Humanity and MHW

The learning objective in the second step is for children to acquire the knowledge that will enable them to understand from examples what the 1-2-3 (What would a good friend say?) practice is and how it can support shared humanity (recognising the qualities of shared humanity in the practice – being non-judgmental, understanding and kind) and thus MHW of others. From KS1, children can also acquire knowledge that will enable them to understand from examples that the 1-2-3 practice (What would a good friend say to me?) can be applied to support their own MHW during times of difficulty.

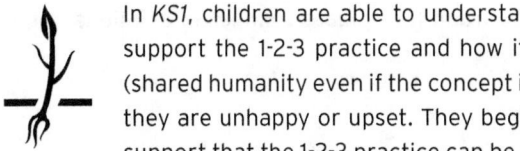 Children in *reception* can begin to understand in basic terms and with support what the 1-2-3 practice is based on examples. They can learn that the practice shows how we can be kind and understanding when a friend is struggling. They also begin to recognise in the examples that the practice can be helpful in making a friend feel better when unhappy or upset. The teacher can use two puppets to provide examples of the 1-2-3 practice to children and encourage them to start remembering what 1, 2, and 3 stand for. Children are also encouraged to recognise in the examples that the responses in the 1-2-3 practice are kind and understanding (shared humanity) of how the other person feels. Children start to recognise that the 1-2-3 technique helped the friend feel better, can use the 'Feels Good' and 'Strength of Emotion' scales to evaluate the change if helpful.

In *KS1*, children are able to understand more readily from examples and with support the 1-2-3 practice and how it can help us be kind and understanding (shared humanity even if the concept is not mentioned explicitly) to others when they are unhappy or upset. They begin to understand from examples and with support that the 1-2-3 practice can be also applied to their own experience when feeling unhappy or upset. The teacher can use activities where children recognise in scenarios involving characters in stories how one of the characters used the 1-2-3 technique to support the other character. In a second reading children are encouraged to raise their hand when they notice that the character is kind and understanding to the other character. And on a third reading teacher can pause and write down on the board using symbols what 1-2-3 stand for in the story. When children are familiar with the story, the teacher can modify it to demonstrate how the 1-2-3 practice can be applied to their own experience too when unhappy or upset, and can use the 'Feels Good' and 'Strength of Emotion' scales to evaluate the change.

In the *lower KS2*, children are able to understand from examples, with some support, what the 1-2-3 practice is about and link this mostly independently to the concept of shared humanity. They can mostly independently identify how the practice can help us be kind, understanding and non-judgmental and this can in turn support others' MHW. They will now also be able to understand with increasing independence from examples that the 1-2-3 practice can be applied to supporting their own MHW. The teacher can use examples from stories to explain the 1-2-3 practice in two different scenarios (e.g. one character being sad or angry and the other character providing support). The teacher then writes on the board what the 1-2-3 stands for and on second reading asks children to identify the 1-2-3 steps in the story by raising their hands and explaining why certain behaviours of a character represent the steps. The same activity can be used to exemplify the application of the 1-2-3 practice to one's own experience when feeling upset or angry. The Pleasantness of Emotion Scale and Intensity of Emotion Scale can be used to evaluate the changes from before to after applying the practice.

Finally, in the *upper KS2*, children will be able to understand from examples what the 1-2-3 practice is about and articulate independently how the practice can help us be kind, understanding and non-judgmental to others, linking this to the concept of shared humanity. They will also be able to explain how the 1-2-3 practice can support MHW of others. They can understand from examples that the 1-2-3 practice can also be applied to one's own challenging experiences and how it can support MHW. The teacher can first explain the 1-2-3 practice to children by using everyday examples from public life or fictional examples and also provide children with a handout explaining the 1-2-3 practice steps plus the three characteristics to be identified. Children can then be provided with short written scenarios. Working in pairs they can identify the 1-2-3 steps and three characteristics in the scenarios. The teacher then explains to the whole class what the 1-2-3 steps in the scenario were and the three characteristics and children compare what they have identified with the teacher explanations. Children can then brainstorm how the 1-2-3 practice can support MHW. A similar approach can be applied to exemplifying how to apply the 1-2-3 practice to own experience. Children can also use the Pleasantness and Intensity of Emotion Graph to evaluate changes in emotions in the scenarios from before to after applying the 1-2-3 practice.

Step 3: Learning Neuroscience Underpinning Shared Humanity and the 1-2-3 Practice

The learning objective in the third step is for children to acquire the knowledge enabling them to understand what happens in the brain when we relate to others (and our experiences) with shared humanity and engage in perspective taking (including the insula, ACC, PFC, TPJ and the mentalising network) such as in the 1-2-3 practice, and how this can support MHW (for others and us).

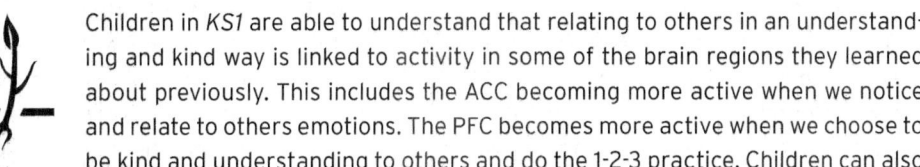

With support and reminders, children in *reception* start understanding that the brain helps us understand what others might be feeling and thinking and we use our brain when relating to others in a kind and understanding way. They can also begin to apply the 1-2-3 practice to help them feel better. Children could learn to point to their forehead as a reference to the PFC. They could be encouraged to learn gestures linked to the 1-2-3 activity which involve also pointing to the brain. The teacher can demonstrate pointing to the forehead as the part of the brain that helps us choose to be kind and understanding to others and to do the 1-2-3 practice supporting others to help them feel better.

Children in *KS1* are able to understand that relating to others in an understanding and kind way is linked to activity in some of the brain regions they learned about previously. This includes the ACC becoming more active when we notice and relate to others emotions. The PFC becomes more active when we choose to be kind and understanding to others and do the 1-2-3 practice. Children can also learn that a new region of the brain called the TPJ is more active when we think about what others are thinking so we can relate to them better. This all helps us in supporting others to feel better when they are feeling unhappy or upset. Children in this age group can also begin to apply, with guidance, their neuroscience knowledge to cases when they do the 1-2-3 practice to support themselves.

To develop their neuroscience knowledge, children could be encouraged to include neuroscience in the activities where they work with scenarios of characters being kind and understanding and applying the 1-2-3 practice. For example, the teacher can write down the relevant brain regions on the board and link them to the relevant parts of the scenarios as children go through the cartoons or stories. Children would then be encouraged to refer to the relevant parts of the brain themselves as they go through the story. They can also be encouraged to use references to the brain when discussing application of the same technique to their own experience using character examples.

In the *lower KS2*, children are able to describe more independently what is happening in the brain when we are non-judgmental, understanding and kind to others while recognising the shared humanity of experience and applying the 1-2-3 practice. This can include references to the insula, ACC, PFC and TPJ, and be linked to supporting MHW of others. Children in this age group can articulate mostly independently and accurately that similar brain processes also happen in our brain when we relate to our own experience with an attitude of shared humanity (and apply the 1-2-3 practice) and can explain with some help how this can support our MHW.

After teacher explains the brain processes underpinning shared humanity to children using examples that include the 1-2-3 practice, children can practise in pairs trying to describe to each other what is happening in the brain during the story examples and different scenarios they are provided with (a handout listing or depicting the relevant brain regions can be helpful). Then the teacher goes over the scenarios and describes the brain processes again solidifying the learning. The teacher can afterwards also provide examples of using neuroscience to explain brain processes underpinning the 1-2-3 practice applied to own experience and children then practise similar explanations to scenarios provided to them in pairs, relating this to MHW benefits.

Finally, in the *upper KS2*, children can explain independently and accurately what happens in the brain when we relate to others with the attitude of shared humanity (non-judgmentally, in an understanding and kind manner), such as in the 1-2-3 practice, and how this can support MHW of others. They use accurate references to the relevant brain regions - the insula, ACC, PFC, TPJ and the mentalizing network - in their explanations. They understand and can also explain independently what happens in the brain when we relate to our own experience with the attitude of shared humanity, including in the 1-2-3 practice, and how this relates to our MHW.

To develop this knowledge, the teacher can build on the everyday examples from public life discussed previously and explain what happens in the brain in those examples and also expand the explanation to include brain processes underpinning the 1-2-3 practice relating its effects to MHW based on brain processes involved. Children then practise in pairs taking turns in explaining to each other what happens in the brain in the scenarios they discussed previously, referring to the 1-2-3 steps, and how this relates to MHW. The teacher then demonstrates how neuroscience can be applied in the case of 1-2-3 practice used to support own MHW and children then work in pairs, building on examples provided previously, practising explanations of neuroscience underpinning the 1-2-3 practice applied to character's own experience and also relate this to supporting the character's MHW.

Step 4: Learning Skills of Shared Humanity in Own Experience

The learning objective in the fourth step is for children to develop the skills that will enable them to recognise from their own experience the shared nature of human experience including its qualities of non-judgment, understanding and kindness. They learn in their own experience how shared humanity can support others' and their own MHW by countering feelings of isolation when experiencing unpleasant and/or intense emotions.

Children are now ready to translate the knowledge they acquired in the three previous steps into skills that can support their own MHW. In *reception*, children begin to recognise in their own experience the meaning of shared humanity, even though the concept is not introduced explicitly. This starts through recognising qualities of understanding and kindness when responding to others and when others are responding to them. With support children begin to recognise that this way of relating to others can make them feel better and less alone when they are feeling unhappy, angry or sad.

To foster these skills, children can engage in guided activities of role playing where one child pretends to feel upset or unhappy and the other child tries to relate to them in a kind and understanding way, applying what children have learned from examples previously. Children then swap their roles. In the next round, children can also use the 'Feels Good' and 'Strength of Emotion' scales to evaluate how it made them feel when the other child was relating to them in a kind and understanding way. This can help them recognise the impact of such a way of relating on their feelings.

Children in *KS1* are able to recognise more readily, but still with support, from their own experience what shared humanity means even though the concept is not introduced explicitly. They are also able to recognise more readily its qualities of non-judgment and kindness and shared nature of feelings. Children are able to understand, with some support, how shared humanity can help make others feel better, particularly less alone, when they are feeling unhappy, sad, angry or have other unpleasant or intense emotions. To develop these skills, children can work in small groups with examples they were provided with earlier, and with support of teaching staff explore what they would do in a similar situation so that the character doesn't feel alone. They then practise recognising in their response qualities of understanding and kindness. Finally, they are encouraged to consider, or use ratings on the 'Feels Good' and 'Strength of Emotion' scales, how the understanding and kind response made the other child feel.

In the *lower KS2*, children are able to recognise mostly independently from their own experience what shared humanity means. They start to use the term shared humanity correctly to describe their own experience and recognise mostly correctly the qualities of non-judgment, understanding, kindness and shared nature of human experience in their own experience. They understand mostly independently from own experience how shared humanity way of relating to others and own experience can counter feelings of isolation when experiencing unpleasant and/or intense emotions

One approach to developing these skills in children is for them to be provided with cartoon-like scenarios where there is a child feeling upset or scared or unhappy or angry and children write on the side (or draw) what they would do to make the child feel better. They then identify using cut out words which aspects of their response were understanding, kind and non-judgmental thus demonstrating shared humanity. In another practice children can imagine that they are feeling unhappy about something and draw or write down a note to themselves that would be kind, understanding and non-judgmental. Children can discuss in small groups how the shared humanity response to others and themselves made them feel. They can also use the Pleasantness of Emotion Scale and Intensity of Emotion Scale, if helpful.

Finally, in the *upper KS2*, children are able to independently recognise from their own experience what shared humanity means. They recognise, and can independently describe, its qualities of non-judgment, understanding and kindness reflecting the shared nature of human experience. They understand independently from their own experience how shared humanity can support others' and their own MHW by countering feelings of isolation when experiencing unpleasant and/or intense emotions.

To cultivate these skills, children can be provided with a written scenario of a situation where a child is angry or upset about something and complete the scenario with how they would respond in a non-judgmental, understanding and kind way (shared humanity). Children can then swap their scenario responses in pairs and discuss what they have found useful in each other's responses. They can then be invited to write a scenario where they feel angry or upset about something small and write what they would say to themselves that is non-judgmental, understanding and kind. Children can be encouraged to use the Pleasantness and Intensity of Emotion Graph to evaluate how they would feel before the shared humanity response and after it to recognise links to MHW (these scenarios would not be shared with others since they are too personal).

Step 5: Learning to Use the 1-2-3 Strategy to Support Others' and Own MHW

The learning objective in the fifth step is for children to be able to use the 1-2-3 practice (What would a good friend say?) to support others MHW. From KS1, children also learn to apply the 1-2-3 practice to support their own MHW (What would a good friend say to me?) during times of difficulty and recognise its benefits to MHW.

With support and reminders, children in *reception* begin to use the 1-2-3 practice to support others when they feel unhappy or upset. They begin to recognise with support the qualities of understanding and kindness in responding using the practice. They also begin to recognise that using the practice in supporting others when they are feeling unhappy or upset can make others feel better. To expand their skills children can do further role play activities where they practise in pairs using the 1-2-3 technique – with one child playing the role of the one who needs support and the other using the 1-2-3 technique to support them (teacher can guide children through the steps of the practice and also use some visual support, such as pointing to 1-2-3 written on the board). Children are then encouraged in small groups to brainstorm about how using the practice made the other child feel. They can also be encouraged/reminded and guided to start using the 1-2-3 practice in everyday situations.

Children in *KS1 are* able to use the 1-2-3 practice more readily, yet still with some guidance, to support others when they feel unhappy, angry or upset. They recognise more readily the qualities of non-judgment and kindness when using the practice. They also recognise more readily that using the 1-2-3 practice to support others can make others feel better. Building on the examples of the 1-2-3 practice they were provided with earlier, children can cultivate these skills by

working with a range of situations, one by one, and practise in small groups how they would respond using the 1-2-3 practice. They can use the 'Feels Good' and 'Strength of Emotion' scales to evaluate how the feelings of the child in the scenarios changed in response to the 1-2-3 practice. They can be encouraged to start using the 1-2-3 practice in everyday situations with reminders and some guidance. Children can also start using the 1-2-3 practice in everyday situations increasingly more readily with some guidance to manage their own thoughts and feelings.

In the *lower KS2*, children are able to use the 1-2-3 practice to support others' MHW mostly independently and can mostly correctly use references to non-judgment, understanding and kindness (and shared humanity) to recognise and describe the relevant aspects of the practice. They begin to be able to apply the 1-2-3 practice mostly independently to support their own MHW during times of difficulty, recognising most of the time its benefits. To further develop the skills of shared humanity, children can work in pairs and come up with everyday examples where the 1-2-3 practice could be useful and take turns practising applying the practice in those different situations, they can use the Pleasantness of Emotion Scale and Intensity of Emotion Scale to evaluate how emotions change from before to after the 1-2-3 practice for the child needing support. Children can then use similar situations to write letters to themselves explaining how they would use the 1-2-3 practice to support themselves in that particular situation and use the Pleasantness of Emotion Scale and Intensity of Emotion Scale to evaluate how this would change their feelings. They begin to use the 1-2-3 practice in everyday situations with some prompts but increasingly independently.

In the *upper KS2*, children are able to use the 1-2-3 practice independently to support other's MHW and can readily recognise and describe the shared humanity qualities of being non-judgmental, understanding and kind when applying the practice. They are also able to use the 1-2-3 practice independently to support their own MHW during times of difficulty recognising its benefits. They begin to use the 1-2-3 practice effectively and independently in everyday situations to support others and own MHW.

To develop these skills, the teacher can provide children with a range of everyday scenarios that can lead to somewhat challenging experiences. Children can then work in small groups where one child enacts the situation and another child applies the 1-2-3 practice to make them feel better. The application of the practice is now more situation-appropriate and complex than in the younger age groups, e.g. the problem solving aspect. The other members of the group provide feedback and suggestions and the whole group can discuss which aspects of the response were non-judgmental, understanding and kind, referring to shared humanity. They can also rate the change in feelings of the person that was provided support using the Pleasantness and Intensity of Emotion Graph. Children can then do a writing practice where they choose from the same scenarios as if they were experiencing them and write to themselves how they would apply the 1-2-3 practice to support themselves and how it would likely change their emotions. This is not to be shared with others, the teacher can provide feedback in writing. Children are also reminded to start applying the 1-2-3 practice in everyday life situations

Step 6: Learning to Apply Neuroscience Knowledge as Part of Shared Humanity Skills

The learning objective in the sixth step is for children to be able to use their understanding of the neuroscience underpinning shared humanity and the 1-2-3 practice in enhancing their new skills in supporting others' and own MHW. Children will also be able to recognise and articulate how using neuroscience in this way can support their MHW.

 With support and guidance, children in *reception* begin to use their understanding of how the brain helps us understand what others might be feeling and thinking, and how we can use the brain, particularly the PFC, to choose to be kind and understanding to others. This can further solidify children's competence in applying the shared humanity attitude and the 1-2-3 practice in everyday situations to support others. These skills can be fostered during previously explained activities where children start applying the attitude of shared humanity and the 1-2-3 practice in everyday situations to support others. Teaching staff can start reminding children about the links between shared humanity and the brain, particularly when children might have difficulty relating to the activity or focusing during the practices. The teacher can start referring to the PFC and pointing to the forehead during such practices for children to have a concrete example of references to the brain and grounding during the practices.

 Children in *KS1* are able to use understanding about relevant neuroscience underpinning shared humanity and the 1-2-3 practice (ACC, PFC and TPJ) with support more readily to recognise and apply the qualities of kindness and understanding to support others MHW. They begin to be able to use the neuroscience understanding in relating to their own experience in an understanding and kind way, including when doing the 1-2-3 practice, to support their own MHW. In developing these skills, Children can further build on examples of applying the qualities of understanding and kindness and the 1-2-3 practice to support others MHW and elaborate the examples with explanations of what is happening in the brain when we are being understanding and kind and doing the 1-2-3 practice. This can serve as a further motivator for children to apply the shared humanity attitude and the practice in everyday situations. Using their neuroscience knowledge when beginning to apply the 1-2-3 practice to their own experience in everyday situations can further help children decentre from their experience, reducing negative affect.

 In the *lower KS2*, children are able to use their understanding of the neuroscience underpinning shared humanity and the 1-2-3 practice (insula, ACC, PFC and TPJ) more independently in recognising the qualities of shared humanity (non-reactivity, understanding and kindness) when supporting others MHW. They are increasingly independently also able to use their neuroscience knowledge in supporting their own MHW when relating to own experience in a non-judgmental, understanding and kind way and applying the 1-2-3 practice to own experience.

To develop these skills, children can expand the pair work in which they were applying the 1-2-3 practice in everyday situations by reminding each other about what is happening in the brain when we are struggling and feeling isolated. They can link this to how we feel, and how this changes when we use some of the brain areas discussed to relate to others with the shared humanity attitude and when doing the 1-2-3 practice with a friend, this may help decentre and motivate the application of the shared humanity attitude and the 1-2-3 practice; similarly children can use references to the brain to describe what the neural processes underpinning the shared humanity attitude and the 1-2-3 practice are when applied to own experience during writing letters to themselves on this topic

Finally, in the *upper KS2*, children are able to use understanding about the neuroscience underpinning shared humanity and the 1-2-3 practice independently and accurately to recognise and apply the qualities of shared humanity (non-reactivity, understanding and kindness) in supporting others MHW. They are also able to use their neuroscience understanding about shared humanity independently to support their own MHW when relating to their own experience in a non-judgmental, understanding and kind way and when applying the 1-2-3 practice to their own experience.

To cultivate their shared humanity skills further, children can build on the activities where they worked in small groups to practice these skills. They can now be instructed to expand the application of the shared humanity attitude and 1-2-3 strategy through references to relevant neuroscience (modelled by their teacher) and explore how this might be helpful in motivating and decentring the conversation with a friend. They can discuss in their small groups the possible usefulness of the neuroscience references in such situations. Children can then be encouraged to apply the same approach in their writing to themselves using the 1-2-3 practice and explore if they find introducing the neuroscience into their considerations helpful in any way, e.g. reducing the unpleasantness and intensity of the emotions they are writing about.

Step 7: Applying Skills of Shared Humanity in Everyday Life

The learning objective in the seventh step is for children to be able to apply their knowledge about shared humanity, relevant neuroscience understanding, and skills in using the qualities of non-judgment, understanding and kindness together with the 1-2-3 practice in supporting others and their own MHW in everyday situations.

In *reception*, children begin to apply, with support and guidance but increasingly more readily, their knowledge about being understanding and kind, including references to the brain and the PFC, and the relevant skills in applying these attitudes plus the 1-2-3 practice in everyday situations. They are able to support others when they are feeling unhappy, or upset in this way with some support and guidance. To further develop these skills, in everyday situations children are encouraged to recognise when they are being kind and understanding to others and when others are being kind and understanding to them (this can include brain and PFC references if helpful). They also apply the 1-2-3 practice to support others when they are feeling unhappy or upset. Children are encouraged to recognise the effect the kind and understanding attitude and the 1-2-3 practice has on others to encourage further more internalised use of the attitude and the practice.

Children in *KS1 are* more readily able to apply their knowledge about the kind and understanding attitude of shared humanity together with relevant neuroscience (ACC, PFC and TPJ) and skills of the 1-2-3 practice to support others when they are unhappy, angry or upset in everyday situations. They begin to apply the kind and understanding attitude and the 1-2-3 practice together with relevant neuroscience in everyday situations to manage their own thoughts and feelings in everyday situations. To facilitate this transfer of the knowledge and skills into everyday life, during everyday situations teachers can remind children before group work or breaks about being kind and understanding and about the 1-2-3 practice (including references to the relevant neuroscience) as a way of supporting each other when they become unhappy, sad or angry. Children can also be reminded and provided with further guidance on using the 1-2-3 practice when they struggle with their own feelings and thoughts in everyday situations.

In the *lower KS2*, children are able to apply their knowledge and skills of shared humanity, relevant neuroscience understanding (including references to the insula, ACC, PFC and TPJ) in supporting others' MHW in everyday situations mostly independently. They are also increasingly able to apply the shared humanity qualities and the 1-2-3 practice together with relevant neuroscience in supporting their own MHW in everyday life.

To foster these skills, children can be reminded to apply them during the morning register and before and after the lunch break. The class can prepare a class wall poster as a reminder of the shared humanity qualities of non-judgment, understanding and kindness and the 1-2-3 practice. Under the poster they can have a chart for each day of the week where they enter two times a day a sticker when anyone has been non-judgmental, understanding and kind to them or if they showed this attitude to others. The teacher can review at the end of the day how many instances of such behaviour the class has done and maybe they will see a gradual increase across the week (praising the class). At the end of the week children can also write a brief report about using the 1-2-3 practice during the week to support themselves (not to be shared with others).

Finally, in the *upper KS2*, children are able to use their knowledge about shared humanity, relevant neuroscience understanding (including the insula, ACC, PFC, TPJ and the mentalising network) and skills including the 1-2-3 practice independently in supporting others MHW in everyday situations. They are also able to apply independently the shared humanity qualities and the 1-2-3 practice together with relevant neuroscience in supporting their own MHW in everyday life.

To fully develop these skills, children can be encouraged to prepare a plan for the week, detailing how they want to implement the shared humanity qualities of non-judgment, understanding and kindness and the 1-2-3 practice together with relevant neuroscience, both in relationships and to their own experience, during their school day and outside of school. They are also encouraged to track their use of shared humanity and the 1-2-3 practice in a log, this can include the Pleasantness and Intensity of Emotion Graph, during the week. The teacher can remind children every day about the shared humanity qualities, the 1-2-3 practice and the log. At the end of the week children reflect in writing on how the application of shared humanity and the 1-2-3 practice went. They particularly consider possible impacts on others and their own MHW, and how they want to keep applying the shared humanity attitude and the 1-2-3 practice further (not sharing the report with others).

Conclusion

Before reading this chapter, just like Claire in the scenario from the case study at the start, you might have been wondering how children can better support each other during times of difficulty and how they can be supported when feeling isolated and self-critical. Now you might have a clearer understanding of why and how cultivating the knowledge and skills of shared humanity could be helpful in addressing these challenges. Recognising the shared nature of human experience can be an effective foundation for supportive communication with a friend, validating their feelings, helping them cope using distractions and problem solving. Older children can also apply the same strategy to supporting their own MHW during times of difficulty, learning to be kind and understanding towards themselves. This can in turn enhance their relational skills and further improve their MHW through social support.

Key chapter points:

- Recognising the shared humanity of experiences, and applying such understanding to our own experience and in relating to others, is an effective way to overcome feelings of isolation linked to poor MHW.
- Shared humanity is underpinned by the mentalising network with TPJ being the key region involved in understanding others' thoughts and emotions and reflecting on our own thoughts and emotions.
- Children can develop the knowledge and skills of shared humanity through the 1-2-3 Practice that can be applied in supporting others and oneself when going through a tough time.
- The 7-Step Approach can enable children to acquire the skills of shared humanity gradually and in a non-probing age-appropriate way.

References

Bluth, K., & Blanton, P. W. (2014). Mindfulness and self-compassion: exploring pathways to adolescent emotional well-being. *Journal of Child and Family Studies, 23*, 1298-1309.

Bluth, K., & Blanton, P. W. (2015). The influence of self-compassion on emotional well-being among early and older adolescent males and females. *The Journal of Positive Psychology, 10*(3), 219-230.

Bluth, K., & Eisenlohr-Moul, T. A. (2017). Response to a mindful self-compassion intervention in teens: A within-person association of mindfulness, self-compassion, and emotional well-being outcomes. *Journal of Adolescence, 57*, 108-118.

Bluth, K., Roberson, P. N., Gaylord, S. A., Faurot, K. R., Grewen, K. M., Arzon, S., & Girdler, S. S. (2016). Does self-compassion protect adolescents from stress? *Journal of Child and Family Studies, 25*, 1098-1109.

Bluth, K., Campo, R. A., Futch, W. S., & Gaylord, S. A. (2017). Age and gender differences in the associations of self-compassion and emotional well-being in a large adolescent sample. *Journal of Youth and Adolescence, 46*(4), 840-853.

Chatterjee Singh, N., & Duraiappah, A. K. (2020). *Rethinking learning: a review of social and emotional learning for education systems*. Mahatma Gandhi Institute of Education for Peace and Sustainable Development.

Dorjee, D. (2024). Conceptualising child and adolescent mental health and wellbeing neurodevelopment: an integrative brain networks framework. Preprint, 4 November. https://doi.org/10.31234/osf.io/7vx45

Liu, G., Zhang, N., Teoh, J. Y., Egan, C., Zeffiro, T. A., Davidson, R. J., & Quevedo, K. (2022). Self-compassion and dorsolateral prefrontal cortex activity during sad self-face recognition in depressed adolescents. *Psychological Medicine, 52*(5), 864-873.

Neff, K. (2003). Self-compassion: an alternative conceptualization of a healthy attitude toward oneself. *Self and Identity, 2*(2), 85-101.

Neff, K. D., & McGehee, P. (2010). Self-compassion and psychological resilience among adolescents and young adults. *Self and Identity, 9*(3), 225-240.

Richardson, H., Lisandrelli, G., Riobueno-Naylor, A., & Saxe, R. (2018). Development of the social brain from age three to twelve years. *Nature Communications, 9*(1), 1027.

Singer, T., & Klimecki, O. M. (2014). Empathy and compassion. *Current Biology, 24*(18), R875-R878.

Sutton, E., Schonert-Reichl, K. A., Wu, A. D., & Lawlor, M. S. (2018). Evaluating the reliability and validity of the self-compassion scale short form adapted for children ages 8-12. *Child Indicators Research, 11*, 1217-1236.

8 Connections

Introduction

Building on the knowledge and skills of shared humanity, the second building block of the ATTEND Pyramid in the third tier of Nurturing CoNnections develops the knowledge and skills of relational mental health and wellbeing (MHW) further. Specifically, the building block of Connections aims to foster the knowledge and skills that enable children to recognise and nourish a wide range of positive connections in their lives in support of their MHW. This includes friend and family relationships, but also connections with community and nature, spiritual connections and recognising the wider interconnected nature of human experience. In this context children explore emotions of gratitude, awe and interconnectedness, expanding further their understanding of shared humanity.

The first part of this chapter presents research evidence in support of fostering a range of connections in schools to enhance children's MHW, relating this to cultivation of the qualities of gratitude and awe. We then explore neuroscience research explaining how developing gratitude and awe may modify the brain. Building on all this research, the following two sections consider possible ways of fostering connections in primary schools and the general principles behind development of corresponding knowledge and skills. Finally, the second part of the chapter specifies how the knowledge and skills of connections can be cultivated in primary school classrooms following the 7-Step Approach, taking into account developmental differences across the key stage groups. But to relate these considerations to the challenges educators face in teaching MHW, let's first consider the following case study.

Case Study: Expanding the Scope of Fostering Relational Wellbeing

Nia is a teacher in year 2 in her primary school. She has been teaching children in her class about positive relationships every school year. Children would learn about what it means to be a good friend, how to be respectful in relationships and set boundaries. But this teaching is usually not directly related to teaching children about MHW. So Nia is wondering if there could be further explicit links to MHW built into the learning.

She was also thinking about expanding her teaching about relationships further. For example, she read this interesting article about the benefits of gratitude to MHW and she thought that this could be linked to learning about relationships. She also thought about the wider range of relationships we build in our lives, like the relationship with school. And she noticed that for several children in her class some of the most supportive relationships in their lives were with animals and nature.

Nia thought it would be good to include more teaching on these different aspects of relationships in her classes but wasn't sure how to organise the content and present it in a coherent way to children. She also wasn't sure whether her intuition of this wider approach to teaching about relationships was supported by relevant research evidence, including the links to MHW.

Questions for reflection:

- What do you include in your teaching about relationships?
- Does learning about relationships in your class include links to MHW?
- Do you think learning about relationships can include learning about gratitude, relationships with community, nature, etc.?

How Are Connections in Our Lives Relevant to MHW?

A robust body of research shows that positive relationships consistently predict better MHW (e.g. Ryff, 1989; Oberle et al., 2018). That's why some wellbeing theories include positive relationships in their models. These conceptualisations often consider 'positive relationships' in terms of immediate personal relationships with family, friends and colleagues. Some of the key prerequisites for developing such positive relationships involve knowledge and skills included in the previous facets two tiers of the ATTEND Pyramid fostering the self-regulation capacity and the in the building block of shared humanity. These skills, for example, encompass the ability to notice and manage own thoughts and emotions in support of non-reactivity that enables effective communication, the ability to take turns during conversations and the ability to recognise, understand and relate kindly to others' and own experiences.

However, our everyday connections go beyond immediate personal relationships. We may feel a strong connection to the place where we live, to our school, cultural community, our country, a sports club, material things we cherish, religious tradition, animals, places in nature we visit or nature in general, spiritual figures or ideals, values, etc. All these different types of connections can be a source of support for our MHW. For example, a sense of connection to their school has been shown to protect pupils' MHW (Aldridge & McChesney,

2018). Similarly, a greater sense of connection with a positive ideal beyond self (such as a positive religious figure, God/Higher Power or greater good/universal goodness) has been also associated with lower rates of anxiety and depression in adolescence (Cotton et al., 2005). Sense of connection with nature has been linked with better mental health (Tillmann et al., 2018), and a sense of expanded non-judgmental sense of self (Birch et al., 2020) in young people.

These different types of connections, if positive, are linked to emotions that can foster MHW. In a basic sense, positive connections are associated with feelings of happiness. Indeed, positive relationships across the lifespan, including in children and adolescents, contribute to happiness linked to life satisfaction (Proctor et al., 2009) which is sometimes referred to as hedonic happiness. Positive relationships are also an essential part of happiness linked to realisation of one's true potential (Ryff, 1989; Oberle et al., 2018) referred to as eudaimonic happiness or eudaimonic wellbeing. However, aside from happiness which is a very broad emotion, there is growing research evidence on positive effects of other emotions related to connections, such as gratitude and awe.

> Questions for reflection:
> - What positive effects can connections to school and nature have on children's MHW?
> - What does the research evidence say about impact of teaching children gratitude skills in schools?
> - How can fostering awe benefit children's MHW?

Gratitude, Connections and MHW

Gratitude can be defined as a tendency to recognise and emotionally positively respond to others' beneficial attitudes, emotions and actions towards oneself. Research on gratitude in adults shows that those higher in gratitude have higher psychological wellbeing, lower stress levels and better sleep (see reviews by Wood et al., 2010; Portocarrero et al., 2020). Importantly, gratitude can be cultivated through simple interventions, most commonly writing a list of up to five things that we are grateful for every day or writing a gratitude letter to someone (regardless of whether it is sent to the person or not) (e.g. Kini et al., 2016).

A meta-analysis of effects of such interventions in adults supported positive effects of gratitude interventions on psychological wellbeing (Davis et al., 2016), sleep quality (Boggiss et al., 2020) and small significant effects on improvement of anxiety and depression symptoms (Cregg & Cheavens, 2021). It is not exactly clear how gratitude exerts these positive effects, with some theories suggesting associations between gratitude and positive coping strategies, and others claiming that gratitude can broaden our attention and expand resources for dealing with stressful situations (Wood et al., 2010).

There is also cumulative evidence that gratitude interventions can improve life satisfaction, positive affect and mental wellbeing in children (Obeldobel & Kerns, 2021). Specifically, a gratitude intervention for 8-11-year-olds, evaluated in a randomised controlled trial, showed significant increase in positive affect up to five months after the intervention (Froh et al., 2014). The intervention in this study consisted of five lessons on gratitude which involved activities such as writing three things one is grateful for and writing gratitude letters. The lessons focused on recognising different feelings associated with gratitude and recognising a benefactor's intention and cost to them, the benefits to the receiver etc. (see descriptions of the lessons in Froh et al., 2014).

An earlier study on gratitude with 11-14-year-olds found more satisfaction with school three weeks after the intervention (Froh et al., 2008), a finding that could be related to greater sense of school belonging and thus protective effect on MHW. The intervention in this study involved listing up to 5 things one is grateful for daily for two weeks. Gratitude has also been found to predict increases in prosocial behaviour in a longitudinal study with adolescents (Bono et al., 2019), with both gratitude and prosociality being positively associated with MHW in other studies.

Awe, Connections and MHW

Aside from gratitude, another emotion that is closely linked to connections in the context of MHW is *awe* and can be described as a self-related emotion resulting from encounters with stimuli that initiate expansion of self (Monroy & Keltner, 2023; Chen & Mongrain, 2021). It is often experienced in response to nature, music, dance, art and contemplative practice (meditation) (Monroy & Keltner, 2023), but can also arise during learning and discovery in the context of science (Gottlieb et al., 2018). There can be both positively valenced awe (in response to viewing vast landscapes or witnessing a moral/virtuous action) and negative awe associated with threat (e.g. gathering of a storm; leader's coercive charisma) (Nakayama et al., 2020). However, positive awe is much more common (Monroy & Keltner, 2023).

Experiences of awe have six main characteristics including change in perception of time, sense of self-diminishment, connectedness, perceived vastness, physical sensations and need for accommodation (Yaden et al., 2019). Some researchers consider the characteristic experience of interconnection to be the key feature of this emotion (Chen & Mongrain, 2021). Awe has been positively linked to prosociality (Stellar et al., 2017), reduction in aggression (Yang et al., 2016), life satisfaction (Rudd et al., 2012), and MHW more generally in adults (Monroy & Keltner, 2023). Specifically, awe may, for example, explain positive impacts of experiences in nature and spiritual/religious connections on MHW (Monroy & Keltner, 2023).

Research on awe interventions with children is very limited, but a recent study documented positive effects of awe on prosocial behaviour and associated positive effects on a psychophysiological index of emotion regulation and the stress response (increases in parasympathetic system activity) (Stamkou et al., 2023). Specifically, in this study with

8-13-year-olds, children either watched movie clips that aimed to elicit awe, joy or a neutral response. Children in the awe condition were more likely to donate 'earnings' to benefit others and showed a physiological response associated with mental wellbeing and social engagement.

Neuroscience of Connections

When we connect with others the brain regions that are activated include those supporting shared humanity. This is because connecting with others involves relating to others' thoughts and emotions in an understanding, non-judgmental and kind way. For example, when we are having a conversation with someone, we need to be able to 'guess' what they are thinking to read between the lines and assess how they are feeling. Otherwise, our responses might not be accurate to what the person intended to say. The mentalising network enables us to understand others' thinking, intentions and emotions.

Research with children and adolescents also links changes in the mentalising network to MHW. For example, some researchers suggested that the mentalising network plays an important role in the emergence of depression in children and adolescents. As a result of maturation of this network children become more self-aware, particularly in social interactions. As a result, they increasingly experience more often emotions such as embarrassment, shame and social rejection which then can lead to excessive self-criticism and spiralling into depression (Luyten & Fonagy, 2018).

However, the mentalising network can also enable development of a healthy perspective on one's identity and relationships with others, such as through development of the knowledge and skills of shared humanity and positive connections. And some of the brain areas involved in the mentalising network are also involved in cultivation of positive emotions, such as gratitude. For example, one study found that adults who were asked to write gratitude letters once a week (20 mins) for three weeks showed an increase in activity in the medial PFC (mPFC) which is part of the mentalising network (Kini et al., 2016). This shift in brain activity persisted up to 3 months after the gratitude training. There are currently no studies that examined such effects in children, but similar findings could be expected.

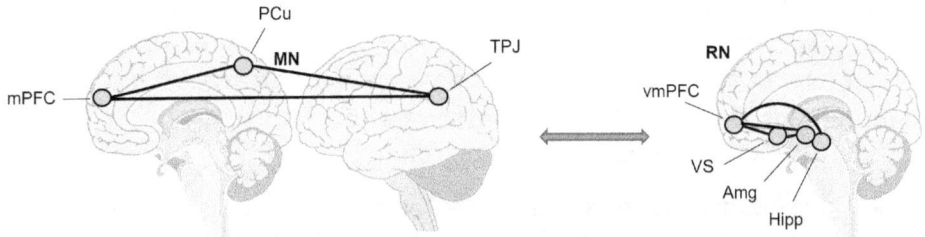

Figure 8.1 Neuroscience of connections. MN - Mentalising network: mPFC - medial Prefrontal Cortex, PCu - Precuneus, TPJ - Temporoparietal Junction; RN - Reward network: vmPFC - ventromedial Prefrontal Cortex, VS - Ventral Striatum, Amg - Amygdala, Hipp - Hippocampus.

Source: adapted with permission from Dorjee (2024)

> **Key Neuroscience Terms for Fostering Connections**
>
> - The mentalising network, and particularly the TPJ, enable us to understand others' thoughts and emotions in social interactions which is a prerequisite of building connections.
> - Activity in regions of the brain underpinning emotional awareness (insula and the ACC) as well as recognising and managing emotions (PFC) further supports building of connections.
> - The reward network, and particularly the VS, increase in activity when we are engaging in positive connections because these are linked to rewarding experiences.
> - Gratitude is associated with activity in the mPFC – a region of the mentalising network.
> - Awe can reduce activity in the default mode network, and this is linked to decreased rumination. Awe can also increase parasympathetic activity in children, thus balance the stress response.

In addition, studies showed that social interactions activate both the mentalising and reward networks. These findings were consistent both in adults and in children (Kawamichi et al., 2016; Alkire et al., 2018). The involvement of the reward network, particularly the ventral striatum, is explained by the positive emotions that typically arise in social interactions. These make connecting with others an inherently rewarding activity which may have evolutionary advantages for humans – positive social interactions with others ensure cooperation and increase chances of survival.

Finally, research on brain correlates of awe suggests that it can reduce activity in the default mode network linked to rumination (van Elk et al., 2019). This might be one of the neural mechanisms underpinning the positive effects of awe on MHW since rumination is a symptom of mental ill-health. In addition, a study with children showed that awe can shift psychophysiological responses in support of emotion regulation by increasing parasympathetic (rest and digest) system activity (Stamkou et al., 2023).

> **Mentalising Network, Reward Network and Fostering Connections in the Classroom**
>
> Now that Nia has deeper understanding of the neuroscience underpinning connections, she can see that fostering connections needs to include cultivation of a wider range of relational skills in children. Such skills are linked to the processes of the mentalising network – being able to understand others' point of view and emotions. They also involve the mentalising network in being able to reflect on which connections support one's own MHW, including connections with animals, nature etc.
>
> Nia is also aware that connections have these positive effects on MHW due to increasing activity in the reward network, that's why engaging in positive connections

feels good. In addition, she remembers the research evidence showing that experiences of gratitude can have longer-term effects on the brain and that awe can downregulate the stress response. Knowing this, she has made a plan to expand her relationship lessons by guiding children in recognising the wider range of positive experiences in their lives and how these make them feel. She is using simple references to neuroscience in this teaching. Nia is also planning to expand her teaching of relationships by supporting children in developing their skills in recognising and nurturing gratitude and awe.

How Can Children Acquire the Knowledge and Skills of Fostering Connections?

Learning the knowledge and skills in recognising and expanding adaptive emotions associated with positive connections, including gratitude and awe, builds on and extends on the self-regulation, perspective taking and other knowledge and skills children acquired in previous facets. The initial learning aims to increase children's awareness of a wide range of positive connections, including and beyond immediate family and friends relationships, such as connections with school, community, nature, religion/spirituality and wider interconnectedness of human experience. In the context of this exploration children are guided and encouraged to particularly notice instances of gratitude and awe and associated feelings and MHW benefits. The learning progresses from accessible examples of connections, gratitude and awe in stories, movies and everyday life, to exploration of the same concepts in own experiences. To achieve this, children are guided in two kinds of activities – the circles of connection and the trails of connections.

The Circles of Connection

The circles of connection is an activity that invites children to place themselves in a central circle and then, in further circles which connect to them, explore different types of connections. These connections include family and friends but also wider connections, such as connections to neighbours and community, sport clubs, school, culture/heritage, nature, religion/spirituality etc. In this context, children are then invited to notice and describe any feelings of gratitude and awe associated with the connections.

Children can be provided with examples of gratitude by their teacher in situations similar to their connections, such as gratitude to someone for being a good friend, or gratitude for feelings of safety and belonging to a school, or gratitude to their teacher, gratitude to nature as a resource, gratitude to religious or spiritual entities/ideals etc. Children can explore with guidance what gratitude feels like and also use the valence/intensity scales to recognise the positive effects of gratitude on their wellbeing.

Similarly, children can be provided with examples of awe using expansive images of nature, art, movies, watching and athletic achievement, examples of technological progress, virtuous acts of others etc. Again, children are guided by their teachers to recognise feelings associated with awe and how these make them feel (using the valence/intensity scales), recognising possible contribution to their MHW. Older children can also be specifically guided in recognising the rumination reducing effects of awe and a possible use of awe-inducing experiences to manage repetitive thoughts linked to worry and negative rumination about the past.

The Trails of Connections

The trails of connections is an activity that further deepens and expands children's understanding of connections, gratitude and awe. In this activity children explore contributions of other people and nature to them having food, clothing or other everyday things. For example, children could explore where the chips they had for lunch came from by drawing a trail of all those who contributed to making the chips, delivering the potatoes, growing the potatoes etc. This could be done with guided questioning such as – Who cooked the chips? What are the chips made from? Who delivered the potatoes to school? Where were they delivered from? Who delivered them to a supermarket? Who packaged them? Who grew them? Where were they grown? Who picked them from the field? And so on.

For each of the connections in the trail children can write down in one circle the answer and then connect it to another circle in the chain. A similar exercise can be done with a class item, for example a chair – if it is a plastic chair children can be guided to question where it was bought, who delivered it, how it was made, where it was made, what plastic is made from, who designed it etc. A pencil or a clothing item children use regularly could also be explored in a similar way etc. Making the trials of connections aims to encourage children to recognise the wide range of people we don't know who contribute to us having things we use every day, and encourage children to explore the associated feelings of gratitude and awe in this context together with feelings of being cared for by many people (thus countering feelings of isolation).

Key Strategies for Fostering Connections

- The Circles of Connection activity invites children to place themselves in a central circle and then, in further circles which connect to them, explore different types of connections in their lives. These connections can be positioned in ever-widening circles (or distinguished by distance from the central circle) and linked to experiences of gratitude and awe.
- The Trails of Connections activity encourages children to explore and recognise the contributions of other people (including and beyond immediate family and friends) and nature to what they use and do everyday. Children are guided to create a trail of 'origin' for the objects or food or clothing they use and often take for granted. This enables children to develop appreciation for people beyond their immediate circle of connections.

- Gratitude lists and posters – Children can be encouraged to write lists of things they are grateful for once and day. The whole class can also prepare a gratitude poster each child contributes to. Their teacher can guide children in recognising feelings of gratitude and their effects on their MHW.
- Recognising and nurturing awe experiences – Teacher can guide children in recognising experiences of awe and how they can support children's MHW. Teacher can also organise activities that induce awe as part of this and include such activities in the school day regularly.

To further deepen children's learning of gratitude and awe, children can be encouraged to make drawings representing gratitude and awe. Older children can also prepare gratitude and awe longs/diaries where they record up to 3 or 5 (age-appropriate number) instances of gratitude and awe. Children can also use Post-it notes on a poster on a wall in the classroom where they write down instances of gratitude and awe during their school day, to encourage them to notice and recognise these emotions more readily in everyday life.

Finally, upper KS2 children can write a reflection report on their experiences of gratitude and awe at the end of the school week to solidify and deepen their understanding of these emotions further (these are not to be shared with others). Whole class activities can encourage children to brainstorm about positive effects of connections, gratitude and awe on MHW they noticed in examples and their own experience (including reduction in feelings of isolation and greater acknowledgement of kindness of others).

Children will also learn about the neuroscience underpinning positive connections, gratitude and awe to further solidify their understanding of positive connections, gratitude and awe, providing further scientific dimension to the associated knowledge and skills. This neuroscience learning particularly aims to deepen their understanding of why and how positive connections, gratitude and awe can benefit our MHW.

Developmental Differences in Fostering the Knowledge and Skills of Connections

As with previous building blocks of the ATTEND Pyramid, there is a developmental progression in terms of complexity and independence of recognising positive connections and associated emotions of gratitude and awe. Younger children will need more guidance with the circles of connection and trails of connections activities, perhaps using pre-made cut outs with pictures of possible connections in circles they can glue on or refer to. Older children can work with their own pictures, can make drawings and write words in the circles during the activities.

Similarly, younger children can use simple gestures to describe emotions of gratitude and awe, with the complexity of descriptions of gratitude and awe and a range of situations where these emotions are experienced increasing with age. Children in KS2 will be increasingly able to notice and describe positive connections and associated emotions of gratitude and awe more independently. Children will also be able to use neuroscience understanding of brain processes underpinning positive connections, gratitude and awe with increasing competence, confidence and accuracy to solidify and deepen their knowledge and skills fostered in this facet.

Acquiring the Knowledge and Skills of Fostering Connections: The 7-Step Approach

As with the previous building blocks of the ATTEND Pyramid, the first three steps of fostering connections involve acquiring the foundational knowledge about connections from external examples. In these first steps children are guided in the Circles of Connection and Trails of Connections practices, to understand the concepts of wider connections and interconnections in relation to MHW. They also learn to recognise gratitude and awe as part of these practices, and learn about the processes in the brain underpinning connections and these emotions. In the following four steps children gradually develop the skills of fostering connections by applying this knowledge to their own experience. Through a range of age-appropriate activities they explore the different connections in their lives, how these connections link to gratitude and awe, and how they can support their MHW. In the final step, children apply their knowledge and skills of fostering connections in everyday life to strengthen their MHW.

Step 1: Learning How Fostering Connections, Including Gratitude and Awe, Relates to MHW

The learning objective of the first step is for children to acquire the knowledge that will enable them to understand, based on examples, that we all can have a wide range of positive connections (using the circles of connection activity) – from family and friends, through school and community, to nature, art and religious/spiritual connections. They will also learn that these connections can support MHW, and in examples recognise gratitude and awe as emotions linked to connections that can support our MHW.

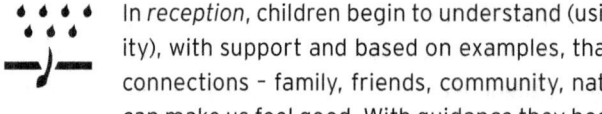

In *reception*, children begin to understand (using the circles of connection activity), with support and based on examples, that we all can have various positive connections – family, friends, community, nature – and that these connections can make us feel good. With guidance they begin to recognise gratitude and awe as emotions linked to connections in examples and begin to notice that these emotions feel good. This can be achieved through the circles of connection activity with children being guided and supported in recognising and selecting corresponding circles with depictions of different connections while listening to a simple story or a cartoon. Children can also be provided with examples of gratitude and awe in stories/cartoons and guided to recognise gratitude and awe in other examples (can use some simple gestures or symbols to refer to gratitude and awe). They start recognising how these emotions make the characters feel in basic terms.

In *KS1* children are able to understand more readily, based on examples and with support, that we all can have different kinds of positive connections (using the circles of connection activity) – from family, friends, through school, community and nature – and that these connections can make us feel good. In examples children begin to recognise more readily gratitude and awe as emotions linked to connections and that these emotions can make us feel better. Teachers can use age-appropriate stories and cartoons as examples to help children recognise a wider range of connections, including family, friends, school, community and nature, during the circles of connection activity where images or simple words can be used to describe the connections. The Feels Good Scale and Emotion Strength Scale can be used to evaluate their emotional qualities. Children are then provided with examples of gratitude and awe and try to recognise these emotions in further examples plus evaluate using the Feels Good Scale and Emotion Strength Scale how these emotions made the characters feel.

In the *lower KS2*, children are able to understand, based on examples and almost independently, that we all can have a wide range of positive connections (using the circles of connection activity) – from family and friends, through school and community, to nature and religious/spiritual connections – and that these connections can support our MHW. In examples, children can also almost independently recognise gratitude and awe as emotions linked to connections that can support our MHW. While listening to a story or watching a movie, children can draw different kinds of connections the characters have (using the circles of connection) and then discuss the connections they identified with the whole class. In this way, they can learn from each other about connections they didn't notice. Guided by their teacher, children can then rate in their drawings how the connections made the character feel using the Pleasantness and Intensity of Emotion Scales. In another activity children can be first provided with examples of gratitude and awe as part of connections and then asked to identify these emotions themselves in further examples and describe how these emotions made the characters feel.

Finally, in the *upper KS2*, children are able to understand independently, based on examples, that we all can have a wide range of positive connections (using the circles of connection activity) – from family and friends, through school and community, to nature, art and religious/spiritual connections – and can articulate how these connections can support our MHW. They can independently recognise instances of gratitude and awe as emotions in examples linked to connections and can articulate how these emotions can support our MHW. To foster such knowledge of connections, children can engage in an activity where they use an example from a story or a movie and draw a map with circles of connection using words in the circles to describe the different connections. Children then discuss in pairs their drawings to see if they can learn about some further connections from each other's examples and also discuss how these connections made the characters feel. In another activity children can be provided with examples of gratitude and awe and then asked to find such examples in stories they read, movies they watch or instances they observe in everyday life. They also evaluate, using the Pleasantness and Intensity of Emotion Graph, how these emotions made the characters feel and how this might have impacted the characters' MHW.

Step 2: Learning about Interconnections and How These Can Support MHW

The learning objective in the second step is for children to acquire the knowledge that will enable them to understand from examples that we are interconnected with many other people and nature in our everyday lives (using the trails of connections activity). They also learn that recognising this interconnected nature of our lives can support our MHW.

 In *reception* children begin to understand (using the trails of connections activity), with support and based on examples, that we are interconnected with many other people and nature in our everyday lives and that recognising this can make us feel good. In examples of interconnection children begin to understand with guidance feelings of gratitude and awe and that they can make us feel better. Children can be guided in the trails of connections activity where they brainstorm about something relevant to all of them (lunch for example) and explore where it came from – recognising all the people that made it possible, and also nature as a resource, for them having their lunch. The teacher can draw the trail of connections on the board. Children are then guided to recognise feelings of gratitude and awe, and can use the gestures or symbols learned previously, realising how many people contributed to their lunch.

 In *KS1* children are able to understand more readily with guidance that we are interconnected with many other people and nature in our everyday lives (using the trails of connections activity) and that recognising this can make us feel good. In examples of interconnection they are able to recognise feelings of gratitude and awe. This can strengthen their understanding of how these emotions can make us feel better. Children can be guided to do the trails of connections activity using an impersonal item that they all use, such as a jumper that is part of their uniform. With support in small groups they can draw a trail of connections that contributed to them being able to wear the jumper on that day and explore how recognising this makes them feel. They are then encouraged to recognise feelings of gratitude and awe in their experience of making the trail of connections and how this made them feel, possibly using the Feels Good Scale and Emotion Strength Scale.

 In the *lower KS2*, children are able to understand from examples mostly independently that we are interconnected with many other people and nature in our everyday lives (using the trails of connection activity) and that recognising this interconnected nature of our lives can support our MHW. In examples of interconnection they can recognise mostly independently feelings of gratitude and awe, strengthening their understanding how these emotions can support our MHW. To foster such knowledge, children can be guided to do the trails of connections activity with focus on an impersonal class item, such as a chair they sit on. In pairs, with the class being guided by their teacher, they brainstorm about the trail of connections that contributed to making it possible for them to use the chair in the classroom. Children can make a poster in pairs outlining the trail and contributors, including people and nature as a resource. Children are then guided to discuss how recognising this made them feel. In the

second part of the activity children are guided to discuss in pairs any feelings of gratitude and awe they experienced and express these emotions via drawings on the poster and also recognise how these made them feel. They can use the Pleasantness of Emotion Scale and Intensity of Emotion Scale, if helpful.

In the *upper KS2*, children are able to understand independently from examples that we are interconnected with many other people and nature in our everyday lives (using the trails of connection activity) and can articulate how recognising this interconnected nature of our lives can support our MHW. In examples of interconnection they can independently recognise feelings of gratitude and awe and can articulate how these emotions can support our MHW. The teacher can guide children in brainstorming about everyday items they all use in school on a daily basis and can make a list of the items on the board. Children can then work in small groups choosing one of the items in each of the groups to describe the trail of connections linked to it and make a poster in groups about this then present it to the whole class group by group (and possibly at assembly). Using google docs children can anonymously write down how recognising all the connections involved with the items they considered made them feel. The teacher can then review this with the whole class and guide the class in recognising particular feelings of gratitude and awe and how these might be relevant to MHW.

Step 3: Learning Neuroscience Underpinning Connections

The learning objective in the third step is for children to acquire the knowledge enabling them to understand what happens in the brain when we experience positive connections (including the previously discussed brain regions involved in emotional awareness - insula, (ACC), recognising emotions (PFC), understanding the perspective of others (TPJ) and rewarding experiences (VS) and associated brain networks - mentalising (upper KS2) and reward networks (lower and upper KS2)). They learn that these brain regions/networks are also linked to positive emotions of gratitude and awe associated with connections, and are able to link their neuroscience understanding of connections to MHW.

In *reception* children begin to understand, with support and reminders, that the brain, including the area of the brain they learned about previously - the PFC, is involved in supporting us in making, noticing and recognising the different types of connections we have. This can be linked to the activities of circles of connection and trails of connections, including recognising feelings of gratitude and awe, and how they make us feel. During the circles of connection and trails of connections activities children can be reminded that their brain is involved in noticing different types of connections and that the PFC particularly is active when we recognise emotions linked to connections such as gratitude and awe. Children can then be guided to link the gestures or symbols they learned for gratitude and awe previously with pointing to the brain and the PFC and how these emotions make us feel. They can make a rhyme or another mnemonic about it.

In *KS1* children are able to understand, with support, that making, noticing and recognising connections is linked to activity in some of the brain regions they learned about previously, including the ACC supporting noticing connections, PFC associated with recognising connections, TPJ involved in relating to what others might be thinking and feeling. They are introduced to a new brain region called the VS they haven't learned about previously which is more active when we experience connections because they make us feel good – they are rewarding. The PFC also enables us to recognise how connections and the emotions of gratitude and awe linked to connections make us feel.

Children can use the drawings from the activities of circles of connection and trails of connections and, with guidance from their teacher, elaborate their drawings further with references to the relevant brain regions which are more active when we are making, noticing and recognising connections and experiencing gratitude and awe – ACC, PFC, TPJ and VS; they can link these regions to the different aspects of experience associated with connections – ACC (noticing), PFC (recognising), TPJ (relating to what others think and feel) and VS (good feelings linked to connections).

In the *lower KS2* children can describe more independently what is happening in the brain during experiences of positive connections, using mostly accurate references to the insula and the ACC underpinning emotional awareness, the PFC linked to recognising emotions and the TPJ that is more active when we relate to the perspective of others. They also learn that the VS they were introduced to when considering habitual thoughts and emotions becomes activated during connections too. This is because VS is sensitive to rewards – positive experiences such as those that arise during positive connections. They are able to link their neuroscience understanding of connections mostly independently to effects of connections, gratitude and awe on MHW.

Building on the previous work children have done with the circles of connection and trails of connections, they can be guided in small groups to add to their posters references to the brain regions that are involved in positive connections. They can practise in small groups taking turns describing to the rest of the group what happened in the brain in an example of gratitude, and then another group member can explain what happened in the brain in an example of awe. Other members of the group then try to link these explanations to MHW. At the end of the activity the small groups feed back to the whole class, the teacher can comment on their neuroscience explanations to deepen their learning further.

Finally, in the *upper KS2* children can describe independently and accurately what is happening in the brain when we experience different types of positive connections. They can use references to the previously discussed brain regions involved in emotional awareness (insula, ACC), recognising emotions (PFC), understanding the perspective of others (TPJ) and the mentalising network. They also understand that a brain region they learned about previously, the VS, together with a brain network it is part of, the reward network, are linked to positive experiences associated with connections. They are able to independently link their neuroscience understanding of connections to effects of positive connections, gratitude and awe on MHW.

To foster this knowledge, children can work in pairs and use the drawings of the circles of connection they created previously to add references to relevant neuroscience processes underpinning the connections, with particular focus on gratitude and awe. Children then explain to each other in neuroscience terms what was happening in the brain when characters were noticing, recognising and experiencing emotions of gratitude and awe associated with connections. In the final step of the activity they discuss with each other how the neuroscience of connections links to MHW effects of gratitude and awe. The teacher can then invite students to share their observations with the whole class and provide feedback on their neuroscience explanations.

Step 4: Learning Skills of Fostering Connections in Own Experience

The learning objective in the fourth step is for children to develop the skills that will enable them to recognise in their own experience the wide range of positive connections in their lives (using the circles of connection activity) – from family, through school and community, to nature, art and religious/spiritual connections – and how these connections can support their MHW. They also learn in their own experience to recognise gratitude and awe as emotions linked to connections and how these can support their MHW.

In *reception* children begin to be able to recognise from their own experience (using the circles of connection activity), with support and guidance, the various positive connections in their lives – family, friends, community, nature – and that these connections can make them feel good. With guidance they also begin to recognise feelings of gratitude and awe in their own experience as feelings linked to connections that can make them feel good. Children can now do the circles of connection activity with focus on their own experience, being guided and supported in recognising connections, and selecting corresponding circles with images relevant to their own life. For example, they can make a glue-on picture of their connections. Children are then guided to recognise feelings of gratitude and awe associated with their own connections, they can also use previously learned symbols to refer to gratitude and awe. They recognise how these emotions make them feel. They can also prepare a gratitude drawing if helpful.

In *KS1* children are able to recognise more readily from their own experience (but still with guidance and support) a wider range of positive connections in their lives, They can use the circles of connection activity to recognise their connections – family, friends, through school, community and nature – and that these connections can make them feel good. They also begin to recognise more readily that gratitude and awe are emotions linked to their own experiences of connections and how these can make them feel good.

To develop these skills, children can prepare a picture depicting their own connections. They can be guided by their teacher to recognise connections including family and friends but also a wider range of connections with the school, community and nature. Children can bring images to school to use in the picture. They can use the Feels Good Scale and Emotion Strength Scale to evaluate how the connections make them feel. Children can be then guided to recognise feelings of gratitude and awe and mark this in the picture using circles of two different colours (corresponding to gratitude and awe) next to the relevant circles of connection). They can also be guided to recognise how this made them feel.

In the *lower KS2* children are able to recognise, almost independently, from their own experience, the wide range of positive connections in their lives (using the circles of connection activity) – from family and friends, through school and community, to nature and religious/spiritual connections. They can also understand, with some guidance, that these connections can support their own MHW. They mostly independently recognise gratitude and awe as emotions linked to their own experience of connections and how these can support their MHW.

To develop these skills children can be guided by a teacher to draw a picture of their circles of connection, including positive connections with family, friends but also school, community and connections with nature and religion/spirituality if relevant. Children are then guided to recognise any instances of gratitude and awe linked to the connections in their picture and to evaluate how these emotions make them feel using the Pleasantness of Emotion Scale and Intensity of Emotion Scale. In addition, everyday of the week (or longer) children are encouraged at the end of the school day to list three things they are grateful for that day and write them down in their workbook. They can reflect in small groups or as a whole class how positive connections and associated emotions of gratitude and awe can support their MHW.

In the *upper KS2* children are able to independently recognise from their own experience the wide range of positive connections in their lives (using the circles of connection activity) – from family, through school and community, to nature, art and religious/spiritual connections – and articulate how these connections can support their MHW. They recognise independently gratitude and awe as emotions linked to their own experiences of connections and can describe how these emotions can support their MHW.

To cultivate these skills, children can draw a map of positive connections in their lives using the circles of connection activity, including family, friends, school, community, nature, art/sports, religious and spiritual connections. They then write next to the circles brief notes about feelings of gratitude and/or awe linked to the connections and rate using the Pleasantness and Intensity of Emotion Graph how these emotions made them feel. Children are then asked to write a gratitude diary every day of the week (either at home or at school), listing up to five things they are grateful for each day. At the end of the week they reflect individually in writing on their gratitude diary and how writing it made them feel (this is not to be shared with the whole class). Children can also have a gratitude poster on the wall in the class where during the school day they can stick Post-it notes describing anything they noticed being grateful for during the day and the whole class can reflect on the notes at the end of the day or end of the week.

Step 5: Learning to Recognise Interconnections and Their Impact on Own MHW

The learning objective in the fifth step is for children to be able to recognise in their own experience the interconnections with many other people and nature in everyday life (using the trails of connections activity) and relate this to the emotions of gratitude and awe. They also learn from their own experience how recognising this interconnected nature of our lives can support their MHW through countering feelings of isolation and recognising kindness of others.

In *reception* children begin to be able to recognise from their own experience, with support and guidance, the interconnections with other people and nature in everyday life (using the trails of connections activity). They begin to understand from their experience how recognising these interconnections can make us feel better. With guidance children begin to recognise in their own experience gratitude and awe linked to interconnections and that these feelings can make us feel good.

Expanding on the trails of connections activity, children are now guided to explore individually the trails of connections for an item of their choosing individually. They start recognising the many different people that contributed to them being able to use that item on that day and also nature as a source of the item. Children can explore, using the gestures or symbols they used previously, feelings of gratitude and awe in recognising these interconnections and how these made them feel. In a separate activity children could also prepare a collage expressing awe in relation to the interconnections, for example nature as a source – awe-related collage.

In *KS1* children are able to recognise more readily, with guidance and support, from their own experience the interconnections with other people and nature in everyday life (using the trails of connections activity). They understand more readily from their own experience how recognising such interconnections can make them feel good, by learning that more people care and are kind to us than we might have thought. Children begin to recognise in own experience feelings of gratitude and awe when noticing interconnections and begin to understand how these can make them feel good.

To foster these skills, with guidance children can prepare a drawing of trails of connections for an item they choose individually and recognise the contributions of other people and also nature as a resource for the item they have. The teacher can explicitly point out how this shows that more people are kind to us than we may notice everyday and then encourages children to recognise feelings of gratitude and awe linked to the interconnections in their trails of connections (they can use the colour coding for gratitude and awe as previously). Children then explore with their teacher's guidance how the interconnections and associated gratitude and awe made them feel. In a separate activity children can explore interconnections through awe experienced when listening to music as a group or watching an athletic achievement etc.

In the *lower KS2* children are able to recognise, almost independently, from their own experience the interconnections with other people and nature in everyday life (using the trails of connections activity). They understand mostly independently from their own experience how recognising this interconnected nature of their lives can support their MHW through countering feelings of isolation and recognising kindness of others. They are also able to recognise mostly independently the emotions of gratitude and awe when noticing interconnections with others and nature, and understand how this can support own MHW.

To foster these skills, children can be guided by their teacher in drawing a trail of connections for an item of their individual choosing, something they use often at school or at home, recognising how many people contributed to them being able to have that item and also nature as a source. Children are then guided in exploring how we sometimes feel isolated but in reality we are interconnected and rely on the kindness of many people we don't know every day. Children then write down on their drawing of the trails of connections about who they are grateful to and why in the context of the trail and also how this made them feel. They also explore any feelings of awe at realising the scale of interconnections and how this made them feel. In a separate activity children can be encouraged to add to their daily gratitude list an awe list with awe experiences (such as realising interconnections, walking through a park, watching something that made them feel awe etc.).

In the *upper KS2* children are able to independently recognise from their own experience the interconnections with many people and nature in everyday life (using the trails of connections activity). They understand and can articulate based on their own experience how recognising this interconnected nature of our lives can support their MHW through countering feelings of isolation and recognising kindness of others. They are able to recognise independently in their own experience the emotions of gratitude and awe when noticing interconnections with others and nature, and can describe how this can support their MHW.

Step 6: Learning to Apply Neuroscience Knowledge as Part of Fostering Connections

The learning objective in the sixth step is for children to be able to use their understanding of the neuroscience underpinning positive connections, interconnections, gratitude and awe in recognising and fostering connections and these emotions as well as their effects on their own MHW in everyday life.

With support and guidance, children in *reception* begin to use their understanding about how the brain and the PFC are involved in supporting us in making, noticing and recognising different types of connections, in recognising positive connections and feelings of gratitude and awe, and how these make us feel in everyday situations. They begin to use references to the brain and the PFC to motivate their recognising of positive connections, gratitude and awe in everyday situations. With guidance and support, children are now encouraged to start recognising positive connections, gratitude and awe in everyday situations and can use references to the brain and the PFC to support the transfer of previous learning into everyday life. In this process children can combine previously learned gestures or symbols for gratitude and awe with references to the PFC and the brain (mnemonic or rhymes they learned about this). Children are also guided to recognise in everyday situations how gratitude and awe made them feel.

In *KS1* children are more readily able to use their understanding about the neuroscience underpinning experiences of positive connections, gratitude and awe (ACC, PFC, TPJ and VS) in noticing and recognising these emotions and their links to how we feel. With support, they are able to use this understanding to motivate/encourage forming positive connections in everyday life. Teachers could use stickers with images of the brain in a circle or with names of the relevant brain regions to remind children to recognise positive connections, gratitude or awe in everyday situations. They can use different background colours in the brain image stickers to distinguish experiences of gratitude and awe and also encourage children to continue noticing gratitude and awe because they make us feel good. With repetition it becomes easier to notice them in everyday situations and children will no longer need the support of the sticker prompts.

In *lower KS2* children are able to use, mostly independently and mostly accurately, their understanding of the neuroscience underpinning experiences of positive connections, gratitude and awe (insula, ACC, PFC, TPJ and VS) in recognising them and their effects on their own MHW in everyday situations. Children can be encouraged during the morning register to remember to recognise instances of positive connections, gratitude and awe in everyday situations during the day (not just at the end of the day when they write their gratitude and awe lists). They reflect at the end of the day together as a class how recognising these instances during the day made them feel using references to the brain in the descriptions, including how connections, awe and gratitude are rewarding. They also reflect on how this is changing their brains and how it is becoming easier with repetition (neural plasticity). Children can also add references to the brain to their gratitude and awe lists at the end of the school day to motivate and sustain their ability to recognise positive connections, gratitude and awe in everyday situations

In *upper KS2* children are able to independently and accurately use their understanding about the neuroscience underpinning experiences of positive connections, gratitude and awe (insula, ACC, PFC, TPJ, VS, reward network and mentalising network) in recognising connections and these emotions as well as their effects on MHW in everyday situations. They can articulate this in relation to their own experience with examples. Children could build on the activities they are already doing, recognising positive connections, gratitude and awe in everyday situations and writing briefly about such instances on Post-it notes where they can also include references to the relevant brain processes. They can also be encouraged to include in their end of the week reflections explanations, using neuroscience, of how recognising positive connections, gratitude and awe in their own experiences impacted on their MHW. The whole class can brainstorm anonymously or via discussion in groups how they applied neuroscience in supporting themselves in recognising positive connections, gratitude and awe in everyday situations and how they will be using neuroscience to motivate themselves in sustaining the practice of recognising connections and these emotions beyond this week

Step 7: Applying Skills of Fostering Connections in Everyday Life

The learning objective in the seventh step is for children to be able to apply their knowledge and skills of recognising and fostering connections and interconnections linked to gratitude and awe, together with relevant neuroscience understanding, in everyday life to support their MHW.

In *reception* children begin to apply, with support and guidance but increasingly more readily, the knowledge and skills in recognising a range of positive connections and interconnections (including references to the brain and PFC) to support their MHW in everyday situations. This will often include starting to recognise the role of gratitude and awe. Children can be reminded in relevant situations about their positive connections - including family, friends, community, nature - to manage their feelings (if feeling sad, left out etc.). They are also reminded of interconnections when taking things for granted or displaying inconsiderate behaviour to things they have or towards others. Children can be reminded in everyday situations, for example during morning register, to remember gratitude and awe during the day (with support of relevant gestures) because this can make them feel good.

In *KS1* children are able to apply more readily, with support, the knowledge and skills of recognising positive connections and interconnections, gratitude and awe, together with relevant neuroscience understanding (ACC, PFC, TPJ and VS) in everyday situations to manage their own thoughts, feelings and behaviour. Since negative emotions are typically associated with narrowing of focus on own experience and feelings of isolation, inviting children to remember the circles of connection and trails of connections drawings during relevant everyday situations might enable them to widen their attention and shift their experience towards positive emotions (e.g. when they withdraw and sit alone during a situation or when they behave in a way that disregards others feelings or property or nature). Children can be also reminded to notice experiences of gratitude and awe in everyday situations and recognise how this made them feel and that they can choose to focus on things that induce gratitude and awe to feel good (e.g. appreciating someone helping them or watching a sunset). They can use neuroscience to motivate themselves to continue practising these new skills.

 In *lower KS2* children are able to, mostly independently, apply the knowledge and skills of recognising positive connections and interconnections, gratitude and awe, together with relevant neuroscience understanding (insula, ACC, PFC, TPJ and VS) in everyday life to support their MHW. Children are encouraged in small groups to brainstorm about practical ways they can use what they have learned in the circles of connection and trails of connections activities, together with relevant neuroscience understanding, to keep supporting their own MHW beyond the lessons. With teacher's support they develop a way to implement the useful ideas in everyday school situations. Children can also be divided into pairs where they will check in with each other briefly on a daily basis. They can also keep on writing their gratitude and awe lists briefly on a daily basis and share tips and experiences of new instances of gratitude and awe they noticed (the pairings can be changed every week to support more diverse learning).

 In *upper KS2* children can apply the knowledge and skills of recognising positive connections and interconnections, gratitude and awe, together with relevant neuroscience understanding (insula, ACC, PFC, TPJ, VS, reward network and mentalising network), independently in everyday life to support their MHW. Teacher can first guide children in a brainstorming activity where they list individually the ways they applied what they have learned from the circles of connection and trails of connections activities and about gratitude and awe in everyday situations in school and outside the school and how this impacted their MHW. They can enter this anonymously in a Google class document that the teacher shares with the whole class and reviews it with the whole class so children can learn from each other. Children can then brainstorm anonymously how they want to continue applying these skills in their lives in the longer term and develop an implementation plan they write about as part of their gratitude and awe reflections at the end of the week. The teacher can support children in implementing their plans either by encouraging further connections/gratitude/awe diaries or by creating a buddy system where children support each other in continuing with the activities (and possibly the Post-it notes activity every week as well).

Conclusion

Connections are central to our lives, therefore recognising and building positive connections plays a key role in children's MHW. If you were, just like Nia, looking for a wider perspective on connections and clearer understanding of links to MHW, this chapter has hopefully provided you with such understanding. We have also considered how connections overlap with experiences of gratitude and awe – two emotions that can enhance children's MHW if they are further supported in developing them both in and outside of school. The chapter provided a detailed outline of how the knowledge and skills of connections, gratitude and awe can be fostered in the classroom across primary school years through a range of activities. The key task now is to sustain this learning through further encouragement and application in children's everyday lives.

Key chapter points:

- Recognising and nurturing a wide range of positive connections in their lives, including and beyond family and friends, can support children's MHW.
- Fostering connections is underpinned by activity in the mentalising network including the TPJ and the reward network including the VS, as well as other brain regions enabling us to become aware of our emotions and manage them skilfully in interactions with others.
- Fostering gratitude and awe can support children in expanding and deepening positive connections in their lives.
- Children can develop their knowledge and skills of positive connections, including gratitude and awe, through the circles of connection and trails of connections activities. They can also engage in writing gratitude lists and recognising/nurturing experiences of awe.
- The 7-Step Approach applied to fostering positive connections can help children systematically develop such knowledge and skills in an age-appropriate way.

References

Aldridge, J. M., & McChesney, K. (2018). The relationships between school climate and adolescent MHW: a systematic literature review. *International Journal of Educational Research*, 88, 121-145.

Alkire, D., Levitas, D., Warnell, K. R., & Redcay, E. (2018). Social interaction recruits mentalizing and reward systems in middle childhood. *Human Brain Mapping*, 39(10), 3928-3942.

Birch, J., Rishbeth, C., & Payne, S. R. (2020). Nature doesn't judge you – how urban nature supports young people's mental health and wellbeing in a diverse UK city. *Health & Place*, 62, 102296.

Boggiss, A. L., Consedine, N. S., Brenton-Peters, J. M., Hofman, P. L., & Serlachius, A. S. (2020). A systematic review of gratitude interventions: effects on physical health and health behaviors. *Journal of Psychosomatic Research*, 135, 110165.

Bono, G., Froh, J. J., Disabato, D., Blalock, D., McKnight, P., & Bausert, S. (2019). Gratitude's role in adolescent antisocial and prosocial behavior: a 4-year longitudinal investigation. *The Journal of Positive Psychology*, 14(2), 230-243.

Chen, S. K., & Mongrain, M. (2021). Awe and the interconnected self. *The Journal of Positive Psychology*, 16(6), 770-778.

Cotton, S., Larkin, E., Hoopes, A., Cromer, B. A., & Rosenthal, S. L. (2005). The impact of adolescent spirituality on depressive symptoms and health risk behaviors. *Journal of Adolescent Health*, 36(6), 529.

Cregg, D. R., & Cheavens, J. S. (2021). Gratitude interventions: Effective self-help? A meta-analysis of the impact on symptoms of depression and anxiety. *Journal of Happiness Studies*, 22, 413-445.

Davis, D. E., Choe, E., Meyers, J., Wade, N., Varjas, K., Gifford, A., ... & Worthington Jr, E. L. (2016). Thankful for the little things: a meta-analysis of gratitude interventions. *Journal of Counseling Psychology*, 63(1), 20.

Dorjee, D. (2024). Conceptualising child and adolescent mental health and wellbeing neurodevelopment: an integrative brain networks framework. Preprint, 4 November. https://doi.org/10.31234/osf.io/7vx45

Froh, J. J., Sefick, W. J., & Emmons, R. A. (2008). Counting blessings in early adolescents: an experimental study of gratitude and subjective well-being. *Journal of School Psychology*, 46(2), 213-233.

Froh, J. J., Bono, G., Fan, J., Emmons, R. A., Henderson, K., Harris, C., ... & Wood, A. M. (2014). Nice thinking! An educational intervention that teaches children to think gratefully. *School Psychology Review*, *43*(2), 132-152.

Gottlieb, S., Keltner, D., & Lombrozo, T. (2018). Awe as a scientific emotion. *Cognitive Science*, *42*(6), 2081-2094.

Kawamichi, H., Sugawara, S. K., Hamano, Y. H., Makita, K., Kochiyama, T., & Sadato, N. (2016). Increased frequency of social interaction is associated with enjoyment enhancement and reward system activation. *Scientific Reports*, *6*(1), 24561.

Kini, P., Wong, J., McInnis, S., Gabana, N., & Brown, J. W. (2016). The effects of gratitude expression on neural activity. *NeuroImage*, *128*, 1-10.

Luyten, P., & Fonagy, P. (2018). The stress-reward-mentalizing model of depression: an integrative developmental cascade approach to child and adolescent depressive disorder based on the Research Domain Criteria (RDoC) approach. *Clinical Psychology Review*, *64*, 87-98.

Monroy, M., & Keltner, D. (2023). Awe as a pathway to mental and physical health. *Perspectives on Psychological Science*, *18*(2), 309-320.

Nakayama, M., Nozaki, Y., Taylor, P. M., Keltner, D., & Uchida, Y. (2020). Individual and cultural differences in predispositions to feel positive and negative aspects of awe. *Journal of Cross-Cultural Psychology*, *51*(10), 771-793.

Obeldobel, C. A., & Kerns, K. A. (2021). A literature review of gratitude, parent-child relationships, and well-being in children. *Developmental Review*, *61*, 100948.

Oberle, E., Guhn, M., Gadermann, A. M., Thomson, K., & Schonert-Reichl, K. A. (2018). Positive mental health and supportive school environments: a population-level longitudinal study of dispositional optimism and school relationships in early adolescence. *Social Science & Medicine*, *214*, 154-161.

Portocarrero, F. F., Gonzalez, K., & Ekema-Agbaw, M. (2020). A meta-analytic review of the relationship between dispositional gratitude and well-being. *Personality and Individual Differences*, *164*, 110101.

Proctor, C. L., Linley, P. A., & Maltby, J. (2009). Youth life satisfaction: a review of the literature. *Journal of Happiness Studies*, *10*, 583-630.

Rudd, M., Vohs, K. D., & Aaker, J. (2012). Awe expands people's perception of time, alters decision making, and enhances well-being. *Psychological Science*, *23*(10), 1130-1136.

Ryff, C. D. (1989). Happiness is everything, or is it? Explorations on the meaning of psychological well-being. *Journal of Personality and Social Psychology*, *57*(6), 1069.

Stamkou, E., Brummelman, E., Dunham, R., Nikolic, M., & Keltner, D. (2023). Awe sparks prosociality in children. *Psychological Science*, *34*(4), 455-467.

Stellar, J. E., Gordon, A. M., Piff, P. K., Cordaro, D., Anderson, C. L., Bai, Y., ... & Keltner, D. (2017). Self-transcendent emotions and their social functions: compassion, gratitude, and awe bind us to others through prosociality. *Emotion Review*, *9*(3), 200-207.

Tillmann, S., Tobin, D., Avison, W., & Gilliland, J. (2018). Mental health benefits of interactions with nature in children and teenagers: a systematic review. *Journal of Epidemiology and Community Health*, *72*(10), 958-966.

Van Elk, M., Arciniegas Gomez, M. A., van der Zwaag, W., Van Schie, H. T., & Sauter, D. (2019). The neural correlates of the awe experience: reduced default mode network activity during feelings of awe. *Human Brain Mapping*, *40*(12), 3561-3574.

Wood, A. M., Froh, J. J., & Geraghty, A. W. (2010). Gratitude and well-being: a review and theoretical integration. *Clinical Psychology Review*, *30*(7), 890-905.

Yaden, D. B., Kaufman, S. B., Hyde, E., Chirico, A., Gaggioli, A., Zhang, J. W., & Keltner, D. (2019). The development of the Awe Experience Scale (AWE-S): A multifactorial measure for a complex emotion. *The Journal of Positive Psychology*, *14*(4), 474-488.

Yang, Y., Yang, Z., Bao, T., Liu, Y., & Passmore, H. A. (2016). Elicited awe decreases aggression. *Journal of Pacific Rim Psychology*, *10*, e11.

9 Making a Difference

Introduction

The final building block in the third tier of the ATTEND Pyramid - Nurturing CoNnections - expands the knowledge and skills of shared humanity and connections further towards making a difference. The aim of learning in this facet is for children to recognise feelings of empathic distress which can sometimes arise in the context of connections and learn how these can be managed by developing compassion and prosocial behaviour in support of their mental health and wellbeing (MHW). Such learning supports children in being able to distinguish between empathic distress and compassion, differentiate types of prosocial behaviour as well as selfish versus compassionate motivation behind it, and recognise how making a difference can foster their MHW.

This chapter first explains how empathy, empathic distress, compassion and prosocial behaviour differ, then relates each of these concepts to MHW. Next, we consider their underpinning neural processes in relation to MHW. Translating this research into the classroom, the chapter then outlines ways compassion and prosocial behaviour can be fostered in primary schools. The rest of the chapter considers the developmental progression of knowledge and skills of making a difference and age-appropriate strategies to cultivate these across the primary school years.

Case Study: Empathy, Caring Behaviours and MHW in the Classroom

Lee is a teacher in year 4. He has been reviewing various guidelines for fostering MHW knowledge and skills in KS2. One of the concepts that he keeps on encountering is empathy. However, most of the teaching materials he came across do not really explain why and how empathy is relevant to MHW. Clearly, empathy could make children more considerate and caring, possibly reduce problematic behaviour, but Lee is wondering if it has direct benefits to children's MHW.

Lee is also wondering if empathy can sometimes be problematic. For example, he found that when children discuss some topics, such as climate change or war, or talk to each other about some difficulties they are facing, some of them become upset. That is understandable and shows that they are empathic, but Lee would like to teach them some strategies to help them manage their emotions when this arises.

Lee also noticed that empathy can sometimes increase children's caring behaviours towards each other, but the behavioural policy in the school encourages considerate behaviour towards others as part of expected discipline, regardless of empathy. He is wondering if there is a difference in these types of behaviours when they arise out of genuine concern for others versus when they are enforced by school behaviour expectations. He is also wondering how such behaviours might link to MHW.

Questions for reflection:
- Do you know how empathy can support MHW?
- Have you come across instances of empathic distress in children in your class?
- Do you think caring behaviours can be beneficial to children's MHW?

How Is Making a Difference Relevant to MHW?

The Facet of Connections demonstrated that we are impacted by many connections we may not have been aware of. Yet, connections can lead to both positive and negative emotions. This is due to empathy, which builds on perspective taking we have discussed in the Facet of Shared Humanity. While perspective taking is a more cognitive 'thinking' way of relating to others' experience, empathy can be described as resonating emotionally with others' experience.

Empathy and Empathic Distress

Empathy has been generally linked to better wellbeing in adolescents (Supervía et al., 2023), and lower empathy is associated with poor mental health in children, particularly in the context of conduct disorders (Frick & Kemp, 2021). However, higher levels of empathy combined with low ability to manage emotions predict higher levels of depression symptoms in early adolescents (Calandri et al., 2021). This is probably because empathy can also result in feelings of *empathic distress* which can be described as 'a strong aversive and self-oriented response to the suffering of others' (Singer & Klimecki, 2014, p. 875).

Empathic distress is self-oriented which means that it focuses on our own feelings of distress and is associated with a tendency to withdraw or avoid situations which would lead to empathic distress; it has also been linked to poor mental health associated with burnout (Singer & Klimecki, 2014). In a wider societal context, empathic distress might be one of the reasons why people prefer to disengage from connections to important but potentially distressing issues, such as news about climate change or war. This can result in increased feelings of disconnection to prevent feeling helplessness, worry and existential uncertainty.

Excessive exposure to experiences that result in empathic distress can feed our negativity bias and undermine our MHW.

Compassion

One way to manage empathic distress is to reduce exposure to distressing news or situations, as we have discussed in the Facet of Distractions. Yet, often it is not possible to completely eliminate such exposure. In addition, excessive and long-term avoidance-based coping can also be unhelpful to MHW in children (Zhang et al., 2022) and adolescents (Frydenberg & Lewis, 2009). In contrast, active coping in general and balanced exposure to others' difficulties, when we are able to use feelings of empathy as a starting point for compassion and prosocial behaviour rather than empathic distress, can be supportive for MHW and also has benefits for those we are responding to.

Compassion is an emotion associated with a feeling of concern for others' suffering but it is accompanied by motivation to help and associated with prosocial approach-oriented behaviour rather than withdrawal. Unlike empathic distress, compassion is an other-oriented emotion that has been linked to positive feelings (such as love and kindness) and better health (Singer & Klimecki, 2014). Research with adults shows that compassion can be trained and can reverse the negative effects of empathic distress (Leiberg et al., 2011; Klimecki et al., 2014). Compassion is also increasingly emphasised as a fruitful approach to treating mental ill health (Foerster & Kanske, 2021). For example, compassion-focused therapy is considered a promising treatment for mood disorders in adults (Leaviss & Uttley, 2015; Craig et al., 2020).

> ### Key Terms
>
> - *Empathy* can be described as not only understanding others' experiences but also resonating emotionally with them.
> - *Empathic distress* can arise in response to empathy; it focuses on one's own feelings of distress and often leads to withdrawal or avoidance of situations that could result in empathic distress. It is linked to poor mental health.
> - *Compassion* is an emotion characterised by concern for others' suffering accompanied by motivation to help. It is a prosocial emotion that often leads to prosocial approach-oriented behaviour rather than withdrawal. It is linked to better mental health.

Jazaieri (2019) explored compassion in the context of education and emphasised that compassion needs to be distinguished from related concepts such as empathy, pity, personal distress, prosociality or well-wishing. She explained that empathy is 'feeling as' others, whereas compassion is 'feeling for others'. Compassion can be considered in terms of four components, including awareness of suffering, sympathetic concern, wish to see the relief of that suffering and responsiveness or readiness to help relieve that suffering (Jazaieri, 2019). Compassion can, and often does, lead to prosocial action, but can also be experienced without the behavioural component.

Research on the effects of training compassion in children and adolescents is limited, but initial findings are encouraging. One study examined the effects of a six-week cognitive-based compassion training programme on psychosocial functioning of adolescents in foster care. A randomised controlled trial didn't find significant benefits for the training group, but there was a significant association between higher frequency of practice and reductions in generalised anxiety as well as increased hopefulness. Qualitative findings reported high acceptability of the programme, with participants reporting that the programme was very helpful generally and also describing instances of managing stressful situations more skilfully as well as relating to others in a more compassionate manner.

Prosocial Behaviour

However, compassion is not the only emotion that can lead to prosocial behaviour. Research shows that compassion can be considered in a cluster of emotions including also gratitude and awe which encourage prosocial behaviour (van Kleef & Lelieveld, 2022). The same authors say that these emotions are self-transcending because they lead to a change in focus from one's own needs and desires to others' needs. Indeed, research suggests that gratitude increases helping behaviours, compassion and awe predict behaviours such as helping and generosity (van Kleef & Lelieveld, 2022).

Across these different emotions and behaviours, *prosocial behaviour* is often described as behaviour that benefits others (Dunfield & Kuhlmeier, 2013). It has been proposed that prosocial behaviour has an evolutionary purpose in supporting cooperation and collaboration for the sake of survival (Cronin, 2012). Some researchers highlighted the importance of prosocial behaviour not only from an individual perspective, but also its importance across societal contexts, including workplace, community and even relations between nations (Helliwell et al., 2017).

There are various *types of prosocial behaviour* sharing, helping, comforting, informing, and cooperating (Dunfield & Kuhlmeier, 2013) and they show different developmental trajectories. For example, simple actions of cooperating appear as early as in the second year of life. Other forms of prosocial behaviour including sharing and helping develop a bit later, but are already manifesting around the time children start primary school. Generally, prosocial behaviour gradually increases during childhood.

Key Terms: Prosocial Behaviour, its Types and Differences in Motivation

- *Prosocial behaviour* is the kind of behaviour that benefits others and it has been linked to better MHW. It is the also the foundation for cooperation and

> collaboration that support survival, so prosocial behaviour may have evolutionary advantages.
> - *Types of prosocial behaviour* are sharing, helping, comforting, informing, and cooperating. They show different developmental trajectories.
> - *Egoistic motivation* for prosocial behaviour drives the behaviour due to goals such as receiving praise or to behave in a socially desirable way.
> - *Altruistic motivation* for prosocial behaviour drives the behaviour due to genuine concern for, or appreciation of, others arising from prosocial emotions such as compassion, gratitude and awe.

Prosocial behaviour can be motivated by ego-centred tendencies (to receive praise or to behave in desirable or normative ways) or arise from a genuine concern for others (compassion) or appreciation of others (gratitude or awe). Based on this motivation distinction, some researchers differentiate between prosocial behaviour with its different motivations and kindness which always arises from genuine compassionate concern for others (Malti & Dys, 2018). Latest research suggests that social foundations of prosocial behaviour seem to form as early as during the first year. For example, 6 months of children have been shown to prefer those who help others to those who interfere with other's goals, and fairness expectations seem to start developing during the second half of the first year (Malti & Dys, 2018).

Importantly, prosociality has been linked to better MHW. For example, a recent study from Canada with children in grades 4-7 found that higher levels of prosocial behaviour at the start of a school year were significantly related to higher optimism and lower depression symptoms at the end of the school year (Oberle at al., 2023). Research during early childhood also showed that better self-regulation can predict higher rates of prosociality (Williams & Berthelsen, 2017) exemplifying links across the self-regulation and self-world capacities. In adolescence, prosociality has been associated with better quality of life (Son & Padilla-Walker, 2020). And research with adults showed that prosocial behaviour such as volunteering is associated with lower mental distress, better quality of life (Mak et al., 2022) and even lower rate of experiences of physical pain (Macchia et al., 2023).

> Questions for reflection:
> - Can you describe the differences between empathy, empathic distress and compassion in relation to MHW?
> - Why is prosocial behaviour relevant to MHW?
> - What are the different types of prosocial behaviour and motivation behind them?

Neuroscience of Making a Difference

The processes in the brain underpinning empathy, compassion and prosocial behaviour are intertwined in some regards and distinct in others. To start with, when considering the neural processes of empathy, it can be useful to distinguish between two aspects of empathy – the cognitive aspect and the affective aspect. The cognitive aspect entails understanding how others' feel, including thinking about others' thoughts and feelings. These processes might remind you of the perspective taking we discussed in relation to shared humanity (Chapter 7). Just like perspective taking, cognitive empathy is underpinned mostly by the mentalising network.

In contrast, affective empathy involves 'feeling' others' emotions. This involves 'mirroring' others' bodily aspects of emotions too. Therefore, one of the key regions involved in affective empathy are insula – particularly their subregion called anterior insula. Among the other regions empathy activates is a part of the ACC – the dorsal ACC (dACC) – involved in noticing emotions. Activating together, the dACC and anterior insula form what some researchers call the empathy network (Fan et al., 2011).

Interestingly, the processes in the mind and brain underpinning cognitive and affective empathy separate during childhood. This involves gradual separation of the mentalising and empathy networks. By the age of three, these two networks are already distinctively activated in children (Richardson et al., 2018) and this process continues during childhood development.

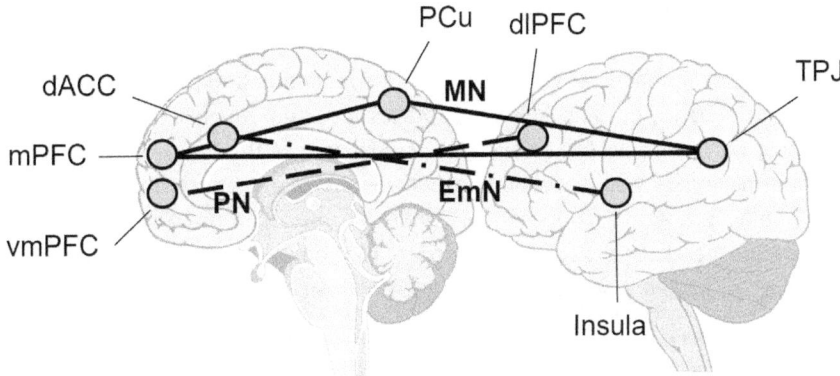

Figure 9.1 Neuroscience of making a difference. MN - Mentalising network: mPFC - medial Prefrontal Cortex, PCu - Precuneus, TPJ - Temporoparietal Junction; EmN - Empathy network: dACC - dorsal Anterior Cingulate Cortex, Insula; PN: Prosocial network: vmPFC - ventromedial Prefrontal Cortex, dlPFC - dorsolateral Prefrontal Cortex.

Source: adapted with permission from Dorjee (2024)

> **Key Neuroscience Terms for Making a Difference**
>
> - The ACC and PFC help us differentiate between empathy, empathic distress, compassion and different types of prosocial behaviours.
> - The empathy network involves the insula (particularly anterior insula), the ACC (particularly dACC) and other brain regions. Together with activation of the mentalising network including the TPJ, the network underpins experiences of empathy and empathic distress.
> - The prosocial network involves ventromedial PFC (vmPFC), dorsolateral PFC (dlPFC) and other brain regions that support planning, decision making and putting plans into action. It underpins prosocial behaviours.
> - The brain regions of the prosocial network linked to action planning are also activated in compassion, together with areas of the reward network including the VS since compassion is a positive emotion.
> - The vmPFC is activated both as part of the prosocial network and as part of the reward network, pointing to overlaps in some functions between the two networks.

And while empathy can be the basis for compassion, neuroscience research also shows that compassion activates a different set of brain regions. In contrast to empathy, compassion tends to activate brain areas of the reward network, including the VS. This is because compassion is associated with positive social connections and positive emotions (Singer & Klimecki, 2014). In addition, compassion tends to activate brain regions linked to action planning – this corresponds to the intentional and motivational components of compassion signalling readiness to help.

With regard to this 'readiness to help' aspect involving action planning, compassion is close to prosocial behaviour and is often its precursor or emotional aspect. Therefore, it is not surprising that prosocial behaviour activates regions in the brain involved in planning and decision making as well 'execution' of behavioural plans. These, for example, involve actions of helping, sharing, cooperation, comforting etc. The brain regions particularly highlighted in research on prosociality are parts of the PFC – the vmPFC and dlPFC – and are considered to form the prosocial network (Bellucci et al., 2020).

> **The Empathy Network, Prosocial Network and Developing Skills of Making a Difference in the Classroom**
>
> Now that Lee knows the difference between empathy, empathic distress and compassion, together with the underpinning neuroscience, he can understand better why some pupils in his class become upset when he is teaching them empathy skills. Lee is aware that the brain activity in the empathy network does not directly link to positive emotions. However, he also knows that expanding empathy towards compassion can

activate the reward network including the VS, and this is linked to positive emotions that can support MHW. And compassion can in turn lead to activation of the prosocial network underpinning prosocial behaviour that can also support children's MHW.

Based on this understanding, Lee has started to incorporate compassion practices into his teaching whenever he is guiding pupils in his class to relate to others or situations from an empathic perspective. He has also included some simple neuroscience explanations of the differences between empathy and compassion in his teaching.

In addition, Lee is now systematically fostering children's prosocial behaviour in the classroom and encouraging his pupils to notice how these behaviours make them feel and how they make others feel. This may motivate children to engage in such behaviours out of altruistic rather than egoistic motivation. He is also using references to the prosocial network to further motivate students in recognising and practising such behaviours. Lee is starting to see greater engagement in these behaviours from pupils and initial benefits to their MHW as a result of these changes.

How Can Children Acquire the Knowledge and Skills of Making a Difference?

Given the rapid development of self-regulation, perspective taking, empathy, and prosociality during childhood, supporting development of the relevant skills underpinning the Facet of Making a Difference can be particularly important and impactful in this age group. The acquisition of the relevant knowledge and skills can start with learning the differences between empathy, compassion and prosocial behaviour in an age-appropriate way with increasingly nuanced learning progressing with age. Based on story, cartoon and movie examples children can start learning about these three concepts and differences between them in an impersonal manner. In this context, children can be introduced to the notion of empathic distress as well and provided with examples of how empathic distress can be countered through compassion and prosocial action. Children can also learn to distinguish between different kinds of prosocial behaviours and those in KS2 can start distinguishing between ego-centred and altruistic motivation behind prosocial behaviour. Throughout learning about empathy, empathic distress, compassion and prosociality from examples children are encouraged to recognise how these emotions and behaviours link to MHW.

Random Acts of Kindness

After acquiring the foundational knowledge about empathy, empathic distress, compassion and prosocial behaviour based on examples, children can start recognising these emotions and behaviours in their own experience. This can be accomplished through group activities guided by teachers first and then prompts to recognise these emotions and behaviours in everyday situations. In the next step, children are encouraged to begin noticing links between these emotions and behaviours and their MHW. Again, this can be first encouraged through non-probing group activities progressing onto application of compassion and prosocial behaviour in everyday situations throughout the school day and also outside of school. Children in KS2 can be encouraged to reflect in writing on their experiences of compassion and prosociality in relation to MHW.

Further learning of these emotions and behaviours can be encouraged through activities such as Random Acts of Kindness (RAK) wall – where children can everyday add Post-it notes on a poster in the classroom briefly describing any instances of compassion and prosocial behaviour they have done on one side and instances where they received compassion and prosocial/kind behaviour from others on the other side. The teacher can review the RAKs of the day everyday with children at the end of the day. In this process, modelling of these emotions and behaviours by the teacher and other school staff will be a key tool in enabling children to recognise and internalise these emotions and behaviours.

Key Strategies for Fostering Skills of Making a Difference

- Random Acts of Kindness (RAK) is an activity encouraging children to recognise instances of compassion and prosocial behaviour they engaged in and received from others. It can be done via RAK wall where children place Post-it notes every day or via logs and diaries older children can write.
- Ripples of Agency is an activity cultivating compassion and prosocial behaviour by guiding children to draw a trail of impact of their acts of kindness on others. This can enable children to recognise how making a small kind act has a ripple effect on others beyond the immediate beneficiary of their action.
- Compassion practices encourage children to recognise differences between empathy, empathetic distress and compassion, and to expand empathy towards compassion by exploring children's feelings of willingness to help and ways of making a difference.

Ripples of Agency

Ripples of Agency (making a difference) is another activity cultivating compassion and prosocial behaviour. Children can draw a trail of impact of their acts of kindness on others, enabling them to recognise how making a small kind act to one person has a ripple effect on others the person encounters and then their contacts, environment etc. This can make children realise the scale of impact their positive actions can have in real life. The activity can be, for example, centred around children recycling their rubbish every day and drawing how the recycled material is made into other things and how it would otherwise end up polluting the environment. Another activity could be about children being kind to a friend and how it changed the day for the friend and the way the friend then related to others making a wider difference. This activity could also be done for a volunteer project children engage in as a group focusing on immediate and wider connections the project impacted.

Compassion Practices

To start with, it is important that children first develop the skills outlined in the self-regulation capacity and previous facets of the self-world capacity to provide grounding for working with emotions that relate to empathic distress and compassion in a safe and non-triggering way. Some of the activities could involve 'spot the difference' encouraging children to find the differences between empathic distress and compassion in examples from stories, cartoons or real life. Other activities could involve relating to news reported on Newsround in a compassionate way linked to prosocial action where relevant.

Here are further suggestions for activities cultivating compassion for primary school children based on Jazaieri (2019) and expanded toward prosocial action. For example, activities involving talking about compassion in response to an event or story could involve questions about what the character/person experienced (cognitive component), sharing how they felt (and recognising the felt sense within their physical bodies, affective component), sharing if they had a wish for the other person (in the case of compassion for others, intentional component), and whether they felt like they wanted to do something to help (motivational component) and what it was they could do to make a difference. Children could also look up or draw images of what compassion and making a difference looks like.

Developmental Differences in Fostering the Knowledge and Skills of Making a Difference

As with activities in all the preceding facets there is a developmental progression in cultivating the skills of empathy, compassion and prosociality. In younger children the activities could focus on recognising that when others are happy we often also feel happy and when others are upset or sad that can make us feel upset or sad too. This can then be expanded to compassion by exploring ways we can wish for the other person to feel better and then prosociality through ways we might be able to contribute to improving the situation. Children in KS1 can start learning the labels 'empathy', 'compassion' and 'acts of kindness' in relation to relevant emotions and behaviour noticed first in examples then in everyday situations in the classroom. They can also start distinguishing basic types of prosocial behaviours (acts of kindness) such as sharing, helping and working together (cooperating). Children are encouraged to recognise more frequent instances of empathy, compassion and acts of kindness and how these make use feel (impact on MHW).

Children in KS2 can be explicitly introduced to the concept of empathic distress, in addition to the concepts of empathy, compassion and acts of kindness (prosociality). The phrase 'making a difference' can also be used to describe prosocial behaviour. Children can also be encouraged to recognise a wider range of prosocial behaviours including helping, sharing, cooperating and also comforting, informing, being generous, volunteering etc. Quizzes (explorative not evaluative) of the 'spot the difference' type could be used to teach children recognise the distinctive features of these emotions and behaviours based on examples. Throughout this learning children are encouraged to recognise how empathy, empathic distress, compassion and acts of kindness make the characters (and then themselves) feel, relating these emotions and behaviours to supporting characters' (and then their own) MHW. In addition, children can explore differences in acts of kindness and how they make us feel based on motivation behind them, doing something out of duty versus doing something because it feels right to do it and one is motivated to genuinely help others without considering reward.

Acquiring the Knowledge and Skills of Making a Difference: The 7-Step Approach

Just like with previous building blocks of the ATTEND Pyramid, children will first acquire the knowledge of making a difference and then associated skills which they will be able to apply in supporting their MW. The first three knowledge steps will focus on teaching children about similarities and differences between empathy, empathic distress, compassion and prosocial behaviour, including underpinning brain processes. They will also learn about ways these qualities can be fostered based on external examples. Next, children will start applying this knowledge in their experience, exploring how fostering these different qualities may support their MHW. In the final step, they are encouraged to use the newly learned strategies of making a difference in everyday life to strengthen their MHW.

Step 1: Learning How Empathy, Compassion and Prosocial Behaviour Relate to MHW

The learning objective of the first step is for children to acquire knowledge that will enable them to understand, based on examples, the differences between empathy, empathic distress, compassion and prosocial behaviour (acts of kindness) and how these emotions and behaviours can support MHW.

In *reception*, children begin to understand, using examples from cartoons or stories, basic differences between empathy (feeling with someone), compassion (wanting to help them) and prosocial behaviour (doing something to help them).

To develop such knowledge, the teacher can use drawings of situations (possibly stills from a cartoon), in three columns, corresponding to empathy, compassion and prosocial behaviour. Simple words like 'caring', 'wanting to help' and 'helping' can be used as age-appropriate names for the categories of empathy, compassion and prosocial behaviour. Or symbols for each of the three categories can be used instead. Then children can try, with support, to sort further stills from other cartoons into the three categories (columns). They start recognising that wanting to help and helping can make us and the other person feel better.

In *KS1* children are able to understand more readily, based on examples and with support, the differences between empathy, compassion and prosocial behaviour. They can also begin to understand what empathic distress means, such as when we feel sad because someone else is sad. They learn that we can feel better and we can help the other person feel better if we want to help them and do something to help them. To foster this knowledge, the teacher can tell children a story and use two puppets, with one experiencing some difficulty and the other experiencing empathy, compassion and engaging in prosocial behaviour. The teacher can use age-appropriate descriptions of the three categories, similar to those in reception. Children then work in small groups, with support, to recognise the three categories of feelings and behaviour in the story example themselves. They practise using further examples the teacher provides. With support, they also start recognising how the three categories of feelings and behaviour made the two characters feel.

In the *lower KS2* children are able to understand based on examples almost independently differences between empathy, empathic distress, compassion and prosocial behaviour. They also recognise mostly independently how these emotions can impact the way one feels. To develop this knowledge, the teacher can use an example from a story or a movie demonstrating the differences between empathy, empathic distress, compassion and prosocial behaviour. The teacher can use visual prompts, showing 'the chain reaction' from empathy, through empathic distress, to compassion and prosocial behaviour. The teacher can briefly describe on the board in four columns corresponding to the four concepts how these emotions and behaviour manifested in the example story or movie. Children can then work in small groups with a new story or short video clip trying to identify the situations corresponding to the four categories. They try to briefly describe these themselves, with some support from teaching staff. They also start recognising how these emotions made the characters feel. They can use the Pleasantness of Emotion Scale and Intensity of Emotion Scale to quantify this if helpful.

Finally, in the *upper KS2* children are able to understand independently, based on examples, the differences between empathy, empathic distress, compassion and prosocial behaviour. They are able to use these terms in describing examples of the corresponding emotions and behaviour in examples. They also recognise the impacts of these emotions and behaviour on MHW in the examples. To cultivate this knowledge, the teacher can show children examples from public life, such as from sports, that demonstrate the differences between empathy, empathic distress, compassion and prosocial behaviour. Children then come up with their own examples they witnessed in public life – sports, movies etc. They share these examples in pairs learning from each other about the differences between the three emotions and prosocial behaviour. They can also write a brief description of the examples, circling or highlighting examples of empathy, empathic distress, compassion and prosocial behaviour in their writing. Then they explore how the three emotions and prosocial behaviour impacted the characters in their examples, recognising links to MHW. They can use the Pleasantness and Intensity of Emotion Graph to quantify the differences.

Step 2: Learning about Different Types of Prosocial Behaviour and Motivation Behind Them

The learning objective in the second step is for children to acquire the knowledge that will enable them to understand and distinguish from examples a range of prosocial behaviour types and start to recognise differences in motivation (egoistic versus altruistic) behind prosocial behaviour and their impacts on our MHW.

 In *reception* children begin to understand with support and based on examples, that there are different types of caring behaviours – such as sharing, comforting and assisting with some activity. They also start recognising how these different behaviours make the one helping and the one being helped feel. To foster this knowledge, the teacher can use the cartoon examples shown to children in the first step and add further cartoon examples with the same characters demonstrating a wider range of prosocial behaviours. Teacher clearly identifies the different types of 'helping behaviour' in the examples. Children then, with support, work with the same examples identifying the different types of 'helping behaviours' themselves. When they are familiar with those examples, the teacher provides a new example and children then work with the new example to solidify their understanding. The teacher also reminds children that these behaviours can make the person helping and the person being helped feel good.

 In *KS1* children are able to understand more readily with guidance that there are different types of 'helping behaviours' – including sharing, comforting, assisting with some activity and informing. They also understand more readily from examples that engaging in such behaviours can make the person helping and the person being helped feel good. The teacher can expand on the previous story examples used in Step 1 and demonstrate the different types of 'helping behaviours'. Children then practise recognising the different types of behaviours in the examples provided and new examples the teacher provides. The teacher can make a poster depicting the four types of 'helping behaviours' and children keep on referring to it when discussing the examples in small groups. They also practise recognising how the person helping and the one being helped felt from before to after the 'helping behaviour'. They can use the Feels Good Scale and Emotion Strength Scale to quantify this.

 In the *lower KS2*, children are able to distinguish in examples mostly independently the different types of prosocial behaviour – sharing, helping, comforting, informing, and cooperating. They are also able to link the emotional effects of these behaviours – on the one acting prosocially and the benefactor – mostly independently. To cultivate this knowledge, the teacher can expand on the movie/video clip or story examples from the first step and exemplify to children the different types of prosocial behaviour. The teacher can write down the different categories of prosocial behaviour on the board. Children then work in small groups to identify the different types of prosocial behaviour in new examples of video clips or stories, with some support from the teaching staff. Children then practise recognising how these behaviours

made the person helping and the recipient feel. They can use the Pleasantness of Emotion Scale and Intensity of Emotion Scale in quantifying the change from before to after the prosocial behaviour, if helpful.

In the *upper KS2*, children are able to understand independently from examples that there are different types of prosocial behaviour, including sharing, helping, comforting, informing, and cooperating. Children also start exploring different motivations behind the behaviours – egoistic versus altruistic. Then they learn about the effects of these behaviours on MHW and can link this to the different types of motivation too (altruistic motivation having stronger positive effects).

To develop this knowledge, as in the first step the teacher can use examples from public life to demonstrate the different types of behaviours. The teacher can write down the names of the different categories on the board or place a poster on the classroom wall. Next, the teacher describes how the behaviours made the person acting prosocially and the benefactor feel, with references to MHW benefits and motivation behind the behaviours. Children then work to come up with their own examples of the five different categories of prosocial behaviour and share these in pairs to practise their descriptions and learn from each other. Next, they discuss the two different kinds of motivation behind the behaviours. After further discussion in the class and reassurance from the teaching staff, they can write a paragraph or two describing the different behaviours, and motivations behind them. They also describe the effects of these behaviours on MHW of the person acting prosocially and the benefactor. They can use the Pleasantness and Intensity of Emotion Graph to quantify the change from before to after the prosocial actions.

Step 3: Learning Neuroscience Underpinning Empathy, Compassion and Prosociality

The learning objective in the third step is for children to acquire the knowledge enabling them to understand what happens in the brain when we experience empathy, empathic distress, compassion and prosocial behaviour – including regions involved in emotional awareness (insula, ACC), recognising emotions (PFC), understanding others' thoughts and feelings (TPJ) and reward network regions including the VS and empathy and prosocial networks. They learn to use their neuroscience understanding in explaining the impact of these emotions and behaviours on MHW based on examples.

In *reception* children begin to understand, with support and reminders, that the brain and particularly the PFC can help us distinguish feelings of caring, wanting to help and different types of caring behaviours – including sharing, comforting and assisting with some activity. To foster this knowledge, children can now be reminded during activities where they practise distinctions between these emotions and types of behaviour to also remember that the brain and the PFC are supporting these. If the teacher is using any images for empathy, compassion and prosocial behaviours (and their types), they can now also add brain symbols to them to remind children that the brain and the PFC are involved in supporting these emotions and behaviours which can make us feel better.

In *KS1* children are able to understand more readily with support what happens in the brain when we feel empathy, empathic distress, compassion and engage in prosocial behaviours, including their different types – sharing, comforting, assisting with some activity and informing. They understand more readily that ACC, PFC, TPJ and insula help us recognise and differentiate these emotions and behaviours. They also recognise, with guidance, that the VS and the prosocial network (new term) are activated because compassion and prosocial behaviours make us feel good. To foster this knowledge, the teacher, and then children, can add brain regions to the different categories of emotions and prosocial behaviour, with ACC and PFC on the top, TPJ and insula being more involved in empathy and empathic distress and VS and prosocial network (new concept) more in compassion and prosocial behaviour. Children can also build on their neuroscience knowledge from the facet of connections.

In the *lower KS2* children can describe more independently what is happening in the brain during empathy, empathic distress, compassion and prosocial behaviours, including their types – sharing, helping, comforting, informing, and cooperating. They are also able to link descriptions of the processes in the brain to effects of these emotions and behaviours on MHW. To foster this knowledge, children can revisit the stories and video-clips they worked with previously and now try to elaborate them further by descriptions of what is happening in the brain. This can be first modelled by the teacher and then children can practise this in small groups.

Children learn that ACC and PFC help us recognise these emotions and behaviours and their effects on our MHW. They also understand that TPJ and insula are particularly involved in empathy and empathic distress – helping us understand how others are thinking and feeling. These brain regions contribute to the empathy network underpinning empathy and empathic distress. Compassion can help us counter empathic distress and together with prosocial behaviours activates brain regions including the VS and the prosocial network (new term) – these are associated with rewarding experiences. That's why compassion and prosocial behaviours make us feel good and can support our MHW.

Finally, in the *upper KS2* children can describe independently and accurately what is happening in the brain during empathy, empathic distress, compassion and prosocial behaviours – including sharing, helping, comforting, informing, and cooperating. They use references to the brain regions they learned about previously and understand that the ACC and PFC help us recognise and differentiate empathy, empathic distress, compassion and prosocial behaviours. These brain regions are also involved in distinguishing egoistic and altruistic motivation for prosocial behaviours. Furthermore, TPJ and insula are particularly involved in empathy and empathic distress as part of mentalising and empathy networks underpinning these emotions. In contrast, compassion and prosocial behaviours activate the VS, reward network and the prosocial network (new term) because they are linked to positive rewarding emotions that can support MHW. Some children may also recognise that the reward and prosocial networks partially overlap, for example, the region of vmPFC is involved in both networks.

To develop this knowledge, children can expand the writings they prepared previously – describing differences between empathy, empathic distress, compassion and prosocial behaviours and their types as well as motivations – with relevant neuroscience descriptions. Using these writings, children can then work in pairs comparing their descriptions and clarifying the differences using neuroscience descriptions to each other. They can also practise linking the brain differences to effects on MHW. Teaching staff can provide children with feedback on their writings and discussions to solidify their understanding.

Step 4: Learning Skills of Empathy, Compassion and Prosocial Behaviour

The learning objective in the fourth step is for children to develop the skills that will enable them to recognise in their own experience the differences between empathy, empathic distress, compassion and prosocial behaviour (acts of kindness) and how these impact their MHW.

In *reception* children begin to be able to recognise with support in their own experience the differences between feeling with someone (empathy), wanting to help them (compassion) and doing something to help them (prosocial behaviour). To foster these skills, the teacher can build on learning from the previous steps and use the drawings of situations (possibly stills from a cartoon) symbolising the three categories. Children can then explore in small groups, with teacher guidance, whether they ever felt like the character in the example, helping them differentiate the two emotions and prosocial behaviour. The teaching staff then helps children to start recognising each of the three categories in their own experience during everyday situations. They can also start preparing a board for recording Random Acts of Kindness (RAK) where children note some of the kind things they have done during the day (for example by placing a magnet on the board). They also start recognising how these made them feel and how they made the other person feel.

In *KS1* children are able to recognise more readily from their own experience (but still with ample guidance and support) empathy, compassion and prosocial behaviour in their own experience. They can also begin to understand in very basic terms what empathic distress means, e.g. feeling unhappy when someone else is unhappy. To cultivate these skills, the teacher can build on the previous examples from a story with puppets. Children can be invited in small groups to explore if they ever felt similar to the puppet, covering all three categories. The teaching staff then reminds children to distinguish the two emotions (and possibly empathic distress too if appropriate), in everyday situations. The classroom prepares a poster or a board for Random Act of Kindness (RAK) where they can start recording instances of being kind, for instance, there can be three different colours for magnets or symbols for empathy, compassion and prosocial behaviour. Children are also encouraged to start recognising how the RAKs made them feel. They can use the Feels Good Scale and Emotion Strength Scale to quantify this if helpful.

In the *lower KS2* children are able to recognise, almost independently, in their own experience, the differences between empathy, empathic distress, compassion and prosocial behaviour. They also recognise in their experience more independently how experiencing these different emotions and behaviours impacts their MHW. To develop these skills, children can build on the movie examples the teacher introduced in the first step and start recognising the 'chain reaction' of the emotions and behaviours in their own experience. They can also use the Pleasantness of Emotion Scale and Intensity of Emotion Scale to support their understanding of the impacts these emotions and behaviours have on them.

Next, the teacher can start the RAK poster/wall with two sides, one for RAKs that children have done themselves and the other for RAKs others have done for them. Children can add Post-it notes briefly describing the RAKs on the wall during the day. At the end of the school day children together reflect on how the RAKs during the day made them feel, both as those doing the RAKs and those receiving them. This can be done anonymously using a rating the teacher reads out and teacher can also reflect on the RAK entries for the day.

In the *upper KS2* children are able to independently recognise in their own experience the differences between empathy, empathic distress, compassion and prosocial behaviour. They are also able to describe these differences and explain from their experience how empathy, compassion and prosocial behaviours can support their MHW. To cultivate these skills, children can build on the examples of these emotions and behaviours from public life which they worked with previously. They can now start reflecting individually, possibly in writing, on whether they themselves ever experienced these emotions and behaviours. They also try to describe how empathy, compassion and prosocial behaviours made them feel, linking these emotions to their MHW. The teacher can then introduce the RAK wall where children are invited to place Post-it notes in two columns, recording the RAKs they have done and those they have received during the day. Children can then work in small groups to review the RAKs at the end of the day and discuss how the RAKs can support their MHW.

Step 5: Learning to Recognise Prosocial Behaviour Types and Their Impact on Own MHW

The learning objective in the fifth step is for children to be able to recognise in their own experience different types of prosocial behaviour and how these impact their MHW. They begin to recognise differences in motivation behind their prosocial behaviour and associated differences in impacts on their MHW these have.

In *reception* children begin to be able to recognise with support in their own experience the different types of helping behaviours - sharing, comforting and assisting with something. They also begin to recognise how these behaviours make them and the one benefiting feel. To foster these skills, children can expand on the examples from cartoons they worked with previously and start identifying the different prosocial behaviours in their own experience. They can use magnets of different shapes

or colours on the RAK board to distinguish the three types of prosocial behaviour. They also start recognising how the different RAKs make ripples - making them feel better and making the other person feel better and then expanding the impact beyond the two persons. The teacher can use a visual example of ripples expanding from some RAKs to demonstrate this and describe to children how their RAKs have similar effects.

In *KS1* children are able to recognise more readily, with guidance and support, the different types of 'helping behaviours' - including sharing, comforting, assisting with some activity and informing - in their own experience. They are also now able to see more readily from their own experience how the helping behaviours can make them and the person benefiting feel good. To develop these skills, the teacher can encourage children to use different shapes of magnets on the RAK board to distinguish the different types of prosocial behaviour. Children can also be guided to draw a picture showing the 'ripples' of their RAKs - depicting how what they did made them feel better and made the other person feel better, and how this them made both of them happier and kinder to others during the day. Children can use the Feels Good Scale and Emotion Strength Scale to make the change they created by engaging in AKRs more visible'.

In the *lower KS2* children are able to recognise, almost independently, in their own experience the different types of prosocial behaviour - sharing, helping, comforting, informing, and cooperating. They also recognise mostly independently the impact these behaviours have on their own and others' MHW. To develop these skills children can start using different colours of Post-it notes for the different categories of prosocial behaviour when placing them on the RAK poster/wall. They can also start noting briefly on the Post-it notes how the RAKs made them feel. Then the teacher can guide children in the Ripples of Agency activity, where children draw a trail of the impacts their RAKs had on themselves and others, beyond the immediate effects. This can include recognising that they were kinder, more patient, more grateful etc. during the day as a result, and how this impacted others they interacted with. They also recognise, mostly independently, the effect this has had on how they feel and how it can impact their MHW in the longer term.

In the *upper KS2* children are able to independently recognise in their own experience the different types of prosocial behaviours - sharing, helping, comforting, informing, and cooperating. They can also articulate based on their own experience how engaging in these behaviours impacted their MHW. Children are able start recognising the egoistic and altruistic motivations behind their behaviours and explore how the differences in motivation can impact how they feel.

To foster these skills, children can start sorting the different types of prosocial behaviours they note on the RAK wall into different categories, using differently coloured Post-it notes. They can also start writing in for the RAKs they engaged in the motivation behind them. They keep on reflecting on the effects RAKs, and the motivation behind them, has on their MHW in writing. Then, children are guided in the Ripples of Agency activity, where they draw the ripples of their RAKs beyond the person they benefited and themselves. They reflect on how engaging in RAKs can make them more tolerant, patient, kinder and happier during the day, impacting their further interactions with others and activities they engage in. Their teacher can now include reflections on types of prosocial behaviours and motivations behind them, as well as ripples of RAKs, in their review of the RAKs and their effects at the end of the school day.

Step 6: Learning to Apply Neuroscience Knowledge as Part of Making a Difference

The learning objective in the sixth step is for children to be able to use their understanding of the neuroscience underpinning empathy, empathic distress, compassion and prosocial behaviour in recognising these emotions and behaviour and how they impact their MHW in everyday life. They are able to use this neuroscience understanding in motivating their empathic and compassionate relating and prosocial behaviour in everyday life.

With support and guidance, children in *reception* begin to use their understanding of how the brain helps us recognise feelings of caring, wanting to help and different types of caring behaviours to motivate their engagement with these emotions and behaviours in everyday activities. To foster these skills, they are encouraged to start referring to the brain and the PFC when recognising these feelings and behaviours. They can also be reminded that feeling these emotions and engaging in caring behaviours also changes the brain and helps us feel better. The teaching staff can use references to the brain to encourage children to recognise feelings of caring and wanting to help and to engage in caring behaviours in everyday activities. To reflect this, brain symbols can be added to the RAK board.

In *KS1* children are able to use their understanding of neuroscience underpinning making a difference more readily to reinforce recognising empathy (empathic distress if relevant), compassion and prosocial behaviours in everyday activities. They also use their understanding of the brain processes to further motivate their engagement with these emotions and in prosocial behaviours, and in recognising how they make them feel. To develop these skills, children can be reminded that ACC, PFC, TPJ and insula help us recognise and differentiate empathy, compassion and prosocial behaviours. When considering how these emotions and behaviours make them feel, children can be reminded that they activate the VS and the prosocial network because these experiences are rewarding (feel good). To strengthen children's integration of neuroscience knowledge into their skills, the teacher can draw brain images and write down the names of the relevant brain regions on the RAK poster or board. Symbols can be used to designate some of the brain regions as primarily supporting recognising of emotions and behaviours and others being involved in the 'feel good' aspects of engaging in these emotions and behaviours. Children can be reminded that experiencing these emotions and behaviours also changes their brain and makes them feel better.

In the *lower KS2* children are able to use their understanding of neuroscience underpinning making a difference, mostly independently and mostly accurately, in recognising empathy, empathic distress and compassion and engaging in prosocial behaviours in everyday life. They are also able to harness their understanding of relevant brain processes in deepening their understanding of the effects these emotions and behaviours have on their MHW. To cultivate these skills, children can add to their RAK Post-it notes the brain regions that were primarily involved in the particular RAK emotion or behaviour. For example, they can note that the ACC and PFC helped them recognise the emotions and behaviours and their effects on their MHW. They can mention the TPJ, insula and the empathy network when referring to empathy on their Post-it notes and more generally to understanding others' thoughts and emotions. And when referring to compassion and prosocial behaviour experiences they can refer to the VS and prosocial network. They are able to link activation of these to the positive effects of compassion and prosocial behaviour on their MHW since these experiences feel rewarding.

Finally, in the *upper KS2* children are able use their understanding about neuroscience underpinning making a difference independently and accurately in recognising empathy, empathic distress, compassion and prosocial behaviours. They can articulate independently how engaging in these emotions links to relevant processes in the brain. They are able to relate their neuroscience understanding to the effects of these emotions and behaviours on their MHW.

To cultivate these skills, children can be encouraged to start referring to the relevant brain regions in their Post-it notes on the RAK wall. They can note down the ACC and PFC in helping them recognise the emotions and prosocial behaviours, as well as motivation behind them. They can also refer to the TPJ and insula, and mentalising and empathy networks, when writing about empathy or recognising how others are thinking or feeling. And when referring to compassion and prosocial behaviours they can also mention the VS, reward and prosocial networks, particularly when noting down how compassion and prosocial behaviours made them feel and supported their MHW. They can also start referring to the vmPFC in this context, as a region involved in both reward and prosocial networks. Children can share tips in small groups about ways they are using their neuroscience understanding in motivating their engagement in empathy, compassion and prosocial behaviours in everyday life.

Step 7: Applying Skills of Making a Difference in Everyday Life

The learning objective in the seventh step is for children to be able to apply their knowledge and skills of recognising and fostering empathy, compassion and prosocial behaviour (including its different types and motivation behind them), together with relevant neuroscience understanding, in everyday life to support their own and others' MHW in the longer term.

In *reception* children begin to apply, with support and guidance but increasingly more readily, the knowledge and skills of caring (empathy), wanting to help (compassion) and engaging in caring behaviours (prosociality), together with references to the brain and PFC, in supporting their and others' MHW in everyday situations. To foster these skills, the teaching staff can use RAK prompts during the day to encourage children to engage in these emotions and behaviours in everyday situations in school. Children are also reminded and guided to repeatedly recognise in these situations how this behaviour makes them and other's feel. Continuing with the RAK board can help maintain this behaviour until it is internalised.

 In *KS1* children are able to apply more readily, with support, the knowledge and skills of recognising and engaging in empathy, compassion and prosocial behaviours, including relevant neuroscience, in everyday situations. They also continue to deepen their experiential understanding that these emotions and behaviours can support their and others' MHW. To cultivate this integrated and more internalised knowledge and skills, children continue with the RAK poster or board activities and can be prompted in everyday situations by teaching staff to engage in these emotions and behaviours. The teacher can also encourage children to engage in RAKs outside of school and can encourage parents to support children in sustaining these skills. Classroom volunteering activities may further support transfer of these skills into everyday life.

 In the *lower KS2* children are able to apply the knowledge and skills of recognising empathy, empathic distress, compassion and engaging in prosocial behaviours – supported by their neuroscience knowledge – in everyday activities mostly independently. They can also mostly independently recognise from their own experience the benefits of fostering these emotions and behaviours to their and others' MHW. To strengthen this knowledge and skills, the teacher can encourage children to continue with the RAK posts on the RAK poster/wall, supported by once-a-day review of the RAKs led by the teacher. Children are also encouraged to kindly remind each other during the day about RAKs when relevant situations arise. The teacher encourages children to continue practising RAKs outside of school too, can involve parents in this as well. Children keep on reflecting on how RAKs are supporting their MHW and can share tips and experiences with each other.

 In the *upper KS2* children can apply the knowledge and skills of recognising empathy, empathic distress, compassion and different types of prosocial behaviours and their motivations, supported by the underpinning neuroscience knowledge, independently in everyday situations. They can also use this knowledge and corresponding skills to increase their engagement in prosocial behaviours in everyday life and can articulate the benefits this provides to their MHW. To strengthen such integrated understanding and skills, children can be

encouraged to continue posting RAKs on the class RAK wall. The teacher can include a new section on engaging in RAKs outside of school and review the responses together with the in-school RAKs at the end of the day. Children can be encouraged to kindly remind each other to engage in RAKs during the day and outside of school. At the end of the week, they can write a reflection piece on how they have been engaging with RAKs in and outside of school and how this impacted their MHW. They can also outline a plan specifying how they will continue embedding RAKs in their everyday lives.

Conclusion

Fostering knowledge and skills involving empathy, compassion and prosocial behaviour can meaningfully extend children's learning in the previous two blocks of the Nurturing Connections tier of the ATTEND Pyramid. This chapter explained why these qualities are relevant to MHW and how they can be cultivated in primary schools. If you were, just like Lee, looking for comprehensive information on how these qualities relate to MHW and how they can be fostered, this chapter may have provided you with a more comprehensive understanding. You may also be able to see more clearly why prosocial behaviour motivated by genuine concern for others, rather than behavioural expectations, is more beneficial to children's MHW. Perhaps you are now in a position to explore implementing some of the strategies that can foster empathy, compassion and prosocial behaviour in your classroom systematically, step-by-step to strengthen your pupils' MHW.

Key chapter points:

- While empathy can benefit children's MHW, particularly in terms of reducing antisocial behaviour, it can also lead to empathic distress.
- Expanding empathy to compassion can increase benefits of empathy to children's MHW.
- Engaging in prosocial behaviour can also support children's MHW, particularly if it arises from genuine altruistic motivation to help.
- Neuroscience research shows that compassion and prosociality, unlike empathy, are underpinned by activity in the reward and prosocial networks that are linked to positive emotions and action planning.
- Activities such as Random Acts of Kindness and Ripples of Agency can support children's development of compassion and prosociality.
- Children can systematically acquire knowledge and skills of empathy, compassion and prosociality via the 7-Step-Approach in an age-appropriate way.

References

Bellucci, G., Camilleri, J. A., Eickhoff, S. B., & Krueger, F. (2020). Neural signatures of prosocial behaviors. *Neuroscience & Biobehavioral Reviews*, *118*, 186-195.

Calandri, E., Graziano, F., Cattelino, E., & Testa, S. (2021). Depressive symptoms and loneliness in early adolescence: the role of empathy and emotional self-efficacy. *The Journal of Early Adolescence*, *41*(3), 369-393.

Craig, C., Hiskey, S., & Spector, A. (2020). Compassion focused therapy: a systematic review of its effectiveness and acceptability in clinical populations. *Expert Review of Neurotherapeutics*, *20*(4), 385-400.

Cronin, K. A. (2012). Prosocial behaviour in animals: the influence of social relationships, communication and rewards. *Animal Behaviour*, *84*(5), 1085-1093.

Dorjee, D. (2024). Conceptualising child and adolescent mental health and wellbeing neurodevelopment: an integrative brain networks framework. Preprint, 4 November. https://doi.org/10.31234/osf.io/7vx45

Dunfield, K. A., & Kuhlmeier, V. A. (2013). Classifying prosocial behavior: children's responses to instrumental need, emotional distress, and material desire. *Child Development*, *84*(5), 1766-1776.

Fan, Y., Duncan, N. W., De Greck, M., & Northoff, G. (2011). Is there a core neural network in empathy? An fMRI based quantitative meta-analysis. *Neuroscience & Biobehavioral Reviews*, *35*(3), 903-911.

Foerster, K., & Kanske, P. (2021). Exploiting the plasticity of compassion to improve psychotherapy. *Current Opinion in Behavioral Sciences*, *39*, 64-71.

Frick, P. J., & Kemp, E. C. (2021). Conduct disorders and empathy development. *Annual Review of Clinical Psychology*, *17*(1), 391-416.

Frydenberg, E., & Lewis, R. (2009). Relations among well-being, avoidant coping, and active coping in a large sample of Australian adolescents. *Psychological Reports*, *104*(3), 745-758.

Helliwell, J. F., Aknin, L. B., Shiplett, H., Huang, H., & Wang, S. (2017). Social capital and prosocial behaviour as sources of well-being. www.nber.org/system/files/working_papers/w23761/w23761.pdf.

Jazaieri, H. (2018). Compassionate education from preschool to graduate school: bringing a culture of compassion into the classroom. *Journal of Research in Innovative Teaching & Learning*, *11*(1), 22-66.

Klimecki, O.M., Leiberg, S., Ricard, M., and Singer, T. (2014). Differential pattern of functional brain plasticity after compassion and empathy training. *Social Cognitive and Affective Neuroscience*, *9*, 873-879.

Leaviss, J., & Uttley, L. (2015). Psychotherapeutic benefits of compassion-focused therapy: an early systematic review. *Psychological Medicine*, *45*(5), 927-945.

Leiberg, S., Klimecki, O., and Singer, T. (2011). Short-term compassion training increases prosocial behaviour in a newly developed prosocial game. *PLoS One*, *6*, e17798.

Macchia, L., Farmer, J., & Kubzansky, L. D. (2023). Prosocial behaviour helps to ease physical pain: longitudinal evidence from Britain. *Journal of Psychosomatic Research*, *169*, 111325.

Mak, H. W., Coulter, R., & Fancourt, D. (2022). Relationships between volunteering, neighbourhood deprivation and mental wellbeing across four British birth cohorts: evidence from 10 years of the UK household longitudinal study. *International Journal of Environmental Research and Public Health*, *19*(3), 1531.

Malti, T., & Dys, S. P. (2018). From being nice to being kind: development of prosocial behaviors. *Current Opinion in Psychology*, *20*, 45-49.

Oberle, E., Ji, X. R., & Molyneux, T. M. (2023). Pathways from prosocial behaviour to emotional health and academic achievement in early adolescence. *The Journal of Early Adolescence*, *43*(5), 632-653.

Richardson, H., Lisandrelli, G., Riobueno-Naylor, A., & Saxe, R. (2018). Development of the social brain from age three to twelve years. *Nature Communications*, *9*(1), 1027.

Singer, T., & Klimecki, O. M. (2014). Empathy and compassion. *Current Biology*, *24*(18), R875-R878.

Son, D., & Padilla-Walker, L. M. (2020). Happy helpers: a multidimensional and mixed-method approach to prosocial behavior and its effects on friendship quality, mental health, and well-being during adolescence. *Journal of Happiness Studies*, *21*(5), 1705-1723.

Supervía, P. U., Bordás, C. S., Robres, A. Q., Blasco, R. L., & Cosculluela, C. L. (2023). Empathy, self-esteem and satisfaction with life in adolescent. *Children and Youth Services Review*, *144*, 106755.

Van Kleef, G. A., & Lelieveld, G. J. (2022). Moving the self and others to do good: the emotional underpinnings of prosocial behavior. *Current Opinion in Psychology, 44*, 80-88.

Williams, K. E., & Berthelsen, D. (2017). The development of prosocial behaviour in early childhood: contributions of early parenting and self-regulation. *International Journal of Early Childhood, 49*, 73-94.

Zhang, Q., Zhou, Y., & Ho, S. M. (2022). Active and avoidant coping profiles in children and their relationship with anxiety and depression during the COVID-19 pandemic. *Scientific Reports, 12*(1), 13430.

PART IV
Finding Direction

10 Purpose in Life and Self-Concept

Introduction

Now that we have built up the first three tiers of the ATTEND Pyramid, the final tier focuses on Finding Direction in life. The first building block of this tier aims to foster knowledge and skills that can enable children to understand what purpose in life is and how having a purpose in life can support their MHW. In acquiring such knowledge and skills, children consider what their strengths are and what causes they may want to contribute to using their strengths. They also learn to distinguish intrinsic and extrinsic goals and their effects on their mental health and wellbeing (MHW). Finally, they start to explore their sense of self, developing an understanding that they can use what they have learned about themselves across facets in developing a healthy flexible sense of self, which is the last building block of the ATTEND Pyramid. Altogether, children learn to recognise how having intrinsic goal-directedness in life aligned with their values and self-concept can support their MHW and ways to cultivate it.

The chapter starts with a review of research explaining the prominent role of purpose in life in our MHW. In relation to purpose in life, we will also examine research showing that having a flexible sense of self can support one's MHW. This understanding is further expanded by considerations about the processes in the brain underpinning purpose in life and self-concept that closely overlap with the processes in the previous tiers of the ATTEND Pyramid. Next, the chapter outlines ways purpose in life can be cultivated in primary school children in age-appropriate ways and foster development of a healthy flexible self-concept. Finally, the chapter provides a detailed overview of how purpose in life can be cultivated in primary schools across age groups following the 7-Step Approach and support children's self-concept development. But first, let's consider the following case study, exemplifying how questions about supporting children in developing a sense of purpose in life and a healthy sense of self can arise in the primary school classroom.

Case Study: Exploring Strengths, Intrinsic and Extrinsic Values, and Purpose in Life

Zoey is a year 5 teacher in her primary school. She recently read an article in the news explaining that young people often lack direction in life and educators should do more to help children find a sense of purpose and healthy self-identity. When looking online for ways to do this in her classroom, she found very little relevant information. But she was surprised to learn that having a strong purpose in life can support MHW in adults. She is wondering if this applies to children too.

Yet, Zoey has some doubts about teaching children in primary schools about purpose in life. It seems to her that this is a topic that is more relevant to adults or possibly to secondary school pupils who are exploring who they want to be, their identity. She is wondering if primary school children have the cognitive capacities to be able to understand what purpose in life is and learn about ways they can cultivate it.

Zoey is also curious about how purpose in life links to cultivating universal values in children. For example, she knows that some children want to become famous and rich, based on the content they have been engaging with online. She is concerned that such ideals may not be healthy and that she should steer children towards more grounded goals in life that can support their MHW. However, Zoey is not sure how exactly she can teach children about this.

Finally, Zoey has been wondering about links between purpose in life and children's self-identity. She noticed that some children seem to 'get stuck' on what others may tell them, particularly when it comes to what could be seen as their 'weaknesses'. This way some children seem to have already internalised that they are 'lazy' or 'clumsy'. Zoey thinks that it is good to be aware of one's weaknesses but also finds some of these perceptions children develop limiting. This could impact on how children view their purpose in life and Zoey would like to know more about ways to work with such perceptions.

Questions for reflection:

- Do you think purpose in life is relevant to MHW?
- Do you think pupils in primary schools are able to engage in learning about purpose in life?
- How would you teach children in your classroom about purpose in life and corresponding skills linked to their self-concept?

How Are Purpose in Life and Self-Concept Relevant to MHW?

Greater sense of purpose in life is a strong protective factor of MHW, and can even be beneficial to physical health. Some studies with adults found that those who have a strong sense of purpose in life have better cardiovascular health, immune system response and live longer (Cohen et al., 2016). Therefore, it is not surprising that purpose in life is one of the dimensions of psychological wellbeing (Ryff, 1989). This is one of the leading wellbeing theories building on Aristotle's concept eudaimonia – state of flourishing arising from leading a virtuous purposeful life as a way of fulfilling one's potential.

The role of purpose in life in MHW is even more central to one of the traditional approaches in psychotherapy. Logotherapy, formulated by Victor Frankl, suggests that humans have a natural tendency to find meaning and purpose in life called 'will to meaning'. Frankl observed that people who lack sense of purpose and meaning in life are much more likely to suffer from depression and anxiety. He also suggested that having a strong sense of purpose in life is a key protective factor during times of personal crises (e.g. serious illness) and wider societal crises such as war – enabling survival under difficult circumstances.

Intrinsic and Extrinsic Values

While meaning in life is about making sense of human existence, purpose in life is more about specific goals one strives towards in life. Sources of purpose and meaning in life can range from personal goals, for example in terms of career or relationships, to contributions to causes such as sustainability, reduction of disease, improvement of living conditions or addressing inequalities. People can also find a sense of purpose in life by connecting with something greater than oneself in a spiritual sense, giving their lives a direction.

Interestingly, the types of goals we choose to strive for matter to our MHW. A recent study compared the relationship between intrinsic goals, which are aligned with eudaimonia, and extrinsic goals in relation to MHW. While intrinsic goals include focus on personal growth, giving to the community and good relationships, extrinsic goals involve striving for wealth, fame and beauty. The findings showed that intrinsic goals are linked to better MHW, whereas extrinsic goals showed the opposite pattern. This was a robust study, the researchers looked at patterns of evidence in over 100 studies, including studies with adolescents, conducted over the past 30 years (Bradshaw et al., 2023).

Purpose in Life in Children

Research in children and adolescents mirrors the positive effects of having a purpose in life reported in adults. For example, a sense of contributing to something greater than oneself has been linked to better wellbeing in adolescents, including reduced symptoms of depression and risk taking behaviour (Cotton et al., 2005). Other studies linked greater sense of purpose in life with greater optimism and resilience in adolescents. In addition, adolescents who have greater sense of purpose beyond self (such as getting into a caring profession) were more likely to persist on a boring learning task and have better academic results (Yeager et al., 2014).

While research on purpose in life in children is much less extensive than in adults or adolescents, initial studies with primary school children also support the protective effects of having a purpose in life. A recent study which also validated a self-report measure of meaning in life in children showed that those with greater sense of meaning/purpose also experienced more positive emotions, less social and emotional difficulties and displayed more prosocial behaviours. The study also reported gender differences, girls had higher self-reported levels of sense of meaning/purpose in life than boys (Shoshani & Russo-Netzer, 2017).

And a recent study showed that meaning/purpose in life and MHW are positively associated even in 3-6-year-olds. The findings indicated that children at this young age are already able to articulate their sense of meaning/purpose in life. The results also showed that sense of meaning/purpose increases with age and is enabled by development of theory of mind – the ability to reflect on one's own and others' thoughts and emotions (fostered in the tier of Nurturing Connections). Stronger sense of meaning/purpose in life was in this study linked to secure attachment of children, better socio-emotional functioning and wellbeing, and greater sense of meaning/purpose of their parents.

Flexible Self-Concept

There are various ways to describe what self-concept or sense of self is, but one of the latest approaches applied in MHW research likens the self to a pattern of our experiences, memories, thoughts, emotions, and ways we perceive and relate to others, society, culture etc. This approach is described as the Pattern Theory of Self (PTS) (Daly & Gallagher, 2019). Importantly, when our self-pattern is rigid and we persist in our ways of thinking, emotionally experiencing and responding even when they are not helpful, this can undermine our MHW. In contrast, when we are able to reflect on our sense of self (who we are) and recognise aspects of ourselves that are helpful and other aspects that we may want to change because they are unhelpful, and work on changing these, this has been linked to a flexible sense of self and better MHW.

> ### Key Terms
>
> - *Purpose in life* describes specific goals one strives towards in life.
> - *Flexible self-concept* refers to the ability to recognise that we can change some aspects of ourselves if we want to and develop some qualities that can support us in moving towards our purpose in life.
> - *Extrinsic values* describe goals in life that depend on others' approval such as fame, wealth and beauty. Striving to achieve extrinsic goals has been linked to poor MHW.
> - *Intrinsic values* describe goals in life that are more within our control, are linked to accomplishing our potential and making a virtuous contribution to society. These are goals such as personal growth, giving to the community and good relationships. Intrinsic goals are linked to good MHW.

Indeed, research shows that rigidity in the pattern of self has been linked with disruptions in some of the aspects of self (e.g. perceptions of one self as defective or unchangeable) and perseverance in associated affective, cognitive, behavioural patterns even when such a pattern of self is maladaptive and undermine one's MHW (Morris & Mansell, 2018). For some mental health disorders the inflexibility of self is particularly salient. In research with adults, an inflexible sense of self has been specifically linked to depression (Daly & Gallagher, 2019), complex trauma (Giommi et al., 2023) and addiction disorders (Garland et al., 2022). In contrast, having a flexible self-pattern characterised by the ability to recognise unhelpful aspects of self and shift them has been linked to positive changes in MHW during psychological interventions (Giommi et al., 2023).

Flexible Self-Concept in Children

While the notion of a flexible sense of self as a transdiagnostic mechanism underpinning MHW is new, the observation that perceiving one's thoughts and emotions as persistent reflections of who one is can undermine MHW has been extensively discussed in psychotherapy before. For example, Martin Seligman (2018), the founder of positive psychology, explained in his book 'The Optimistic Child' that attributing failures and general perception of experiences and thoughts as pervasive and permanent are the main reasons for children's learned helplessness which can lead to poor MHW.

Children often internalise their perceptions of who they are based on what those they have close relationships with tell them. This includes parents, siblings, other family members but also teachers, peers and role models. In this way, children can start perceiving themselves as clever, lazy, trouble-makers or funny. While such attributions are a part of children's identity development, they can also result in an inflexible sense of self if they are reinforced and children are not offered opportunities to reflect on who they are – what their strengths are and what aspects of themselves they may want to work on.

This can be closely related to children's sense of purpose in life. Children often follow a path of purpose that is expected of them, based on who their parents/caregivers want them to be, particularly when it comes to their professions. Enabling children to recognise their strengths and exploring a sense of purpose that they are passionate about, particularly one that is linked to intrinsic values, is essential both for supporting them in finding direction in life and for supporting their MHW.

While purpose in life and sense of self is rarely discussed in the primary school context, some recent interventions showed that a healthy self-concept can be fostered in schools and can protect MHW. For example, one randomised-controlled trial investigated the effects of a programme based on a dialectical behaviour therapy with elements of mental health literacy (Katz et al., 2020). In the programme children (grades 3-12 in Canada) acquired knowledge and skills in mindfulness, distress tolerance, emotion regulation and interpersonal skills. The findings showed improvements in children's self-concept, understood primarily as a combination of self-awareness and self-esteem, after the intervention, alongside improvements in coping. This suggests that a flexible sense of self can be fostered even in primary school children and protect their MHW.

218 Making Sense of Mental Health and Wellbeing in Primary Schools

Questions for reflection:

- What does the research evidence say about links between purpose in life and MHW in children?
- How are extrinsic and intrinsic values linked to MHW?
- Why is flexible self-concept relevant to MHW?

Neuroscience of Purpose in Life and Flexible Self-Concept

The knowledge and skills linked to fostering purpose in life and flexible self-concept rely on complex processes across the brain networks we discussed in the previous tiers of the ATTEND Pyramid. The mentalising network is specifically involved in formulation of purpose in life and thinking about self-identity. This involves reflecting on one's thoughts, emotions, memories and relationships with others, connections more broadly and ways one can make a difference. These processes also involve the default-mode network which overlaps with the mentalising networks (Yang et al., 2018) and the salience network which enables us

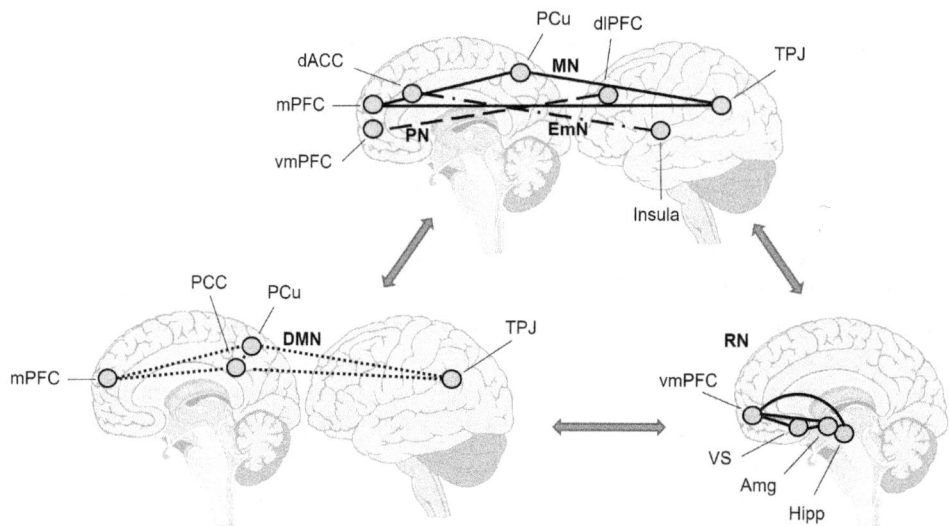

Figure 10.1 Neuroscience of purpose in life and flexible self-concept. MN - Mentalising network: mPFC - medial Prefrontal Cortex, PCu - Precuneus, TPJ - Temporoparietal Junction; EmN - Empathy network: dACC - dorsal Anterior Cingulate Cortex, Insula; PN: Prosocial network: vmPFC - ventromedial Prefrontal Cortex, dlPFC - dorsolateral Prefrontal Cortex; DMN - Default mode network: mPFC - medial Prefrontal Cortex, PCC - Posterior Cingulate Cortex, PCu - Precuneus, TPJ - Temporoparietal Junction; RN - Reward network: vmPFC - ventromedial Prefrontal Cortex, VS - Ventral Striatum, Amg - Amygdala, Hipp - Hippocampus.

Source: adapted with permission from Dorjee (2024)

to notice our thoughts and emotions. The empathy network supports self-reflection when it involves affectively relating to one's own and others' experiences.

In the absence of relevant neuroscience research with children, studies with adolescents showed that considerations about values are central to development of purpose in life and self-identity and such considerations are particularly linked to brain activity in the vmPFC (Pfeifer & Berkman, 2018). This brain region is involved in mentalising, default mode, reward and prosocial networks. These overlaps indicate the shared nature of processes linked to self-reflection, connecting with others and finding purpose in life as part of developing self-identity. They also highlight some possible reasons why purpose in life can have protective effects on MHW – since it is associated with rewarding experiences.

There is further neuroscience evidence in support of the notion that purpose in life, particularly when focused on intrinsic goals, can be linked to activity in the reward network and better MHW. A study with adolescents examined their brain activity when they were making eudaimonic decisions of prosocial nature and selfish decisions (Telzer et al., 2023). The findings indicated that greater brain activity in the VS region of the reward network in response to the eudaimonic decisions was linked to less depression symptoms in adolescents one year later. In contrast, greater activity in the VS to selfish decisions was associated with more depression symptoms one year later.

Key Neuroscience Terms for Purpose in Life and Flexible Self-concept

- Mentalising and default mode networks support reflections on purpose in life and flexible self-concept because they underpin thinking about others' and own thoughts, emotions and behaviours, as well as our values and goals. Such reflections can also involve the empathy network when they include reflecting on emotions.
- The ACC and PFC, involved in salience and executive networks, are active when children practise recognising strengths, as well as differentiating and setting goals.
- The vmPFC, involved in both reward and prosocial networks, and the VS of the reward network are particularly activated when considering values as part of purpose in life and self-identity. This can partially explain why purpose in life and having flexible self-concept support MHW.
- The HPA axis is downregulated and children are able to stay in the green zone more readily when they have a clear purpose in life and flexible self-concept which further supports their MHW.
- Neural plasticity underpins the ability to set and work towards goals as part of one's purpose in life. Neural plasticity also supports flexible self-concept by enabling us to work on some aspects of ourselves that we may want to change or develop further.

Another study linked greater engagement with ethical and moral issues to greater coordination in default mode and executive control network (Gotlieb et al., 2024). The study particularly highlighted the involvement of the default mode network in identity-related biographical and reflective thinking and suggested that the involvement of the executive control network is due to its role in focused thinking. The study showed that the increased coordination between the default and executive networks predicted self-identity development in later adolescence and also greater life satisfaction when the study participants were young adults.

Finally, greater sense of purpose in life has also been linked to downregulation of the HPA axis. Indeed, findings from studies with adults suggest that those who have a stronger sense of purpose in life also have lower cortisol levels and better sleep, with both being strong indicators of better HPA functioning (being in the green zone) (Ryff et al., 2004). There is no research relating purpose in life to HPA activity in children yet, but it is likely that similar findings might be expected given the association between greater purpose in life and more positive affect as well as greater life satisfaction in children (Shoshani & Russo-Netzer, 2017).

> **Brain Networks, Purpose in Life and Flexible Self-concept in the Classroom**
>
> Based on what Zoey learned about purpose in life, flexible self-concept and their roles in supporting children's MHW, as well as the underpinning neuroscience, she now feels better equipped in supporting her pupils in developing these qualities. She understands that children can build on all the MHW learning they acquired across the tiers of the ATTEND Pyramid because purpose in life and flexible self-concept engage nearly all of the brain areas and brain networks they learned about previously.
>
> Building on this understanding, Zoey prepared an overview of neuroscience content children learned and used it in teaching them about the roles the different brain regions and networks play in fostering purpose in life and flexible self-concept. She found that this was a useful way for children to both integrate their learning across the building blocks of the ATTEND Pyramid and to motivate their new learning about purpose in life and flexible self-concept. Zoey felt that this approach also made it easier to explain this more advanced topic to children in an age-appropriate way and link it to MHW.

How Can Children Acquire the Knowledge and Skills of Finding Purpose in Life and Developing a Flexible Self-concept?

Helping children explore their purpose in life is closely linked to the knowledge and skills children acquired in the previous facets of the self-world capacity. For example, research shows that children who practise gratitude in their life are also more likely to contribute to causes beyond self-benefit. Other studies show that experiences of awe and compassion can connect us with greater good causes and build an emotional foundation for finding our sense of purpose in life. And those who have a greater sense of altruism and prosocial behaviour are also more likely to have a greater sense of meaning and purpose in life. Finally, purpose in life beyond self-focus is also linked to personal growth which is a hallmark of building a flexible sense of self. So learning in the previous facets prepared the foundations for children to start developing their sense of purpose in life and a flexible self-concept.

Knowing Your Strengths

The first activity in this facet encourages children to learn to recognise their strengths and explore greater good causes they want to contribute to using their strengths. Such learning starts with examples of strengths of characters in stories, cartoons or real life to provide children with understanding what is meant by 'strengths'. Children can make a list of different strengths they noticed in the examples.

Then they try to develop skills in recognising their own strengths. In this process, they can start with the list they prepared based on external examples first or they may be provided with a list of possible strengths they may choose from by their teacher. Children try to identify which strengths apply to them and come up with their own. Older children can create their *Map of Strengths* – a mind map where they include the range of strengths they have with an empty centre which will later include their 'big goal', their purpose in life with links to their strengths.

This learning is then expanded towards recognising how the characters in stories or cartoons apply their strengths to impact the world in wholesome ways. Children can also make a list of greater good causes they observed in the example stories, cartoons, movies or real life. They also notice how the characters applied their strengths in pursuing the causes. For older children, the concept of purpose in life can be introduced here, linking the use of one's strengths by the characters to pursuit of causes in the examples.

Next, children explore which causes they would like to make a difference to. Again, they can build on the list of causes they observed in the examples and also come up with further causes that were not mentioned in the examples. They brainstorm how they could use their strengths to contribute to some of the causes they care about in order to make a positive difference to others or nature and positively impact the world. They can write possible causes they care about in the middle of their Map of Strengths and then highlight the one they chose as their 'Big Goal', their purpose in life.

Older children can also explore if there are any further skills they need to develop to contribute to their 'Big Goal'. If they identify some such skills, they can write them down on the periphery of their Map of Strengths and after further reflection highlight the skill or skills they want to work on in the coming months or years. Children also need to be reminded that the 'Big Goal' can change as they grow and the strengths and skills they need to work on can change too.

Throughout the process children explore how understanding their strengths and having a purpose in life made the characters feel, how it impacted the characters' MHW. Then they explore how acknowledging their own strengths and having a sense of purpose in life makes them feel, noticing any benefits to their own MHW. They may also notice, for example, a greater sense of hope about the future, more resilience in overcoming obstacles and determination to work towards the 'Big Goal'.

> **Key Strategies for Fostering Purpose in Life and Flexible Self-concept**
>
> - Knowing your Strengths is an activity that enables children to recognise their strengths and explore causes ('big goals') they want to contribute to using their strengths. The activity progresses from examples of strengths in characters from stories or public life to exploration of own strengths. Children also explore how knowing their strengths and having 'big goals' to strive towards makes them feel.
> - Map of Strengths is a mind map children can create where they include a range of strengths they have and leave an empty centre which will later include their 'big goal', their purpose in life with links to their strengths. Children can add qualities they want to develop or strengthen in working towards their purpose in life on the periphery of the map.
> - Exploring Goals in Life activity introduces children to the differences between intrinsic and extrinsic goals and their consequences for one's MHW. Children practise distinguishing different types of goals in the two categories in examples and then are supported in selecting goals for themselves that are in the intrinsic category.

Exploring Goals in Life

The second activity aims to introduce children to differences between intrinsic and extrinsic goals and their impacts on MHW, in age-appropriate ways. This can be framed in terms of exploring goals in life that can make us happy and goals that can make us unhappy.

To start with, children can be provided with examples from stories, cartoons, movies or real life which exemplify pursuit of extrinsic goals and pursuit of intrinsic goals. To exemplify extrinsic goals, the teacher could use a story where the character aims to be wealthy disregarding others' needs, or they want to be famous. To explain intrinsic goals, the teacher can use examples of characters striving to make a positive difference in the world – through caring for others (animals or nature), helping others, doing research that will help others, advising other people etc. These can be examples used in the previous activity about strengths. The teacher can explain to children the difference between the two categories of goals. Children then try to categorise new external examples of goals into the two categories.

Next, the teacher can provide children with examples of consequences extrinsic goal focus and intrinsic goal focus can have. These can involve elaboration of the examples of extrinsic and intrinsic goals provided previously with primary focus on how working towards the two different categories of goals made the characters feel, how it impacted their MHW. In the older age groups (particularly upper KS2) this can include examples children encountered in public life – for example sports personalities or celebrities reflecting on the effects of fame and wealth on their MHW. In this age group the differences between extrinsic and intrinsic goals can also be linked to egoistic and altruistic motivation they learned about previously.

It is important not to misrepresent the considerations about extrinsic goals. Of course, everyone wants to be able to earn enough money to cover their needs and not have to struggle financially. Also, there is nothing wrong with trying to make a difference in the world through becoming a public person that is known to others. The key consideration here is the negative impact of self-focused pursuit of extrinsic goals on one's own MHW and disregarding the needs of others. Another key consideration is the mistaken perception that excessive wealth and fame are the main means to leading a happy life.

Finally, children explore whether the goals they have chosen would be more in the extrinsic or in the intrinsic goals category. They reflect further on the consequences the goals may have for their own MHW. Then children can explore if any of their goals need adjusting, so that they support their MHW in the longer term. Finally, they can further refine their plans of working towards the goals they have chosen, building on their strengths and considering any further skills they need to develop to pursue their goals in life (purpose in life).

Developmental Differences in Fostering the Knowledge and Skills of Purpose in Life and Flexible Self-concept

As explained earlier in the chapter, fostering purpose in life and flexible self-concept rely on a range of cognitive processes, particularly reasoning about one's own thoughts, emotions, actions and their impacts on others. It also involves empathy and skills supporting prosocial behaviour. And all these skills build on one's ability to manage own thoughts, emotions and behaviours in alignment with one's goals cultivated in the first two tiers of the ATTEND Pyramid to strengthen children's self-regulation. So exploration of purpose in life and flexible self-concept bring together children's learning across the tiers and building blocks of the Pyramid.

Since considerations about purpose in life and flexible self-concept particularly involve the theory of mind processes, children's ability to engage with the activities in this tier needs to be aligned with the development of their mentalising skills. Therefore, younger children will require a lot of teacher guidance in considering strengths and goals of a cartoon character and the range of strengths and goals considered will also need to be restricted to a small group of qualities children can relate to – such as being patient, brave, kind, clever etc. Drawings depicting the strengths can be particularly helpful in supporting children in thinking about different kinds of strengths and how the characters are using them to help others or animals or nature etc.

Based on such examples, children can start exploring their own strengths and possible ways they want to impact the world. This can involve considerations about children's future careers but should not be restricted to it. One's goals in life can involve fostering good relationships with others or developing some skills, such as learning to play an instrument for one's own and others enjoyment. They can also involve developing qualities one can apply in everyday relating to others, work etc. – such as being patient, considerate, tolerant, kind, courageous etc.

Older children (KS2) will be able to explore a greater range of possible strengths in external examples and then for themselves. They will also be able to brainstorm about a range of possible causes in the world that matter to them and may want to contribute to. They will be able to reflect with more nuance on their strengths and possible ways of using these in pursuing one's purpose in life – to impact the world in positive ways. They will be able to recognise impacts of pursuing wholesome goals on MHW more readily and in more depth. They may also realise that working towards worthwhile goals may also enhance their sense of agency and foster hopefulness. The Ripples of Agency exercise from the previous chapter could make the effects of one's actions in pursuit of purpose in life more visible.

Finally, older children will be also able to engage with considerations about internal and external goals more directly and relate them to real-world issues they are encountering. In the process of exploring a flexible sense of self, they will be able to also start considering qualities they would like to develop further to support their pursuit of goals aligned with their purpose in life. They may start recognising differences between the goals others may want them to pursue versus goals they want to pursue and start acknowledging that it is ok if others have different expectations of them, as long as the goals they themselves care most about are intrinsic. They may also start observing that one's goals can change over time.

Acquiring the Knowledge and Skills of Developing Purpose in Life and Flexible Self-concept: The 7-Step Approach

Translating the research presented in this chapter into teaching practice, the first three steps of the 7-Step approach specify the knowledge children need to acquire to develop purpose in life and flexible self-concept. This involves learning from external examples about different types of strengths and ways one can use their strengths in finding and pursuing a sense of purpose in life, and how this can foster MHW. Children also learn to recognise the differences between extrinsic and intrinsic goals, and their different impacts on one's MHW. Solidifying this knowledge, children develop understanding about the neural underpinnings of purpose in life and flexible self-concept.

The next four steps then translate this knowledge into skills children can use to cultivate their own sense of purpose in life and flexible self. They first explore their own strengths and consider ways they can apply them in finding and pursuing their own purpose in life. They also explore how this impacts their MHW. Then they distinguish intrinsic and extrinsic goals in their own experience and explore consequences of pursuing these different goals for their own MHW. Older children also examine alignment between their goals and expectations others place on them, and possible skills they need to develop to pursue their goals in life. Finally, children apply their knowledge and skills, including their neuroscience knowledge, in fostering a greater sense of purpose in life and flexible self-concept in their everyday activities.

Step 1: Learning How Recognising Own Strengths and Finding Purpose in Life Relates to MHW

The learning objective in the first step is for children to acquire the knowledge that will enable them to understand, based on examples, the range of strengths one can have and how one's strengths can be applied in finding and pursuing purpose in life. They also learn that having a sense of purpose in life can support MHW.

 In *reception*, children begin to understand, with support and based on examples, that we all have some strengths. They also begin to understand that everyone's strengths can be used in ways that can positively impact the world. They begin to recognise, with support, that engaging in activities where one works towards a bigger goal and uses their strengths can make them feel good. To foster this knowledge, the teacher can use cartoons to exemplify a range of strengths and how these can be used in contributing to a worthwhile goal in one's life. The teacher can use images from cartoons children watched previously to remind them about the strengths they learned about and goals the characters worked towards. Children can then, with teaching staff support, practise recognising strengths in the examples they worked with and in some simple new examples. They also explore how working with strengths towards a goal made the characters feel. They can use the Feels Good Scale and Emotion Strength Scale to evaluate this.

 In *KS1*, children are able to understand more readily, based on examples and with support, that everyone has some strengths. They can recognise a greater range of strengths in examples and understand more readily that one can use such strengths in working towards a worthwhile goal of one's choice. They also recognise with support that using our strengths in this way can make us feel good. To cultivate this knowledge, the teacher can use a story from a storybook, or come up with an original story, that exemplifies strengths of a story character and ways the character used them in finding and pursuing their 'big goal in life'. Children can then try to identify the strengths in the story on their own, with guidance. Finally, children can work in small groups with a new story where they practise identifying strengths of the story character and the 'big goal' the character is working towards. Children are also guided to recognise how using one's strengths in this way and finding one's 'big goal' in life made the character feel. They can use the Feels Good Scale and Emotion Strength Scale to support their understanding of the impact strengths and purpose in life can have on how one feels.

 In the *lower KS2*, children are able to understand mostly independently based on examples that we all have strengths and that we can use them in pursuing worthwhile goals in life that we chose. This way we can positively impact the world and also strengthen our MHW. To develop this knowledge, children can watch a short movie where the characters use their strengths to find and pursue their purpose in life. The teacher can guide children to recognise the character's strengths and ways they use them in finding and pursuing their purpose in life. Children can then work with another short movie in small groups and practise recognising the character's strengths and purpose in life with some guidance. They can also brainstorm about

a range of strengths they noticed other characters have in stories, movies or people in everyday life. Children work in their small groups to recognise how applying their strengths in pursuit of purpose in life made the character feel. They can use the Pleasantness of Emotion Scale and Intensity of Emotion Scale to quantify the change in character's emotions from before to after recognising their strengths and finding a purpose in their life.

In the *upper KS2*, children are able to understand independently based on examples that everyone has some strengths and we all can use our strengths to find and pursue a goal in life that gives our life purpose. They can recognise a wide range of strengths in examples and can articulate how finding purpose in life and using one's strengths to pursue it can support MHW. They can describe in their own words using the examples what having a purpose in life means. To cultivate such knowledge, children can be provided with real world examples of strengths - from news stories, athletes, celebrities - and be guided in recognising these and linking them to purpose in life those in the examples found and pursued. They can make a list of strengths they observed. Children are then asked to come with their own examples of strengths and purpose in life they can identify in public life or their community. They can add these to the list they started. They share their examples with each other in pairs and also explain how the strengths and having purpose in life made those in their examples feel, how it supported their MHW. They can use the Pleasantness and Intensity of Emotion Graph to quantify the change the person in their example experienced from before to after having a clear purpose in life.

Step 2: Learning about Intrinsic and Extrinsic Goals and Their Impact on MHW

The learning objective in the second step is for children to acquire the knowledge that will enable them to understand from examples the differences between extrinsic and intrinsic goals and how the different types of goals can impact MHW.

In *reception*, children begin to understand, with support and based on examples, that there are two main categories of goals. One group of goals is when one wants things like lots of toys or money just for oneself, or when somebody wants to be famous and doesn't care about others. The other group of goals is when we want to do something that makes both us and others happy – such as creating things together that we can all benefit from, caring for others or learning new things so we can help others, animals or nature. The teacher can use the labels 'helpful goals' and 'unhelpful goals' if children can engage with those.

To foster such knowledge, children can be provided with cartoon examples of extrinsic and intrinsic goals and their consequences. As an example of extrinsic goals there can be a character who wants everything for themselves and doesn't want to share, then ends up lonely and unhappy. In contrast, there can be a character who has goals that make him happy and benefit others too. Children can have a vote about who they think is happier. They can practise distinguishing the 'goals that make us happy' and 'goals that can make us unhappy' in other examples. The teacher can create a symbol or sticker that means 'helpful goals' and another one that means 'unhelpful goals' to support children's learning.

In *KS1*, children are able to understand more readily with guidance the differences between extrinsic and intrinsic goals, and their consequences for how one feels. This can be explained in an age-appropriate way based on examples from stories children might be familiar with, e.g. The Grinch and many others, with children clearly distinguishing between the two categories of goals. These examples will be more nuanced than those in reception, and children can keep practising 'sorting' character's goals into the two categories. These can be labelled as 'helpful goals' and 'unhelpful goals' as in reception. Children can also use the Feels Good Scale and Emotion Strength Scale to make the differences between how the characters pursuing 'helpful goals' and those pursuing 'unhelpful goals' feel.

In the *lower KS2*, children are able to understand mostly independently from examples the difference between extrinsic and intrinsic goals and their consequences for MHW. To foster this knowledge, children can first work with the examples introduced in Step 1 and put them into one category of goals – 'wholesome goals' that benefit oneself and others too. Then the teacher can provide children with examples of 'unwholesome goals' that focus only on oneself and disregard others' needs. The teacher then guides children in exploring how the two categories of goals impact MHW of the characters in the two examples. Children can use the Pleasantness of Emotion Scale and Intensity of Emotion Scale to distinguish how the characters pursuing the two different types of goals feel. Children can then be provided with further examples where they practise the skills in distinguishing 'wholesome goals' and 'unwholesome goals' and their consequences for the characters' MHW.

In the *upper KS2*, children are able to understand independently from examples the difference between intrinsic and extrinsic goals and they are able to use these goal category labels correctly. They can also articulate accurately and independently the impact of intrinsic and extrinsic goals on the persons' MHW in the examples. To cultivate this knowledge, children can first work with the goals characters pursued in examples from public life in Step 1. The teacher can describe the characteristics of intrinsic goals – that they benefit oneself and others – and children try to recognise these characteristics in the examples. This can also be linked to the altruistic motivation children learned about previously. Then the teacher explains the characteristics of extrinsic goals – mostly being self-focused – and this can be linked with egoistic motivation. Children can then evaluate the impact of intrinsic and extrinsic goals on the persons' MHW in the examples using the Pleasantness and Intensity of Emotion Graph. They can practise making links to MHW on further examples, working in pairs and explaining the differences to each other.

Step 3: Learning Neuroscience Underpinning Purpose in Life and Flexible Self-concept

The learning objective in the third step is for children to acquire the knowledge enabling them to understand what happens in the brain when we reflect on purpose in life and flexible self-concept and why this can support our MHW. They learn that such considerations involve all the brain areas and brain networks they learned about in the previous building blocks of the ATTEND Pyramid and are able to explain why.

In *reception*, children begin to understand, with support and reminders, that the brain, including the PFC, can help us recognise our strengths and goals. To foster this knowledge, the teacher can start reminding children that the brain and the PFC enabled the characters in the examples they worked with previously to recognise their strengths and use them in working towards a bigger goal. The brain and the PFC also help us distinguish how different goals make us feel – they help us differentiate the 'helpful goals' and 'unhelpful goals'. Children can then practise integrating neuroscience knowledge into their understanding of purpose in life and flexible self with further examples.

In *KS1*, children are able to understand more readily with support that exploring one's strengths and a 'big goal' one wants to contribute to, as well as distinguishing between 'helpful goals' and 'unhelpful goals', involves activity in the brain regions they learned about previously. The ACC, PFC, TPJ and insula help us think about our strengths, 'big goals' and distinguish happy and unhelpful goals. The VS and the prosocial network are activated when we use our strengths in working towards 'big goals' that make us feel good. To develop this knowledge, children can work with the story examples they were introduced to in Steps 1 and 2 and expand them with references to what is happening in the brain of the characters when they are exploring their strengths and using them in working towards 'big goals' (ACC, PFC, TPJ and insula). Children can also explore how activity in the VS and the prosocial networks underpins the 'feel good' aspects of 'helpful goals' because those experiences are rewarding and connect us with others.

In the *lower KS2*, children are able to understand mostly independently what is happening in the brain when one is recognising one's strengths, reflecting on their purpose in life and distinguishing 'wholesome goals' and 'unwholesome goals'. They also understand mostly independently how this relates to MHW. They understand that the ACC, PFC, TPJ and insula help us think about our strengths, purpose in life and self-concept. This sometimes also involves empathy because of connecting with others and wanting to help them as part of our goals in life – this is linked activity in the empathy network. Children understand that finding purpose in life and working towards wholesome goals leads to rewarding experiences that support MHW – and this is reflected in the increased activity in the VS and in the prosocial network.

To cultivate this knowledge, children can work with the short movie examples they were introduced to in Steps 1 and 2. They can practise in small groups elaborating these examples with explanations of what is happening in the brain, based on an example the teacher provides. They can also link the activity in the VS and the prosocial network to the changes in the Pleasantness of Emotion Scale and Intensity of Emotion Scale they noted previously. They can start applying the neuroscience explanations to new examples the teacher provides, further strengthening their knowledge.

In the *upper KS2*, children are able to understand and describe independently and accurately what is happening in the brain when one is exploring strengths, reflecting on purpose in life and flexible self-concept. They can relate this understanding to the effects of pursuing extrinsic and intrinsic goals, linked to egoistic and altruistic motivation, respectively. They are able to use references to the brain regions and brain networks they learned about in all the previous building blocks of the ATTEND Pyramid. This includes understanding that reflections on purpose in life and flexible self primarily involve the mentalising and default mode networks since these networks support thinking about others and own thoughts, emotions and behaviours. This can also involve the empathy network when such considerations include reflecting on emotions.

Children also recognise that the ACC and PFC, involved in salience and executive networks, are active during recognising strengths, as well as differentiating and setting goals. They understand that the vmPFC, involved in both reward and prosocial networks, is particularly activated when considering values as part of purpose in life and self-identity, this can explain why purpose in life and having flexible self support MHW. Finally, they recognise that having purpose in life and a flexible self-concept (self-identity) can also help us stay in the green zone (manage stress and reactivity) and thus downregulate the HPA axis. They can also recognise that developing new skills they may need to pursue their goals involves neural plasticity.

To foster this knowledge, children can revisit the examples from public life they worked with previously and try to explain the effects of exploring strengths, finding purpose in life and engaging in pursuit of extrinsic vs intrinsic goals in relation to MHW using their neuroscience understanding. The teacher can first model such explanations and then children can practise this in pairs with further examples they previously came up with.

Step 4: Learning Skills of Recognising Own Strengths and Exploring Purpose in Life in Own Experience

The learning objective in the fourth step is for children to develop the skills that will enable them to recognise their own strengths and explore their purpose in life, in relation to their MHW.

In *reception*, children begin to be able to recognise, with support, their own strengths and start exploring 'big goals' they may want to contribute to, in order to positively impact the world. They begin to recognise with guidance that engaging in activities where they can use their strengths to contribute to a bigger goal can make them feel good. To foster these skills, the teacher can remind children about the strengths characters in the cartoons they watched previously had. They can use the images from cartoons to remind children. Then the teaching staff can guide children in exploring if they also have some of the strengths the characters had or maybe other strengths that were not mentioned previously. Children can then be reminded of the goals the characters worked towards and explore if they would like to contribute to any of those goals too. Finally, children are supported in exploring how recognising their strengths and using them in working towards a 'big goal' made them feel.

In *KS1*, children are able to recognise more readily with support their own strengths and possible 'big goals' they may want to contribute to using their strengths. They also recognise more readily with guidance that using their strengths to contribute to a 'big goal' can make them feel good. To cultivate these skills, the teacher can build on the stories children were introduced to in Step 1. Children explore in small groups with guidance if they might have any of the strengths the characters in the stories had or any other strengths that were not in the stories. Once they have identified a few of their own strengths, they explore if any of the goals the characters pursued would be goals they also want to contribute to and impact the world in a positive way. They can also come up with their own goals. Children then explore with support how recognising their strengths and goals made them feel. They can use the Feels Good Scale and Emotion Strength Scale to make it more explicit how knowing their strengths and goals can make them feel good.

In the *lower KS2*, children are able to recognise mostly independently their own strengths and worthwhile goals in life that they want to pursue. They also recognise from their own experience that knowing their strengths and using them to contribute to a goal that can improve the world can support their MHW. To develop this knowledge, the teacher can revisit the short movie examples from Step 1 and encourage children to explore if any of the strengths the characters identified apply to them too and if they can recognise any further strengths in themselves that haven't been discussed previously. Next, children can explore if any of the goals in life the characters pursued using their strengths may also apply to them, or identify other goals that they would like to pursue (the teacher can use the term purpose in life if children are sufficiently familiar with it). Finally, children can explore how recognising their strengths and identifying goals they can work towards in their life makes them feel. They can use the Pleasantness of Emotion Scale and Intensity of Emotion Scale to quantify this.

In the *upper KS2*, children are able to independently recognise their own strengths. They also recognise that they can use their strengths in pursuing a goal in life that gives them purpose and contributes to improving the world. They recognise from their own experience that knowing their strengths and pursuing their purpose in life can support their MHW. Based on their experience, they can describe the links between recognising their own strengths, finding purpose in life and their MHW. To develop these skills, children can revisit the list of strengths they previously prepared based on examples and explore if any of those strengths apply to them. They can also explore if they recognise further strengths

Purpose in Life and Self-Concept 231

in themselves not mentioned in the list. Children can work in pairs where they write down the strengths they observed in the other person on a piece of paper and then exchange the notes. They can discuss in pairs the strengths mentioned on the notes. Based on all these considerations, they can create their 'Map of Strengths'. Then the teacher can remind children about the different types of goals linked to purpose in life the characters in the examples pursued and invite children to reflect on how they could use their strengths in finding their purpose in life and goals to contribute to. They can write down their possible purpose in life (or a few goals) in the middle of their Map of Strengths. Finally, children explore how knowing their strengths and exploring their purpose in life impacted their MHW. They can use the Pleasantness and Intensity of Emotion Graph to quantify this.

Step 5: Learning Skills of Recognising Intrinsic and Extrinsic Goals in Own Experience and Their Impact on Own MHW

The learning objective in the fifth step is for children to be able to recognise intrinsic and extrinsic goals in their own experience. They also learn to recognise the different impacts these two groups of goals can have on their MHW, how to change extrinsic goals into intrinsic goals, and what qualities they may want to develop (aside from their strengths) in working towards their intrinsic goals linked to their purpose in life.

In *reception*, children begin to be able to recognise with support in their own experience the difference between helpful goals and unhelpful goals and how they make them feel. To foster these skills, children can be reminded of the examples used in Step 2 to distinguish between helpful and unhelpful goals. They then reflect if their goals (explored in Step 4) are in the helpful or unhelpful group. Most likely, their goals will be in the helpful group, but if any of them fall into the unhelpful group, the teaching staff can support children in reformulating the goal in a way that would make it a helpful goal. For example, if some children say they want to have lots of money, they can explore what they would do with the money to see if they could use it to positively impact the world. They can also explore how it would make them feel if they just kept the money all to themselves in comparison to how they would feel if they shared it with their friends and family. Finally, children can start exploring with support, in very simple terms, if there is any further skill (aside from their strengths) they need to learn to accomplish their goals.

In *KS1*, children are able to recognise more readily with support the difference between helpful and unhelpful goals from their own experience and can also recognise more reality how the two different types of goals make them feel. To cultivate these skills, children can revisit the examples from stories they were introduced to in Step 2. Then they start exploring if the goals they chose in Step 4 fall into the helpful goals category or the unhelpful goals category. It is very likely that the vast majority of their goals will belong to the helpful goals category, but if any of them choose a goal that could fall into the unhelpful goal category, the teaching staff can support children in reframing the goal into a helpful goal. For instance, if children say that their main goal is to be famous, the teacher can guide them in exploring whether that would just make them happy or whether they could be famous so that they also improve the world – for example by entertaining people or being able to help others with a wide reach. Children also explore further how the goals they chose make them feel. Finally, they can explore with guidance whether there are any skills they need to develop, in addition to the strengths they already have, to pursue their chosen helpful goal/goals.

In the *lower KS2*, children are able to recognise mostly independently the difference between wholesome and unwholesome goals, and how they impact their MHW. They are also able to recognise mostly independently any further skills or qualities they may need to develop in working towards their goals. To develop these skills, children can first revisit the movie examples of goals they worked with in Step 2 where they sorted them into the wholesome goals and unwholesome goals categories. Then, children explore if the goals they chose in Step 4 would fall into the wholesome or unwholesome goals category. If some children's goals will be in the unwholesome goals category, the teaching staff can work with children in exploring how the goals could be reframed to be more wholesome. For example, if the goals focus on fame or wealth, children can explore ways how these goals could be adjusted so that they benefit both oneself and also positively impact the world. Then children explore further how the wholesome goals they selected could support their MHW. Finally, they can consider if they need to develop any new skills (e.g. learning about animals or learning to juggle) or qualities (e.g. being more patient or outspoken), aside from their strengths, in working towards their goal/goals.

In the *upper KS2*, children are able to recognise independently whether their goals fall into the intrinsic goals or extrinsic goals category, and how the goals may impact their MHW. They are also able to recognise and articulate independently whether they need to develop any further qualities and skills in working towards their intrinsic goals as part of their pursuit of purpose in life. To cultivate these skills, children can first revisit the examples of goals they divided into the intrinsic and extrinsic goals categories in Step 2. They can also be reminded about the altruistic motivation mostly driving the intrinsic goals and the egoistic motivation behind extrinsic goals. Then children can work with their Map of Strengths and explore if their goals/purpose in the centre of the map would fall into the intrinsic or extrinsic goals category, and how the goals they chose make them feel. If some children's goals fall into the extrinsic goals category they can work with the teaching staff in brainstorming how the goals could be modified so that they benefit both oneself and others, and thus fall more into the intrinsic goals category. Finally, children explore whether there are any qualities and skills, aside from their strengths, they may need to develop in working towards their goals and purpose in life. They can write these qualities/skills on the periphery of their Map of Strengths.

Purpose in Life and Self-Concept 233

Step 6: Learning to Apply Neuroscience Knowledge as Part of Finding Purpose in Life and Developing Flexible Self-concept

The learning objective in the sixth step is for children to be able to use their understanding of the neuroscience underpinning purpose in life and flexible self-concept in exploring their strengths and purpose in life and its impact on their MHW.

 In *reception*, children begin to use, with support, their understanding about involvement of the brain and the PFC in recognising their own strengths and exploring 'big goals' they want to contribute to. They can also begin to use references to the brain and the PFC in distinguishing helpful and unhelpful goals. To foster these skills, their teacher can expand the guidance in activities where children explore their strengths and 'big goals' with references to the brain and PFC. Children can also be encouraged to refer to the brain and the PFC as the brain regions enabling them to distinguish helpful and unhelpful goals. With support, they are able to link their considerations about neuroscience underpinning their exploration of strengths and 'big goals' to how this makes them feel.

 In *KS1*, children are able to use their understanding of neuroscience underpinning exploration of strengths and 'big goals' and distinguishing helpful and unhelpful goals more readily in deepening their skills of recognising their own strengths and 'big goals'. They are also able to link their neuroscience understanding to the effects of recognising their strengths and 'big goals' on how they feel. To develop these skills, the teacher can invite children to think about brain areas that are active when they are working in small groups exploring their strengths and 'big goals'. They may refer to the ACC, PFC, TPJ and insula as helping them notice and recognise their strengths and 'big goals'. They may then mention the VS and the prosocial network being activated when they notice how this makes them feel, particularly when they consider contributing to 'helpful goals', since such feelings are typically positive and rewarding.

 In the *lower KS2*, children are able to use their understanding of neuroscience underpinning recognising one's strengths, reflecting on purpose in life and distinguishing 'wholesome goals' from 'unwholesome goals' mostly independently in deepening their exploration of own strengths and 'wholesome goals' they want to contribute to. They are also able to use their neuroscience knowledge in strengthening their understanding of the effects recognising their strengths and 'wholesome goals' can have on their MHW. To cultivate these skills, teaching staff encourages children to consider which brain areas they used when they were considering their strengths and a 'wholesome goal' or goals they want to contribute to. Children can then practise describing that this involves activity in the ACC, PFC, TPJ, insula and sometimes also activates the empathy network if our goals involve connections with others. Children are then encouraged to use references to relevant brain regions when linking recognising their strengths and wholesome goals to MHW. They may be reminded that positive emotions they may experience when recognising their strengths and a 'wholesome goal'

activate the VS and the prosocial network. Next, children can practise in pairs describing to each other what is happening in their brain when they are recognising their strengths, 'wholesome goal' and how this makes them feel.

In the *upper KS2*, children are able to use their understanding of neuroscience underpinning exploring one's strengths, reflecting on purpose in life and flexible self concept, and distinguishing extrinsic and intrinsic goals independently in strengthening their exploration of their own strengths and purpose in life. They are also able to use their neuroscience understanding in deepening their skills of linking exploration of strengths, purpose in life and flexible self to supporting their MHW.

To develop these skills, children can use the Map of Strengths they prepared previously and note down in the map which brain regions supported their exploration of strengths and purpose in life. This can involve noting down that reflections on purpose in life and flexible self involve the mentalising and default mode networks. This can also include the empathy network when the goals include connections with others. Children can then note that the ACC and PFC, as part of salience and executive networks, helped them recognise their strengths and differentiate if their goals were intrinsic or extrinsic. In addition, they can write down that the vmPFC is involved in the positive emotions that arise as a result of recognising one's strengths and using them in pursuit of one's purpose in life. This can in turn help them stay in the green zone through downregulating the HPA axis. And developing new skills they may need to pursue their purpose in life involves neural plasticity. Next, children can practise explaining to each other in pairs what is happening in their brain using their Map of Strengths. Or they can write a short description of this.

Step 7: Applying Skills of Finding Purpose in Life and Flexible Self-concept in Everyday Activities

The learning objective in the seventh step is for children to be able to apply their knowledge and skills of recognising their strengths, finding purpose in life and fostering flexible self-concept, including relevant neuroscience understanding, in everyday life to support their MHW.

In *reception*, children begin to apply, with support and guidance but increasingly more readily, their knowledge and skills in recognising their strengths and using them in working towards a helpful 'big goal' in everyday life. They use their neuroscience understanding (references to the brain and the PFC) in motivating their use of strengths in this way and in recognising how this can make them feel better. To foster these skills, children can be reminded at the start of the day to remember their strengths and their 'big goal' and think about ways to use their strengths in this way during the day. Then, in everyday situations, teaching staff can remind children to remember their strengths and use them in managing challenges (they can also use all the different skills they learned in the previous building blocks of the ATTEND Pyramid). At the end of the school day, children can reflect on how they were using their strengths to move towards their 'big goal'. They also reflect on how this made them feel.

In *KS1*, children are able to apply more readily with support the knowledge and skills of recognising their strengths and using them in working towards a helpful 'big goal' or goals in everyday life. They are also able to use their neuroscience understanding (ACC, PFC, TPJ, VS) in motivating their use of strengths during the day and in recognising how this makes them feel (VS and prosocial network). To foster these skills, during the morning register the teacher can take a moment for children to remember their strengths and their 'big goal'. They can also be reminded to use their strengths in everyday situations, when focusing on a school task or resolving a disagreement. They can also build on the knowledge and skills they learned across all the building blocks of the ATTEND Pyramid. At the end of the day children can reflect on how they worked towards their 'big goal' during the day and how that made them feel. The teacher provides encouraging positive feedback to children to reinforce their learning further.

In the *lower KS2*, children are able to apply their knowledge and skills of recognising their strengths, working towards a worthwhile goal and fostering flexible self-concept mostly independently in everyday life. They are also able to use their neuroscience understanding (ACC, PFC, TPJ, insula, VS, empathy and prosocial networks) to motivate the use of their new skills in everyday situations and to recognise how this can support their MHW. To develop these skills, children can prepare a simple plan for the week, describing how they want to use their strengths during the week to work towards their 'big goal' and start developing new skills that they can use in pursuing their goal. They can then revisit their plan at the beginning and at the end of each day of the week, first to remind themselves to use their strengths in that way during the day and then to reflect on how it went at the end of the day. They can write some further notes on what they learned at the end of each day and use them to build up their learning gradually. Children are also reminded throughout the day to use their strengths during tasks or challenging situations (and other skills they learned previously in the other building blocks of the ATTEND Pyramid). Finally, children reflect on how the use of their strengths in this way and working towards their goal supported their MHW.

In the *upper KS2*, children are able to apply their knowledge and skills of recognising their strengths, working towards an intrinsic purpose in life and fostering flexible self-concept independently in everyday life. They are able to use their neuroscience understanding (mentalising and default networks, ACC and PFC - salience and executive networks, empathy network, vmPFC involved in reward and prosocial networks, the HPA axis and neural plasticity) in motivating their use of these skills in everyday life and in internalising their understanding that this can support their MHW.

To develop these skills, the teaching staff can make copies of each child's Map of Strengths and children can then use the copies to write notes for themselves on how they want to use their strengths during the day each day and write further notes at the end of the day on how it went. They can circle or tick the strengths they used most everyday and at the end of the week they will be able to see a pattern of which strengths they have been using most. They can also circle the skills on the periphery of their map, those are skills they want to develop further to help them pursue their purpose in life. After a week or two of daily reviews, children can start revisiting their Map of Strengths at the end of each term and explore if anything needs changing, or maybe draw a new Map of Strengths if they like. They can also reflect on how they have been using all the different skills in the other building blocks of The ATTEND Pyramid to pursue their purpose in life (a teacher can make a poster with all the different skills and make a handout children can work with based on it). Children can write a reflective essay on this topic at the end of each term.

Conclusion

Purpose in life is one of the main predictors of MHW across the lifespan. If you were, just like Zoey, wondering if purpose in life can be fostered in children of primary school age, hopefully this chapter provided you with a clear 'Yes' answer and helpful tips on how this can be done in a primary school classroom. To this aim we have explored ways to guide children in recognising their strengths, considering possible 'big goals' they want to contribute to and distinguishing between intrinsic and extrinsic goals, and their effects on MHW. The chapter also provided an opportunity to start exploring, in a more implicit way, a flexible sense of self through reflecting on possible skills children may want to work on in their pursuit of the 'big goal' (which can also change with time). The chapter also encouraged integration of learning across the building blocks of The ATTEND Pyramid. The next step could be for children to develop a working plan on how they want to maintain the skills they learned across the ATTEND Pyramid topics. They can revisit the plan at the beginning and the end of each term and keep working with the help of the posters, prompts and other tools they were using across the ATTEND Pyramid. As with any skills, practice is the key to sustaining the benefits of these skills to MHW in the long term.

Key chapter points:

- Purpose in life has been consistently linked to better MHW across the life-span, even though the research evidence in children is limited.
- Having a flexible self-concept, understanding that we can change some aspects of ourselves if we want to, can also support MHW.
- Neuroscience underpinning purpose in life and flexible self-concept involves most of the brain regions and brain networks children learned about in the previous tiers of the ATTEND Pyramid, and thus integrates their neuroscience understanding.
- Children can develop their sense of purpose in life even in primary schools in an age-appropriate way through activities such as 'Knowing your Strengths', 'Map of Strengths' and 'Exploring Goals in Life'.
- Children's knowledge and skills of purpose in life and flexible self-concept can be systematically fostered in these activities following the 7-Step-Approach.

References

Bradshaw, E. L., Conigrave, J. H., Steward, B. A., Ferber, K. A., Parker, P. D., & Ryan, R. M. (2023). A meta-analysis of the dark side of the American dream: evidence for the universal wellness costs of prioritizing extrinsic over intrinsic goals. *Journal of Personality and Social Psychology, 124*(4), 873.

Cohen, R., Bavishi, C., & Rozanski, A. (2016). Purpose in life and its relationship to all-cause mortality and cardiovascular events: a meta-analysis. *Biopsychosocial Science and Medicine, 78*(2), 122-133.

Cotton, S., Larkin, E., Hoopes, A.. Cromer, B. A. & Rosenthal, S. L. (2005). The impact of adolescent spirituality on depressive symptoms and health risk behaviors. *Journal of Adolescent Health, 36*(6), 529.

Daly, A., & Gallagher, S. (2019). Towards a phenomenology of self-patterns in psychopathological diagnosis and therapy. *Psychopathology, 52*(1), 33-49.

Dorjee, D. (2024). Conceptualising child and adolescent mental health and wellbeing neurodevelopment: an integrative brain networks framework. Preprint, 4 November. https://doi.org/10.31234/osf.io/7vx45

Garland, E. L., Hanley, A. W., Hudak, J., Nakamura, Y., & Froeliger, B. (2022). Mindfulness-induced endogenous theta stimulation occasions self-transcendence and inhibits addictive behavior. *Science Advances, 8*(41), eabo4455.

Giommi, F., Bauer, P. R., Berkovich-Ohana, A., Barendregt, H., Brown, K. W., Gallagher, S., ... & Vago, D. R. (2023). The (In) flexible self: psychopathology, mindfulness, and neuroscience. *International Journal of Clinical and Health Psychology, 23*(4), 100381.

Gotlieb, R. J., Yang, X. F., & Immordino-Yang, M. H. (2024). Diverse adolescents' transcendent thinking predicts young adult psychosocial outcomes via brain network development. *Scientific Reports, 14*(1), 6254.

Katz, J., Mercer, S. H., & Skinner, S. (2020). Developing self-concept, coping skills, and social support in grades 3-12: a cluster-randomized trial of a combined mental health literacy and dialectical behavior therapy skills program. *School Mental Health, 12*(2), 323-335.

Morris, L., & Mansell, W. (2018). A systematic review of the relationship between rigidity/flexibility and transdiagnostic cognitive and behavioral processes that maintain psychopathology. *Journal of Experimental Psychopathology, 9*(3), 2043808718779431.

Pfeifer, J. H., & Berkman, E. T. (2018). The development of self and identity in adolescence: neural evidence and implications for a value-based choice perspective on motivated behavior. *Child Development Perspectives, 12*(3), 158-164.

Ryff, C. D. (1989). Happiness is everything, or is it? Explorations on the meaning of psychological well-being. *Journal of Personality and Social Psychology, 57*(6), 1069.

Ryff, C. D., Singer, B. H., & Dienberg Love, G. (2004). Positive health: connecting well-being with biology. *Philosophical Transactions of the Royal Society of London. Series B: Biological Sciences, 359*(1449), 1383-1394.

Seligman, M. (2018). *The optimistic child: a revolutionary approach to raising resilient children*. Hachette UK.

Shoshani, A., & Russo-Netzer, P. (2017). Exploring and assessing meaning in life in elementary school children: development and validation of the meaning in life in children questionnaire (MIL-CQ). *Personality and Individual Differences, 104*, 460-465.

Telzer, E. H. (2023). Association of habitual checking behaviors on social media with longitudinal functional brain development. *JAMA Pediatrics, 177*(2), 160-167.

Yang, X. F., Pavarini, G., Schnall, S., & Immordino-Yang, M. H. (2018). Looking up to virtue: averting gaze facilitates moral construals via posteromedial activations. *Social Cognitive and Affective Neuroscience, 13*(11), 1131-1139.

Yeager, D. S., Henderson, M. D., Paunesku, D., Walton, G. M., D'Mello, S., Spitzer, B. J., & Duckworth, A. L. (2014). Boring but important: a self-transcendent purpose for learning fosters academic self-regulation. *Journal of Personality and Social Psychology, 107*(4), 559.

11 Implementing the ATTEND Framework

Introduction

The ATTEND Framework aims to systematically foster the 'root systems' underpinning mental health and wellbeing (MHW) of children via a progression of knowledge and skills cultivated in the four tiers of the ATTEND Pyramid – from Guiding Attention, through Managing Emotions and Nurturing Connections to Finding Direction. The previous chapters presented the research underpinning each building block in the four tiers of the Pyramid, together with neuroscience of the 'root systems' and ways to foster MHW skills across primary school years following the pedagogy of the 7-Step Approach. The framework offers a comprehensive way of cultivating MHW knowledge and skills of children during a developmental period that can impact children's lifelong MHW trajectories. The aim of this chapter is to consider how the ATTEND Framework can be effectively implemented in primary schools to fully harness its potential.

To enable you to introduce the ATTEND Framework in your school impactfully, this chapter first provides answers to key questions you might have about its implementation. These could be questions about trainability of the self-regulation and self-world capacities or questions about ways to integrate the ATTEND framework with other programmes fostering social-emotional development, resilience or mindfulness. Next, the chapter explores how the ATTEND Framework can be embedded in your school as a whole school approach, given the advantages of such implementation to children, school staff and school community. Finally, the chapter positions the ATTEND Framework in the context of the current societal crises – including climate change, political instability and war conflicts – discussing how the knowledge and skills cultivated in the framework may protect children's MHW during these volatile times. But first, let's consider a case study exemplifying the opportunities and challenges of implementing the ATTEND Framework in a primary school.

Case Study: How to Implement the ATTEND Framework Effectively

Fiona is a deputy headteacher in her primary school and is currently developing a new MHW strategy for her school. She is familiar with the guidelines from the Department of Education encouraging schools to foster MHW via a whole school approach. Fiona likes the nuanced progression of learning in the ATTEND Framework and would like to recommend its implementation in her school, but she isn't sure how the framework would work as a whole school approach.

Fiona is also wondering how to integrate the ATTEND Framework with other approaches they have already implemented in her school. Some of these programmes – like those that foster social-emotional development of children in early years or those that teach children mindfulness skills – seem to work quite well, so it would be good to keep them or some elements of them. However, she does not want to duplicate learning that is already outlined in the ATTEND framework.

Finally, Fiona is wondering if the ATTEND Framework could improve children's resilience. She found that there is a lot of emphasis on resilience in the government guidance on fostering MHW in schools. Fiona also saw further discussions in the media about the importance of cultivating resilience in children and young people in the face of the current societal crises. Fiona knows from her own experience that even children in primary schools are increasingly worried about climate change and the impact of possible war conflict on their families and themselves. She would like to know if the ATTEND Framework offers any specific guidance on how to support children's resilience from this wider societal perspective.

Questions for reflection:

- Do you think the knowledge and skills detailed in the ATTEND Framework can support children's social-emotional development? If so, how?
- Can you envision the ATTEND Pyramid to be implemented as a whole school approach in your school?
- Do you think the knowledge and skills fostered in the ATTEND Framework can support children's resilience? Can you describe why and how?

Two Approaches to Implementing the ATTEND Framework

There are two main approaches to implementing the ATTEND Framework in your school. The first approach involves following closely the content in the chapters in this book and translating the guidance into lesson plans you can then implement in the classroom. In this process, it is best to follow the progression of the tiers and building blocks of the ATTEND Pyramid because they gradually build up children's MHW knowledge and skills. Skipping some of the building blocks will likely make the learning less effective. Similarly, the progression of the 7-Step Approach ensures that children's MHW knowledge and skills are fostered gradually in an accessible and trauma-sensitive way, thus minimising the likelihood of triggering effects.

The second approach to implementing the ATTEND Framework still follows the progression of the tiers and building blocks of the ATTEND Pyramid and the progression and principles of the 7-Step Approach, but uses them both as a more overarching guidance on implementing MHW learning in your school. This means, for example, applying the research-based content outlined in the previous chapters explaining the reasoning behind the building blocks and the progression of the tiers of the ATTEND Pyramid as a form of CPD training for you and your staff. Such training would deepen your understanding of what 'roots systems' MHW universal interventions in schools need to foster, why and how this can be done. This may in turn enable you to see beyond the labels of programmes – such as resilience or social-emotional learning (SEL) – and focus on the 'root systems' of MHW which need to be fostered systematically across primary school years. In this way, the ATTEND Framework can be considered a *meta-framework*, creating a roadmap for a range of MHW curriculum frameworks where the tiers and building blocks of the ATTEND Pyramid are closely followed – but ways to foster the knowledge and skills of the building blocks may differ to some extent.

Using the ATTEND Framework as a meta-framework, you can then try to map existing MHW initiatives in your school onto the 10 building blocks of the ATTEND Pyramid, to see which building blocks might the current initiatives be already covering and where the gaps are. You can also compare the approaches you have already implemented to the strategies detailed in the book. Next, you may use the guidance on the 7-Step Approach in assessing if the MHW initiatives you are currently implementing in your school are delivered gradually and in a trauma-informed way, or whether they need some improvements. Based on this understanding, you may then try to develop a bespoke approach tailored to your school's needs, preserving elements of MHW learning which you have found helpful in the past and covering any missing elements. This can ensure that children's MHW knowledge and skills are fostered in an age-appropriate way effectively and safely across primary school years.

The decision to follow the first or the second approach depends on your individual classroom or school circumstances. If you are looking for a new comprehensive approach that can build up children's MHW knowledge and skills year-by-year and step-by-step, applying the first approach to implementing the ATTEND Framework might be the best choice. However, if you already have successfully implemented some MHW learning initiatives in your school and would like to expand or refine them or improve the developmental progression of learning, you may want to apply the second approach to implementing the framework.

Questions for reflection:

- Does the first or the second approach to implementing the ATTEND Framework fit the needs of your school better?
- Will you be able to implement all the building blocks of the ATTEND Pyramid in your school in the recommended progression?
- Is it possible to implement the ATTEND Framework in your school with children's learning building up across primary years?

The ATTEND Framework FAQs

Whether you choose the first or the second approach to introducing the ATTEND Framework in your school, just like Fiona from the case study at the start of the chapter, you may have further questions about specifics of implementing the framework in your school. It might be useful for you to write some of these questions down before you proceed to reading this section. Here are answers to some of the most common questions:

Are Self-regulation and Self-world Capacities Trainable?

With the growing research on genetic components of traits relevant to MHW knowledge and skills, particularly self-regulation, some teachers are questioning whether teaching such skills in schools can make a difference to children and adolescents. There is indeed research supporting strong genetic contribution to self-regulation as a neurodevelopment trait, particularly when considering poor self-regulation in relation to attention deficit hyperactivity disorder (ADHD), impulsive behaviour, antisocial behaviour and substance use (e.g. Karlsson Linnér et al., 2021).

However, interpretation of such research findings from genetics research in a deterministic way is inaccurate and unhelpful. First, it is important to understand that this research is probabilistic – pointing to a possible likelihood of certain behaviour manifesting, rather than confidence that it will manifest. Second, it is essential to acknowledge that manifestation of a genetic predisposition is strongly impacted by environmental influences – particularly stress – influencing whether, and if so to what extent, a genetic predisposition manifests in behaviour.

Chapter 4 discussed different types of stressors children can be exposed to, from poverty through discrimination to bullying and family stress. Mitigating these stress factors is paramount to reducing genetic risk factors to self-regulation and other MHW capacities. The chapter also outlined how the stress response impacts MHW and how children can acquire skills in adaptively managing it. Understanding the role of the stress response in triggering genetic predispositions adds further weight to the importance of cultivating these skills in children.

Key Points: Genetics and Malleability of the MHW Capacities

- Genetic contribution to self-regulation (or other neurodevelopmental traits) should not be interpreted in a deterministic way.
- Manifestation of a genetic predisposition is influenced by environmental factors, particularly strong acute stress or chronic stress.
- Extensive research shows that self-regulation knowledge and skills can be acquired through effective learning in schools.
- The processes of the self-world capacity are also malleable and associated knowledge and skills can be learned.

How mitigation of some of the environmental stress factors together with equipping children with opportunities to improve their self-regulation skills may reduce the impacts of genetic predispositions and environmental stress has been examined in neuroscience research. One study specifically investigated the interactions between the effects of low socio-economic status as a stressor, unfavourable genetic predisposition for self-regulation (long 5-HTT-LPR allele) and self-regulation training in children (the training involved both a parenting intervention and self-regulation training for children) (Isbell et al., 2017).

The study specifically looked at changes in a brain marker of top-down self-regulation derived from brain wave data. At the baseline, before the training, children with the unfavourable genetic predisposition showed a diminished pattern of self-regulation brain responses in comparison to children with a favourable genetic predisposition. However, after the training the self-regulation brain responses of children in both groups were comparable. In other words, children in the group with the unfavourable genetic predisposition no longer showed the deficit in their self-regulation brain responses. This demonstrates that despite unfavourable genetic predispositions, the 'root systems' underpinning MHW are malleable by training. However, there are very few training approaches and studies on how the initial training benefits can be sustained in the longer term. The ATTEND Framework aims to encourage such long-term training and research.

Similarly, extensive research on acquisition of social-emotional competencies, which overlap with the facets of the self-world capacity, shows that these can be effectively cultivated in schools. For example, a recent robust research synthesis of findings across 424 studies found that social and emotional learning interventions in schools can improve children's interpersonal skills including perspective taking and empathy, peer relationships, prosocial behaviours and ethical/moral reasoning (Cipriano et al., 2023). The previous chapters also provided specific examples of research studies showing that the knowledge and skills linked to the facets of the self-world capacity – including a sense of connection, gratitude, compassion, prosocial behaviours and purpose in life – can be effectively fostered in primary schools.

Can the ATTEND Framework Support Social-Emotional Development of Children?

Social-emotional development refers to the developmental progression of children's abilities to manage their emotions and relate to others. Such abilities are particularly underpinned by processes of emotion regulation as part of self-regulation and being able to understand and reflect on one's own and others thoughts, emotions and behaviours (perspective taking). The ATTEND Framework aims to effectively foster these processes and specifies a nuanced systematic research-based approach for cultivating corresponding social-emotional skills during child development.

Specifically, the self-regulation capacity underpinning the first two tiers of the ATTEND Pyramid involves processes of managing one's attention, emotions and behaviour in alignment with one's goals. And the self-world capacity underpinning the third and the fourth tier of the ATTEND Pyramid focuses on processes supporting the development of children's a connected, purposeful, ethically-grounded and flexible sense of self (Dorjee, 2024a). Thus the ATTEND Framework aims to foster children's social-emotional development, with particular emphasis on how these processes contribute to prevention of mental ill-health and enhancement of children's MHW.

> Questions for reflection:
> - Can you link the knowledge and skills cultivated in each of the building blocks of the ATTEND Pyramid to specific aspects of children's social and emotional development?
> - How can the ATTEND Framework strengthen the current approach to fostering children's social and emotional development in your primary school?

How Is the ATTEND Framework Different from Social-Emotional Learning?

Social-emotional learning (SEL) describes the learning process of acquiring competencies, attitudes and skills of managing emotions, positive relationships and responsible decision making (Chatterjee Singh, 2020). In other words, SEL is a process of fostering children's social-emotional development. While there are over 130 SEL frameworks, one of the first and most widely applied frameworks is the CASEL – Collaborative for Academic, Social and Emotional Learning – developed in the USA (Kaspar & Massey, 2023). In this framework the main focus is on cultivating five SEL competencies – self-awareness, self-management, responsible decision making, social awareness and relationship skills.

Relating the competencies of the CASEL framework to the ATTEND Framework, one can see alignment with fostering of the attention and emotion regulation skills as part of the first two tiers of the Pyramid and overlaps with the skills fostered in the last two tiers of the Pyramid. However there is also a difference between the CASEL and ATTEND approaches. For example, the ATTEND Framework places greater emphasis on relevance of the knowledge skills to MHW and progression of their fostering. It also expands the scope of competencies fostered in SEAD towards specific strategies for managing distractions, reactivity of rumination, as well as relational qualities of shared humanity, prosociality and purpose in life.

Understanding these similarities and differences can support teachers in meaningfully integrating SEL and ATTEND approaches based on particular learning objectives. For instance, if the primary focus of learning is on developing MHW knowledge and skills, it might be useful to expand SEL learning with further learning based on the ATTEND framework, possibly following the second implementation approach explained above. The ATTEND framework can also be expanded further to cover both MHW and SEL skills by content focusing on problem solving or team work skills. The MHW knowledge and skills fostered in the ATTEND Pyramid will most likely further catalyse SEL learning.

Can the ATTEND Framework Foster Children's Resilience?

Another concept that is often highlighted in both MHW curricula and social-emotional development is resilience – the ability to bounce back from adversity. Resilience is usually described in terms of internal and external protective factors. The internal protective factors involve strong self-regulation and social skills, prosocial behaviour, groundedness in ethical/moral beliefs, optimism and hopefulness etc. The external protective factors include strong social support from family and friends, community and cultural belonging, as well as positive school relationships.

School-based universal interventions that aim to foster resilience typically develop children's skills of decision making and problem solving, cooperation and communication and their coping skills (Dray et al., 2017). Looking closer at this list of skills, as well as at the description of the internal and external protective factors, it becomes clear that the concept of resilience closely overlaps both with SEL approaches and with the ATTEND Framework. The main differences may lie in less focus on examples of 'bouncing back' in SEL and the ATTEND Framework, and more focus on fostering social competencies and a range of MHW skills in these two approaches, respectively. Nevertheless, both SEL (LaBelle, 2023) and training in skills detailed in the ATTEND Framework such as self-regulation (Keane & Evans, 2022), have been shown to increase resilience in children. This further highlights the need to look beyond labels and examine processes and skills cultivated across these approaches to meaningfully combine them.

> Questions for reflection:
> - Can you identify any overlaps between the knowledge and skills cultivated in the ATTEND Framework and knowledge and skills in resilience programmes implemented in your school?
> - Are there ways the ATTEND Framework can enrich resilience training in your school, for example through more systematic progression of learning within and across years?

Is the ATTEND Framework Aligned with Teaching Children Mindfulness Skills?

Over the decade and a half mindfulness-based approaches have been increasingly implemented in schools to support children's MHW. Mindfulness practice, which originated in Buddhist philosophy and meditation, is in its secular form described as guiding and sustaining attention intentionally on present moment experience with an accepting non-judgmental attitude (Kabat-Zinn, 2003). Such accepting attention to one's experience is a central therapeutic component of mindfulness-based approaches including the Mindfulness-Based Stress Reduction (MBSR) and Mindfulness-Based Cognitive Therapy (MBCT). Rigorous evidence from studies with adults shows that MBSR is effective in reducing stress and anxiety

(Khoury et al., 2015) and MBCT in reducing symptoms of anxiety and depression (Hofmann et al., 2010) and preventing depression relapse in recurrent depression (Kuyken et al., 2008).

The beneficial effects of MBSR and MBCT inspired adaptations of these approaches to children and adolescents, in both clinical and non-clinical contexts. The latter includes universal mindfulness-based programmes that can be implemented in primary schools. Many current SEL and resilience programmes also include mindfulness elements. Research evidence on effectiveness of mindfulness-based programmes in primary schools suggests that they can reduce negative affect in children (Vickery & Dorjee, 2016) and strengthen brain processes underpinning effective emotion regulation (Nguyen & Dorjee, 2022). However, our understanding of the long-term effects of these interventions is still limited.

The ATTEND Framework encourages children from the start to cultivate an accepting and non-judgmental attitude towards their experience, and gradually deepens children's understanding and skills of relating to their experience in this way throughout the tiers of the ATTEND Pyramid. Thai is because a non-judgmental accepting attitude is essential for effective and non-triggering (trauma-informed) acquisition of MHW knowledge and skills of the ATTEND Pyramid. It is also commonly applied in therapeutic approaches including and beyond MBSR and MBCT.

So the ATTEND framework is aligned with mindfulness-based and other therapeutic approaches fostering a non-judgmental accepting attitude towards one's own experience. Some of the strategies children train in, particularly those in the building block of managing reactivity, are aligned with mindfulness practices one can find in a mindfulness programme. The ATTEND Framework also introduces children to simple practices in which they ground their attention on neutral external sensory anchors, which are similar to some MBSR and MBCT techniques. Providing children with further training in mindfulness may deepen their skills of non-judgmental attending to their present moment experience and can be delivered alongside MHW learning in the ATTEND Framework.

Is the ATTEND Framework Trauma-Informed?

When delivering MHW programmes in schools, the key requirement is that they do not trigger or worsen mental ill-health symptoms in children. This requirement is particularly salient in the context of supporting children with adverse childhood experiences (ACEs) which may have resulted in trauma. These experiences typically involve acute high-intensity stressors such as a traumatic event exposure or repeated chronic stressors including family or community violence, maltreatment, family member incarceration etc. Worldwide estimates of ACEs prevalence are as high as 60% of the population (Madigan et al., 2023). Given that over a half of children in a classroom are likely to have had ACEs, there is the need for trauma-informed delivery of MHW approaches in schools and adoption of trauma-informed teaching practices in general (Downey & Greco, 2023).

Trauma-informed teaching is based on the premise that ACEs lead to changes in the stress response in children with wide reaching negative impacts on their ability to self-regulate – including focus on tasks, managing reactivity and adaptive social interactions.

Therefore, trauma-informed teaching aims to create a learning environment that may mitigate children's stress response and provide them with tools that could support them in cultivating adaptive responses to stress. This can be achieved through implementation of trauma-informed practices in schools involving staff training to deepen their understanding of what ACEs are and how they impact children's attention, emotions and behaviour. The next step should then be development of policies and practices in the school to minimise re-traumatisation of children with ACEs (Downey & Greco, 2023).

The ATTEND Framework applies a trauma-informed approach to MHW teaching in schools throughout its building blocks, the four tiers and the 7-Step Approach. Indeed, the progression of the ATTEND Framework aims to minimise trauma-triggers by building up children's MHW skills by starting with least probing learning and progressing onto more complex MHW skills. For example, children first develop emotional awareness from a non-judgmental accepting perspective together with a simple emotional regulation strategy of naming emotions. This can reduce the likelihood of increased emotional awareness triggering mental ill-health symptoms, yet this is often not acknowledged in policy recommendations to train children in emotional awareness. Similarly, children start working with more challenging emotions linked to stress only in the third facet of the ATTEND Pyramid, after they have acquired foundational MHW skills they can fall back on if working with stress and reactivity becomes too challenging. Again, this is not a common approach in education, teaching children about stress and reactivity is often done in isolation without teaching children foundational MHW skills.

> **Key Points: Trauma-Informed Learning and the ATTEND Framework**
>
> - Over a half of children in each classroom is likely to have had adverse childhood experiences (ACEs) which are often linked to trauma.
> - Trauma-informed teaching creates an environment that fosters adaptive stress responses and reduces likelihood of re-traumatising.
> - The ATTEND Framework is trauma-informed – it is strengths-based, uses non-probing language and activities, and builds up children's MHW knowledge and skills gradually.
> - Trauma-informed delivery of the ATTEND Framework requires the teaching staff to relate to children and their experiences in a non-judgmental, empathic and compassionate way.

In addition, the progression of learning in the 7-Step approach aims to introduce children to MHW knowledge and skills in a trauma-informed way, by first working with external impersonal examples and then gradually exploring applicability of any of the learning to their own experience. And throughout the building blocks of the ATTEND Pyramid, the strategies children acquire using the 7-Step Approach are strengths, rather than symptom, focused. This is one of the key features of trauma-informed approaches. Finally, specific strategies across the ATTEND Pyramid have been adapted to be least triggering. This for example involves the recommendation to introduce children to paced breathing practices and progressive-muscle relaxation with their eyes open and while sitting, not lying on the floor which is a more vulnerable position (e.g. Treleaven, 2018). There are also recommendations throughout the ATTEND Framework on how to invite children to reflect on their experience in a confidential and respectful way (e.g. not sharing deeper personal experiences with the class).

However, trauma-informed delivery of the ATTEND Framework in your classroom involves first and foremost creating an environment where children can feel safe and understood, with zero-tolerance of ridicule or shaming which can have re-traumatising effects. This also involves use of accepting and non-judgmental language by the teaching staff, encouraging and inviting children to explore the different strategies and their experience. Thus trauma-informed delivery of the ATTEND Framework inevitably requires strengthening of social-emotional competencies of the teaching staff. The teaching can't be simply delivered from a prescriptive didactic perspective, but requires empathic and compassionate relating to children's experiences. Developing skills in relational teaching methods such as PACE – Playfulness, Acceptance, Curiosity and Empathy – can be particularly suitable both for trauma-informed delivery of the ATTEND Framework and other teaching in your school.

The Whole School Implementation of the ATTEND Framework

Supporting the MHW of children in primary schools involves more than just delivery of a MHW curriculum in classrooms. In schools children are embedded in a complex system of relationships including their peers, teachers, specialist support staff and other school staff, school ethos and wider school community including parents. If we consider children as being at the centre of these complex interactive relationships, it becomes clear that supporting children's MHW effectively also needs to take into account the impacts these relationships have on them. Fostering this wide network relationship can further facilitate children's MHW learning. That is why there has been increasing emphasis on implementing MHW initiatives in schools in a whole-school format (Department for Education, 2025).

Indeed, research shows that teachers' MHW is intertwined with their pupils' MHW. For example, one study found that increased levels of burnout in teachers were associated with an increase in the stress hormone cortisol in primary school children (Oberle & Schonert-Reichl, 2016). Thus supporting children's MHW needs to include supporting teachers' MHW too. This is a challenging task given that 86% of teachers in a 2024 survey in the UK reported that their job negatively impacted their mental health over the preceding 12 months (NASUWT, 2024). Reasons for this pattern are complex, including long hours, poor pupil behaviour, and little control over policy changes and associated implementation pressures.

The systemic contributors to teacher stress clearly need urgent addressing. Alongside them, there is a need for interventions that can support teachers' MHW, and such interventions can be effective (Beames et al., 2023). They often include fostering a very similar range of knowledge and skills to those fostered in MHW programmes for children, including mindfulness and resilience. Research shows that teachers' MHW can also benefit when they are delivering such programmes to children (Schoenert-Reichl, 2017). To enable these benefits to manifest in schools, teacher training in MHW knowledge and skills needs to be facilitated by sufficient support and funding at the school leadership and policy levels.

However, a whole school implementation of MHW strategies in primary schools would go even further – beyond direct involvement of teachers, pupils and school leadership. It would include all teaching staff and also other staff in a school – so that children engage in consistently supportive interactions with everyone in their school. This would be reflected in the school ethos and support children's sense of school belonging which is, together with teacher-pupil relationships and peer relationships, another key predictor of children's MHW (Aldridge et al., 2018). Finally, a whole school implementation would also impact on how the school staff interacts with parents and involves them in supporting children's MHW. This can be further enhanced by constructive engagement with the wider community in which a school is positioned, through mutual support and involvement, for example through volunteering and enrichment activities. An MHW programme that is embedded across these multifaceted child-school relationships has the stronger potential of making a true difference to children's long-term MHW trajectories.

> Questions for reflection:
> - Have you implemented a whole-school MHW approach in your school? If so, what elements does it have?
> - Does your approach cover all the dimensions of the whole-school implementation checklist outlined in Figure 11.1?

Whole School Implementation Checklist and the ATTEND Framework

The ATTEND Framework is a universal curriculum-based MHW programme or meta-framework which can be implemented in schools both as part of a regular curriculum or as a whole school approach. Given the advantages of a whole school implementation outlined above, we will now consider what such implementation would entail. The MHW programme implementation checklist presented in Figure 11.1 can help you make practical decisions about implementing the ATTEND Framework in your school and will guide our considerations in what follows.

Integrating the ATTEND framework with targeted MHW and SEN support

The first question in the checklist asks about a universal versus targeted nature of the MHW programme you will be implementing. In the case of the ATTEND Framework the programme is intended for a whole classroom delivery, thus universal. But you may be wondering, from

Implementation dimension	Tick	
Where on the spectrum from targeted to universal does the MHW programme fall?	T	U
Does the programme follow a developmental progression? Is it suitable for the age group?	Yes	No
Does the programme develop skills supporting MHW or does it rely on knowledge-based learning?	K	K+S
Does the programme address MHW of teachers as well as wellbeing of pupils?	Yes	No
Is the programme implemented only in separate lessons, or does it involve more embedded implementation?	L	E
Does the programme involve the whole school and wider school community?	Yes	No
Does the programme include guidance on long-term sustainability of its benefits?	Yes	No

Figure 11.1 The whole-school implementation checklist for MHW programmes

a whole school perspective, how the framework can support pupils who need specialised MHW support, including students with special education needs.

To start with, the trauma-informed formulation of the ATTEND Framework makes it suitable for delivery to both students with general and more specific MHW and special educational needs (SEN). However, students with further needs, may benefit with some adjustments to some of the practices though. For example, some students with SEN may find it more challenging to engage with some of the neuroscience content or practices that emphasise reflection on one's own or others' thoughts and behaviours. Simplifying the practices using recommendations for a younger age group, may make it easier for some pupils to engage with the practices.

In addition, some pupils who need further MHW support may benefit from being reminded that they should engage with the strategies and practices only to the extent they feel comfortable with. Throughout the programme there is an emphasis on pupils choosing strategies that work best for them, rather than forceful engagement with all strategies. This applies to all students, regardless of their further needs, so this approach can accommodate students who need further MHW support readily.

Moreover, both children with and without further MHW and educational needs are likely to benefit from fostering self-regulation and relational MHW skills of the self-world capacity. This is because such skills are often cultivated both in universal and more targeted interventions tailored to pupils' with further MHW needs and SEN. Thus their learning in the ATTEND Framework may complement the tailored support they might be receiving in small groups or one-to-one settings.

Therefore, to support a whole-school implementation of the ATTEND Framework, it is recommended that all teaching staff – including specialist staff working with children who need further MHW support and children with SEN – to familiarise themselves with the framework if it is implemented in the school as a universal approach. Closer understanding of the framework may allow specialist SEN support staff to skilfully combine the knowledge and skills children acquire in universal classroom settings with more targeted support they receive. In this way the two approaches may work in complementary ways to catalyse children's MHW learning.

Developmentally Nuanced and Skills-Based Learning in the ATTEND Framework

The second question in the whole-school implementation checklist for MHW programmes asks whether the programme is age-appropriate and includes a developmental progression of cultivating children's MHW. This aspect of implementation is a key to fostering children's MHW knowledge and skills in a way that can have long-term positive impact on their MHW trajectories. Simply put, while short MHW programmes implemented in a particular school year are better than no MHW training, their long-term benefits are very unlikely to be sustained unless the acquired knowledge and skills are systematically reinforced and deepened further. This principle is being readily applied in any other learning in schools, from acquisition of reading and writing skills through maths skills to science. As highlighted in the first chapter, we should start approaching MHW learning in the same way if we want to build up children's MHW knowledge and skills effectively and impactfully.

The ATTEND framework follows this principle closely and provides a clear horizontal and vertical progression of systematic age-appropriate MHW learning. The horizontal progression in learning refers to the build up of MHW knowledge and skills across the building blocks of the ATTEND Pyramid and its four tiers. The horizontal progression of learning also applies to the 7-Step Approach which gradually scaffolds children's acquisition of specific MHW knowledge and skills within each building block of the pyramid. The vertical progression of learning refers to the build up of children's knowledge and skills across primary school years, reinforcing and expanding their learning within each building block from one key stage to another. This approach is aligned with whole-school strategies of fostering MHW knowledge and skills systematically across school years.

Finally, it is important to highlight that effective MHW learning needs to include acquisition of both relevant knowledge and skills. Current MHW learning seems to be 'skewed' towards teaching children *about MHW* rather than teaching them *how to develop MHW skills* that they can apply in their everyday life. This might be one of the reasons why such teaching has limited impact on children's MHW. As was highlighted throughout this book, children can develop a range of MHW skills that can enable them to manage their thoughts, emotions, behaviours and relationships skilfully. Systematic reinforcement and internalising of such skills is a key to children's long-term MHW. Recognising this, the ATTEND Framework is designed to effectively develop and sustain such skills through its horizontal and vertical progression of learning.

The ATTEND Framework and Teacher MHW

As discussed at the beginning of this section, teacher and pupil MHW is closely intertwined. Therefore whole-school approaches encourage fostering of teacher MHW alongside children's MHW when introducing such programmes in schools. Implementing the ATTEND Framework in your school is no exception. While the framework is clearly designed for delivery to pupils, effectiveness of its delivery will depend both on teachers' understanding of the relevant research and strategies, and their own MHW knowledge and skills.

For these reasons, the implementation of the ATTEND Framework should ideally be preceded by teacher training that will enable teachers to develop the MHW knowledge and skills described in the framework themselves. However, in the absence of such tailored training programmes, it is up to teachers to develop relevant MHW knowledge and skills via available training programmes. These can include mindfulness-based programmes which have been shown to reduce teacher stress and burnout as well as foster the non-judgmental accepting attitude to own experience that is cultivated throughout the ATTEND Framework. Training in social-emotional competencies for school teachers can also be effective in supporting teachers' MHW and equipping them with foundational MHW skills they can apply when teaching the ATTEND Framework. Importantly, any such training should entail development of MHW skills as well as knowledge, which can then be expanded through the learning in the ATTEND Framework detailed in this book.

Embedding the ATTEND Framework as a Sustainable Whole-School Approach

Finally, you will need to make some decisions about implementing the ATTEND Framework in your school to align it more closely with a whole-approach to MHW learning. The first decision involves considering whether the framework will be delivered solely as part of lessons or whether it will be more broadly embedded into the school life. A whole-school implementation approach encourages an embedded implementation, where the learning children acquire in lessons can be applied and reinforced outside of the classroom.

This is also the approach championed as part of the ATTEND Framework, where the last step of the 7-Step Approach in each building block of the ATTEND Pyramid encourages children to apply their new MHW knowledge and skills throughout the school day and outside of school as well. Such learning is more likely to lead to impactful long-term enhancements of children's MHW. However, effective embedding of the ATTEND Framework requires all teaching staff to become familiar with the framework and development of a coordinated strategy detailing how the embedding will be supported and encouraged across school contexts (e.g. during breaks, on the playground, during mealtimes, field trips etc.).

Such embedding can also be expanded to include the wider school community, beyond the teaching staff. For example, this can involve preparing resources for parents that will inform them about the MHW knowledge and skills children are developing and ways to support them in practising the skills outside of school. In a way, this approach is no different from other types of 'homework' children receive for other school subjects. However, what makes it different is the potentially sensitive nature of such learning, therefore any resources shared with parents need to be accessible and trauma-informed.

Wider embedding of the ATTEND Framework can also involve exploration of alignment of different aspects of the framework with the school ethos. For example, if the school ethos encourages cultivation of qualities such as patience or kindness or courage, this can be readily linked with the learning of self-regulation, shared humanity and 'making a difference' skills. Such skills can also be fostered through engagement with the wider community via volunteering and further enrichment activities. In this way the learning can increase children's sense of school belonging and their connection to the wider community, supporting their MHW further.

Finally, the implementation strategy needs to include a clear plan for sustaining children's newly acquired MHW knowledge and skills long-term to maximise the likelihood of the learning having tangible impact on children's life-long MHW trajectories. Here it can be useful to remember that children's self-regulation and self-world capacities predict their health, academic and social outcomes into adulthood. Therefore, investing in reinforcing and internalising the MHW knowledge and skills is most likely to have lasting impact on children's prospects and is worth the effort.

The ATTEND Framework, with its horizontal and vertical progression of learning, is designed to sustain and gradually expand children's acquisition of MHW knowledge and skills throughout primary school years. Embedded whole-school implementation of the framework can provide further opportunities for children to practise and reinforce these skills. Therefore, it is the recommended approach to introducing the framework in your school effectively and sustainably.

The Big Picture: The ATTEND Framework in Society

Humanity is currently facing several existential crises including climate change, political polarisation, war conflicts and challenges linked to artificial intelligence (AI) developments. It is rarely acknowledged that these crises are intertwined – with political polarisation which is associated with growing decline of democracy and governance of societies at their centre. For example, insufficient action on climate change is the result of some political views linked to distrust towards science. Similarly, lack of political agreement is undermining efforts to address current war conflicts and prevent new ones. And both climate inaction and political disagreements are fuelled by online disinformation and misinformation enabled by AI developments.

These interlinked crises have an impact on child and adolescent MHW both directly and indirectly. The direct impacts for those young people exposed to climate disasters or war include acute trauma, chronic stress and resulting increased risk of long-term anxiety disorders and depression. And even for those not directly impacted, concerns about the current crises are significantly undermining their MHW. For example, a recent study in Germany found that concerns about global crises – including the Covid-19 pandemic, climate change and war in Ukraine – were linked to nearly a third of anxiety symptoms in 12-16-year-olds (Lass-Hennemann et al., 2024).

In the face of unpredictable political developments exacerbating these crises, there are growing calls for schools to equip children with the knowledge and skills they need to strengthen their resilience. This includes educating children more effectively to recognise disinformation and misinformation, but also fostering their psychological resilience in case of natural disasters or war. In addition, children need to be equipped with a stronger understanding of democracy and how it differs from autocracy, given the increasing attempts at undermining democratic societies.

The ATTEND Framework, Climate Anxiety, Digital Literacy and Democracy Education

The current societal challenges and the associated calls for resilience education in schools raise the question whether the ATTEND Framework could play a role in these efforts. The knowledge and skills of MHW cultivated in the ATTEND Framework closely overlap with knowledge and skills of internal protective factors of resilience as discussed earlier in this chapter. Therefore, learning in the four tiers of the ATTEND Pyramid is very likely to strengthen children's psychological resilience in various contexts, including in the face of societal crises.

For example, in the context of managing climate anxiety linked to climate change, children can build on their skills of emotional awareness and naming emotions as well as strategies for managing reactivity in the moment. They can also use the skills cultivated in the building blocks of Connections and Making a Difference, to transform their empathic distress into compassionate climate action which can give them the sense of hopefulness and purpose that many young people currently struggle with. Such application of the MHW knowledge and skills to climate anxiety can usefully complement teaching climate literacy in schools.

Similarly, children can be guided in using the MHW skills they acquired in the ATTEND Framework to enhance their digital literacy skills. Currently, we often separate teaching children about online disinformation and misinformation from teaching them MHW skills. Such separation of learning is likely undermining the effectiveness of digital literacy teaching. This is because disinformation and misinformation often uses emotional content, such as survival fears or appeals to in-group out-group belonging, to capture one's attention. This makes it difficult to disengage one's attention from the content. Therefore, children need to apply their skills of noticing emotions, managing reactivity and managing distractions to resist disinformation and misinformation content online (Dorjee, 2024b). This can be most effective if such learning is combined with effective action by governments and social media companies to reduce children's exposure to harmful content online (Dorjee, 2025).

> **Key Points: Ways the ATTEND Framework Can Support Children's Resilience in the Face of Global Crises**
>
> - Children can use their MHW skills of emotional awareness and managing reactivity to down-regulate their climate anxiety, and skills of nurturing connections and making a difference in contributing to climate action and increasing feelings of hopefulness.
> - Children's MHW skills of emotional awareness, managing reactivity and managing distractions can usefully complement their digital literacy learning and increase their ability to recognise and resist disinformation and misinformation.
> - Fostering children's MHW skills of shared humanity, nurturing connections, making a difference and finding purpose in life beyond self-focus can contribute to their understanding of democratic values and ways to defend democracy against autocratic threats.

In addition, feelings of existential uncertainty linked to societal crises make us more susceptible to conspiracy theories because they offer ways of making sense of events or threatening developments as a way of coping. Any explanation is better than none when we are trying to reduce the feeling of stress arising from existential uncertainty. Children are increasingly exposed to conspiracy theories online too. Applying their skills of managing the stress response and staying in the 'green zone' may reduce their susceptibility to such manipulation online. And if these MHW skills become internalised habits, they can protect children's MHW and increase their resilience in the longer term.

Finally, teaching children about the virtues of democracy in comparison to autocracy needs to include more than knowledge of the differences. When researchers examined psychological profiles of people who stood up to rising autocratic powers in the build up to World War II and during the war, they found that these people shared some key characteristics. They were more empathic, compassionate and committed to moral values, and they were also more inclusive and likely to embrace universalist views – that justice and equality apply to everyone. Unlike the majority of current MHW frameworks, the ATTEND Framework aims to develop the knowledge and skills linked to these characteristics in children, particularly in the last two tiers of the ATTEND Pyramid fostering the self-world capacity. Hence, the framework can support democracy education in schools too.

During this volatile time of societal crises, when schools are being asked to play an active role in fostering children's resilience, one of the key determinants of the success of these efforts will be whether they manage to meaningfully integrate effective MHW learning with fostering climate, digital and democracy literacy in children. As the examples in this section show, this is because MHW knowledge and skills build an indispensable foundation for such literacy knowledge and skills. The ATTEND Framework has the potential to effectively and impactfully contribute to developing the wide range of resilience skills children need to navigate current societal challenges, alongside timely systemic changes in policy and economy – addressing inequalities and toxic online influences on children's lives. Hopefully this book has provided you with useful nuanced guidance on why and how the key MHW knowledge and skills enhancing children's resilience can be fostered in your primary school classroom.

Conclusion

If you were, just like Fiona in the case study presented at the start of this chapter, wondering how to effectively implement the ATTEND Framework outlined in the previous chapters in your classroom or school, this chapter provided answers to the most common questions you might have been asking. First we considered two main approaches to introducing the ATTEND Framework in a primary school. The chapter then considered FAQs about the framework implementation, such as its contribution to fostering children's social emotional development and resilience. We have also discussed reasons why the framework is trauma-informed and why it needs to be delivered by teachers from a trauma-informed relational perspective. Next, the chapter explained how the ATTEND Framework can be embedded in your school in a whole-school format, to maximise its effectiveness. Finally, we considered how the ATTEND Framework can contribute to fostering children's resilience in the current volatile world of societal crises. Overall, the chapter brought together the explanations of the 'why and how' of fostering children's MHW skills presented in this book to support you in effectively implementing the ATTEND Framework in your primary school.

Key chapter points:

- The ATTEND Framework provides a systematic and developmentally nuanced approach to introducing or enhancing MHW curriculum in your school.
- The ATTEND Framework can foster social emotional development and resilience of children.
- The framework is trauma-informed and needs to be delivered from a trauma-informed perspective.
- The ATTEND Framework will be most effective if implemented via a whole-school approach.
- The framework can meaningfully complement learning of climate, digital and democracy literacy skills and enhance it to support children's resilience in the face of global crises.

References

Aldridge, J. M., McChesney, K., & Afari, E. (2018). Relationships between school climate, bullying and delinquent behaviours. *Learning Environments Research, 21*, 153-172.

Beames, J. R., Spanos, S., Roberts, A., McGillivray, L., Li, S., Newby, J. M., ... & Werner-Seidler, A. (2023). Intervention programs targeting the mental health, professional burnout, and/or wellbeing of school teachers: Systematic review and meta-analyses. *Educational Psychology Review, 35*(1), 26.

Cipriano, C., Strambler, M. J., Naples, L. H., Ha, C., Kirk, M., Wood, M., ... & Durlak, J. (2023). The state of evidence for social and emotional learning: a contemporary meta-analysis of universal school-based SEL interventions. *Child Development, 94*(5), 1181-1204.

Chatterjee Singh, N., & Duraiappah, A. K. (2020). *Rethinking learning: A review of social and emotional learning for education systems*. Mahatma Gandhi Institute of Education for Peace and Sustainable Development. https://mgiep.unesco.org/rethinking-learning

Department for Education (2025). Promoting and supporting mental health and wellbeing in schools and colleges. www.gov.uk/guidance/mental-health-and-wellbeing-support-in-schools-and-colleges

Dorjee, D. (2024a). Conceptualising child and adolescent mental health and wellbeing neurodevelopment: an integrative brain networks framework. https://doi.org/10.31234/osf.io/7vx45

Dorjee, D. (2024b). Existential uncertainty: how it affects your mind – and what you can do about it. https://theconversation.com/existential-uncertainty-how-it-affects-your-mind-and-what-you-can-do-about-it-24119

Dorjee, D. (2025). Why resilience won't solve the mental health crisis among young people. https://theconversation.com/why-resilience-wont-solve-the-mental-health-crisis-among-young-people-24682

Downey, J., & Greco, J. (2023). Trauma sensitive schools: A comprehensive guide for the assessment planning and implementation of trauma informed frameworks. *Children and Youth Services Review, 149*, 106930.

Dray, J., Bowman, J., Campbell, E., Freund, M., Wolfenden, L., Hodder, R. K., ... & Wiggers, J. (2017). Systematic review of universal resilience-focused interventions targeting child and adolescent mental health in the school setting. *Journal of the American Academy of Child & Adolescent Psychiatry, 56*(10), 813-824.

Hofmann, S. G., Sawyer, A. T., Witt, A. A., & Oh, D. (2010). The effect of mindfulness-based therapy on anxiety and depression: a meta-analytic review. *Journal of Consulting and Clinical Psychology, 78*(2), 169.

Isbell, E., Stevens, C., Pakulak, E., Hampton Wray, A., Bell, T. A., & Neville, H. J. (2017). Neuroplasticity of selective attention: research foundations and preliminary evidence for a gene by intervention interaction. *Proceedings of the National Academy of Sciences, 114*(35), 9247-9254.

Kabat-Zinn, J. (2003). Mindfulness-based interventions in context: Past, present, and future. *Clinical Psychology: Science and Practice, 10*(2), 144-156. https://doi.org/10.1093/clipsy.bpg016

Karlsson Linnér, R., Mallard, T. T., Barr, P. B., Sanchez-Roige, S., Madole, J. W., Driver, M. N., ... & Dick, D. M. (2021). Multivariate analysis of 1.5 million people identifies genetic associations with traits related to self-regulation and addiction. *Nature Neuroscience, 24*(10), 1367-1376.

Kaspar, K. L., & Massey, S. L. (2023). Implementing social-emotional learning in the elementary classroom. *Early Childhood Education Journal, 51*(4), 641-650.

Keane, K., & Evans, R. R. (2022). Exploring the relationship between modifiable protective factors and mental health issues among children experiencing adverse childhood experiences using a resilience framework. *Journal of Child & Adolescent Trauma, 15*(4), 987-998.

Khoury, B., Sharma, M., Rush, S. E., & Fournier, C. (2015). Mindfulness-based stress reduction for healthy individuals: a meta-analysis. *Journal of Psychosomatic Research, 78*(6), 519-528.

Kuyken, W., Byford, S., Taylor, R. S., Watkins, E., Holden, E., White, K., ... & Teasdale, J. D. (2008). Mindfulness-based cognitive therapy to prevent relapse in recurrent depression. *Journal of Consulting and Clinical Psychology, 76*(6), 966.

LaBelle, B. (2023). Positive outcomes of a social-emotional learning program to promote student resiliency and address mental health. *Contemporary School Psychology, 27*(1), 1-7.

Lass-Hennemann, J., Sopp, M. R., Ruf, N., Equit, M., Schäfer, S. K., Wirth, B. E., & Michael, T. (2024). Generation climate crisis, COVID-19, and Russia–Ukraine-war: global crises and mental health in adolescents. *European Child & Adolescent Psychiatry, 33*(7), 2203–2216.

Madigan, S., Deneault, A. A., Racine, N., Park, J., Thiemann, R., Zhu, J., ... & Neville, R. D. (2023). Adverse childhood experiences: a meta-analysis of prevalence and moderators among half a million adults in 206 studies. *World Psychiatry, 22*(3), 463–471.

NASUWT. (2024). Wellbeing survey briefing. www.nasuwt.org.uk/static/17ad7ef2-879e-40d4-96b3c014e605746a/Teachers-Wellbeing-Survey-Report-2024.pdf

Nguyen, T. U., & Dorjee, D. (2022). Impact of a mindfulness-based school curriculum on emotion processing in Vietnamese pre-adolescents: an event-related potentials study. *Developmental Science, 25*(6), e13255.

Oberle, E., & Schonert-Reichl, K. A. (2016). Stress contagion in the classroom? The link between classroom teacher burnout and morning cortisol in elementary school students. *Social Science & Medicine, 159*, 30–37.

Schonert-Reichl, K. A. (2017). Social and emotional learning and teachers. *The Future of Children*, 137–155.

Treleaven, D. A. (2018). *Trauma-sensitive mindfulness: practices for safe and transformative healing.* W. W. Norton & Company.

Vickery, C. E., & Dorjee, D. (2016). Mindfulness training in primary schools decreases negative affect and increases meta-cognition in children. *Frontiers in Psychology, 6*, 2025.

INDEX

ACC see anterior cingulate cortex (ACC)
adrenal cortex 75, 77, 78
adverse childhood experiences (ACEs) 35, 245-246
affect 30, 52; affective empathy 191; affective processes 144; longer-term affective experiences 31; negative 122, 145, 158, 245; positive 145, 166, 220; short-lived 30, 31
age of child 3, 9, 15, 23, 24; and connections, fostering of 171, 172, 184; and distraction management 61, 68, 69; and emotional awareness 29, 35, 36, 37, 39, 41, 44, 48; and habitual thoughts and emotions, dealing with 98; implementing ATTEND Framework 240, 250; learning objectives 58; and making a difference 186, 193, 196, 197; neuroscience knowledge 2, 80; and purpose in life/flexible self-concept 213, 220, 222, 227, 236; and reactivity, managing 73, 96; and rumination and worry, dealing with 139; and shared humanity 147-148, 161; stories and cartoons 173; vocabulary 35, 36, 39, 44; see also KS1 (5-7 year-olds), learning of MHW skills; lower KS2 (7-9 year olds), learning of MHW skills; reception age group (4-5 year-olds), learning of MHW skills; upper KS2 (9-11 year-olds), learning of MHW skills
agency, facet of see making a difference
amygdala/amygdalae: and distraction management 53, 57, 62, 66; and emotional awareness 33; and habitual thoughts and emotions, working with 102, 103, 109, 110, 113, 114; and reactivity, managing 75-79, 86, 87, 92-95; right and/or left 13, 79; and rumination and worry, dealing with 122, 123, 130, 131, 136; self-regulation processes 13-15

anterior cingulate cortex (ACC) 14, 23, 24; and connections, fostering 168, 175, 176, 181-183; and distraction management 53-55, 61, 62, 66, 68; dorsal part (dACC) 33, 147, 191; and emotional awareness 33, 35, 41, 42; and habitual thoughts and emotions, working with 102, 103, 106, 109, 110, 113, 114; and making a difference 191, 192, 199, 200, 204, 205; and purpose in life and self-concept, encouraging 219, 228, 229, 233-235; and reactivity, managing 78, 86, 87, 92-95; and rumination and worry, dealing with 122, 123, 130, 131, 136; self-regulation 14, 53; and shared humanity, fostering 146, 153, 154, 158, 160
ATTEND Pyramid/Framework for school MHW curricula: as acronym for Guiding **ATT**ention, Managing **E**motions, Nurturing Co**N**nections and Finding **D**irection 18-19; 'big picture' 25; on brain regions in emotional awareness 33; building blocks 105, 106, 139, 171, 196, 220, 228, 229, 234-236, 239, 240, 243, 246, 250, 251; developmental continuity of MHW learning 9; developmentally nuanced and skill-based learning 250-251; facets of see connections, fostering; distraction management; emotional awareness; habitual thoughts and emotions, working with; making a difference; purpose in life and self-concept, encouraging; reactivity, managing; rumination and worry, dealing with; shared humanity, fostering; illustration of tiers **19**; implementing see implementing ATTEND Framework; integrating framework with targeted MHW and SEN support 248; and mindfulness 245; NDeTeC theory 18; progression of tiers 240; reasoning/

research evidence behind 18-21; and resilience 244, 254-255; and social-emotional learning 243; strategies 247; Tier 1 - Guiding Attention (Facets of Emotional Awareness and Managing Distractions) 3, 19, 20, 22, 29, 48, 50, 73, 123, 139, 143, 213, 218, 220, 223, 236, 238, 242, 253; Tier 2 - Managing Emotions (Facets of Managing Reactivity, Habitual Thoughts and Emotions, and Managing Rumination and Worry) 3, 20, 68, 98, 118, 123, 139, 143, 213, 218, 220, 223, 236, 238, 242, 246, 253; Tier 3 - Nurturing Connections (Facets of Shared Humanity, Connections and Making a Difference) 20, 68, 143, 144, 163, 164, 172, 186, 207, 213, 218, 220, 236, 238, 242-243, 253, 254; Tier 4 - Finding Direction (Facets of Purpose in Life and Flexible Self) 18-19, 21, 68, 143, 144, 213, 220, 238, 242-243, 253, 254; see also 7-Step approach, implementing ATTEND Framework through; strategies
attention economy 52
autonomic nervous system see nervous system, sympathetic/parasympathetic

blue zone 76, 80, 82-84; expanding 120
bottom-up self-regulation 13, 15
brain hemispheres see corpus callosum (brain hemispheres)
brain/brain regions 1, 18, 20, 77, 245; activity patterns 31; brain waves 242; and connections, fostering 163, 167, 168, 169, 172, 175-177, 180-182; development 9; developmental vulnerabilities 52; and distraction management 53, 55, 57, 61-62, 66-67; drawing of 41, 42, 62; and emotional awareness 29, 31-33, 35-37, 41, 42, 45, 46; and habitual thoughts and emotions, working with 101, 104, 105, 109, 110, 113, 114; and HPA axis, downregulating see HPA axis; and making a difference 191, 192, 196, 199-201, 204-206; maladaptive activity 139; maps 62, 66, 67, 87, 109, 136; maturation of areas 37, 52; models of 41, 46, 62, 67, 110; networks 15, 18, 175, 176, 218, 220, 228, 229, 236; processes underpinning MHW 2, 5, 8, 9, 11, 25, 32, 50; and purpose in life and self-concept, encouraging 219, 220, 228, 229, 233, 234, 236; and reactivity, managing 75-78, 81, 86, 87, 92, 93; reward network see reward network; root system processes 8; and rumination and worry, dealing with 118, 121-123, 126, 130, 131, 135-137, 139; salience network 23, 35; self-regulation capacity 12-15, 16, 33, 242; self-world capacity 18; and shared humanity, fostering 146, 147, 149, 153, 154, 158, 159; stickers 135, 181; stress response 75; symbols of 199, 204; temporal lobes 101; transdiagnostic processes 8; see also mentalising network; neuroscience; salience network; specific regions of the brain
breathing exercises 81, 82, 86, 96, 123; deep breathing 78; flower-bubbles breathing 90, 92, 93, 94; 4-6 breathing see 4-6 breathing, reactivity management; paced 15, 20, 78, 79, 101, 108, 112, 114, 115, 119, 247; prolonging the outbreath 78

capacities underpinning MHW see self-regulation capacity; self-world capacity
cartoons and stories, use of in teaching 22, 23; connections, fostering 173; distraction management 57, 61, 63; emotional awareness 37; habitual thoughts and emotions, working with 110; reactivity, managing 86; shared humanity 148
case studies: distraction management 50-51; emotional awareness, teaching across primary school years 29-30; MHW, choice of approach 7, 25; negativity bias and learning to savour experiences in classroom 99; reactivity, managing 73-74; relational wellbeing, expanding scope of 163-164; rumination and worry, dealing with 119; shared humanity 143-144
charts, in classrooms 95, 115, 160
circles of connection 169-170
cognitive defusion 144; distraction management 53, 56, 57, 60-62, 65, 67-69; habitual thoughts and emotions, working with 105, 108, 112, 115
compassion 188-189; distinguished from empathy 17, 20, 186, 192, 193, 195-197, 200, 202, 204-207; practices 195; relating to MHW 196-197; self-world capacity 16
connections, fostering 163-185; and VS 168, 175, 176, 181-183; and ACC 168, 175, 176, 181-183; acquiring knowledge and skills through 7-Step Approach 172-183; ATTEND Pyramid 20; awe, connections and MHW 166-167, 172-173; case study 163-164; circles of connection 169-170;

developmental differences in fostering knowledge/skills of in children 171-172; drawings 170, 171, 173, 175, 176, 177, 178, 179, 180, 182; Emotion Strength Scale (reception/KS1) 173, 174, 177; Feels Good Scale (reception/KS1) 173, 174, 177; gratitude, connections and MHW 165-166, 172-173; how children can acquire knowledge and skills of 169-171; how relevant to MHW 164-167; and insula/insular cortex 175, 176, 181, 183; key strategies 170-171; in KS1 173, 174, 176, 177, 179, 181, 182; in lower KS2 173, 174, 176, 178, 180, 181, 183; and mentalising network 175, 176, 181, 183, 184; nature, with 10-11; neuroscience 167-169; and PFC 167, 168, 175, 176, 180-183; Pleasantness and Intensity of Emotion Graph (upper KS2) 173, 178; Pleasantness of Emotion Scale and Intensity of Emotion Scale (lower KS2) 175, 178; in reception 172, 174, 175, 177, 179, 180, 182; reward network 168-169, 175, 176, 181, 183, 184; and TPJ 168, 175, 176, 181-184; trails of connection 170-171; in upper KS2 171, 173, 175, 176, 178, 180, 181, 183

corpus callosum (brain hemispheres) 35, 101

corticotropin releasing hormone (CRH) 76

cortisol: purpose in life and self-concept, encouraging 220; reactivity, managing 76, 77, 87, 93, 95; rumination and worry, dealing with 123, 131, 136; and teacher MWH 247

developmental continuity of MHW learning 9-10

developmental differences in fostering MHW knowledge/skills in children: connections, fostering 171-172; distraction management 57; emotional awareness 36-37; habitual thoughts and emotions, working with 105-106; making a difference 195-196; purpose in life and self-concept 223-224; reactivity, managing 81-82; rumination and worry, dealing with 126; shared humanity 149

distraction management: and VS 53, 57, 62, 66; and ACC 53-55, 61, 62, 66, 68; acquiring knowledge and skills through 7-Step Approach 57-68; and amygdala/amygdalae 53, 57, 62, 66; ATTEND Pyramid 19; attention economy 52; case study 50-51; developmental differences in fostering knowledge/skills of in children 57; drawings 62; Emotion Strength Scale (reception/KS1) 58, 60, 63, 64; executive network/managing distractions in the classroom 53-54; external distractions 58-59, 62-64; Feels Good Scale (reception/KS1) 58, 60, 63, 64; how children can acquire knowledge and skills of 55-57; how relevant to MHW 51-53; and insula/insular cortex 53, 61, 62, 66; internal distractions 59-61, 64-65; key strategies 56; in KS1 57-61, 63, 64, 66, 67; in lower KS2 58-61, 63, 65-67; neuroscience 53-55; and PFC 53-55, 57, 61, 62, 66, 68; Pleasantness and Intensity of Emotion Graph (upper KS2) 60, 64, 65; Pleasantness of Emotion Scale and Intensity of Emotion Scale (lower KS2) 59, 60, 63, 65; and positive effects of distractions 52-53; 'real world,' contextualising MHW learning in 10, 16; in reception 57-61, 63, 64, 66, 67; salience network 53, 55; self-regulation processes 15; in upper KS2 58-60, 62, 63, 65, 66, 68

dorsal anterior cingulate cortex (dACC) 33, 35, 147, 191

dorsolateral PFC (dlPFC) 192

drawing: of the brain 41, 42, 62; connections, fostering 170, 171, 173, 175-180; distraction management 62; emotional awareness 38, 40-43; gratitude 177; habitual thoughts and emotions, working with 113; making a difference 196, 201, 203; purpose in life and self-concept, encouraging 223; reactivity, managing 84, 92; rumination and worry, dealing with 137

emojis 24, 80, 83; and 'Feels Good' scale 39, 40; and Pleasantness and Intensity of Emotion Graph 93; and Pleasantness of Emotion Scale and Intensity of Emotion Scale 92; stickers 86; and zones of reactivity 84, 88, 90

Emotion Strength Scale (reception/KS1): connections, fostering 173, 174, 177; distraction management 58, 60, 63, 64; emotional awareness 39, 40, 44, 47; habitual thoughts and emotions, working with 108, 110; making a difference 198, 201, 203; purpose in life and self-concept, encouraging 225, 227, 230; shared humanity, fostering 150-152, 155, 157

emotional awareness 29-49; and VS 33; and ACC 33, 35, 41, 42; acquiring knowledge and skills through 7-Step

Approach 37-47; and amygdala/amygdalae 33; ATTEND Pyramid 19, 20; cognitive component 30-31; developmental differences in fostering knowledge/skills of in children 36-37; distinguishing emotions, feelings and mood 30-31; drawings 38, 40, 41, 42, 43; Emotion Strength Scale (reception/KS1) 39, 40, 44, 47; emotion vocabulary, learning 36, 39-41; feelings and emotions, terminology 37; Feels Good Scale (reception/KS1) 40, 44, 47; healthy kinds 32; how children can acquire knowledge and skills of 35-36; how relevant to MHW 31-33; and insula/insular cortex 33, 35, 42, 46, 47; key strategies 36; in KS1 37, 38, 40-45, 47; in lower KS2 37-40, 42-44, 46, 47; naming of emotions *see* naming of emotions, benefits of; neuroscience of 33-34, 35; non-judgmental 31; noticing of thoughts and emotions *see* noticing of thoughts and emotions, relation to MHW; overpathologising of normal emotional experience 32; and PFC 20; in the playground 34; Pleasantness and Intensity of Emotion Graph (upper KS2) 40, 41, 45, 47; Pleasantness of Emotion Scale and Intensity of Emotion Scale (lower KS2) 40, 47; in reception 36-46; reward network 110; salience network 24, 33, 34-35, 37, 42, 46, 47; self-regulation processes 15; strength and intensity of emotions 41-42; and Tier 1 of ATTEND Pyramid *see* ATTEND Pyramid/Framework for school MHW curricula; in upper KS2 37, 39-43, 45-47

empathy/empathic distress 4, 145-147, 186-188, 194, 206; affective empathy 191; cognitive and affective aspects 191; distinguished from compassion 17, 20, 186, 192, 193, 195-197, 200, 202, 204-207; and making a difference 187, 199; and mentalising 191; networks 192-193, 205; neural processes 191; and prosocial networks 18, 196, 197, 199, 200, 201, 202, 204, 205, 206, 207; recognising 204; relating to MHW 196-197; self-world capacity 16

feelings and emotions: distinguishing emotions, feelings and mood 30-31; terminology 37; *see also* emotional awareness
Feels Good Scale (reception/KS1): connections, fostering 173, 174, 177; distraction management 58, 60, 63, 64; emotional awareness 40, 44, 47; habitual thoughts and emotions, working with 107, 108, 110; making a difference 198, 201, 203; purpose in life and self-concept, encouraging 225, 227, 230; reactivity, managing 83, 88, 90; rumination and worry, dealing with 128, 129, 134, 138; shared humanity, fostering 150, 151, 152, 155, 157
fight, flight, freeze response 75, 78, 86, 87
flexible self-concept: ATTEND Pyramid 21; self-world capacity 17; 7-Step approach 216-217, 233-236; *see also* purpose in life and self-concept, encouraging
flower-bubbles practice, reactivity management 80, 82, 84, 86, 90, 92-94, 96
4-6 breathing, reactivity management 80, 82, 85-87, 90-95; *see also* breathing exercises

gratitude 16, 165-166, 172-173
green zone 76, 80, 87, 220, 254; expanding 80, 81, 82, 84, 85, 87-89, 91-96, 122; feeling what it is like to be in 88, 89; movable boundaries 81, 82; as optimal 83, 86; and progressive muscle relaxation, practice of 80, 85, 87, 92, 94, 95; recognition of 94; reducing 95, 120; shifting to 88; staying in 219, 229, 234, 254
Guiding **ATT**ention, Managing **E**motions, Nurturing Co**N**nections and Finding **D**irection *see* ATTEND Pyramid/Framework for school MHW curricula

habitual thoughts and emotions, working with 98-117; and VS 102, 103, 105, 110, 113, 114; and ACC 102, 103, 106, 109, 110, 113, 114; acquiring knowledge and skills through 7-Step Approach 106-115; and amygdala/amygdalae 102, 103, 109, 110, 113, 114; ATTEND Pyramid 20; case study 99; developmental differences in fostering knowledge/skills of in children 105-106; drawings 113; Emotion Strength Scale (reception/KS1) 108, 110; Feels Good Scale (reception/KS1) 107, 108, 110; hippocampus 102; how children can acquire knowledge and skills of managing 104-105; how relevant to MHW 99-100; and insula/insular cortex 102, 109, 110, 113, 114; key strategies 104-105; in KS1 107-110, 112-114; in lower KS2 107-109, 111-113, 115; managing in classroom

103; negativity bias, relation to MHW 98, 99, 100, 103–116; and neural plasticity 98, 100, 101, 103, 105, 106, 109, 110, 113, 120; neuroscience 101–102; with paced breathing 101, 108, 112, 114, 115; and PFC 102, 103, 109, 110, 113, 114; Pleasantness and Intensity of Emotion Graph (upper KS2) 107, 113; Pleasantness of Emotion Scale and Intensity of Emotion Scale (lower KS2) 107, 108, 111, 112; in reception 106, 108–110, 111, 113, 114; reward network 116; self-regulation processes 15; in upper KS2 107, 108, 110–112, 114, 115

hippocampus: and habitual thoughts and emotions, working with 101, 102, 109, 110, 113, 114; and neural plasticity 103, 131, 136; and reactivity, managing 75, 76, 77, 86; receptors 101; and rumination and worry, dealing with 123, 130, 131, 136, 137; self-regulation processes 13

HPA (hypothalamic-pituitary-adrenal axis): downregulating through mental health strategies 78–79, 219, 220, 229, 234; imbalances in 75–76, 79; and purpose in life and self-concept, encouraging 219, 220, 229, 234, 235; and reactivity, managing 75–80, 86–87, 92–96; and rumination and worry, dealing with 121–124, 131, 136; stress response, linked to 76–77, 78, 79, 92, 93, 122, 124

implementing ATTEND Framework 238–255; approaches 239–240; climate anxiety 253–255; compared with social-emotional learning 243; democracy education 253–255; developmentally nuanced and skill-based learning 250–251; digital literacy 253–255; effectiveness 238–239; embedding as a sustainable whole-school approach 251–252; FAQs 241–247; genetics and malleability of MHW capacities 241; resilience, whether fostering in children 244; Self-Regulation and Self-World capacities, whether trainable 241–242; social-emotional development of children, supporting 242–243; in society 252–255; supporting children's resilience in global crises 254; and teacher MWH 251; teaching children mindfulness skills, whether aligned with 244–245; trauma-informed, whether 245–247; and trauma-informed learning 246; whole school implementation 247–252; see also ATTEND Pyramid; ATTEND Pyramid/Framework for school MHW curricula; 7-Step Approach, implementing ATTEND Framework through

insula/insular cortex 23, 24; anterior insula 191, 192; and connections, fostering 175, 176, 181, 183; and distraction management 53, 61, 62, 66; and emotional awareness 33, 35, 42, 46, 47; and habitual thoughts and emotions, working with 102, 109, 110, 113, 114; and making a difference 191, 192, 199, 200, 204, 205; and purpose in life and self-concept, encouraging 228, 233, 235; and reactivity, managing 87; and rumination and worry, dealing with 122, 123, 131, 136; self-regulation processes 14, 53; and shared humanity, fostering 146, 153, 154, 158, 160, 168

Jacobson, Edmund 81

Key Stage 1 see KS1 (5-7 year-olds), learning of MHW skills
Key Stage 2 see lower KS2 (7-9 year olds), learning of MHW skills; upper KS2 (9-11 year-olds), learning of MHW skills
KS1 (5-7 year-olds), learning of MHW skills: connections, fostering 173, 174, 176, 177, 179, 181, 182; distraction management 57–61, 63, 64, 66, 67; Emotion Strength Scale see Feels Good Scale (reception/KS1); emotional awareness 37, 38, 40–45, 47; Feels Good Scale (reception/KS1) see Feels Good Scale (reception/KS1); habitual thoughts and emotions, working with 107–110, 112–114; making a difference 195, 197, 198, 200, 201, 203, 204, 206; purpose in life and self-concept, encouraging 225, 227, 228, 230, 231, 233, 235; reactivity, managing 80, 83, 84, 86, 88, 90, 92, 94; rumination and worry, dealing with 127, 129, 130, 132, 134, 136, 137; shared humanity, fostering 149, 151, 153, 155, 156, 158, 160

lower KS2 (7-9 year olds), learning of MHW skills: connections, fostering 173, 174, 176, 178, 180, 181, 183; distraction management 58–61, 63, 65–67; emotional awareness 37–40, 42–44, 46, 47; habitual thoughts and emotions, working with 107–109, 111–113, 115; making a difference 197, 198, 200, 202, 203, 205, 206; Pleasantness of Emotion Scale and Intensity of Emotion Scale see Pleasantness of Emotion Scale and Intensity of Emotion Scale (lower

KS2); purpose in life and self-concept, encouraging 225, 227, 228, 230, 232, 233, 235; reactivity, managing 83, 85, 86, 88, 90, 92, 94; rumination and worry, dealing with 127, 129, 131, 133, 134, 136, 138; shared humanity, fostering 149, 150, 152, 153, 155, 157, 158, 160

making a difference 186–209; and ACC 191, 192, 199, 200, 204, 205; acquiring knowledge and skills through 7-Step Approach 196–207; ATTEND Pyramid 20; caring behaviours 186–187; in classroom 186–187, 192–193; compassion 188–189, 195; developmental differences in fostering knowledge/skills of in children 195–196; drawings 196, 201; Emotion Strength Scale (reception/KS1) 198, 201, 203; empathy/empathic distress 187–188, 192–193; Feels Good Scale (reception/KS1) 198, 201, 203; how children can acquire knowledge and skills of 193–195; how relevant to MHW 187–190; and insula/insular cortex 191, 192, 199, 200, 204, 205; key terms 188; in KS1 195, 197, 198, 200, 201, 203, 204, 206; in lower KS2 197, 198, 200, 202, 203, 205, 206; and mentalising network 191, 192, 200, 205; neuroscience 191–193; and PFC 192, 199, 200, 204–206; Pleasantness and Intensity of Emotion Graph (upper KS2) 197, 199; Pleasantness of Emotion Scale and Intensity of Emotion Scale (lower KS2) 197, 199, 202; prosocial behaviour and motivation 189–190, 192–193; random acts of kindness 193–194; in reception 196–199, 201, 202, 204, 206; reward network 192, 193, 199, 200; Ripples of Agency 194–195, 203, 207, 224; self-world capacity 17; and TPJ 192, 199, 200, 204, 205; in upper KS2 197, 199, 200, 202, 203, 205, 206
Map of Strengths 221, 234
MBCT (Mindfulness-Based Cognitive Therapy) 244, 245
MBSR (Mindfulness-Based Stress Reduction) 244, 245
medial PFC (mPFC) 18, 122, 167
meditation 166, 244; see also mindfulness
mental health and wellbeing (MHW) see MHW (mental health and wellbeing)
mentalising network 18; in classroom 147; and fostering connections 167–169, 175, 176, 181, 183, 184; and making a difference 191, 192, 200, 205; and purpose in life/flexible self-concept 218, 223, 229, 234, 235; and shared humanity 146, 147, 153, 154, 160
MHW (mental health and wellbeing): ATTEND Framework see ATTEND Pyramid/Framework for school MHW curricula; implementing ATTEND Framework; 7-Step approach, implementing ATTEND Framework through; and awe 166–167, 172–173; biomedical model 10; brain processes underpinning 2, 5, 8, 9, 11, 25, 32; capacities underpinning 11–18; case study 7; choosing right approach for classroom 6–26; genetics and malleability of capacities 241; and gratitude 165–166, 172–173; implementing ATTEND using 7-Step approach see 7-Step Approach, implementing ATTEND Framework through; mental ill-health prevention and learning MHW skills 10; overlaps across MHW concepts 12; pillars of (three) 8–11; relevance of distraction management 51–53; relevance of emotional awareness 31–33; relevance of fostering connections 164–167; relevance of making a difference 187–190; relevance of purpose in life and self-concept 214–218; relevance of reactivity management 74–76; relevance of shared humanity 144–145; relevance of working with habitual thoughts and emotions 99–100; relevance of working with rumination and worry 119–120; self-world capacity 16–18; social factors 10; targeted support 248; in teachers 251; three pillars 8–11; see also NDeTeC (Neurodevelopmental Theory of MHW Capacities)
mindfulness 3, 7, 12, 14, 144; and ATTEND Framework 245; emotion regulation 122; and emotional awareness 33; and flexible self-concept 145; implementing ATTEND Framework 238, 239, 244–245; Mindfulness-Based Cognitive Therapy 244, 245; mindfulness-based programmes 245, 251; Mindfulness-Based Stress Reduction 244, 245; in primary school 245; and reactivity, managing 78, 79; and resilience 7, 245, 247–248

naming of emotions, benefits of 22–24, 32–33, 39–41, 44–47; acquisition of knowledge 35; age-appropriate emotion vocabulary, use of 36; developmental differences in fostering MHW knowledge/skills in children 36; Guiding **ATT**ention in the ATTEND Pyramid 29; intensity of emotions 36; pleasantness of emotions 36; tracking on logs 24; *see also* Emotion Strength Scale (reception/KS1); emotional awareness; Feels Good Scale (reception/KS1); noticing of thoughts and emotions; Pleasantness and Intensity of Emotion Graph (upper KS2); Pleasantness of Emotion Scale and Intensity of Emotion Scale (lower KS2)

NDeTeC (Neurodevelopmental Theory of MHW Capacities): and ATTEND Framework 18; self-regulation capacity 11; transdiagnostic processes 8-9

negativity bias, relation to MHW: and attention, fostering 19; classroom management 99; defining 116; in everyday situations 115; excessive 19; habitual thoughts and emotions, working with 98, 99, 100, 103-116; impact 115; and making a difference 188; and mental health conditions 100; rumination and worry, dealing with 120, 122, 123; self-regulation capacity 15; strategies to counter 105

nervous system, sympathetic/parasympathetic 75, 76-77, 78, 79

neural plasticity: connections, fostering 181; defining 102; habitual thoughts and emotions, working with 98, 100, 101, 103, 105, 106, 109, 110, 113; and hippocampus 103, 131, 136; purpose in life and self-concept, encouraging 219, 229, 234, 235; reactivity, managing 81, 82; rumination and worry, dealing with 120, 122-124, 126, 130, 131, 136, 137

Neurodevelopmental Theory of MHW Capacities *see* NDeTeC (Neurodevelopmental Theory of MHW Capacities)

neurophysiological changes 31

neuroscience: connections, fostering 167-169; and distraction management 53-55; educating children about 23, 24; and emotional awareness 33-34, 35; and habitual thoughts and emotions 101-102; and making a difference 191-193; and purpose in life and self-concept 218-220; and reactivity, managing 76-79, **77**, 78; and rumination and worry, dealing with 120-124; self-regulation capacity 12-15; self-world capacity 18; and shared humanity 146-147; terminology 35, 55, 78, 122, 146, 168, 192, 219; *see also* amygdala/amygdalae; anterior cingulate cortex (ACC); brain/brain regions; corpus callosum (brain hemispheres); dorsal anterior cingulate cortex (dACC); hippocampus; HPA axis; insula/insular cortex; pre-frontal cortex (PFC); temporo-parietal junction (TPJ); ventral striatum (VS)

noticing of thoughts and emotions, relation to MHW 22, 24, 29, 38-39, 42-43; *see also* emotional awareness; naming of emotions, benefits of

1-2-3 practice (what would a good friend say?): shared humanity facet 148-149; Step 2 151-152; Step 3 153-154; Step 5 156-157; Step 6 158-159; Step 7 159-161; *see also* shared humanity

PACE (Playfulness, Acceptance, Curiosity and Empathy) 247

paced breathing 15, 20, 119, 247; habitual thoughts and emotions, working with 101, 108, 112, 114, 115; reactivity, managing 78, 79

pair work/group activities 23, 24, 130, 131, 159; connections, fostering 173, 174, 175, 177, 183; distraction management 59, 60, 66; emotional awareness 38-39, 40; habitual thoughts and emotions, working with 108; making a difference 197, 199, 201; purpose in life and self-concept, encouraging 226, 227, 229, 231, 234; reactivity, managing 95; rumination and worry, dealing with 129, 130, 131; shared humanity, fostering 152, 154, 156, 157

parasympathetic nervous system 75, 76-77, 78, 79

PFC *see* prefrontal cortex (PFC)

pillars of MHW school curricula (three): contextualising MHW in the 'real world' 10-11, 16; developmental continuity of MHW learning 9-10; 'root systems,' nourishing 8-9

plasticity, brain *see* neural plasticity

Pleasantness and Intensity of Emotion Graph (upper KS2): connections, fostering 173, 178; distraction management 60, 64, 65; emotional awareness 40, 41, 45, 47; habitual thoughts and emotions, working with 107, 113; making a difference 197, 199; purpose in life and self-concept, encouraging 226, 227, 231; reactivity, managing 85, 87, 89, 91, 93, 95; rumination and worry, dealing with 133, 135, 139; shared humanity, fostering 151, 152, 156, 157, 161

Pleasantness of Emotion Scale and Intensity of Emotion Scale (lower

KS2): connections, fostering 175, 178; distraction management 59, 60, 63, 65; emotional awareness 40, 47; habitual thoughts and emotions, working with 107, 108, 111, 112; making a difference 197, 199, 202; purpose in life and self-concept, encouraging 226, 227, 229, 230; reactivity, managing 83, 85, 87, 88, 90, 91, 92, 94; rumination and worry, dealing with 129, 133, 135, 138; shared humanity, fostering 150, 152, 155, 157

prefrontal cortex (PFC): and connections, fostering 167, 168, 175, 176, 180-183; and distraction management 53-55, 57, 61, 62, 66, 68; dorsolateral 192; and emotional awareness 20; and habitual thoughts and emotions, working with 102, 103, 109, 110, 113, 114; lateral 55; and making a difference 192, 199, 200, 204-206; medial 18, 122, 167; and purpose in life and self-concept, encouraging 219, 228, 229, 233-235; and reactivity, managing 75-79, 86, 87, 92-95; and rumination and worry, dealing with 122, 123, 125, 130, 131, 136, 137; self-regulation processes 14, 15; self-world capacity 18; and shared humanity, fostering 146, 153, 154, 158-160; ventromedial 102, 192

progressive muscle relaxation (PMR): case study 79; defining 81; development of 81; emotional awareness 20; everyday practice 101; and green zone, expanding 80, 85, 87, 92, 94, 95; guiding, by teacher 81, 88, 92; habitual thoughts and emotions, working with 101, 112; implementing ATTEND Framework 247; reactivity, managing 80, 81, 82, 83, 84, 85, 88, 89, 92, 93, 94, 95, 96; rumination and worry, dealing with 123

prosocial behaviour 201; in the classroom 192-193; distinguished from empathy 18, 196, 197, 199-202, 204-207; motivation behind 189-190, 198-199; relating to MHW 196-197; self-world capacity 16; types 198-199

purpose in life and self-concept, encouraging 213-237; and ACC 219, 228, 229, 233-235; acquiring knowledge and skills through 7-Step Approach 224-236; ATTEND Pyramid 21; brain network 220; in classroom 220; developmental differences in fostering knowledge/skills of in children 223-224; drawings 223; Emotion Strength Scale (reception/KS1) 225, 227, 230; exploring goals in life 222-223; exploring strengths and intrinsic/extrinsic values 213-214; Feels Good Scale (reception/KS1) 225, 227, 230; flexible self-concept 17, 216-217, 233-236; how children can acquire knowledge and skills of 220-223; how relevant to MHW 214-218; HPA axis 219, 220, 229, 234, 235; and insula/insular cortex 228, 233, 235; intrinsic and extrinsic values 215; key strategies for working with 222; in KS1 225, 227, 228, 230, 231, 233, 235; in lower KS2 225, 227, 228, 230, 232, 233, 235; and mentalising network 218, 223, 229, 234, 235; neural plasticity 219, 229, 234, 235; neuroscience 218-220; and PFC 219, 228, 229, 233-235; Pleasantness and Intensity of Emotion Graph (upper KS2) 226, 227, 231; Pleasantness of Emotion Scale and Intensity of Emotion Scale (lower KS2) 226, 227, 229, 230; in reception 225-229, 231, 233, 234; reward network 219; self-world capacity 16, 17; strengths, knowledge of 221; and TPJ 228, 233, 235; in upper KS2 222, 226, 227, 229, 230, 232, 234, 235

Random Acts of Kindness (RAKs) 35, 193-194, 201; board, poster or wall 194, 202-207;

reactivity, managing 20; and ACC 78, 86, 87, 92-95; acquiring knowledge and skills through 7-Step Approach 82-95; and amygdala/amygdalae 75-79, 86, 87, 92-95; ATTEND Pyramid 20; case study 73-74; classroom management 79; developmental differences in fostering knowledge/skills of in children 81-82; drawings 84, 92; Emotion Strength Scale (reception/KS1) 83, 88, 90; Feels Good Scale (reception/KS1) 83, 88, 90; flower-bubbles practice 80, 82, 84, 86, 90, 92-94, 96; 4-6 breathing 80, 82, 86, 87, 90-95; how children can acquire knowledge and skills of 80-81; how relevant to MHW 74-76; HPA axis 75-80, 86-87, 92, 93, 94, 95, 96; and insula/insular cortex 87; key strategies 80-81; in KS1 80, 83, 84, 86, 88, 90, 92, 94; in lower KS2 83, 85, 86, 88, 90, 92, 94; and mental health 75-76; neural plasticity 81, 82; neuroscience 76-79, **77**; paced breathing 78, 79; and PFC 75-79, 86, 87, 92-95; Pleasantness and Intensity of Emotion Graph (upper KS2) 85, 87, 89, 91, 93, 95; Pleasantness of Emotion Scale and Intensity of Emotion

Scale (lower KS2) 83, 85, 87, 88, 90, 91, 92, 94; in reception 80, 81, 83, 84, 86, 88, 90, 92, 93; self-regulation processes 15; three zones of reactivity 76; in upper KS2 82, 84, 85, 87, 89, 91, 93, 95; when reactivity is useful 74-75; *see also* zones of reactivity

'real world,' contextualising MHW learning in 10-11, 16

reappraisal: cognitive 15, 57, 123; and mindfulness 122, 123; and rumination and worry, dealing with 118, 122-126, 128-131, 133-139; and sensory-focus strategies 122-124, 126, 129, 131, 137-139; of thoughts and emotions 9, 118

reception age group (4-5 year-olds), learning of MHW skills: connections, fostering 172, 174, 175, 177, 179, 180, 182; distraction management 57-61, 63, 64, 66, 67; Emotion Strength Scale *see* Feels Good Scale (reception/KS1); emotional awareness 36-46; Feels Good Scale *see* Feels Good Scale (reception/KS1); habitual thoughts and emotions, working with 106, 108-110, 111, 113, 114; making a difference 196-199, 201, 202, 204, 206; purpose in life and self-concept, encouraging 225-229, 231, 233, 234; reactivity, managing 80, 81, 83, 84, 86, 88, 90, 92, 93; rumination and worry, dealing with 127, 128, 130, 132, 134, 135, 137; shared humanity, fostering 150, 151, 153, 154, 156, 158, 159

red zone 76, 80, 82-84, 86-88, 93; expanding 120

resilience 3, 238, 239; in adolescents 215; and ATTEND Framework 244, 254-255; curriculum 4; and habitual thoughts and emotions 102-103; and mindfulness 7, 245, 247-248; programmes 245; psychological 253; and purpose in life/flexible self-concept 221; and self-regulation 9, 12; strengthening 253; teaching in schools 253

reward network: abnormalities in 103; connections, fostering 168-169, 175, 176, 181, 183, 184; developmental differences in fostering MHW knowledge/skills in children 105; emotional awareness 110; habitual thoughts and emotions, working with 116; making a difference 192, 193, 199, 200; purpose in life and self-concept, encouraging 219; rumination and worry, dealing with 121, 122, 131; self-world capacity 18; shared humanity 103; and ventral striatum 102

Ripples of Agency 194-195, 203, 207, 224

root systems of MHW 8-9; and emotional awareness 32; self-regulation capacity 12; self-world capacity 16

rumination and worry, dealing with 118-140; and ACC 122, 123, 130, 131, 136; acquiring knowledge and skills through 7-Step Approach 126-139; and amygdala/amygdalae 122, 123, 130, 131, 136; ATTEND Pyramid 20; case study 119; default mode network 123-124; developmental differences in fostering knowledge/skills of in children 126; drawings 137; Emotion Strength Scale (reception/KS1) 128, 129, 134, 138; Feels Good Scale (reception/KS1) 128, 129, 134, 138; how children can acquire knowledge and skills of 124-126; how relevant to MHW 119-120; HPA axis 121, 122, 123, 124, 131, 136; and insula/insular cortex 122, 123, 131, 136; key strategies 125; in KS1 127, 129, 130, 132, 134, 136, 137; in lower KS2 127, 129, 131, 133, 134, 136, 138; negativity bias, relation to MHW 120, 122, 123; and neural plasticity 122-124, 126, 130, 131, 136, 137; neuroscience of 120-124; and PFC 122, 123, 125, 130, 131, 136, 137; Pleasantness and Intensity of Emotion Graph (upper KS2) 133, 135, 139; Pleasantness of Emotion Scale and Intensity of Emotion Scale (lower KS2) 129, 133, 135, 138; and reappraisal 118, 122-126, 128-131, 133-139; in reception 127, 128, 130, 132, 134, 135, 137; reward network 121, 122, 131; self-regulation processes 15; and TPJ 121; in upper KS2 128, 129, 131, 133, 136, 138

salience network 24; distraction management 53, 55; emotional awareness 33, 34-35, 37, 42, 46, 47; illustration **34**; in the playground 34-35; purpose in life and self-concept, encouraging 218; rumination and worry, dealing with 120, 122, 123, 131; 7-Step approach, description 23, 24

self-compassion, cultivating 13, 16; in adolescents 145, 147; compared with shared humanity 144-145; concept 145; mindful 145; in primary school 145

self-regulation capacity 11-15; and ACC 14, 53; bottom-up processes 13, 15; brain regions involved 13; defining self-regulation 11; facets of 15; NDeTeC theory 11; neuroscience of 12-15; overlaps across MHW concepts **12**; and resilience 9, 12;

top-down processes 14, 15; trainable, whether 241-242
self-world capacity 16-17; facets of 17; neuroscience of 18; trainable, whether 241-242
SEN (Special Educational Needs) 248, 249, 250
sensory-focus strategies, and reappraisal 122-124, 126, 129, 131, 137-139
7-Step approach, implementing ATTEND Framework through 3-4, 25; connections, fostering 172-183; distraction management 57-68; emotional awareness 36, 37-47; habitual thoughts and emotions, working with 106-115; making a difference 196-207; objective of 21; principles 22; purpose in life and self-concept 224-236; reactivity, managing 82-95; reasoning/research evidence behind ATTEND Framework 21-24; rumination and worry, dealing with 126-139; shared humanity, fostering 149-161; see also Step 1 (learning key MHW concept of a facet and its relation to MHW); Step 2 (learning about strategies linked to key MHW concept and how they support MHW); Step 3 (learning neuroscience underpinning key MHW concept/associated strategies); Step 4 (applying knowledge about key MHW concept to own experience in support of own MHW); Step 5 (starting to apply knowledge about strategies linked to key MHW concept in support of own MHW); Step 6 (starting to use neuroscience knowledge underpinning key MHW concept and associated strategies in supporting own MHW); Step 7 (applying new knowledge/skills about key MHW concept and associated strategies to everyday life)
shared humanity 143-162; 1-2-3 practice (what would a good friend say?) 148-149, 151-152, 156-157; acquiring knowledge and skills through 7-Step Approach 149-161; ATTEND Pyramid 20; case study 143-144; developmental differences in fostering knowledge/skills of in children 149; how children can acquire knowledge and skills of 147-149; how relevant to MHW 144-145; key strategies 148; and mentalising network 146, 147, 153, 154, 160; neuroscience 146-147
shared humanity, fostering: and ACC 146, 153, 154; Emotion Strength Scale (reception/KS1) 150-152, 155, 157; Feels Good Scale (reception/KS1) 150, 151, 152, 155, 157; in KS1 149, 151, 153, 155, 156, 158, 160; in lower KS2 149, 150, 152, 153, 155, 157, 158, 160; and PFC 146, 153, 154, 158-160; Pleasantness and Intensity of Emotion Graph (upper KS2) 151, 152, 156, 157, 161; Pleasantness of Emotion Scale and Intensity of Emotion Scale (lower KS2) 150, 152, 155, 157; in reception 150, 151, 153, 154, 156, 158, 159; and TPJ 146, 153, 154, 158, 160, 161; in upper KS2 149, 151, 152, 156, 157, 159, 160
Siegel, Dan 76
social-emotional competencies 145, 242, 247, 251
social-emotional development 16, 238, 239, 244; and ATTEND Framework 242-243
social-emotional learning (SEL) 240, 243
Special Educational Needs see SEN (Special Educational Needs)
'spot three things' practice 53, 54, 56, 69
Step 1 (learning key MHW concept of a facet and its relation to MHW) 22; cartoons and stories, use of 22, 38; connections, learning how relate to MHW 172-173; empathy, compassion and prosocial behaviour, relating to MHW 196-197; external distractions and impact on MHW 58-59; habitual thoughts and emotions management relating to MHW 106-107; learning how recognising own strengths/finding purpose relates to MHW 225-226; reactivity management, relation to MHW 82-84; rumination and worry, relation to MHW 127-128; shared humanity, learning relation to MHW 150-151
Step 2 (learning about strategies linked to key MHW concept and how they support MHW) 22-23; cartoons and stories, use of 39; interconnections, learning how supporting MHW 174-175; internal distractions and impact on MHW 59-61; intrinsic goals, learning impact on MHW 226-227; learning emotion vocabulary and benefits of naming emotions 39-41; negativity bias, relation to MHW 107-109; prosocial behaviour, learning about types and motivation behind 198-199; reactivity, learning to recognise/manage 84-85; rumination and worry, learning strategies to manage 128-130; shared humanity, learning how 1-2-3 strategy supports 151-152
Step 3 (learning neuroscience underpinning key MHW concept/associated strategies) 23; connections,

neuroscience underpinning 177; distraction management 61–62; emotional awareness 41–42; empathy, compassion and prosocial behaviour, relating to MHW 199–201; neuroscience 109–110; purpose in life and self-concept, neuroscience underpinning 228–229; reactivity, managing 86–87; rumination and worry, neuroscience underpinning 130–131; shared humanity, learning how underpinning neuroscience supports 153–154

Step 4 (starting to apply knowledge about key MHW concept to own experience in support of own MHW) 23; cartoons and stories, use of 23; connections, learning to foster in own experience 177–178; emotional awareness 42–43; empathy, compassion and prosocial behaviour, learning skills of 201–202; external distractions 62–64; habitual thoughts and emotions, working with 109–110; pair/group activities 23; reactivity, managing 88–89; recognising own strengths/exploring purpose in life in own experience 229–231; rumination and worry, management skills 132–133; shared humanity, learning skills in own experience 154–156

Step 5 (starting to apply knowledge about strategies linked to key MHW concept in support of own MHW) 24; cartoons and stories, use of 24; emotional awareness 42–43; habitual thoughts and emotions, learning to shift 111–113; interconnections, learning to recognise/impact on own MHW 179–180; internal distractions 64–65; pair/group activities 24; prosocial behaviour, learning to recognise/impact on own MHW 202–204; reactivity, learning to recognise/manage 89–91; recognising intrinsic and extrinsic goals/impact on own MHW 231–232; rumination and worry, learning to apply strategies to support 133–135; shared humanity, learning to use 1-2-3 strategy to support others' and own MHW 156–157

Step 6 (starting to use neuroscience knowledge underpinning key MHW concept and associated strategies in supporting own MHW) 24; connections, fostering 180–182; distraction management 65–67; emotional awareness skills 45–46; finding purpose in life/developing flexible self-concept, applying neuroscience to 233–234; habitual thoughts and emotions, using neuroscience to manage 113–114; making a difference, learning neuroscience as part of 204–205; reactivity management, learning to apply neuroscience knowledge in relation to 91–93; rumination and worry, learning to apply neuroscience as part of managing 135–137; shared humanity, applying neuroscience as part of skills 158–159

Step 7 (applying new knowledge/skills about key MHW concept and associated strategies to everyday life) 24; applying skills of finding purpose in life/flexible self-concept in everyday activities 234–236; distraction management in everyday life 67–68; emotional awareness and naming of emotions 46–47; habitual thoughts and emotions, managing in everyday life 114–115; making a difference, applying skills in everyday life 205–207; reactivity, applying management skills in everyday life 93–95; rumination and worry, applying skills to managing in everyday life 137–139; shared humanity, applying skills to everyday life 159–161

strategies: connections, fostering 170–171; distraction management 56; emotional awareness 36; habitual thoughts and emotions, working with 104–105; purpose in life and self-concept 222; reactivity, managing 80–81; rumination and worry, dealing with 125; shared humanity, fostering 148; *see also specific Steps*

Strength of Emotion Scale *see* Emotion Strength Scale (reception/KS1)

stress response: acute 77; adaptive 246; and adverse childhood experiences 245–246; chronic 77, 78; and connections, fostering of 166, 168, 169; downregulating 169; emotional awareness 31; HPA axis, linked to 76–77, 78, 79, 92, 93, 122, 124; impact on MHW 241; increased 122; reactivity, managing 75, 76–77, 78, 79, 80, 81, 82, 86, 87, 92, 93, 95, 96; rumination and worry, dealing with 121, 122, 123, 124; and staying in green zone 254; and trauma-informed teaching 246; *see also* emotional awareness; nervous system, sympathetic/parasympathetic; reactivity, managing; rumination and worry, dealing with

sympathetic nervous system 75, 76–77, 78, 79

temporo-parietal junction (TPJ): and connections, fostering 168, 175, 176, 181-184; defining function of 146; and making a difference 192, 199, 200, 204, 205; and purpose in life and self-concept, encouraging 228, 233, 235; and rumination and worry, dealing with 121; self-world capacity 18; and shared humanity, fostering 146, 153, 154, 158, 160, 161

theory of mind 18

top-down self-regulation 14, 15

TPJ *see* temporo-parietal junction (TPJ)

trails of connection 170-171

trauma-informed teaching 245-247

upper KS2 (9-11 year-olds), learning of MHW skills: connections, fostering 171, 173, 175, 176, 178, 180, 181, 183; distraction management 58-60, 62, 63, 65, 66, 68; emotional awareness 37, 39-43, 45-47; habitual thoughts and emotions, working with 107, 108, 110-112, 114, 115; making a difference 197, 199, 200, 202, 203, 205, 206; Pleasantness and Intensity of Emotion Graph *see* Pleasantness and Intensity of Emotion Graph (upper KS2); purpose in life and self-concept, encouraging 222, 226, 227, 229, 230, 232, 234, 235; reactivity, managing 82, 84, 85, 87, 89, 91, 93, 95; rumination and worry, dealing with 128, 129, 131, 133, 135, 136, 138; shared humanity, fostering 149, 151, 152, 156, 157, 159, 160

values, extrinsic and intrinsic 215

ventral striatum (VS) 109; and connections, fostering 168, 175, 176, 181-183; defining function of 102; and distraction management 53, 57, 62, 66; emotional awareness 33; and habitual thoughts and emotions, working with 102, 103, 105, 110, 113, 114; and HPA axis, downregulating 78; and making a difference 192, 193, 199, 200, 204, 205; and purpose in life and self-concept, encouraging 219, 228, 229, 233-235; and reactivity, managing 78, 79; and rumination and worry, dealing with 131, 136; self-regulation processes 13, 14

ventromedial PFC (vmPFC) 102, 192

VS *see* ventral striatum (VS)

Well Minds Lab 23

whole school implementation of ATTEND Framework 247; checklist 248-252; integrating framework with targeted MHW and SEN support 248

World Health Organization (WHO) 1-2

zones of reactivity: blue 76, 80, 82-83, 120; emojis associated with 84, 88, 90; green 76, 80-89, 91-96, 120, 122, 219, 220, 254; making a graph of 81; movable boundaries 81; recognition of 88, 95; red 76, 80, 82-84, 86-88, 93, 120; *see also* reactivity, managing

For Product Safety Concerns and Information please contact our EU representative GPSR@taylorandfrancis.com
Taylor & Francis Verlag GmbH, Kaufingerstraße 24, 80331 München, Germany

www.ingramcontent.com/pod-product-compliance
Lightning Source LLC
Chambersburg PA
CBHW060258240426
43661CB00060B/2824